FEEDING GOTHAM

FEEDING GOTHAM

THE POLITICAL ECONOMY AND GEOGRAPHY OF FOOD IN NEW YORK, 1790–1860

Gergely Baics

PRINCETON UNIVERSITY PRESS
PRINCETON AND OXFORD

Copyright © 2016 by Princeton University Press
Published by Princeton University Press, 41 William Street,
Princeton, New Jersey 08540
In the United Kingdom: Princeton University Press, 6 Oxford Street,
Woodstock, Oxfordshire OX20 1TR

press.princeton.edu

Jacket image: Matthew Dripps, *Plan of New York City, from the Battery to Spuyten Duyvil
Creek. Based on the surveys made by Messrs. Randall & Blackwell, and on the special survey
by J. F. Harrison*. Published by Matthew Dripps, 1867. From The Lionel
Pincus & Princess Firyal Map Division, The New York Public Library

All Rights Reserved

ISBN 978-0-691-16879-1

Library of Congress Control Number 2016942620

British Library Cataloging-in-Publication Data is available

This book has been composed in Charis

Printed on acid-free paper ∞

Printed in the United States of America

1 3 5 7 9 10 8 6 4 2

To Caterina and Emma

Contents

Illustrations and Tables

FIGURES

MAPS

COLOR INSERT MAPS

TABLES

Acknowledgments

This book began in an unexpected way during graduate school, when I stumbled upon the vernacular sketch of African American dancing contests at Catharine Market in 1820, which provides the opening scene of chapter 4 in this book. I was touched by this drawing, for it captured, in the most intimate sense, the cosmopolitan character and dynamic public spaces of New York, the city I had wished to call home ever since I first visited it. It took me years to realize that behind that small sketch lay a vast and complex landscape of food provisioning in a rising metropolis, a problem that would occupy my mind for ten years.

Helping me find this intellectual path, and guide me through the challenges, from dissertation stage to the book's completion, I have been supported by the most extraordinary mentors at Northwestern University, Josef Barton and Joel Mokyr. Joe and Joel have worked with me closely and patiently on every aspect of the project: from the first ideas to the last word and beyond. They pushed me through all the hoops, from countless manuscript revisions, talks, and applications to giving me perspective and much-needed support at periods of self-doubt. In the process, they have become true friends, or perhaps, more accurately, family away from family. I have no words to express my gratitude and respect for them. If there is any way I could return what I have been given, it is to be as good a mentor to my students as they have been to me.

Many other colleagues supported my research and writing at Northwestern. I am especially thankful to Henry Binford and David Van Zanten, who did several close readings of the manuscript and offered invaluable advice. David and I have kept up our conversations on cities, and I am most pleased that our exchange and friendship have continued over the years. Ken Alder was closely involved in the original Catharine Market paper and has remained a friend ever since. Brodwyn Fischer introduced me to Latin American cities, helping me further my transnational urbanist perspective. In general, I am thankful to the Northwestern History Department, which supported me, intellectually and financially, for six years. Additionally, the Workshop in Economic History provided an inspiring intellectual community for someone invested in social science history. I also learned a tremendous amount from my friends at graduate school, especially Min Kyung Lee, Umud Dalgic, Juan Olmeda, Nicole Fabricant,

Emily Shafer, Jarod Roll (who also read and commented on parts of the manuscript), and Rhiannon Stephens, who is now my colleague at Columbia.

After graduate school, I had the good fortune of joining the faculty at the History Department and Urban Studies Program at Barnard College, Columbia University. Working in such an inspiring environment, in the city I love and study, has been the most rewarding experience. First, I owe my gratitude to my home departments for providing all the support needed to write this book. Special thanks go to my reading committee, Deborah Valenze, Robert McCaughey, and José Moya, for their thoughtful suggestions; to my chairs, Joel Kaye and Lisa Tiersten, for their support; to Herb Sloan for our delightful conversations; to Nara Milanich and Carl Wennerlind for all their guidance; to Pablo Piccato, Madeleine Zelin, and Rebecca Kobrin for their good advice and friendship. At Urban Studies, I am most grateful to my chairs, Flora Davidson and Kimberley Johnson, who have always looked out for me and protected my time to work on this book, and to Meredith Linn for being an outstanding colleague.

Barnard-Columbia is home to a thriving economic history group. David Weiman has mentored me since the day I arrived and has become a true friend over the years: he has read closely and critically everything I have written, guided my thinking toward structure and clarity, and has made this book infinitely better. My colleague and friend Alan Dye also read the manuscript word by word and suggested invaluable revisions, for which I am deeply thankful. Our Columbia Seminar on Economic History has provided intellectual community both to discuss my work and to be inspired. From the seminar members, I extend special thanks to Jason Barr, with whom we swapped ideas and shapefiles on Manhattan GIS.

Barnard-Columbia is also home to a large community of urbanists. Above all, I am deeply thankful to Betsy Blackmar for her mentoring over the years, her close and critical reading of my manuscript, and whose example as a scholar and teacher has been an inspiration. I am also grateful to Kenneth Jackson, who welcomed me at Columbia as a fellow urbanist. The Columbia Seminar on the City, where I have presented my work and participated in many discussions, has provided an important intellectual venue. My coauthor on other projects, fellow GIS enthusiast and friend Leah Meisterlin, played an important part in the mapping analysis: she helped develop some of the book's maps, taught me advanced GIS techniques, and inspired me to see maps as artwork, to be designed with care. Toward this goal, I had the privilege to work with outstanding student research assistants: Gabrielle Lewis helped with data entry, Somala Diby with geocoding, and Rachael Dottle created the final design of the book's numerous maps and graphs. Rachael deserves special recognition for her dedication, technical skills, and creativity in transforming my original ArcGIS maps into their current design, a work that took us eight months to complete.

In between Northwestern and Barnard, I benefited from a number of fellowships in support of this project. An ACLS dissertation completion fellowship allowed me to fully devote my last year of PhD studies to writing, and to take up a visiting research associate position at the McNeil Center for Early American Studies at the University of Pennsylvania. I am thankful to Daniel Richter and the McNeil Center community in 2008–9, with a special note of thanks to Jason Sharples and Megan Walsh for making this a most productive year. At Penn, I had the great honor of discussing my work and receiving invaluable comments on it from the late Michael Katz, who had been an inspiration ever since my undergraduate studies. Mark Stern and Domenic Vitiello also graciously welcomed me into Penn's vibrant urbanist community. My one year in Philadelphia was made infinitely better by the friendship of João Rangel de Almeida and Dóra Vargha. João read countless iterations of what was back then a dissertation, and his suggestions made this book much better.

After Philadelphia, I took up a Max Weber Postdoctoral Fellowship at the European University Institute in Firenze, Italy. Being part of a community of more than forty postdoctoral fellows from across the social sciences and all over the world shaped my thinking tremendously. I am thankful to Ramon Marimon for this wonderful year, to Giovanni Federico and Antonella Romano for many inspiring conversations, and to the other fellows, especially Elaine Fahey, Shikeb Farooqui, Raphaël Levy, Naomi Beck, and Nai Rui Chng.

While at Barnard, I spent one year on leave as an Andrew W. Mellon Foundation Fellow at the New-York Historical Society. I could not have hoped for a better setting than the rich collections of the N-YHS to wrap up my manuscript. I am most grateful to Valerie Paley for this wonderful opportunity. I also wish to acknowledge our group of fellows, especially Nick Yablon and Steven Moga, and the knowledgeable and most helpful library staff there, especially Nina Nazionale and Edward O'Reilly. This is also the place to extend the same recognition to the several archivists and librarians who supported my work at other collections, in particular, the New York Public Library and the Municipal Archives of New York City. At the city archives, special thanks go to Leonora Gidlund, Tobi Adler, and Barbara Hibbert, who moved mountains of documents for me. Further, I wish to acknowledge the input of so many colleagues at various venues where I presented my work. In particular, I thank Timothy Leunig at the London School of Economics and Naomi Lamoreaux and Timothy Guinnane at Yale University for inviting me to their economic history workshops.

I could not have found a better publisher for my first book than Princeton University Press. I am thankful to senior editor Eric Crahan for all his solid advice and guidance; to the anonymous readers for their careful reading and insightful comments; to production editor Brigitte Pelner for the seamless publication process; to Cathy Slovensky for her thoughtful and meticulous copyediting; and to illustration manager Dimitri Karetnikov for taking good care of my maps. Parts of this book have been published in different formats: an earlier version of chapter 2 was published in "Is Access to Food a Public Good? Meat Provisioning in Early New York City, 1790–1820," *Journal of Urban History* 39, no. 4 (2013), 643–68; some of the ideas in chapter 2 have been previously published in "The Geography of Urban Food Retail: Locational Principles of Public Market Provisioning in New York City, 1790–1860," *Urban History* (2015); and portions of chapter 6 appeared in "Meat Consumption in Nineteenth-Century New York: Quantity, Distribution, and Quality, or Notes on the 'Antebellum Puzzle,' " in *Institutions, Innovation, and Industrialization: Essays in Economic History and Development*, ed. Avner Greif, Lynne Kiesling, and John Nye (Princeton, NJ: Princeton University Press, 2015), 97–127. I am grateful for their permission to reproduce here.

There are other colleagues who deserve recognition, even if they were not directly involved with this book. Though I left Hungary thirteen years ago, I have kept many connections. I thank Károly Halmos, Gábor Sonkoly, György Granasztói, Attila Melegh, András Lugosi, György Kövér, Tamás Magyarics, and Tibor Frank for their different ways of helping me find my path as an urban social and economic historian. I spent one year as an exchange student at Trinity College in Hartford, Connecticut, where Eugene Leach guided me with dedication. My collaborator on other projects and friend Mikkel Thelle has kept me engaged with European cities. My deepest gratitude belongs to Gyula Benda, an outstanding historian and most generous teacher, who mentored me for many years and shaped my work profoundly. Though he passed away just about the time I began this project, each and every page bears his influence.

In completing my PhD, taking up a postdoc and a faculty position, and relocating each time, I have made many friends. While not all of them have contributed to this book, their friendship has made all the difference. I wish to especially thank Bryson Brodie, Sayra Player, Geoffrey Scott, Aaron Cedolia, Pantelis Anastasakis, Dezső Birkás, and Hava Mendelberg. In New York, I have had the good fortune to become close friends with István and Gloria Deák. István also invited me to join the Hungarian roundtable: our monthly lunch with this remarkable group has been a cherished aspect of my social life. Despite all the moves, Budapest has remained my home, and my friends have everything to do with this. I would like to thank our close-knit group of high school friends, especially Péter Gáti (Oszkár), Andrea Tóth, and Gáspár Gombos, for two decades of friendship.

The most enduring support I have received throughout my life is from family, and I am fortunate to have the love of many. My sincere thanks go to my aunt's family (Gyöngyi, János, Márta, and Péter Zafír), my uncle's family (Léna Szilvási, Gábor, and Balázs Kertesi), and to my Italian family (Giovanna, Giuseppe, and Mauro Pizzigoni, and Luciano Guagenti). My American family (Allison, Dave, Katie, and David McClay) has given me a second home in the United States and has changed my life more than they could ever imagine. I am thankful for the love of my sister and her family (Judit, Noémi, and Norbert Corell). I am most grateful to my stepfather, Ákos Fehér, who raised me and never let me down, and to my mother, Erzsébet Kertesi, who loves me so dearly. Even though we live in different countries, my parents have always been there for me. While I know they would prefer me living closer, they never second-guessed my choice to leave and supported me all the way. I cannot wait to give them a copy of this book, to be proudly placed on the shelf next to the one authored by Caterina Pizzigoni.

I met my wife, Caterina, a fellow historian at Columbia, in my first year as faculty. Cate has been deeply involved with my book from day one. She has read and commented on each chapter, page, and word countless times, and supported me through the process intellectually and emotionally. I would never have finished without her. Whether she ever wished to know this much about *Feeding Gotham*, I dare not ask. I have no words to express how lucky I feel to have met her. If New York City has become my new home, it is thanks to her. To our greatest happiness, two months ago, our daughter, Emma Feher Pizzigoni, was born, opening a new chapter in our lives just as I am bringing this book to a closure. I dedicate this book to my wife, Caterina, and to our daughter, Emma.

To my deepest sadness, my grandmother, Margit Kertesi, passed away at ninety-four, a year before I could finish this book. To her last day, she was involved with this project, just as she was involved with every aspect of my life. It gives me solace to think that her prayers were ultimately answered: this book is now finished and Emma has landed.

FEEDING GOTIIAM

Introduction

POLITICAL ECONOMY: FROM PUBLIC TO PRIVATE

Feeding Gotham presents the story of New York's transition from a tightly regulated public market system of provisioning in the Early Republic to a free-market model in the antebellum period.[1] It examines what a municipal market system was and how it worked to supply urban dwellers, how and why access to food moved from the public to the private domain by the 1840s, how these two distinctive political economies shaped the physical and social environments of a booming city, and, above all, what the social consequences of deregulation were for residents of America's first metropolis. On the whole, the book offers a comprehensive account based in political economy and the social and geographic history of the complex interplay of urban governance, market forces, and the built environment in provisioning New Yorkers.

The narrative follows the expansion of free-market relations in this vital sector of the urban economy and public policy. It explores how the rise of unregulated exchange in the selling and buying of food amounted to a "market revolution" in provisioning, to borrow from a leading interpretation of the antebellum United States.[2] To situate this transition in context, however, it is important to recognize a countervailing development in the political economy of the period: the expansion of government activity in a range of infrastructures, services, and regulatory bodies, the theme of which is particularly evident when looking at urban history. Facing unprecedented challenges from accelerating growth, municipalities expanded robustly in the domain of public goods.[3] They increased infrastructural investments and brought critical aspects of the built environment under their police power. Like many other sectors of the economy, food provisioning underwent deregulation in antebellum New York City. But this transition occurred in the broader setting of expanding municipal services to address other pressing problems.

To make these contrary trends more concrete, consider two other basic necessities of urban life besides food provisioning: the supply of water and housing. Sanitation, in fact, presents the most prominent case in which antebellum city councils, among them New York, expanded the public realm by building extensive water and sewer networks.[4] The Croton aqueduct, opened with great fanfare in October 1842, amounted to Gotham's largest public works until that moment and by an enormous margin. Bringing in clean water from a huge distance, the aqueduct also signified a profound increase of municipal capacity to address intensifying urban challenges. Lacking the authority to require that landlords subscribe to Croton water undoubtedly resulted in uneven access, which weakened the system's public benefits and especially hurt the tenement poor. Further, the Croton put additional pressure on New York's flimsy sewers, driving intensifying investments in that infrastructure after 1850. Still, the project was a landmark achievement, a major leap toward a broadened public domain. Yet in January 1843, within a few months of this enormous municipal venture, the city liberalized the food system and left provisioning in the hands of unregulated markets. So close a conjunction of the contrary strategies to expand the public domain in one arena and to shrink regulation in another demonstrates how the boundary between public and private goods was endlessly negotiated in the antebellum political economy.

Housing offers another instructive case.[5] In this sector, newly emerging and fully unregulated real estate markets reigned supreme, while Gotham's relentless growth created virtually insatiable demand. The conditions of crowded and unsanitary living in antebellum New York are familiar from both contemporary and historical accounts. In fact, the tenement evil became the defining trope of public health treatises. Decades of consistent critique at last resulted in some legislative steps, even if as timid as the first Tenement Housing Act of 1867. Twenty years later, Jacob Riis still denounced the suffocating environment of Lower East Side tenements, and only the Tenement House Act of 1901 had enough teeth to bring the housing market under meaningful regulatory control. Still, the chronology is telling. For even as social reformers and public health experts mobilized from the 1840s to extend the state's police power over the housing sector, access to food became marginalized in municipal policy. By 1867, the food economy was wholly liberalized, all surviving regulations were a dead letter, and the only development to speak of was to push slaughterhouses into the city's outskirts. The contrast with the housing question epitomizes the realignment of public priorities, whereby shelter gained urgency and provisioning fell out of the agenda.

This book is neither about the water supply nor housing, areas well covered by other historians. These pointed comparisons serve both to underscore the specific transition of food access from a public to private good in America's leading city and to provide benchmarks for the case within the political economy context. Historians have long grappled with the complex and dynamic interplay between government and markets, public and private matters in the Early Republican and antebellum United

States.[6] The most influential thesis to make the case for a strong government presence was developed by William Novak in his seminal book, *The People's Welfare*, which offers a useful point of departure.[7]

Novak's concept of the "well-regulated society" provides a comprehensive account of social and economic policy making and political culture in nineteenth-century America.[8] It is also particularly well suited for the nation's highly decentralized governmental regulatory structure. At the center of the well-regulated society were the widely asserted police powers of local governments, originating mainly from the common law tradition, which served to sustain the "people's welfare." Accordingly, state and local governments intervened in a wide array of policy arenas, limiting private property rights for "public safety," regulating market relations for the "public economy," seizing control of "public ways" to help economic development, asserting control over "public morality," and stepping up local policing for "public health." In Novak's view, nineteenth-century public power was vigorously exercised and ubiquitously felt. It was locally based, self-governing, and regulatory in character. Further, it sought to balance private interests and the public good, and did not recognize a clear division between the two.

Most pertinent for this book are the concepts of "public economy" and "well-ordered market," referring to the myriad regulatory interventions in economic relations meant to sustain the common good.[9] The public market model that structured the provisioning of New York and other northeastern cities in the colonial and Early Republican era sits particularly well with this framework. Local governments were expected to maintain well ordered markets in urban food supplies to guarantee their availability in adequate quantities and quality to citizens.[10] Public markets served as privileged spaces designated for this purpose, bringing together vendors and customers to exchange life's necessities under the watchful eye of the municipal government. Participation was limited to licensed groups of vendors, including butchers, fishmongers, farmers, and hucksters, each with their own specific trade rights, places, and corresponding status within the marketplace. Where market-houses represented the infrastructural ground on which the model rested, market laws sanctioned its principles by extending the state's police power to regulate private interests for the public good. In theory, market laws curbed unethical trade practices;[11] enforced vendors' use of legal weights and measures; protected licensed vendors from unlicensed competition; regulated the daily conduct of marketing, ranging from the uses of market space to the fixing of market-days and hours; promoted welfare by various means, such as price controls in certain commodities or granting licenses to those in need; and, most important, safeguarded the wholesomeness of the food supply to preserve public health.

New York's version of the public market model emerged with the city's charters, reflecting the precedents of English municipal corporations and mirroring similar arrangements in other colonial American cities. It was fully institutionalized by the Montgomery Charter of 1730.[12] The public markets belonged to the City Corporation's property, much like its ferry rights and water lots, which also served important public purposes. The corporation managed its market property for the welfare of residents and licensed vendors; it also collected revenues to this end. Public and private interests overlapped. Much like the ferry rights, which were leased out to chartered companies, vendors paid rents for the exclusive right to retail at the public markets. In exchange for this privilege, they were to supply New Yorkers with adequate and wholesome provisions. As New York set a path toward a new era of urbanization after the late eighteenth century, the Common Council was responsible for expanding the market infrastructure for the welfare of its growing population.

The municipal provisioning model, therefore, exemplifies Novak's idea of the well-ordered market, at least in theory. It is also true that in New York City this framework was officially dismantled in 1843, when the Common Council repealed the key clause of the market laws that restricted the sale of meat to licensed butchers. Gotham's decision to deregulate its food system was followed by other cities at the time, pointing to a broader transition in political economy that modifies Novak's chronology. Further, the disintegration of the public economy of provisioning was a piecemeal process, well under way by the second quarter of the century. New York had already abolished its assize of bread in 1821, two decades prior to the general liberalization of its food economy.[13] The latter development also unfolded gradually, first taking place on the ground and only later being legitimized by municipal policy. Outside the public markets, a vigorous informal economy emerged by the 1830s.

From a broader perspective, the deregulation of the urban food sector was part of a larger transition toward a more liberal regime in a variety of industries in New York State and nationally. Best known is the case of banking, which fueled some of the most heated political debates of Andrew Jackson's presidency.[14] Following the president's veto in 1832 of the bill to recharter the Second Bank of the United States, portrayed by Jackson as an aristocratic monopoly, the late 1830s heralded what is often called the "free banking era," which lasted until 1864. One state after another moved to the free entry model, whereby setting up a bank no longer required a special charter from the state legislature. The intricate process of special chartering also gradually gave way to general incorporation laws not only in banking but across the nation's economy before the Civil War.[15] New York State, with one of the nation's earliest free banking laws dating from 1838, was among the leaders in such liberal reforms.

One common thread between the case study of *Feeding Gotham*, and such national themes of antebellum economic history as free banking or the proliferation of private corporations, is the era's growing distrust of monopolistic privileges and greater embrace of open entry and free competition. Special charters guaranteed investors exclusive protections in exchange for provisioning quasi-public goods, like ferries, bridges, or banking, at an early stage of economic development. By the antebellum era, as the national economy expanded robustly, such monopolistic protections came to be regarded as no longer necessary and indeed as unfair. Free banking and general incorporation laws served to open up the process of setting up businesses to a wider constituency of citizens. Open access aimed to benefit the public by stimulating investments in goods and services and intensifying competition.

The analogy with New York's public market system and its deregulation is directly relevant. The public markets sustained a vital service for the city by supplying residents with life's necessities at an early stage of urban development. Much like special charters, the system instituted certain monopolistic protections: public markets were the only places where fresh food, meat in particular, could be retailed, and only licensed vendors, like the regular butchers, had the right to participate. Those selling food outside of the system were excluded from this lucrative economy. Similarly, those residing too far from a public market were inconvenienced in their daily routine of provisioning. In an emerging metropolis, with thousands of aspiring entrepreneurs and a vastly expanding customer base, such restrictions were beginning to lose legitimacy with the public, and so the voices in favor of open access and competition became ever louder. Tellingly, the critics of the public market system invariably exploited the antimonopoly rhetoric. By the 1830s the term "market monopoly" summed up all that seemed wrong with the municipal model, whether from the perspective of city officials, marginalized vendors, or dissatisfied customers.

To be sure, the penetration of market relations in economic and social life was a transformative development in Early Republican and antebellum history. At the same time, various layers of government were actively involved in building the infrastructures that made the market revolution possible.[16] The construction of turnpikes, canals, and railroads depended on all varieties of public and private partnerships, enabling the consolidation of far-reaching and more deeply integrated markets. Internal improvements like the era's vast canal networks, most famously, the Erie Canal, completed in 1825, required hitherto unprecedented scales of public investments. Cities were among the leading sites of public works, and New York boasted some impressive achievements. The vitally important Croton Waterworks, Manhattan's ambitious street grid, the underground arteries of water and sewer mains, or Central Park's great urban outdoors were all major investments in the public domain.[17]

New York's prodigious urbanization depended on such public goods and services. Without the Erie Canal, linking up the nation's vast interior directly to the New York port, thereby reducing west-to-east transportation costs most dramatically, it may not have become America's gateway to the world, on which position thrived its commercial and industrial economy. Without the Croton, channeling in fresh water from farther upstate to quench the city's thirst, it could not have sustained its exponential growth, absorbing hundreds of thousands of immigrants. As urbanization altered the city's scale, turning a colonial port into a major city in one generation, and pushing it to the threshold of a metropolis in another, public officials faced novel challenges. The question was not whether or not the municipal government had an important role to play but rather in what areas of economic and social life public investments and regulatory oversight should be extended and where free-market relations should prevail. The point is that the balance of public and private goods was contested and open-ended, leading to opposing developments in the antebellum political economy. By necessity, America's cities were at the center of these deliberations, given the scale, novelty, and urgency of their problems.

Certainly, public opinion shifted as New Yorkers gradually endorsed free-market relations in one of the largest and most critical sectors of the economy. The provisioning of food, deemed an essential municipal service by generations, was increasingly thought best left to private initiative. Formerly symbols of Gotham's well-regulated and abundant food supplies, the public markets were ever more often criticized by shoppers, food purveyors, and municipal officials for being outmoded and restrictive institutions in which to exchange life's necessities. Where before fairness in trade was to be enforced by municipal oversight, dissatisfied customers and excluded food vendors now protested such unwarranted meddling in the transactions between buyers and sellers. Similarly, where before the urban community sanctioned the legitimate rights and due obligations of licensed vendors, the market model's many critics now decried these as monopolistic privileges that favored the few over the many, who deserved an equal opportunity to open a shop and make a living.

Yet again, New Yorkers, who by and large demanded the deregulation of the market system, voted in favor of the Croton bonds in 1835, $5 million in value, thereby raising the city's debt several times.[18] Similar expansions of public services, from policing to park space, surged ahead in the antebellum decades. The municipal government expanded and professionalized, with specialized departments addressing its broadening responsibilities. Most spectacularly, public health emerged as one of the most critical and comprehensive areas of urban policy. The vitally important and wholly unregulated housing market was but one field where the state's police power was augmented, hesitantly at first, to assert a renewed awareness of public health. In short, the public domain was enlarged considerably in certain areas just as the market revolution was generally given freer rein in the urban economy. Access to food, the subject of this book, epitomizes the liberalizing trajectory from a public to a private good.

To appreciate the extent of this transition, it should be noted that in the area of food access, liberalization was pushed to an extreme. Considering the already discussed matrix of public and private goods, the Croton Waterworks belonged to the other end of the spectrum. To supply Manhattan with safe drinking water, the city established a publicly owned and operated monopoly. Labeling the public market system as a monopoly, while an effective critique, was in all fairness a misnomer, for the system is best described as a government-managed public marketplace. It was certainly not a free market, like free banking would become, for it lacked the features of open access and free competition. The point is that in theory, deregulation could have led to a transition from a municipally managed public market to a free-market environment with access open to all entrants under appropriate municipal health and trade regulations. Instead, liberalization was not matched by a new regulatory regime, either at the retail level or higher up in the provisioning system, at slaughter and wholesale, probably because this would have required creating an entirely new infrastructural and legal framework. And whereas antebellum health and social reformers were devoted to laying down the intellectual foundations for such a regulatory system for housing, they were not similarly engaged with food access as a matter of urban policy.

The provisioning of food in America's first metropolis at its defining moment of urbanization is an important problem in its own right. Set against the backdrop of shifting public and private goods, like water supply and housing, it also brings the subject in dialogue with larger questions of antebellum political economy, both within the urban setting and nationally. How did New York arrive at a fully unregulated food system? And what does this history reveal about the changing boundaries of public and private? A study of the development of New York's public market system, its expansion in the Early Republic and deregulation in the antebellum decades, in particular, why and how these changes of municipal governance and regulation occurred, provides new insights for urban economic and social history.

FOOD ACCESS: INFRASTRUCTURE, GEOGRAPHY, LIVING STANDARDS

Decades of public market investment followed by liberalization set the terms of New Yorkers' food access in the first half of the nineteenth century. Just as New York transformed into a bourgeoning and heterogeneous metropolis, residents faced profound changes in the institutional setting and daily practice of household provisioning with direct consequences for their living standards. For this book, which foregrounds the economic, social, and geographic dimensions of food provisioning and access, the central questions are the following. How did the contrasting models of public market versus free-market provisioning perform under the pressure of rapid urbanization? How did these distinctive infrastructural arrangements shape the city's growth and its built and social environments? What were the welfare costs and benefits of the two models of food access? In particular, how did deregulation affect the material well-being and living standards of New Yorkers? Grappling with these questions, this book expands the scope of the scholarship from its preoccupation with the debates surrounding provisioning to the actual consequences of specific policy choices.

In this effort, *Feeding Gotham* is a history of food access in nineteenth-century New York rather than a history of food. Existing literature, including more recently Cindy Lobel's *Urban Appetites*, mainly concerns the city's food and restaurant cultures.[19] Though this scholarship has enriched our knowledge of urban eating and dining, it provides limited understanding of how food access, as a matter of governance and economy, shaped the city's built environment and impacted residents' living standards. By placing the problem of residents' access to food into the foreground, this book pursues a comprehensive account from both ends of supply and demand. As for supply, the discussion centers on how urban governance and changing policies shaped the institutional framework and built environment of provisioning. As for demand, the book explores how New Yorkers negotiated their daily access to supplies, and how changes in the infrastructural and geographic setting of the food system affected this vital aspect of their living standards. The three themes—infrastructure, geography, and living standards—therefore structure the book's research and analysis.

The history of urban provisioning infrastructures, and more recently of urban food systems planning, provides useful context.[20] In particular, the subjects of urban slaughtering and meat supplies have attracted considerable attention. Informative works on European and American cities explore the expansion of government and public health oversight of this key industry in some cities during the nineteenth century, especially at its latter end.[21] Similarly, the history of public markets has become a more widely researched topic. Scholars have detailed the expansion of munici pal market-halls in certain European cities, like Paris, Berlin, Barcelona, and Budapest in the century's second half, or conversely, the decline of traditional marketplaces, more typical of northwestern Europe, including many cities in England.[22]

For American cities, the mid-nineteenth century brought about the general decline of public markets, despite their traditionally central role in food provisioning since the colonial era.[23] As already noted, New York's transition from a public to a free-market model is representative of other northeastern cities, like Philadelphia. Gotham's experience with deregulation has been explored in some detail by historians.[24] Thanks to these works the specifics of the narrative and the anchoring role of the meat trade in the American public market system, as well as the regulatory matters at stake, are largely familiar. In general, the liberalizing trajectory of New York City in the mid-nineteenth century is typical of America, even as it stands in contrast with many continental European cities, such as Paris. Whatever the balance of government involvement, the point to keep in mind is that major nineteenth-century cities faced similar challenges and engaged in similar policy debates about the organization and regulation of their food systems.

The infrastructural research, while rich in exploring the connections between urban governance and food systems, is far from complete. One limitation is the tendency to examine the individual elements of the infrastructure as discrete pieces. In general, more has been discovered about large-scale facilities, such as public abattoirs or central wholesale markets, than the smaller institutions at the retail end of food distribution. In the case of Early Republican and antebellum New York City, the different layers of the provisioning system are disjointedly covered by the literature. The history of slaughterhouses, for instance, is treated in only one article-length study focusing on the late eighteenth and early nineteenth centuries.[25] Gotham's wholesale and retail markets are more widely explored, albeit not primarily from the angle of provisioning history and food access.[26] As for the rest of the retail infrastructure of independent shops or unlicensed vendors, their contribution to the food system remains only patchily researched.[27]

Yet it was the retail spaces of food distribution—the public markets with their municipally managed stalls, the provision shops that proliferated under a free-market economy, and the street peddlers with their ambulatory trade—that constituted New Yorkers' daily points of access. The retail end also underwent the most consequential changes, fragmenting from a tightly managed world of municipal markets where customers negotiated a gathering of food vendors into a free-for-all landscape of private retailers where residents assembled provisions from dispersed locations. Overall, the book brings together the different layers of the urban food system in one comprehensive analysis.[28] The public market model and its deregulation present the main narrative. Yet just as important, the research attends to the wholesale markets and slaughterhouses, as well as the sprawling landscape of independent provision shops and street vendors. In fact, from the infrastructural perspective, the most intriguing question concerns the dynamic relations between the elements. Specifically, how did changing regulatory regimes in the midst of New York's metropolitan transition reconfigure the infrastructure and built environment of food access?

What holds the different layers of the food system together conceptually is space, a focusing lens of the book. The premise is that in the urban context, food access was to a large degree a matter of neighborhood geography. New Yorkers negotiated a complex landscape of markets, shops, and ambulatory vendors to procure food supplies. The spatial relations of food shopping not only transformed during this period but also increasingly differed by neighborhood, social class, and ethnicity, enabling some residents and constraining others in finding adequate, healthy, and affordable provisions. Just as current debates about "food deserts" highlight the adverse health effects of living too far from convenient access to affordable and nutritious food options, this book directs attention to the critical role of space in mediating food access.

In Early Republican and antebellum New York, still primarily a walking city before the availability of modern refrigeration, food shopping constituted one of the most taxing daily household chores. Convenient access to varied and wholesome food supplies constituted a basic necessity, much like housing, water, or sanitation. Conversely, obstacles to access introduced substantial distress in urban living standards. How did the public market system facilitate the distribution of supplies across neighborhoods? Was municipal control a suitable arrangement to mediate the spatial challenges of food access under the pressure of urbanization? Deregulation profoundly altered the landscape of provisioning. How did the free-market geography of food distribution differ from the municipally managed one, and what were the costs and benefits? Further, how did these structural changes affect residents' daily routines of household provisioning?

Examining the city's complex, layered, and changing food geography and access demands a comprehensive mapping analysis. Specifically, geographic information system (GIS) research documents the public market system's evolution over time and its relations to New York City's expansion and constantly changing population distribution. GIS mapping extends to the spatial experience of food shopping, including the interior spaces of some marketplaces and the exterior environment of urban neighborhoods. Tracing how deregulation restructured the daily conditions of household provisioning also entails the plotting of thousands of private food shops sprawling across the city. Further, the changing geography of the meat supply system, from slaughter to retail, is examined, nailing down the locations of this noxious industry, which alarmed contemporary public health reformers and puzzled historians. Overall, GIS mapping provides a theoretical framework, a methodological approach, and an empirical base on which the book's analysis rests. The numerous maps are not merely illustrations but provide the backbone of the book's arguments and conclusions.[29]

The third aspect of food access as an approach, besides infrastructural and geographic analysis, concerns the linkage between residents' unequal access to food supplies and their living standards. This is a central problem, often touched upon and assumed rather than carefully studied in food histories, including the literature on nineteenth-century New York.[30] Yet one field of scholarship, economic history, has extensively examined food consumption, its historically changing amounts, and its shifting composition. In the past few decades, joined by demographic historians, economic historians have explored the impact of changing nutritional conditions on the biological standard of living. Their interest was prompted by the counterintuitive discovery, commonly referred to as the antebellum puzzle, that the three decades prior to the Civil War in America were characterized by a combination of rapid economic growth and rising per capita income on the one hand, and worsening biological standards of living, in particular, declining physical stature and soaring mortality, on the other.[31] Research has documented that agricultural supply conditions by and large became unfavorable in the antebellum era, contributing to declining nutritional standards. The largest drop in per capita consumption rates occurred in the supply of meat, in part accounting for the widely observed decline in adult physical stature. Cities, generally dependent on agricultural imports for their food supplies, were especially affected.

This book extends the historical record by presenting new meat consumption estimates for the yet undocumented period of the Early Republic. Further, by exploring the interplay of municipal governance, political economy, and the changing infrastructure and geography of provisioning, it probes less-studied but equally pressing issues about the role of food supplies in residents' living standards. Beyond quantity, the book attends to the overlooked subject of food quality, especially in the contexts of an unregulated food economy and worsening urban disease environments. In addition, it traces the uneven geographies of food distribution across different neighborhoods, documenting how food access became an important and enduring factor of structural inequality, much like the more familiar problems of housing and sanitation. To be sure, the book's findings are specific to New York City, while the antebellum puzzle draws on national-level research, which makes direct comparisons difficult. At the same time, this focused case study opens up new areas of inquiry and a more rounded approach to assessing how structural changes in access to food supplies impacted nineteenth-century urban living standards.

CASE STUDY: NEW YORK CITY AND THE FOOD ECONOMY

New York presents an optimal case for addressing these large questions. Gotham's unparalleled growth, from a population of 30,000 in 1790 to 800,000 in 1860, turned the former colonial port into America's largest and the Western world's third-largest metropolis after London and Paris, putting into sharp focus the challenges of meeting residents' most essential needs. New York not only became the most populous but also the most heterogeneous American city, with large and diverse populations of immigrants arriving from overseas and across the nation, and a society increasingly stratified along various socioeconomic groups. It is in this context of immigration-driven urbanization and rising inequality that dismal housing conditions and their adverse health effects constituted key areas of urban policy, reverberating across America's cities, or that the Croton aqueduct was built, inspiring similar public waterworks elsewhere. Even if food was a far more ambiguous matter, New York faced novel but by no means unusual challenges about how to manage the proper provisioning of residents. By definition, municipal concerns centered on issues of distribution, quality, and slaughter, while the decision to liberalize food markets in 1843 not only fueled Gotham's most heated public debates but was also paralleled by developments elsewhere. Subsequently, in a liberalized food economy, the problem of food access by and large fell out of the domain of urban governance and policy. Certainly, New York was, and has ever been, a unique city in America: the largest, most complex, and heterogeneous. Yet a study of food access in New York during the city's onset of modern urbanization highlights central issues of urban development with both specificity and wider relevance.

Feeding Gotham also offers more than a case study in urban history. It is equally a focused history of a vital industry that experienced rapid growth and profound regulatory changes. The city's food economy was transformed by demographic developments, the transportation revolution, and, much less recognized, by liberal political economy reforms. In fact, one may read this book's account of food provisioning as a case study in one of the largest and most critical sectors of the urban economy. To keep the scale in perspective, about one-third of commercial businesses in mid-nineteenth-century New York operated in the food trade. Readers interested in economic history, but more familiar with other sectors like manufacturing or finance, will find informative parallels in this less-studied field. In fact, the food economy presents a distinctive opportunity to explore larger themes, such as how regulatory changes reshaped an entire industry, how an insurgent informal economy challenged established businesses, how rapid growth and open access altered the city's land use and commercial geography, and what these and other changes meant to New Yorkers.

Within the food economy, one industry in particular, meat provisioning, is featured prominently. There are several good reasons for this. To begin with, it was the most critical sector of the municipal model, the anchoring trade on which the public market monopoly rested legally and economically. This reflected the prominent status of butchers as craftsmen, and the central role of meat in the diet of urban Americans. Early Republican cities sustained high levels of meat consumption by any standard, with fresh beef becoming a staple for ordinary citizens. Moreover, butchery and the meat trade were the most affected by political economy changes in the antebellum era. The growth of informal commerce and the disintegration of the market monopoly were both concentrated in this sector. As the public markets' anchoring business shattered, the free-market regime reconfigured the geography and daily routine of household provisioning. Further, antebellum dietary pressures were most evident in the supply of meat. As will be shown, this entailed not only declining quantities of meat consumption but also deteriorating quality. Public health concerns about nuisance trades and food supplies also centered on butchers, especially their practice of slaughtering. All in all, at each juncture—from regulation to infrastructure, geography, and living standards—meat provisioning occupied prime importance, thus exemplifying larger developments in Gotham's food system in that period.

At last, a brief note on sources. Among America's cities, New York offers the best-documented case for its nineteenth-century food system, especially as concerns the public markets and meat supplies. This is in part thanks to the Jefferson Market butcher Thomas F. De Voe (1811–92), who in his free time devoted himself diligently to reconstructing the history of Gotham's food markets from their earliest days through his own time. His two published books, along with the corresponding archives, present a rich and exceptional resource, complementing more conventional municipal and other records available for other cities as well.[32] Additionally, the book's GIS analysis requires the availability of geospatial data. Most of these data were created by the author, but the process was greatly enhanced by the New York Public Library (NYPL) and the New-York Historical Society's (N-YHS) recent efforts to digitize some of their collections. The NYPL has done extraordinary work, relying on crowdsourcing to construct a database of georeferenced historical maps.[33] Their digitization of the Perris Fire Insurance Atlas (1852–54) made it possible to build a reliable address locator necessary to geocode historical addresses.[34] In turn, pulling the addresses for specific trades or professions was expedited by the N-YHS's initiative to make their collection of city directories electronically searchable.[35] Creating the book's geospatial data for a city as large as New York was a considerable investment, which only a few years ago may have proven excessively difficult.

PLAN OF THE BOOK

Feeding Gotham is organized in three parts. The first part consists of one chapter, covering the book's entire chronology and setting up its narrative. First, it provides a new account of the political economy of the public market system of provisioning, exploring how the common good of citizens' access to food was forged out of the conflicting and converging interests, rights, and responsibilities of the three constituent parties involved: residents, market vendors, and city officials. Second, it then discusses the process of market deregulation, exploring how and why citizens' access to food was gradually pushed from the public to the private domain through the expansion of informal retail from the 1830s, followed by the market laws' repeal in 1843. Further, chapter 1 details the shifting ground of public and private goods, outlining the fiscal connections between the liberalization of New York's formerly tightly regulated food economy and the city's huge investments in the Croton Waterworks.

The book's second part, comprising three chapters, shifts the discussion from the institutional framework of the public market system to its daily functioning and performance in supplying New Yorkers, focusing on the period between the 1790s and 1820s. Presenting new meat consumption estimates and using GIS mapping, chapter 2 examines the geography of food access. It establishes that Early Republican New York drew on sufficiently expanding supplies, while the public market system also succeeded in distributing provisions to residents across all neighborhoods in a rapidly growing city. Additionally, a case is made that the municipal model had meaningful redistributive effects, because it played a central role in ensuring basic food quality standards.

Chapter 3 addresses the problem of time by examining the temporal geography of household provisioning, a more unconventional subject. It scrutinizes the seasonal, weekly, and daily schedules of food shopping, outlining how complementary rhythms provided steady supplies to customers, while also sustaining permanent and stable trade at the public markets. Last, chapter 4 examines the neighborhood setting, which provided the immediate economic, social, and cultural contexts of the public markets. Through a case study of Catharine Market, the chapter documents the piecemeal process by which the neighborhood marketplace was assembled, along with the consolidation of its economic agglomeration, internal social and spatial order, everyday functioning, formal and informal management, and daily relations to customers. Overall, this three-pronged approach of space, time, and neighborhood serves to fully appreciate the complex dynamics, benefits, and trade-offs that defined the municipal model of provisioning in the Early Republic.

The third part propels the discussion into the antebellum period. It interrogates the geographic, social, and economic consequences of a changing political economy of food access with the decline of the public market system and its replacement by a free-market regime of provisioning. Chapter 5 provides a systematic GIS analysis of the city's food infrastructure, encompassing the wholesale and retail public markets and the newly sprawling landscape of private provision shops. Additionally, it maps the retail food economy in relation to the city's land-use environment and broader commercial geography while also situating food access within its local neighborhood context. In general, the analysis reveals the development of a novel, highly fragmented, and differentiated provisioning landscape, whereby residential location increasingly defined one's options of food access. At the end, the narrative returns to Catharine Market in the mid-nineteenth century, finding the public market's status as the economic, social, and cultural hub of its area compromised by the emerging retail corridor of Catharine Street as the new center of consumption and public space in the neighborhood.

If the underlying premise of chapter 5 is that political economy and geography are closely connected, chapter 6 completes the discussion by looking at the impact of these changes on the living standards and social inequalities of New Yorkers. At a time of worsening supply conditions and rising food prices, the final chapter contends that the city's surrender of oversight of the entire provisioning system contributed to the deterioration of food quality, thereby putting additional pressure on urban diets, especially among poorer residents. Layer by layer, the GIS research exposes how in a rapidly growing, immigrant, and working-class city, unequal access to adequate quantity and quality of food supplies mapped onto an ever more segregated landscape, compounding other sociospatial inequalities such as class, ethnicity, sanitation, or housing. The book provides evidence of how growing disparities in food access coalesced with better-known ones in health and housing to become structural sources of inequality that defined and shaped the nineteenth-century urban environment.

PART I

Political Economy of Urban Provisioning

CHAPTER 1

Is Access to Food a Public Good?

From Public Market to Free-Market System, 1790–1860

A Market Suitable for the Metropolis of the Union

On January 21, 1822, the *New York Gazette* triumphantly announced: "The Public are informed that Fulton Market will be opened on Tuesday, the 22d instant. . . . The Fulton Market, take it in the whole, is the most spacious and costly one in the country; and as it is to be a productive one to the city, may it also be so to the butchers, and other occupants of this market, in proportion to their respective merits." The next day, the *Gazette* followed up with details. The marketplace "was ornamented with the handsomest exhibitions of beef, mutton, pork, &c., ever presented to the public. We passed through it in company with several gentlemen from Europe, who were unanimous in the opinion that they had never seen anything of the kind to equal it, in all respects."[1]

Fulton Market was long in the making. As early as 1815, the Common Council contemplated the need to replace Gotham's largest marketplace, the dilapidated and narrow Fly, inconveniently situated next to a sewer, with a more commodious place. By January 1816, the Finance Committee had prepared its cost assessments of erecting "a spacious market on an enlarged scale and suitable to the taste, opulence & standing of the Metropolis of the Union."[2] Given the usual bureaucratic turns that characterized the fragmented decision making of Early Republican municipal governance, the project was put off for years. The main problems were the appropriation of land and finances. By the fall of 1820, despite the grounds being "vested in the Corporation for the purpose of a market," the project was abandoned due to lack of funding.[3]

At this point, quite literally, Fulton Market was resurrected from the ashes. A major conflagration in January 1821 destroyed most of the buildings on the site, leaving no other choice for the council than to pursue its original plans.[4] Certainly, Fulton Market remained a contentious matter, compelling local residents, property owners, market vendors, and the wider public in general to engage in an unprecedented scale of petitioning in favor of or against its construction.[5] What made the project exceptionally divisive was that never before had the city dug so deep into the public purse to improve its provisioning infrastructure. Total costs reached a staggering $220,000, making Fulton not only New York's most expensive public market but also one of the costliest public works the city had hitherto undertaken.[6] The price alone explains why its opening was accompanied by such a public spectacle.[7]

From this perspective, Fulton Market epitomizes the culmination of a subtle but important development in the history of New York's public market model of provisioning. The willingness of city officials to consistently expand the market system to sustain Gotham's accelerating growth after the War of 1812 resulted in a gradual transition, for lack of better words, from a "communal" to a "public" infrastructure. Whereas traditionally, marketplaces functioned as neighborhood institutions—funded, built, and managed by the local community of stakeholders of residents and market vendors—from the 1810s, they increasingly consolidated into an infrastructural system falling directly under the fiscal and administrative responsibility of the government. The completion of Washington Market in 1813 was already a move in this direction, but Fulton Market raised the stakes and committed the Common Council to a public market system.[8] Underlying this development was the city government's expanding public powers and responsibilities in response to urban growth.[9]

Common markets had served New Yorkers for generations as the primary sites to purchase provisions. That they should remain so even after the city set out on a path to a new age of feverish growth, however, was not self-evident. In fact, the Commissioners' Plan of 1811, arguably the most influential document to anticipate New York's rise as the "Metropolis of the Union," had already outlined an alternative vision to erect one central wholesale market in the northern suburbs, and to relocate the retail of food supplies from neighborhood marketplaces to unregulated and dispersed private shops.[10] Even the completion of Fulton Market was a fluke insofar as the fire turned the appropriated site useless. Had Fulton not been built, city officials might have felt less compelled to erect additional markets. At least, this is what one group of petitioners objecting to the plan contended when they warned that Fulton Market would "be used as a pretext for the removal of the Catharine-Market, the building of a new Market in the southerly part of the city, and the opening and extending of Beekman-Street; which . . . will add about three hundred thousand dollars to our present debts, already enormous and oppressive."[11] Such improvements, they warned, would lead to further engagement of municipal funds for the expansion of the market system and other public works.

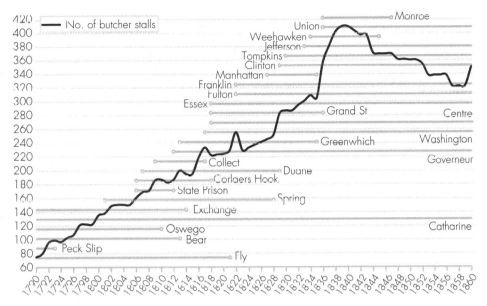

FIGURE 1.1. Expansion of the public market system, 1790–1860. (*Sources*: See text and appendix B)

To the petitioners' credit, this is by and large what happened. In the next fifteen years, existing marketplaces were upgraded while additional ones were built to supply urbanizing neighborhoods. Figure 1.1 documents the period of operation of the individual public markets between 1790 and 1860, and also traces the total number of butcher stalls within the system.[12] Two periods are outlined by the chart. First, in the two decades between the opening of Washington Market in 1813 and the building of Monroe and Union in 1836, the market system went through a period of expansion.[13] It appears that the council devoted considerable municipal resources for the improvement of its provisioning system. But this was followed by a second period from the mid-1830s, when the development of the infrastructure reached a standstill.[14] In fact, not a single new public market was opened after 1836.[15] Despite New York's relentless growth from 300,000 to 800,000 residents, two aging marketplaces were even shut down after 1845.[16]

If the construction of Fulton Market marks the zenith of the public market system, its demise is most effectively captured by the Common Council's decision on January 20, 1843, to repeal the market laws after two years of heated public debates.[17] What this legislative change actually meant was that public markets were no longer the exclusive sites for the retail of meat supplies. Instead of limiting the sale of fresh meat to licensed market butchers, the council now permitted anyone to open a private shop. At first, this may appear a rather insignificant change, but given the centrality of meat in the American urban diet, and its anchoring role in agglomerating the trade of all fresh food supplies and other provisions in and around the public markets, deregulation in effect meant the disintegration of the very foundation of the municipal provisioning model. The transition from a municipally managed to a wholly unregulated food economy, in turn, had far-reaching consequences for the geography of food access, the daily routines of household provisioning, and the living standards of residents. While no one could have anticipated these outcomes, all constituent parties, city officials, food purveyors, and residents alike grasped the significance of this decision.

From the long-term perspective, the repealing of the market laws represented a historical departure from the colonial heritage of tightly regulated food markets. Already, from the 1670s on, the council allowed only licensed butchers to retail fresh meat at the marketplaces, and as noted in the introduction, the legal ground for the model was asserted by the Montgomery Charter of 1730.[18] The 1735 market laws declared that no person "shall buy, or cause to be bought, any *Victuals* or other *Provisions* . . . within the said City of *New-York* . . . before the same shall be brought into one of the said Markets, ready to be there Sold." To eliminate the middlemen, the laws also prohibited anyone "to sell the same again in his, her or their Shop or Shops, or in any of the Markets or other Places."[19] The council furnished retail butchers with individual stalls in exchange for market fees, forging an enduring alliance with them.[20] By the Early Republican period, as the 1793 market laws reveal, the categories of butcher's meats—"Beef, Pork, Veal, Mutton or Lamb"—were also firmly established.[21] Moreover, by prohibiting any butcher from selling his goods in any other part of the market "than at his own licensed Stall or Standing," the laws further cemented the butchers' dependence on their assigned places.[22] Subsequent market laws in 1812, 1814, and 1833 reiterated the butchers' monopoly over the retail of fresh meat, a clause that increasingly served as the legislative cornerstone of the municipal provisioning model. This was precisely the passage that came under intense public scrutiny by the 1830s, and was finally repealed in 1843.

Of course, the public market system was never as airtight as the laws would have it.[23] To begin with, each market had a separate country section where visiting farmers could sell meat or other provisions, grown on their own farms, without having to pay fees.[24] This concession aimed at keeping food prices low by eliminating the middlemen. One unforeseen consequence was that "shirk butchers" also occupied the country markets, and, posing as farmers, retailed meat without licenses.[25] Another concern was that given the city's rapid growth, thinly urbanized northern districts might have been temporarily left without markets. To address this, the council licensed butchers case by case from the early nineteenth century in such frontier areas to sell meat in street stalls or from their own homes, hence establishing a precedent for meat shops.[26] Permits were provisional and kept few in number, even as nonmarket vendors were subject to the same rules and fees as market butchers. By 1817, the council integrated this system through a simple spatial logic: outside vendors could sell meat only north of the "market boundaries," in thinly populated districts. As urbanization and the market facilities caught up, these boundaries were pushed northward, reaching Fourteenth Street by 1840.[27] This was a systematic albeit small exception to the market laws: compared to the 376 market butchers, the number of licensed nonmarket butchers was thirty in 1840.[28] One last accommodation concerned grocers, who were permitted to sell fresh pork after 1817.[29] Yet fresh pork was a minor part of an average New Yorker's diet and thus represented a small modification to the overall intent of the market laws.

A much greater challenge to the market system was the numerous violations that occurred outside of the regulatory framework. The frequent reiterations of the market laws are themselves suggestive that unlicensed food distribution by nonmarket vendors must have continued throughout the period. There appears to be a consensus among historians that by the late 1830s, this unregulated economy reached such proportions that "it was becoming clear that the marketing laws were virtually a dead letter."[30] Whether or not this was the case will be explored later. What matters here is that, insofar as city officials shared this perspective, the revoking of the market laws in 1843 was the formalization of an existing informal economy. If so, the chronology suggests that the council's inattention to its market infrastructure from the mid-1830s on was in part to blame for the proliferation of an informal sector, constituted by unlicensed vendors and customers, a development that undermined the city's traditional public market–based provisioning system.

While this is a persuasive account, it leaves one question unexplained: Why did city officials become reluctant to expand the market system? The discontinuity is puzzling given that from the early 1810s onward they allocated considerable sums for the infrastructure's improvement. In the next quarter century, they opened the modern Fulton Market, upgraded existing facilities, and erected new ones in urbanizing areas. Yet their views changed by the mid-1830s, reflecting an ideological shift in antebellum political economy in favor of open access and free competition. Indeed, frustrated by the endless petitions of butchers to preserve the market laws, city comptroller D. D. Williamson bluntly summarized the new administrative position in December 1842: "the age has gone by, when a Market monopoly will be tolerated in this community, and the sooner that part of the Market Law is repealed the better."[31] Legislation followed within a month, leading to the market laws' repeal, effectively destroying the regulatory pillar of the municipal system.

In the next decade, officials came less and less to consider the public market system, and access to food in general, as a public good to be managed by the city government. As market incentives were given free rein, profitability became the sole criteria by which to judge a public market's utility. In 1854, introducing a new cost-benefit calculation, Comptroller A. C. Flagg, a firm believer in unregulated provision markets, established that the public markets were losing money for the city and suggested leasing them to private investors.[32] The council went further, entertaining the idea of privatizing all facilities, a strategy also endorsed by Mayor Fernando Wood in 1856.[33] And while at the end public markets were neither leased nor sold, it is evident that, after the mid-1830s, the municipal model of provisioning had been gradually dismantled.

But how and why did city officials come to regard the public market system, arguably New York City's oldest and socially most embedded municipal service, in such a negative light? Why did its perception change from a vital public good to a symbol of unfair trade monopoly and a financial burden for the city and taxpayers?[34] The expansion of free-market ideology in antebellum America, no doubt, played an important role, and other scholars have turned to this interpretation.[35] This view is also compatible with the previously mentioned account that an informal economy, emerging in the niches left open by insufficient market facilities, propelled authorities toward deregulation. After all, what was the informal economy if not the free market in action, only outside of municipal regulation? Given that unlicensed vendors had proven their worth and resilience, it was not without foundation to assume that the free market was able to organize the distribution of food supplies, letting the council off the hook to sustain a critical and complex infrastructure.

Certainly, a growing faith in free markets prevailed in the council's decision to deregulate the provisioning system in 1843. Comptrollers Williamson and Flagg and Mayor Wood made no secret about their preferences. Still an overarching shift to free-market ideology is too simple a framework on two grounds. First, according to this narrative, the free-market consensus overturned the traditional municipal model of provisioning, the core institutions of which were the city's public markets with their various trade privileges and obligations.[36] One problem is that this narrative outlines an imprecise chronology. It depicts the public market model as unchanging and overlooks the subtle but important shift between 1813 and the mid-1830s, when neighborhood marketplaces consolidated into a citywide system to serve a much larger population. The point is that deregulation did not simply overturn a traditional provisioning model; rather, it reversed the market system's partial development to become a modern municipal infrastructure, much like the Croton Waterworks would later become.

This leads to the second issue, namely, that the market system's deregulation did not happen in isolation but was part of an ongoing negotiation over public and private goods in the antebellum political economy. Was it mere coincidence that just as citizens' access to food was pushed from the public to the private domain, the provisioning of water was increasingly socialized?[37] Evidently, city officials felt confident in handing over to the free market a policy area long regarded as a municipal responsibility, even as they recognized the need to invest in massive public works to address another. For the problem of food provisioning, the question of "Why deregulation?" should hence be complemented by "Why no further socialization?" The answer to this, in narrower terms, resides with the city's changing fiscal condition by the 1840s. More broadly, the contrary trajectories in the provisioning of these two essential goods demonstrate the reality of antebellum municipal governance, whereby ever-changing urban problems resulted in different policy decisions. The labyrinthine narrative of how food access shifted from communal to public to private good from the 1790s to the 1840s provides an illuminating account of these complex negotiations.

Public Markets as Neighborhood Institutions

In the introduction, William Novak's concepts of the public economy and well-ordered market were used to describe the principles of the municipal model of provisioning.[38] Others have turned to E. P. Thompson's theory of the "moral economy" or relied on such terms as "paternalism" to interpret this institutional arrangement.[39] Whichever concept is used, there is a consensus that the model's rationale was to ensure that citizens had access to adequate, healthy, and affordable provisions, and that, to this purpose, it fell upon the municipal government to sustain fair and well-regulated markets in food supplies.[40] These accounts emphasize how public markets and market laws served to balance private, corporatist, and public interests for the general welfare of residents.[41]

Indeed, the municipal model was an institutional arrangement by which urban communities sought to control the exchange of life's necessities under a tightly knit legal, social, and economic order with well-defined rules and responsibilities, and spatial and temporal boundaries.[42] While this interpretation provides a useful starting point, it has certain limitations. First, both the moral economy and well-ordered market are normative concepts, better at capturing the rationale and justification of the public market model than its practice and reality. The moral economy theory, in particular, has been used by scholars in a variety of contexts to describe an alternative, fairer, and socially more embedded economic system than free-market capitalism, one not driven by private gain and profit but by reciprocal rights and obligations.[43] The risk is to mistake these ideals for the reality by focusing too much on what the public markets were supposed to achieve instead of how they actually functioned on the ground. The benefit of the well-ordered market concept is that it is more limited to the model's regulatory environment.

Another and related point is that the moral economy lens tends to accentuate cooperation over competition, consensus over conflict.[44] However, when shifting the focus to the ground, the public market system may be best described as a tripartite model of political arbitration, where the three constituent parties of customers, vendors, and city officials relied on a range of mechanisms—including petitioning, regulations, the allocation of public funds, and informal control—to constantly renegotiate the common good of urban provisioning. From this viewpoint, competition and conflict between and within the parties were just as central to the public market model's functioning as were cooperation and consensus. Further, deregulation presented a historical departure, not so much by changing the motives and incentives of the food economy's participants but by moving the arbitration process from the realm of decentralized local politics to self-regulating free markets.

From the political economy perspective, the question is how the urban community financed the construction, expansion, and maintenance of its food infrastructure.[45] Traditionally, public markets in New York were erected not by the city government but through voluntary subscriptions of concerned parties, especially local residents and property holders. Catharine Market serves as a case in point: in 1786, Henry Rutgers, along with other prominent residents in the vicinity, "prayed permission to erect a public market-house at Catharine Slip, at their own expense."[46] The subscribers were both to furnish the grounds and cover the construction costs, leaving the council only to appoint a committee "to determine the place and the manner of building the market-house."[47] Within a month, Rutgers reported the marketplace ready for the accommodation of the butchers and farmers. From this point on, the council assumed greater responsibility, allocating municipal funds to enlarge, renovate, and rebuild Catharine Market, as well as to invest in complementary infrastructures.[48] Still, voluntary contributions by local stakeholders continued to play a role in any market's life. For example, the expansion of Fly Market, the city's oldest and largest, galvanized numerous subscribers in 1789.[49] Similarly, in 1793, the council endorsed the petition of residents in Bear Market's vicinity to enlarge their own marketplace.[50]

This Early Republican version of a public-private partnership in financing the market infrastructure could assume many arrangements. Besides erecting a marketplace with local contributions, subscribers often solicited the council to match private collections with public funds.[51] In 1788, a group of inhabitants "of the Neighborhood of the Exchange" requested permission to erect a market "at their own expense." The council approved the project, and soon the construction began. Yet the costs exceeded the available funds, and the next year, the subscribers petitioned "for aid of the Corporation in the finishing of the market-house lately erected; to which the Board granted £15 towards its completion."[52] Similarly, in 1812, Mr. Bergh asked the council to cover the sizable shortfall between his own expenses of erecting Governeur Market and the amount collected. "From a belief that a work of so general utility would require but little solicitation to obtain subscription adequate to defray the expenses," he overestimated his neighbors' generosity.[53] The construction of Greenwich Market in 1812–13 was unique in that funds originated from three sources at the outset: expenses were divided about equally between the treasury and local subscribers, while the ground on which the market stood was ceded free of charge by Trinity Church.[54]

On the whole, between 1786 and 1813, New York's population quadrupled to reach nearly 100,000. Meanwhile, nine new markets were built, even as only three were closed, and the construction of all of them relied on neighborhood subscriptions, at times bolstered by public funding.[55] One should note that this model of financing originated from an earlier era. For example, voluntary subscriptions built the large-scale Bear Market in 1771,[56] and one year later, local residents raised £300 through a neighborhood lottery to erect Oswego Market, while to purchase the ground, they turned to voluntary subscriptions.[57] Several other cases could be cited that would push the chronology further back. In fact, in his 1854 report, Comptroller Flagg criticized the alleged wastefulness of the market system of his own time by comparing it to this more frugal period. In researching the subject, he found that "commencing with 1699, the inhabitants built the market-houses at their own cost . . . and it is believed that the first market built at the expense of the Corporation, after 1699, was in 1812, when the present Washington market was built." From this he opportunistically concluded that back then the "inhabitants were competent for self-government, so far as the business of conducting their own markets is concerned."[58]

This neighborhood-centered model of financing the construction of public markets may appear as evidence of community cooperation in the logic of a moral economy. To be sure, a sense of civic engagement was central to the process. Just as important, there were well-defined particularistic interests at work. Evidently, residents of each vicinity depended on a municipal market to provision their households. In almost every case, petitioners justified their request for a new marketplace by declaring that they lived too far from convenient access to one.[59] Given that market construction was funded by voluntary subscriptions, in theory, there could have been as many market-houses as there were communities willing to pay for them. Yet two factors, both deriving from spatial conditions, limited their overall number. First, there was the scarcity of land: after all, markets had to be built on either public or private grounds. Most often, they stood in the middle of the street as this was "freely" available land insofar as the council endorsed their construction.[60] But there they interfered with traffic, so a legitimate demand had to justify why the council would reserve a specific piece of public space for provisioning.

A more complex issue was that market vendors supplied residents insofar as they sustained reasonable profits. In practice this meant that there was a limit to the overall number of vendors in the city and at each marketplace, given that markets relied on a regular pool of customers from their respective neighborhoods. Market vendors, especially the best-organized trade of butchers, ardently protected their alleged spheres of interest, pressuring the council to ensure that the catchment areas of the individual markets did not overlap. Petitions to erect a new marketplace often triggered vehement protests from vendors at nearby locations.[61] In fact, any change to the marketplaces prompted a cacophony of conflicting demands. By and large, the political mandate that all citizens were entitled to convenient access to food supplies had to be balanced by the legitimate business interests of various groups of vendors. In practice, it fell upon the council to negotiate the number, locations, and sizes of the public markets, thereby limiting the total supply of vendors, and all of this under the pressure of accelerating urbanization.

Further, locational considerations meant that just like obtaining other utilities—gas lighting, street pavement, or water pumps—neighborhoods competed with one another to build or enlarge their market facilities even if until 1812 they bore most of the costs. Notably, such competition was not solely motivated by residents' need for convenient access to food supplies. Subscribers were often not local tenants but prominent residents, especially property holders from the vicinity, who considered the public market a worthwhile investment.[62] Building a market was critical to settling and developing frontier areas, thereby increasing the value of real estate there, generating higher rents for landlords. The principle that those who benefited the most from a public improvement should cover the costs gained traction in Early Republican municipal governance.[63] Indeed, special assessments on real estate were increasingly used to fund public works from streets to parks.[64] Similarly, the initiative behind the opening of new marketplaces shifted from residents to property holders. Whereas the lottery scheme that funded the building of Oswego Market in

1772 dispersed expenses among 2,500 inhabitants, only 121 subscribers signed up for the construction of Exchange Market in 1789, while in the case of Greenwich Market in 1812, donations were pulled from only fifty-nine citizens. Such declining participation from neighborhood inhabitants likely reflected deeper changes in the Manhattan housing market, whereby an increasing share of local populations became tenants as opposed to owner-occupants. What powered this transition toward urban tenancy was rapid urban growth, which turned Manhattan land into a highly profitable investment.[65]

Built by a specific alignment of competing and complementary interests, the urban marketplace was a genuinely neighborhood venture. With the endorsement of the Common Council, however, it also became a public infrastructure. This process is best documented in the case of Crown Market. In 1772, the local stakeholders informed the board that they "had erected a building as a market-house . . . and were desirous of conveying the same to the Corporation for public use." Others were "requesting the Board to accept this market-house," and after the owners released the ground on which the market stood, it was accepted: "the Board do hereby establish the same building as a publick market-house accordingly."[66] The tradition of handing over communally built market-houses to the city appears to have dated back to 1735, when a "provision was made for the Common Council to take charge of all the markets," for which purpose the Market Committee was created.[67] Even if the boundaries between municipal and communal ownership and control remained fluid,[68] from this point on, to borrow Comptroller Flagg's words, "the market-houses . . . although built at the expense of private individuals, were considered public markets."[69] It is important to underline the word "considered," for it conveys how much these market-houses stood at the intersection of public and private interests.

Further complicating matters, butchers constituted yet another group of prominent stakeholders with both formal and informal claims over the marketplaces. Market space was divided into stalls, and butchers, unlike the other vendors, sold meat from these individually assigned retail spaces. When the city took charge of the public markets in 1735, it numbered the stalls with the original intent to lease them.[70] Its first attempt to earn taxes through stall rents, however, was abandoned in five years, and the council returned to the old method of collecting excise taxes on the amount of butcher's meats sold until 1822.[71] The largest and busiest Fly Market became one curious exception. In 1796, the council renovated and enlarged the lower market-house, and since there were far too many butchers applying for the fourteen new stalls available, it resorted to selling those via public auctions to "licensed Butchers subject to such regulations & fees as the Corporation may direct from time to time."[72] They sold for remarkably high sums, contributing an impressive £3,470 to the treasury. Within less than a month, nine more vacant stalls at the less desirable upper market were also sold in the same fashion for a total of £498.[73]

From 1735 on, the butchers were associated with their respective marketplaces, and within those the specific spaces from where they sold their goods. The auction of twenty-three out of Fly Market's seventy-one stalls further cemented this relationship. In effect, butchers became "shareholders" of Fly Market. As a 1799 report remarks, the Fly Market butchers "understand the right to the stalls is vested in them, their heirs and assigns forever."[74] Even though they needed the council's consent to transfer their stalls to other butchers, their widows, or heirs, this became a common routine, generally approved by the Market Committee.[75] To be sure, butchers traded stalls informally in other markets as well, even if in those cases no property rights were passed from the council to the butchers in the first place.[76] The issue here is not to sort out who exactly held the property rights in what cases but to note how butchers, paying taxes to the council and retailing meat daily by their stalls—even in those public markets, where they had never purchased nor leased stalls—regarded them as their properties. Such informal claims were not always respected by the council. But those of the Fly Market butchers had to be. In 1822, when Fly was replaced by Fulton Market, a group of these butchers sued the city for the damages they had suffered for losing their properties. The verdict favored the butcher who filed the test case, and soon after the city settled on compensating all the other plaintiffs in "the amount paid for the stalls which they held at the time the market was pulled down, together with the interests from that time to the present." Total compensations exceeded $10,000, demonstrating the significant real estate value of market space.[77]

To conclude, public markets in New York City from the eighteenth through the early nineteenth century were neighborhood institutions that belonged to three groups of stakeholders: the local community of customers, especially the subscribers; the licensed vendors, in particular, the butchers; and the City Corporation, which legally owned and managed the infrastructure. It is worth noting that, until 1821, the clerks and later the deputy clerks of the markets, whose duty it was to collect fees and enforce the laws and regulations, were also stakeholders, for they were not salaried officials but were entitled to 10 percent of the revenues.[78] Property rights, demands, and duties were not clearly differentiated or set in stone but often overlapped and were subject to renegotiations. In the public markets' political economy, private, communal, and public spheres often converged. Yet just as important, the public markets were the products of myriad competing interests asserted through local politics.

Consequently, no master plan underlay the expansion of this vital infrastructure. Initiatives for opening a new public market always originated from the bottom up. In principle, the model was responsive to demands on the ground precisely because the marketplace was a neighborhood-level compromise among the parties involved. The markets added up to a system only insofar as the Market Committee arbitrated agreements, not only at the level of individual facilities but across the city. How well this model worked to sustain the provisioning of a rapidly growing city will be studied in chapter 2. Yet from the fiscal standpoint, the model was flexible and capable of growth. Through the political economy lens, what is important to note is that in an effort to bring the city's food supplies under government control, the public market model replaced the free-market coordination of supply and demand with a decentralized, complex, and at times contentious political arbitration, whereby stakeholders could press their legitimate needs. The moral economy idea pertains more to the consensus reached at the end. Yet the deliberative process was just as much the public market model as the resultant infrastructure.

THE MARKET SYSTEM AS MUNICIPAL INFRASTRUCTURE

The first market-house to be built entirely by the public purse, Comptroller Flagg correctly noticed, was Washington Market in 1812–13. Plans to "erect a substantial and commodious Market house" to replace Bear Market, which was "in a state of decay" were first proposed in 1805.[79] Seven years later, city officials decided to pursue the project. The Market Committee reported that the lots taken up by Bear Market "if disposed of constitute a fund sufficient to erect an accommodating market on a spacious & elegant plan." Notably, this new marketplace was to "occupy the square bounded by Washington, West, Partition & Vesey Streets & forming a hollow square in the center for the resort and convenience of the Vegetable & Fruit dealers."[80] Construction began in the summer of 1812, and even if the scale of the project was reduced considerably, for the committee found that "one half of said plan at present will answer all purposes," Washington, completed by the end of 1813, was by far Gotham's largest public market.[81] It was also the most expensive one, with overall costs reaching an impressive $22,500.[82]

The building was an elegant brick structure: two stories high, with the second floor additionally serving as a watchhouse, supported by imposing stone pillars and furnished with a cupola and a bell.[83] Importantly, it was the first market in New York not situated on a public street but inside the block, occupying a square-shaped ground plan. Scholars have distinguished two conventional market types in Early America.[84] The street market, typically standing in the middle of a street, was the simpler and more popular design. Preceding Washington, all market-houses in New

York were frame or brick street markets, which, by virtue of occupying public space, were cheaper to build. Their disadvantage was that they obstructed traffic, not only by blocking passage through a densely built city but also in terms of carting goods in and out of the marketplace. Furthermore, their limited size and often narrow, elongated shape could make shopping a crowded experience. Yet these were small inconveniences compared to the benefit that they did not require a valuable piece of land to be withdrawn from the real estate market. At the same time, an elegant, spacious, and expandable market like Washington had to be built on a city block and on a square-shaped ground plan. Conveniently in this case, the city owned the lots, which significantly reduced the construction costs.[85]

Washington Market also signals a more consequential shift from the marketplaces' operation as neighborhood institutions to their consolidation as a public infrastructure system, both in terms of political economy and function. This was a gradual development, not limited to Gotham's food system but more generally corresponding to the municipality's broadening public powers and responsibilities under the pressure of accelerating growth.[86] Reflecting this citywide perspective, in 1820, for the first time, the City Corporation appraised the value of its market property. Tellingly, Washington Market alone represented three-fourths of the real estate value of the entire system.[87] If city officials were to continue to erect comparably spacious markets, community-based funding was no longer viable. Notably, this shift to increased public investments was not self-evident. Only a year before, the Commissioners' Plan of 1811 proposed a different vision to address the provisioning needs of the future metropolis: a single wholesale market up north that supplied a network of dispersed, private retail shops.[88] To be sure, Washington was more than just a neighborhood market. Standing by the Hudson River, it could, and in a few decades it did, acquire wholesale functions, despite its southwestern location not being optimal as a central hub to distribute supplies. One outcome of erecting Washington Market was that the council had to build a set of additional small markets to supply developing northern vicinities. Another was that it set the precedent and necessitated a far more ambitious project to replace the dilapidated Fly Market with a more modern building on the opposite side of the island by the East River.

As for small neighborhood markets, in the next decade, the council built three such facilities, two of which were to replace old decaying buildings. These were Centre, Grand, and Essex Markets, all supplying sprawling northern districts. Importantly, despite their modest construction costs, in all three cases residents no longer asked for permission to erect their own marketplace but instead requested one from the council, which built it with public funds.[89] For instance, Essex Market was built in response to a petition by local residents declaring that "the rapid increase of population in this ward . . . render it necessary in our opinion, that a market should be erected for our accommodation."[90] In other words, even if the demand still originated from the neighborhood, the construction process and its financing, once the responsibility of interested local stakeholders, was now relegated to the wider public. Insofar as the council was to limit its commitment to similarly modest market-houses, while incrementally upgrading older ones, its market system would have remained a low-cost infrastructure for taxpayers.

It was in this context that Fulton Market was a paradigm changer, for the expenses, nearly all of which occurred in 1821–22, were astronomical. With total costs reaching $216,768, three-fourths of which was spent on purchasing the lands, Fulton Market was by far the city's most expensive market-house,[91] as well as the third most costly public works project, only behind the new Almshouse and the new City Hall.[92] Funding such an "improvement" was not just beyond the scale of subscriptions, but with total expenses reaching 30 percent of annual revenues, it also exceeded available public funds.[93] The original financial plan of 1816 was designed to "incur (no permanent debt) and create no necessity for the imposition of additional taxes."[94] The city would draw on $140,000 of federal government funds, while an additional $80,000 would be borrowed at a yearly interest of 10 percent.[95] Rents earned at Fulton Market, a projected $22,600 annually, would redeem this loan in five years, "after which period the entire revenue can be appropriated to the *sinking fund* which together with the permanent income it now has will in a few years extinguish the whole funded debt of the City." For the first time, the building of a public market was conceived as a long-term infrastructural investment. The financial plan, in particular to issue city stocks to borrow the missing sum, mirrored the state-funding schemes of massive canal networks like the Erie, constructed at the same time as Fulton Market, and anticipated future municipal public works like the Croton aqueduct or Central Park.[96]

Moreover, the plan treated the building of a new and modern public market as a viable strategy to increase public revenues and therefore fund the city's growing debt burden. Construction failed to advance as planned. Bureaucratic dead-ends sidetracked the project, while by 1820, the federal funds had been "applied to other purposes." At the same time, the council was committed to purchasing the grounds, while a Special Committee found "little probability" that rents would "produce the Revenue upon which the above calculation is founded."[97] The least bad option, it seemed, was to abandon the scheme and resell the lots, at which point, the conflagration in January 1821 saved Fulton Market.[98] Left without a viable exit option, the city forged ahead to build Fulton, and with notable speed. By

March the project was authorized, this time with no pretense that it would cost nothing to taxpayers. "Resolved, that Fifteen thousand dollars be raised annually for Ten years by tax, which together with the income from the said Market, shall be appropriated to the sinking fund, for the extinguishment of the debt created by the purchase of the said ground, and the erection of suitable buildings for a Market." The council then issued $200,000 worth of city stocks at a yearly interest of 5 percent, thereby raising the total value of the municipal debt by about 20 percent.[99] No later than the end of that year, Fulton Market was finished. Occupying an entire city block, and consisting of three stories, including a basement with thirty-two cellars, it was an incomparably more imposing building than Washington Market.[100] Even with the twists and turns of its financing, it was a powerful symbol of the Common Council's investments in the city's provisioning infrastructure.

To complete the account, over the next fifteen years, eight new markethouses were built, four of which replaced old, decrepit structures. The initiative always came from local residents customarily demanding more convenient access and better facilities through petitioning. Given the city's relentless growth, six of the eight new markets opened in northern districts: Manhattan (1827), Tompkins (1829), and Jefferson (1833) served communities that hitherto lacked access to a marketplace, whereas Weehawken (1834), Union (1836), and Monroe (1836) replaced aging structures. The only new public market in the city's southern part was Franklin (1822), a sensible addition after Fly's removal. Construction costs were borne by the taxpayers in all cases. Admittedly, none of these buildings came close to the scale and opulence of Fulton Market. Rather, they remained modest buildings meant to supply their respective vicinities, albeit no longer standing in the middle of the street but within the block. Even if the council had to acquire the lots, their smaller footprints ensured that building costs remained manageable.[101]

One exception was Clinton Market, erected in 1828 to replace the old Spring Street Market sheds. Standing by the Hudson River at the city's central-western zone, it was the most expensive of the eight new markethouses by a considerable margin. Total construction costs reached nearly $60,000, that is, about 50 percent more than the second-costliest Jefferson, or three times higher than the third-most expensive Tompkins Market. While certainly not as spacious and imposing as Fulton or Washington, Clinton Market also took up an entire city block and had a unique triangular-shaped ground plan. In addition to opening new public markets, the council also had the responsibility to maintain existing facilities, and in some cases, it approved major reconstruction works. For instance, Essex Market, first enlarged in 1822–23, was completely rebuilt in 1836–37, with a more spacious market-house on a rectangular plan, and one year later, the old Centre Market was upgraded with a similarly large modern facility.[102]

Overall, by 1838, among Gotham's thirteen public markets, no less than five occupied valuable lots and had extensive ground plans. When assessing the city's portfolio of public markets, the system looked much different from the situation prior to the building of Washington Market in 1813. Whether the council's investments were adequate to sustain a population that tripled to reach 300,000 is yet to be seen. Evidently, the political economy context had shifted, for public markets were no longer the responsibility of local stakeholders primarily. Once community institutions of neighborhood residents and market vendors, they had consolidated into a public infrastructure system, funded and managed solely by the city government. Fulton Market was unique in that no other markethouse cost a comparable sum, and in no other case did New Yorkers have to take on so much debt. Just as important, Fulton presented another turning point: with its completion, the council managed to overhaul its method of collecting market revenues to finance its much-enlarged provisioning system.

Traditionally, the council charged fees on the amount of butcher's meat sold. It fixed different rates for beef, veal, lamb and mutton, and pork, which were then collected by the market clerks, who kept 10 percent, while the rest was divided equally between the treasury and the mayor. Several attempts were made to boost revenues.[103] In 1790, the council proposed to lease out butcher stalls for yearly rents based on their respective values.[104] In a month, the plan fell through on the butchers' protest that this would hugely augment their tax burden.[105] Another attempt came in 1796 and 1798 with the sale of Fly Market stalls.[106] This implied a notable change, for it affected property rights, while the sums collected were twice the amount of annual market fees.[107] Still, the reform was partial because sales involved only twenty-three out of Fly Market's seventy-one and the city's 122 butcher stalls. Then again, after Washington Market was built, the council sought to increase revenues, a matter especially urgent once marketplaces depended entirely on public funds, and the city's debt obligations had sharply risen. In July 1813, the sinking fund was created to redeem the city stocks issued for building the new Almshouse and City Hall, and market fees, along with other corporation properties that earned revenues, were directed there, thereby becoming an important income stream to repay the debt.[108] Since there was always a shortage of vacant stalls, in 1816 the council proposed to sell "at auction . . . to the highest bidder . . . at annual rent, payable quarterly" all newly available stalls, a standard practice for the allocation of market cellars.[109] The butchers, again, fiercely protested. Forty of them remonstrated that this would cause them "great inconvenience and distress." For the last time, the council retreated, returning to its original custom of allocating stalls by lottery and collecting excise taxes.[110]

Fulton Market ushered in an overhaul of the fiscal foundations of the public market system. From the outset, it was planned as a major infrastructural investment, where retail leases played a central part in the project's financial viability. Significantly, the same legislation that approved Fulton Market's construction in March 1821, and stipulated that "the Stalls for the Butchers and the Stands for the Fishermen, Country people and sellers of Vegetables, and fruit shall be rented at Auction for one or more years," also resolved "that the aforesaid regulations shall apply to all the Markets in the City."[111] As expected, the city's butchers mobilized, and when Fulton Market stalls were auctioned on December 18, 1821, they attended only to boycott the event, except for one renegade butcher, a certain Leonard, who was grabbed by the others and "thrown in the river, and came near being drowned." Shortly after, the butchers humbly prayed "that instead of selling the stands at auction, the Corporation should affix a rent upon their respective stands as they should deem just."[112] By the second auction two weeks later, however, they caved in and placed their bids for five-year leases for each of the eighty-six stalls in the value of $18,865 of annual rents. Further, twenty-one market cellars for leases up to three years for a total annual rent of $9,575, and thirty-four huckster stands for three-year leases at an annual rent of $1,320, were auctioned.[113] Fishermen, country folk, and hucksters were to generate additional revenues. In total, Fulton Market alone should have earned $45,000 yearly income, almost five times the value of annual market fees in the late 1810s.[114]

These were overly optimistic calculations. Just within a few months, Fulton Market butchers demanded lower rents, and by November, no less than fifty-seven stalls were vacated, while many incapable of paying the amounts they owed pleaded for relief from the city jail.[115] Already in June, the council had given up on selling stalls at the other markets. Instead, it fixed annual rents for each stall based on their relative value within and across the public markets, which were then leased out to the butchers by individual contracts, a method also applied to the vacated Fulton Market stalls.[116] By the beginning of 1823, the new market revenue system at last shaped up. Henceforth, the council earned three sources of income. First, butchers paid annual stall rents, fixed by the Market Committee, in monthly and later weekly sums; market cellars were also leased out in this fashion. Second, all the other vendors, including fishermen, hucksters, and country folk, paid market fees, collected daily by the clerks. Third, the auction system was limited to so-called premium stalls. Despite the suggestion that these were prime retail spaces, in fact, the council used premiums to lease out recently vacated stalls to extract additional taxes from the butchers on top of their rents. Auctions for premiums began in 1822 but remained limited until 1829. That year Clinton Market opened, and each of its stalls were auctioned. Premiums were constantly decried by the butchers and were finally abandoned in 1835 after generating significant extra revenue.

How did the new revenue system perform? One matter is how rents, fees, and premiums altogether performed relative to the original model of market fees as excise taxes. On this account the record looks strong from the council's perspective, for by changing its method of taxation, it nearly quadrupled market revenues between 1818 and 1824, while the population grew by just 45 percent.[117] In comparison, between 1790 and 1818 market fees rose in proportion to the population (see figure 2.1 in chapter 2). Another consideration is the share of the market income within the municipal budget. In 1790, market revenues appear to have covered about 4.3 percent of all city expenses. By 1800, expenditures grew more than fourfold, while market fees only doubled, hence, they contributed to a declining portion of municipal revenues, which was compensated by a greater reliance on real and personal property taxes.[118] By 1813, market fees continued to decline to 1.7 percent, and by 1818 to 1.3 percent of all incomes. It is also true that by then they were transferred to the sinking fund, set up to finance the city's growing debt, where they comprised a considerable 21.7 percent of the revenues.[119] The reform in 1822 restored the market incomes' share of the municipal budget to the 1790s level. In 1824, they again represented no less than 4.1 percent of the City Corporation's and 52.9 percent of the sinking fund's income.[120]

A third and equally relevant measure concerns the balance of market revenues and expenditures. Precise and complete figures for market-related outlays prior to 1823 are not available, hence, figure 1.2 looks at annual balances between 1823 and 1845.[121] It documents how revenues by and large surpassed expenses over this period, except for 1828 and from 1834 until 1838, when significant sums were dispensed to purchase new grounds or renovate older facilities.[122] On the whole, the market system paid for itself; in fact, it even generated a positive balance: between 1823 and 1845, the surplus came close to $400,000. Yet before jumping to the conclusion that the system was designed to maximize profits, one should remember that between 1812 and 1821, the council had access to inadequate fees to cover mounting costs, especially when it borrowed $200,000 to build Fulton Market.

Unfair taxation was an allegation frequently made by the butchers in their opposition to auctions and premiums, and not without some justification. However, their stance that the council violated the market laws' principles, or, as one historian would interpret it, allowed the moral economy to disintegrate, overlooks the deeper political economy context.[123] A

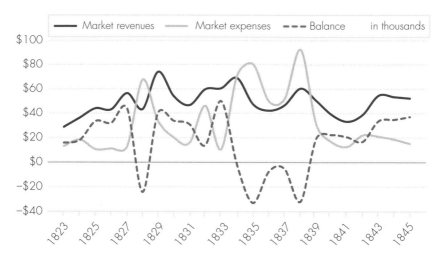

FIGURE 1.2. Market revenues and expenses, 1823–45. (*Sources*: See text and appendix B)

fair assessment would be that the new model of taxation served to revamp the market system as a financially sustainable, although hardly profitable, public infrastructure. Precisely because the council sought out ways to increase market revenues, it was able to build the magnificent Fulton Market in 1821, and to expand this vital infrastructure through the mid-1830s. In other words, if the moral economy, or, more accurately, the traditional neighborhood-based arbitration, was falling apart, it was not so much because the council sought to maximize revenues but rather because the urban scale was changing, and in that context marketplaces were developing into a system of modern public infrastructure. From this view it is even more interesting to grasp why in 1843 city officials dropped the ball and opted to deregulate the public market model. This was a major legislative shift, because deregulation meant the abandoning of the traditional consensus that provisioning was a public good, a municipal responsibility to be sustained by the council's police power and its close monitoring of the food supplies through its public markets.

DEREGULATION FROM BELOW

The public market model was described above as an institutional framework by which local residents, market vendors, and city officials pressed their interests and concerns to arbitrate the public good of provisioning.

The transition from neighborhood facilities to a system of public infrastructure changed this equation in subtle ways. Above all, taking on the responsibilities of building, overseeing, and the daily running of the public markets, the council became more directly invested in ensuring New Yorkers' access to food supplies. The market butchers remained key stakeholders; in fact, their personal leases and rising taxes gave them greater control over their respective marketplaces and vending spaces. Local residents, on the other hand, became less invested. Already by the late eighteenth century, subscriptions had shifted mainly to landowners, who financed market construction to boost the value of their properties. With municipal financing, residents withdrew one step further. Certainly, they remained equally reliant on public markets for their food supplies. But this relationship became less centered on their active involvement as stakeholders and more on their experience as customers, while the public markets became increasingly treated as one of several important urban amenities.

From the customers' perspective, the main question was how successfully the public markets ensured access to adequate quantities and quality of provisions at affordable prices. In theory, the market system could fall short of residents' expectations in two principal ways. First, given the costs of maintaining the infrastructure, it could inflate retail food prices. Butchers and other vendors paid substantial rents and fees for the right to sell at the markets, which costs in turn they shifted to customers. Second, the market system had an inbuilt spatial limitation. In a rapidly growing city, certain areas could be left underserved by market buildings. Even if the council had insisted on opening new facilities in urbanizing frontier districts, below a certain population, they made little sense, a problem to be explored in later chapters. Importantly, from the 1830s the public market system showed signs of malfunction on both fronts.

To begin with the first issue of taxation, in their memorial of March 19, 1830, titled "Liberty & Principle," the "General Executive Committee of Mechanics, Workingmen, and those friendly to their interests" confronted the council directly on the matter. "Why are our *provision markets* 25 percent higher on an average, than the markets in any city north of the Potomac possessing they do . . . the choicest productions of the most fertile districts in the world?" The answer, they found, was the dreadful state of municipal finances in general, and the public market system in particular. "What is the practical effect of this system," they asked, then replied with considerable clarity:

> The tax collected, is charged on the articles sold, and in due order paid by the consumers. . . . The rent and other dues, paid by the Butcher, and justly charged by him upon his meat, is also paid by

the consumer, and the practical result of your whole system is, that the meat market is forestalled—the vegetable huxsters forestall the vegetables, and the countryman's meats and vegetables are excluded from a free sale—your markets worse supplied, and articles dearer, not only by the tax and the expenses attending its collection, frauds etc. but also by the exclusion. And who are the consumers? We reply all the citizens.

These consumer citizens then pressed their case by highlighting the regressive nature of imposing sales taxes on basic necessities. "For nearly half a century the poor have been burthened and oppressed by the payment of a most unequal proportion of those exorbitant taxes, and that the just and republican principle, has been entirely lost sight of that taxation should follow property."[124]

Whether or not the mechanics' grievance was accurate, that retail food prices in New York were unjustifiably high, their complaints followed sound logic, for the public markets certainly introduced a form of taxation. The question is what was the alternative? As for the petitioners, they no longer requested the system's improvement but, reminiscent of the 1811 Commissioners' Plan, insisted on its complete overhaul based on a free-market model. They demanded that the city "sell all its properties in the markets"; "that it abolish all laws against forestalling, in as much as they cannot be enforced"; "that it establish in one or more places, country markets, where . . . every article may be sold free of Corporation tax"; "that Butchers and Huxters be permitted to sell meats and vegetables, in every part of the City"; and, most important, "that it abolish all market taxes."[125]

Citizens asserted ever more frequently that the public market system imposed unjust taxes on consumers, whereas free markets would deliver lower food prices. Popular sentiment was shifting in favor of open access and free competition, reflecting the emerging market ethos of antebellum America. City officials were not blind to such critiques. The Law and Market Committees, for example, acknowledged this argument with regards to premium stalls, and, on their guidance, the council abandoned their auctions in 1835.[126] Yet food prices began to rise from the mid-1830s (see figures 6.2–6.3 in chapter 6), further intensifying antimonopoly and anti-tax rhetoric aimed at the public markets. In 1836, the Butchers' Committee requested that the council reduce rents, for "an impression has gone ahead and gained some credit that the present high price of eatables is conclusively owing to our present market regulations and high rents."[127] Three years later, the Market Committee also commented that "the late high prices of beef may have given some foundation for the belief that some different policy should be resorted to from the present."[128] Others opposed taxation on ideological grounds, such as the Equal Rights Party, which in 1836 remonstrated that the public market system was an "odious monopoly," defying the principles of free trade while also inflicting an "unequal oppressive and unjust tax on the useful and poor classes of the community."[129] Hundreds of grocers and food purveyors seized upon this point, stressing that "a very large part of our Citizens, are from nature of their occupations, compelled to live upon daily supplies from the Grocers and nearest Meat Shops, as a matter of economy and in short, necessity."[130]

Excluding the issue of premiums, the council by and large avoided confronting allegations of unfair taxation. It fell upon the Market Committee, the main supporter of the market laws, to defend the system on the ground that it preserved the public health of the community, even as it produced key revenues to fund the municipal debt.[131] Other officials less friendly to the market vendors—members of special committees, the Finance Committee, or the comptroller—leaned toward repealing the market laws, not only because they violated the principle of free trade and were troublesome to enforce but also because they failed to generate sufficient incomes.[132] Municipal officials on both sides of the argument understood that the public market system implied some taxation; their views mainly differed whether this was fair or unfair, and whether the revenues amounted to major or trivial sums. Either way, the Common Council faced mounting pressure from below in the form of an emerging public consensus that an alternative model of provisioning, defined by open entry and free competition among food purveyors, would benefit consumers.[133] Shifting public opinion must have swayed many in government to reassess their commitment to the public market system. Indeed, the people's voice weighed more heavily on the minds of elected officials as the franchise was expanded to include all white men in New York State in 1826, and New Yorkers at last acquired the right to elect their mayor directly in 1834.[134]

Moving on to the second problem, the public market system's spatial limitations, intriguingly, this subject was also framed within the discourse of taxation, for insofar as the market laws were a given, not having a marketplace near one's home could be regarded as an unfair tax burden. The underlying point that "one hour spent in market is frequently worth more than the whole of . . . purchases" had already been established by the Commissioners' Plan in 1811 to make the case for a system of dispersed private shops.[135] It was articulated again in 1818, when local inhabitants requested that the council erect Essex Market. The petitioners described themselves as "persons of moderate circumstances," and argued that the "market hours generally interfere with the hours of labour, and is a heavy tax upon those who live so great a distance from it," especially for the poor, who "can only purchase small quantities at a time as they came in possession of the means."[136] By 1837, citizens more explicitly argued that the market laws deprived a "class of persons . . . from earning a livelihood for themselves and their families," while for those living too far from a public market, "imposing a tax upon their time."[137]

To be fair, the market laws did address this extra burden on time by the option to license butchers case by case to retail out of street stalls or shops in underserved areas. On their part, local customers endorsed trusted vendors enthusiastically. For instance, in 1810, inhabitants of a northeastern district requested a "special license" for Blaze Tenbrook, "who has been regularly taught the art of butchering." They further recommended "licensing, at least, two stalls in this and every other appropriate vicinity at too great a distance from a public market."[138] In 1817, the council established market boundaries, restricting nonmarketplace vendors to north of First Street east of the Bowery, and north of Thirteenth Street west of Broadway, that is, to thinly urbanized frontier areas.[139] Over the next two decades, market butchers tried to push these boundaries northward, whereas nonmarket butchers and their customers resisted. Not until two years later, in 1828, did the Centre Market butchers persuade the council against the objection of the Bowery butchers to redraw the line at Tenth Street east of Broadway.[140] By this time, hundreds of resident petitioners defended their nonmarket suppliers, a sign that the market laws were starting to lose public support.[141] As part of the regular process, albeit with some delays, the new Tompkins Market was opened to supply the vicinity.[142] Yet by the mid-1830s, the expansion of market facilities clearly fell behind the city's growth. In 1836, quite tellingly, well over a hundred residents endorsed street butcher Daniel Hyde's endeavor to "enlarge his establishment."[143]

Provisioning one's household through licensed butchers outside of the public markets was not very different from the alternative of relying on unlicensed vendors. The council did not keep an updated register of licensed street and shop butchers, nor did it closely monitor their operations.[144] Their number remained small, however, an estimated thirty north of Fourteenth Street in 1840, by then the market boundary, licensed only to remedy the market infrastructure's temporary spatial limitations.[145] In other words, they originally provided a complementary and marginal arrangement. Yet by the mid-1830s, there is growing evidence that unlicensed street vendors, shop butchers, and grocers, many of whom once held permits, created a parallel system of informal retail. To be sure, informal food trade always existed in the city. Shirk butchers crowded into the country markets, pretending that they were farmers, while fresh meat and fish were occasionally hawked through the streets or sold at outdoor stands and stores by vendors without permits.[146]

What changed by the mid-1830s was that, despite prior investments in the market infrastructure, in certain areas this informal economy gradually moved from the margins into the center. Nonmarket vendors, licensed or not, attended to both problems of the municipal model. Being spatially flexible, they swiftly responded to unmet demand. Avoiding rents, they could also undersell market vendors. The sources are unanimous that unlicensed food retail was on the rise. In 1835, for the first time, city officials acknowledged "that it is already impossible to prevent meat from being sold in other places than the Markets."[147] From this point, the Market Committee's main concern became how to address the "increasing evil of unlicensed butchers selling meat at shops in various parts of the city in open violation of the law."[148] Efforts to repress the practice failed for "the difficulty in bringing those persons to punishment . . . from the want of any evidence."[149] The Market Committee pursued tougher enforcement. In 1837, two market superintendents were employed; two years later, the street inspectors and health wardens were enlisted; by 1842, two special marshals patrolled the streets as well: all of this to no avail.[150] Meanwhile, members of the other committees began to seriously consider the option of legalizing unlicensed vendors by lifting the market laws' restrictions.[151] In the final years of the public market system, the council concurrently pursued stronger policing while also exploring the legal ramifications of repealing the market laws, in particular, how to compensate those butchers who paid out large sums for premium stalls.[152]

Prolonged confusion galvanized public support as groups of citizens protested the repression of nonmarket butchers. In one unusually confrontational petition from 1837, echoing the bitter political battles surrounding the Bank War, 108 signatories declared that "the meat shops, so far from being nuisances, are a great public convenience; and they hope that the Corporation will pause before they cause them to be hunted down by a system of espionage."[153] Others humbly requested that "the Bye Law prohibiting the sale of fresh meats, at places other than the public markets" be repealed.[154] Grocers and other nonmarket vendors seized the momentum. In 1837, no less than 377 of them, with names and addresses listed, pleaded for revoking the market monopoly.[155] By 1841, even shirk butchers felt at ease to demand equal rights.[156] Whereas dozens of petitions favoring deregulation have survived, not a single record of residents taking side with the market butchers is available from the archives. It appears that licensed butchers were on their own when fighting for the market laws, which they did with impressive organization. In 1840, for instance, 306, or 80 percent, of them petitioned the council to uphold the system. In their words, a few "disorganizers" were trying "to create an impression, that the high prices of meats were exclusively owing to the market monopoly," falsely suggesting "that the law is unconstitutional." As for reinforcement, they enlisted 324 of their apprentices, who asked the council not to "violate or abolish, as we believe[,] the best regulated publick markets in the world."[157] Yet discord already penetrated this new generation of butchers, and eighty of them, frustrated by their inability to acquire stalls, decided to endorse the meat shop system.[158]

Overall, the analysis supports the view held by some historians that the unyielding expansion of unlicensed trade in the 1830s was a decisive experience that helped sway the council to deregulate the public market system in 1843.[159] It also confirms that an ideological transition in favor of free markets, as it gained popularity among shopkeepers, residents, and city officials alike, played an equally important part, as scholars have also suggested.[160] More and more New Yorkers came to believe that the public markets fell short of their mandate to supply their households with wholesome and affordable provisions, while nonmarketplace vendors, not unjustifiably, felt excluded from the food economy.[161] In the end, a growing body of citizens asserted that rather than promoting the public good, the market laws imposed unfair taxes on customers while also serving as a system of rent-seeking for the butchers. Even the language employed to justify the market laws' repeal originated from the bottom up. In December 1842, when Comptroller Williamson triumphantly predicted the end of the "Market monopoly," he tactfully adopted the discourse of the enemies of the market system.[162] Paradoxically, in their petition from two years earlier, the market butchers also found themselves borrowing the derogatory term of "market monopoly," which, more than anything, conveys how much the ideological ground had shifted.

THE FISCAL CALCULUS

If the public market system once worked as a tripartite model of arbitration, by the end of the 1830s, one party, that of consumers, seemed to have left the table, while another, that of Gotham's food vendors, appeared disunited in their loyalties. But if the system imposed considerable taxation, as the critics charged, why would city officials jeopardize such an important source of revenue? Even if deregulation did not necessarily mean the shutting down of public markets, the freedom to retail fresh meat and other provisions by anyone at any place would have no doubt depressed the rental value of market space, which was the source of all market incomes. Given that markets on the whole produced a positive balance, one would assume that the council had an interest in sustaining the system. In fact, this was one point asserted by the Market Committee to defend the market laws.[163] Notably, the comptroller, the

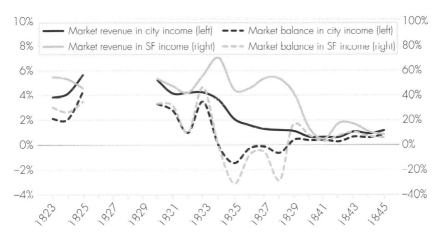

FIGURE 1.3. Contribution of markets to city and sinking fund incomes, 1823–45. (*Sources*: See text and appendix B)

official in charge of municipal finances, was least supportive of the market monopoly.[164]

To appreciate better the comptroller's perspective, figure 1.3 explores the weight of public market revenues in municipal finances. Specifically, it traces the contribution of annual market revenues as a share of both corporation and sinking fund incomes from 1823 until 1845. Even if data from the late 1820s are not available, the trends are evident. Whereas until 1834, market revenues represented a significant 1 to 6 percent of all city incomes, from the mid-1830s, their share declined gradually and considerably to under 1 percent. A similar story can be told about the sinking fund, where market revenues belonged since 1813. Until the late 1830s, public markets generated about half, at times even more, of all sinking fund incomes, thus playing a central role in financing the municipal debt. Yet by the early 1840s their share fell to only 10 percent. Further, one should recall that the market system itself cost considerable sums to maintain and expand. Including the expenses as well, the system's contribution to either corporation or sinking fund incomes not only trended downward, but in some years, the net contribution amounted to deficits.

Evidently, from the mid-1830s onward, the system's fiscal contribution was diminishing considerably. This was not because public markets earned less income but rather that other revenue sources, above all, property taxes, became increasingly prominent. In other words, were deregulation to reduce the rental value of market space, this would have virtually no bearing upon the city budget, and would not even make much of a dent in funding the debt obligations. Just as the system came under popular attack on the ground of taxation, both the comptroller and the commissioners of the sinking fund found that the public markets were no longer indispensable fiscal resources. With momentum on the side of deregulation, for many in public office it seemed easier to do away with the municipal model than to struggle in vain to preserve the increasingly unpopular and unenforceable market laws.

To be fair, this is an incomplete assessment, for the market system's fading fiscal performance in part originated from the same issue of inadequate public investments that was spurring the expansion of informal trade. Had the council developed the infrastructure more forcefully over the late 1830s by opening new marketplaces in northern areas, hundreds of new vendors and tens of thousands of new customers would have been integrated into the formal provisioning system. To be sure, such an approach would have required reinvesting a greater share of the market revenues. Instead of generating surpluses, even if modest ones, the markets may have incurred temporary losses or increased the debt burden. Furthermore, one should keep in perspective that the public markets were a municipal amenity in the first place. Their raison d'être was not to maximize revenues but to ensure the common good of provisioning residents. Temporary deficits were not untenable losses but social investments. Earlier they had not stopped city officials from taking on new loans for building Fulton Market. In theory, the social benefits of sustaining public control over the urban food supply outweighed the temporary financial sacrifices that the expansion of the market system would have required. Was there any specific reason why comparable deficits were no longer justifiable?

The municipal records do not reveal any explicit reason why city officials became unwilling to allocate adequate funds for the public market system from the late 1830s. Yet their decision to socialize the provisioning of another basic good, the supply of water, by building the Croton aqueduct, changed the fiscal calculus, and this in turn became an indirect factor in the council's reconsidering its role in the supply of food. For decades New York had struggled with how to build a water supply system adequate for its population, in the process deliberating on one scheme after another. In comparison, by 1830 Philadelphia's Fairmount Waterworks achieved a technological state that made it the nation's model for a municipal water system. In the meantime, New York City was not alone in depending on a private water monopoly, for the same was the case in Boston and Baltimore until midcentury. What was distinctive about Gotham was the degree to which the Manhattan Company, chartered in 1799 to supply the city with "pure and wholesome water," but in reality serving as a cover for Aaron Burr to set up a bank, failed in its original mandate while jealously holding on to its monopoly. For decades, even as it became America's first city, New York found itself at an impasse, with a deeply flawed water supply consisting of a hodgepodge of increasingly polluted wells, springwater carted expensively from Upper Manhattan, and a water monopoly interested in supplying banking, not water.[165]

By the 1830s a sense of alarm, exacerbated by a devastating cholera epidemic in 1832, overtook authorities, the city's elite, and the public in general. Plans converged on the Croton River solution, a project to bring water from a distance of forty-one miles via a massive aqueduct. In March 1835 the Common Council and the mayor approved the Croton plan for popular referendum, which only three weeks later was confirmed by a large majority of the voters. At last, the road seemed to be paved for a governmental solution. Much like in the case of Fulton Market earlier, however, one last push was needed, which again took the form of burning flames. Indeed, the Great Fire of 1835, which destroyed much of the city's commercial center in one of the worst conflagrations in New York's history, provided the final impetus to spur the completion of this much-delayed and desperately needed public works.[166] Broad political and public consensus ensured the Croton's completion, despite the fateful conjunction of the beginning of construction and the severe recession of 1837. It was probably no accident that this was also the last year when a new public market was built in antebellum New York City.

As the Croton's construction progressed, city officials and the public alike became increasingly concerned about the resulting growth of the municipal debt. In March 1839, a civic-minded "taxpayer" published an open appeal about the worrisome state of public finances.[167] Most alarming were the rapidly rising taxes and spiraling debts, which, after remaining steady for three years, ballooned from $715,000 in 1834 to about $8.2 million by 1838.[168] A closer look at present and future city expenditures was warranted. Within three months, the Special Committee, entrusted with the task, prepared its own detailed report, arriving at the same conclusions.[169] Surveying all government functions, it documented rapidly rising expenses across the board, along with notable cases of wasteful spending. After a brief comparison with Philadelphia and Boston, the committee concluded:

> Our municipal expenses are far greater than the public interests require; and that the government could be as well administered, the peace and health of the city as well preserved, its improvement advanced in proportion with that of other American cities, and, as far as the public interests require, with a much less expenditure of the public money, and much fewer burdens to the public.[170]

By the time the Croton Waterworks was inaugurated on October 14, 1842, total expenses, all of them funded by public loans, added up to an astronomical $12 million, making it by far the most expensive public works New York City had yet undertaken.[171] Certainly, the water stocks had a unique legitimacy since the voters themselves endorsed the project, although they only approved a $5 million budget originally.[172] In any case, over the eight years between 1834 and 1842, the municipal debt multiplied by an astounding eighteen times, reaching $13.7 million.[173] Understandably, the mayor and the comptroller became deeply concerned about how to manage this massive debt.[174] It is telling that over the next fifteen years, until the construction of Central Park began in 1857, the council did not authorize any new large-scale public works, except, of course, the construction of essential infrastructures such as the street, water, and sewer networks, already a significant financial commitment. Partly because of this relative municipal inactivity in the 1840s and early 1850s, the debt burden remained roughly the same amount of $13.9 million in 1852, out of which $3 million was managed by the commissioners of the sinking fund, where the public market property belonged.[175]

It would be a stretch to postulate a direct causal relationship between the contrary developments: just as citizens' access to water was being redefined as a public good, access to food was left increasingly to private enterprise. To be sure, neither city officials nor the wider public asserted such a connection directly. Instead, the two processes were linked indirectly through the fiscal calculus. One lasting consequence of building the Croton was that because of the project's immense costs, it foreclosed any further large-scale infrastructural improvement Gotham may have otherwise undertaken. It was hardly a coincidence that all public market construction halted for about fifteen years once the authorities fully appreciated the financial burden they had assumed.[176] Prolonged inaction under the pressure of rapid urban growth inevitably resulted in a deficient market system, which fueled popular support for deregulation while also feeding the expansion of informal trade. The recession of 1837–43 further barred the release of municipal funds for public projects. On the contrary, the council now found itself with a pressing need to identify additional sources of revenue. The Market Committee's claim that public markets produced indispensable incomes for the sinking fund was in theory a powerful argument. In an 1840 report, the committee even attempted to directly link market revenues to water loans:

> The debt of the City of New York is at this time large, and by necessity must be gradually increased until the final completion of the Croton Water Works. . . . Whatever portion of the revenue, other than the annual taxes, are taken away, a deficiency in the annual receipts will be created, which can be supplied only by resort to new loans, or to taxation. . . . That the repeal of the existing Market Laws will have the effect of greatly diminishing, and perhaps entirely de-

stroying, that branch of the public revenue, your Committee entertain no doubt.[177]

The problem was that this argument no longer rang true to city officials in charge of public finances. It was not only that by the late 1830s the markets had generated too small a share of either corporation or sinking fund incomes, but also that municipal real estate seemed like an easy place to start when looking for additional revenues.[178] As the Croton increased the public debt to previously unknown heights, the comptroller regularly appraised the value of city property.[179] Markets were assessed at roughly $1.2 million in 1838, and, after undergoing a temporary loss during the depth of the recession of 1837–43, their value eventually stabilized at about $1.1 million during the 1840s and early 1850s.[180] In 1846, this comprised no less than 4.4 percent of the value of all municipal real estate. This time, the comptroller identified $2.6 million worth of "property available for the purposes of sale."[181] Much of this must have been disposed of over the years that followed, because in 1851 the same $1.1 million worth of market property amounted to 5.7 percent of the value of all corporation property.[182]

Appraising the value of city real estate was hardly an impartial exercise. In fact, it enabled Comptroller Flagg, an ideological opponent of the public markets, to redefine the method by which to judge their profitability. In a detailed report of 1854, he put forth a new approach, accounting for opportunity costs, to compute the market balance. Accordingly, in 1853 the markets were assessed at the value of $1,041,000. They produced a total of $84,251 revenue, while overall outlays amounted to $44,018. After a simple subtraction, one may conclude that their net balance was $40,233, perhaps not a huge amount but certainly a profit. At least this had been the way to calculate the item for decades. Not this time, for Flagg introduced an "interest, at seven per cent on the estimated value of the market grounds and buildings" to account for the amount of rent any city real estate should have earned. In other words, he treated the public markets as any other investment, intended to earn a reasonable yearly return.[183] Having included this interest of $72,870 into the loss column, the market system now ended up generating a deficit of $32,637.[184] Suddenly, public markets were proven a failure in yet another way. Not only did they represent unwarranted taxation and government interference in free markets and generate trivial incomes in a new era of mounting fiscal liabilities, but they also produced persistent deficits for the taxpayer. The method of accounting for revenues not earned was quickly adopted by other officials. Among those was Mayor Wood, another opponent of the market system, who even included the property taxes, not collected, on top of these immaterialized rents into the loss column.[185]

Having conveniently discovered that the public market system was "losing" money, while the treasury was in need of additional revenues, Comptroller Flagg proposed a sweeping solution: to attract private investments by leasing out "Fulton, Franklin, or any other public market . . . for a fixed annual rent, to be paid into the city treasury, leaving all the market arrangements to be made on enlightened, liberal and simple business principles." In addition, he suggested that new markets should be built based on the same logic of renting "grounds for a period of ten years, with the market franchise" to private investors.[186] Prompted by Flagg's report, the council went one step further, and in a few months instructed the Finance Committee "to inquire into the expediency of selling all the public markets belonging to the Corporation."[187] Armed with the comptroller's verdict of the public markets' unprofitability while also standing firmly on the principles of laissez-faire, holding "that government shall not interfere with private enterprise; that that is the best government which governs the least," Mayor Wood suggested "the abolition of the present system, and the sale of the market property, and the adoption of the free trade principle" in an 1856 communication.[188] In the end, the council did not pursue this approach to privatization either. Instead, Gotham's once proud public markets were left to linger on without any consequential reform or investment. Some were kept up piecemeal, whereas others were simply left to decay.

CONCLUSION

By the time the butcher-turned-historian Thomas F. De Voe published *The Market Book* in 1862, the landscape of food provisioning was profoundly transformed by a free-market regime of grocers, meat shops, and other food purveyors supplying residents out of shops or selling on the streets. An entire new generation of native-born New Yorkers and hundreds of thousands of immigrants from abroad or across the nation came to experience household provisioning in the context of a free-market economy. They may have shopped at some of the surviving markets, but those did not amount to a comprehensive municipal infrastructure. Rather, market vendors, a shrinking constituency, complemented and competed with a larger and expanding private sector. By midcentury, it can be firmly stated, access to food in New York City was redefined from a public to a private good. Nothing about this outcome was self-evident. As this chapter has shown, the decision to deregulate the market system in 1843 was highly contingent.

In the three decades after the Revolution, New York City's municipal markets were neither public nor private institutions. Rather, preserving their colonial heritage from the Montgomery Charter, they functioned as communal institutions in terms of their regulation, financing, construction, upkeep, and management. In essence, they were the joint ventures of three constituents of stakeholders: the local community of residents and property holders; the licensed market vendors, especially the butchers; and city officials, above all the Common Council's Market Committee. For a small city, such a decentralized model of community-based provisioning proved flexible and responsive enough to arbitrate the converging and conflicting needs of the parties involved, even as it sustained the common good of citizens' access to food.

New York's rise as the "metropolis of the Union" in the 1810s changed the equation. Gotham's expanded scale and unrelenting growth necessitated greater municipal investments, as well as the integration of neighborhood markets into a public infrastructure system. Fulton Market represented the culmination of this new political economy from both an infrastructural and fiscal standpoint. At the same time, officials had to remain responsive to local needs on the ground, which became a more complex challenge. Indeed, the success of the public market model depended on a delicate balance between population growth, urban development, and sustained infrastructural investment, carefully calibrated to protect vendors' interests while also promoting convenient access to food supplies in all neighborhoods. In effect, the market infrastructure was under intensifying pressure from urbanization, and significant delays to the system's development undermined its legitimacy and dominant position.

Whenever market facilities were wanting, economic niches opened up for excluded vendors to create a parallel informal economy. Real or perceived failures, whether they concerned the price of food or the distance of travel to shopping, were translated into the language of unfair tax burden on citizens. Growing belief in free-market ideology further destabilized the legitimacy of the public market system, especially its underlying trade privileges, which were now referred to as the market monopoly. The system's funding came under scrutiny as well, at times on the ground of excessive taxation, at other moments because the public markets produced trivial revenues, especially once the Croton altered the fiscal calculus. The social provisioning of water certainly did not directly undermine the social provisioning of food, but by creating a huge public debt, it made deregulation the easier option. By the early 1840s, too many factors converged—in political economy, public opinion, and on the ground—to halt the pendulum's swing from a public market to a free-market system. Still, it needs to be stressed that deregulation gained momentum partly as a result of inadequate infrastructural investments in the first place. Had the council invested the necessary resources to expand and modernize its provisioning system, the ground would not have shifted, at least not to this extent.

Recognizing this history contributes to our understanding of antebellum political economy and urban development in New York and beyond. First, it warns that the agent of change was not some impersonal market revolution or even the political elites, but more subtle shifts in popular ideology, consumer preferences, and business attitudes that gradually tilted the balance in favor of open access and free competition in this and other sectors of the economy. New Yorkers, including citizen consumers, market and nonmarket vendors, and city officials, struggled with the most fundamental dilemma of any democratic society: how to define the boundaries of public and private. What is most noteworthy about the negotiations surrounding food access is how pervasive and open-ended the public debate was. Contrasting the case of food with that of water highlights the range of possible outcomes in such political economy debates. Indeed, New Yorkers reached the opposite conclusions, with the market monopoly of food losing its historic legitimacy, even as the government monopoly of water gained public support.

Second, following the public market system's development reveals that what was abandoned in the early 1840s was not the moral economy of provisioning but the prospect of building a modern and comprehensive municipal food system, with hierarchically distinct wholesale and retail market-halls, centralized abattoirs, and improved transportation linkages. By the century's second quarter, the public market system was halfway into the transition from communal facilities to municipal infrastructure, while still holding on to the vestiges of an earlier regulatory framework. In theory, in the next decades officials could have pursued a robust infrastructural expansion and regulatory reform to boost public oversight of food supplies while at the same time repealing old privileges. The fact that the municipal government did not take this road, not only in New York but across the nation, meant that access to food did not become a public good like sanitation, green space, or schooling did in the nineteenth-century American city.[189] Retrospectively, it seems inconceivable that a city approaching a million would have not built a public water supply. On the contrary, the failure to create a comprehensive municipal food infrastructure until the twentieth century has not warranted explanation. Like all developments, this one has its history, and one should bear in mind that until the 1830s, the case was the reverse, with food access being a public and water access a private good. It was in these antebellum political economy debates that the fate of nineteenth-century urban food systems was decided in favor of unregulated free markets.

Third, for the specific case of New York City, reframing the problem in these terms brings into focus the stakes involved in these political economy decisions made and not made. Should food deregulation be regarded a failure of antebellum urban governance, or was it a sensible policy under the circumstances? Addressing this question leads to a different level of research and analysis focusing on the socioeconomic conditions of provisioning, which is the focus of the book's next chapters. Specifically, how did the public market model perform to ensure citizens' access to food? What were its social costs and benefits? How did its geography evolve under the pressure of accelerating urban growth? And how did it shape the daily routines of household provisioning? Further, how did deregulation reconfigure the spatial conditions of food access in a booming city? What did this mean for the urban built environment? And most important, what were the consequences of liberalization on residents' living standards and material well-being in an emerging metropolis, with an increasingly diverse, immigrant, and working-class population?

PART II

Public Market System of Provisioning, 1790s–1820s

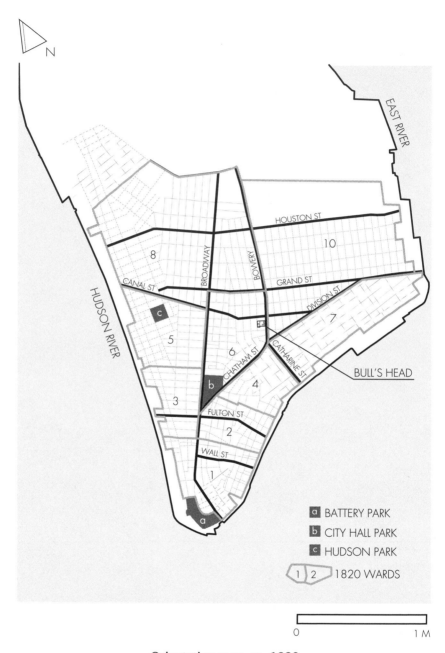

Orientation map, ca. 1820

CHAPTER 2

The Landscape of Municipal Food Access

The Fattest Cattle Ever Exhibited in This City

"Fat Oxen," an announcement trumpeted loudly on Saturday, March 29, 1828, enticing New Yorkers to savor the meat of two magnificent cattle from Gotham's abundant hinterlands. The public notice was prepared by the young butchers John Ackly and Henry Hyde to increase traffic at their modest Essex and Governeur Markets, which supplied the city's then northeastern districts. Boasting about their merchandise, the butchers proudly declared that their pair of seven-year-old oxen were "superior to any thing of the kind ever offered in this market . . . In the opinion of thousands, who have seen them, they are not surpassed in the United States." They did not fail to bring attention to their supplier: the "cattle were reared by Mr. Ariel Lathrop . . . , the worthy and industrious farmer" from the town of Danube in Herkimer County, Upstate New York, whose excellence in feeding "has set an example worthy of imitation."[1]

The animals' sheer size was critical to the spectacle: "the above pair of Cattle are so extremely fat, they cannot be drove about the city." To those who wished to witness the splendid beasts alive, they would "be exhibited in the Park on MONDAY AFTERNOON." Two days later, away from the public eye, the butchers would perform their skillful labor to slaughter the animals in Hyde's killing shed on Essex Street, between Rivington and Stanton, at the eastern edge of the meatpacking district. The final act, when the beef was "offered for sale" to the public "at stalls No. 1 Gouverneur Market . . . and No. 13 Essex Market," was scheduled for Saturday, in order to take full advantage of the weekly peak in market traffic. Leaving little to chance, the young butchers also secured endorsements from two of the city's grand old butchers—Thomas Gibbons of Fulton Market, who had been in business for at least three decades, and Henry Astor, elder brother of John Jacob Astor and once a butcher at Fly Market—who vouched their "opinion that the above Cattle are the fattest that were ever exhibited in this city."

It was a well-crafted public relations event meant to enhance the reputation of the butchers, promote their lesser-known marketplaces, and, more immediately, boost sales on April 5. Given the enormous size of these oxen, and the circumstance that all fresh meat had to be disposed of the same day, Ackly and Hyde had to find a way to sell at least twice the usual amount of beef on this particular Saturday. Their announcement was informative about the complexities of their craft: how they bought livestock each week at the Bull's Head from the drovers, linking agricultural hinterlands to urban food markets; how they skillfully slaughtered the animals in their killing shed to prepare their meat for local consumption; and how they stood each day by their stalls to serve residents. It was this last step at the public markets, Ackly and Hyde fully appreciated, on which their entire success depended. Their transactions with the drovers, or their labor at their slaughterhouses, were preparations for the final act of delivering delicious cuts of meat to a population accustomed to abundant supplies of wholesome, fresh meat at affordable prices. The public markets structured these transactions, and, by extension, they defined Gotham's landscape of provisioning, so it is no wonder that Ackly and Hyde seized the opportunity to bring awareness to their small marketplaces at the city's northern fringes.

Chapter 1 put forth the argument that the raison d'être of the municipal market system was to sustain the public good of citizens' access to food. To what extent the corresponding market infrastructure succeeded in fulfilling this political mandate is the focus of this chapter. The analysis therefore shifts the discussion from the realm of political economy to evaluating the public markets' performance on the ground. It studies how Early Republican New Yorkers were in fact provisioned, and how effectively the public market model supported this vital aspect of their living standards.[2] From this more pragmatic perspective, the issue to bear in mind is that urban provisioning was by definition a mediated process. Urban dwellers, as the story of Ackly and Hyde illustrates, depended on complex supply chains linking their city to hinterlands, and a range of market intermediaries to ensure their daily food access. Under the municipal model, the public markets were the key infrastructure of provisioning. As such, their challenge was to coordinate the delivery of adequate quantity and quality of food supplies at affordable prices to all districts. In evaluating the public market system, this chapter pursues supply side and spatial analyses. Did New Yorkers gain access to adequate quantities of food supplies? Were all neighborhoods well provisioned, or were some areas unfairly burdened by too taxing a distance? And did the model muster effective means to sustain food quality? At the center of the inquiry is the geographic mandate of the public market system, which determined its success in meeting socially agreed-upon and politically mediated provisioning standards.

This chapter advances through three connected discussions. The first subject to be addressed concerns New York City's supply conditions. In particular, it explores the supply of meat reaching Gotham's markets in order to assess the dietary conditions of residents. The second section moves the discussion from the availability of supplies to their distribution across the neighborhoods. Specifically, it presents a geographic analysis of the public market system by focusing on its expansion and spatial organization in the context of accelerating urban growth. The third section concludes the analysis by assessing the beneficiary effects of the public market model. It interrogates the ways in which the city's marketplaces served to control food quality, how they helped mitigate potential public health risks deriving from private slaughtering, and the degree to which they supported the settlement of newly urbanizing, more marginal districts to promote urban development.

SUPPLY CONDITIONS

As discussed in chapter 1, the retail trade of licensed butchers provided the statutory cornerstone of the public market model. The basis of this institutional setting was the central place of meat in the American urban diet. Indeed, the daily consumption of butcher's meats represented an essential component of the nutritional standards of Early American city dwellers. More broadly, it defined a key aspect of their living standards.[3] Accordingly, the supply of meat presents an especially telling case study to assess how well New Yorkers were provisioned in general, and how successfully the municipal model fulfilled its mandate to distribute food supplies to residents in all neighborhoods. Additionally, because of the central role of butchers in the provisioning system, it offers the best-documented food item.

A unique set of sources bears upon the supply of butcher's meats in New York City, making it possible to estimate urban meat consumption levels in the Early Republic, a previously undocumented period.[4] The critical records are the aggregate sum of market fees collected from the butchers by the Common Council between 1786 and 1818, and the market clerk's monthly returns of actual meat sales at Fly, Washington, and Catharine Markets in 1816 and 1818. The surviving sales figures are sufficient to generate trustworthy estimates of the total number of cattle, calves, sheep, and hogs slaughtered for sale in New York City in these two years. By incorporating market fees into the calculation, per capita butcher's meat consumption rates can also be established for almost three decades. There is one limitation to this source material. Provisioning records were generated by the council as a product of the municipal market system's regime of public finances, which collected revenues by taxing the retail trade of fresh butcher's meats. Other sources of meat, including poultry, fowl, and game, which were sold by the farmers and hucksters at the marketplaces, as well as processed and preserved meats, such as ham, sausage, lard, salted pork and beef, smoked beef, or corned beef, which were also regularly retailed by the grocers, fell outside the remit of municipal taxation. Any attempt to study per capita meat consumption at the time is therefore centered on fresh red meat, leaving a substantial portion of the meat supply unaccounted for.[5]

To begin, the analysis attends to both long-term trends and short-term changes in New York City's food supplies. Figure 2.1 compares the city's population growth to that of the aggregate amount of market fees collected by the market clerks between 1786 and 1818.[6] While the time series has some gaps, especially for the period after 1807, it provides an indispensable record of the supply of meat reaching New York City in the Early Republican era. At first glance, the evidence suggests that Gotham's accelerating growth at the turn of the eighteenth and nineteenth centuries, which made the city the nation's largest, was supported by favorable agricultural supply conditions, with market fees increasing at the same rate as did the population. Evidently, no trend change in the city's provisioning chains occurred, which would have significantly altered residents' access to food supplies.

A closer look, however, reveals less stable conditions. Shifting the attention from long-term trends to short-term changes, the market fees highlight one essential constraint of urban provisioning. Specifically, any city's provisioning chains, by necessity, were highly sensitive to exogenous supply shocks, which could result in temporary shortages. Above all, the War of 1812 caused a veritable collapse in meat sales in 1813, a shortage that lasted into the following year, until the war finally ended. De Voe himself commented that the prices of provisions became very high at the commencement of the war, and remained so for a few years after, resulting in a notable scarcity of supplies.[7] Yet exorbitant prices were only one side of the story, since meat sales swiftly recovered by 1816, despite food prices staying high for some time. The war not only depressed farming output in New York's hinterlands, undermining the city's regular imports of fresh provisions, but it also disrupted the daily functioning of the city's market intermediaries across the provisioning chain, from slaughter to retail.[8] It took some time for supply chains and market infrastructure to fully recover, when the butchers and other food purveyors resumed normal trade.

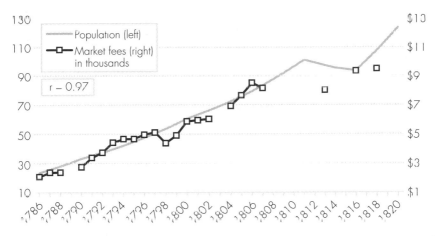

FIGURE 2.1. Population and market fees, 1786–1820. (*Sources*: See text and appendix B)

Even though the War of 1812 presented the deepest and longest period of relative scarcity, New York City's supply chains were not immune to other exogenous shocks. After nearly a decade of steady growth, the supply of meat stagnated between 1794 and 1795, when yellow fever came to New York for the first time after the Revolution, claiming the lives of 1.6 percent of the population. Three years later, market fees dropped by a considerable 14.2 percent compared to the previous year, as the most devastating yellow fever epidemic in Gotham's history wiped out 4 percent of the inhabitants, scattering thousands of others into the countryside, where many of them also lost their lives. Indeed, the 1798 epidemic brought severe disruptions to the city's economy, causing the provisioning system to virtually collapse. Addressing both shortages and problems of distribution, the council operated three provision centers that fed between 1,600 to 2,000 poor citizens on a daily basis at the peak of the epidemic, while another 800 were supplied at the Almshouse, and about 500 families obtained free rations at temporary stores.[9] A few years later, the Embargo Act of 1807 also corresponded to a notable drop in market fees. Gotham's fresh meat derived from regional sources, and a maritime trade ban did not directly affect these supply chains. But for America's leading commercial port, the interruption of foreign trade networks, the lifeblood of the city's economy, presented a serious economic setback, which indirectly manifested in a 4.2 percent decline in the total volume of meat sales.[10]

Overall, the records on market fees offer ground for two conclusions. Focusing on the long-term trend, they confirm the steady growth of New

York City's meat supplies between 1786 and 1818. The evidence is clear that Gotham's takeoff was sustained by prolific supply chains that tapped into expanding hinterlands, ensuring that most residents did not need to forego their customary dietary standards, even as the population increased fourfold in one generation. Even so, periodic shortfalls in the availability of provisions, triggered by the yellow fever epidemic of 1798, the Embargo Act of 1807, and the War of 1812, suggest a less comfortable situation, underlining the vulnerability of the same supply chains. For example, an epidemic could bring urban food markets to a standstill as provisioning institutions shut down, the movement of goods and people came to a halt, and drovers and farmers failed to transport supplies into the city in fear of contracting the disease. Similarly, in wartime situations, military operations could disrupt farming activity, divert surpluses to armies, and isolate the city from its hinterlands. The evidence points to the mediated and dependent nature of urban provisioning: even as New Yorkers gained access to adequately expanding supplies, they nevertheless had to rely on supply mechanisms beyond their control, which exposed them to comparatively greater hardship in periods of crisis.

Establishing a strong correspondence between population growth and the city's meat supplies in one generation still falls short of documenting how well New Yorkers were actually provisioned. Fortunately, the market clerks' surviving returns, complemented by De Voe's notes, allow for estimating the total number of cattle, calves, sheep, and hogs slaughtered for sale at the New York markets in 1816 and 1818. From these data it becomes possible to estimate per capita butcher's meat consumption annually. According to the calculations, New Yorkers on average consumed between 85.9 to 92.1 pounds of beef, 16.9 to 19.6 pounds of veal, 28.6 to 34.1 pounds of lamb and mutton, and 10.7 to 13.5 pounds of pork—for all species of meat, 1816 representing the upper and 1818 the lower bound.[11] On the whole, per capita fresh red meat consumption reached 159.3 pounds in 1816 and 142 pounds in 1818.[12] Are these estimates realistic, and how do they compare to more established twentieth-century figures? Research by Roger Horowitz offers reliable benchmarks.[13] Taking into account that the estimates presented here exclude processed and preserved meats and poultry, it appears that New Yorkers in the 1810s consumed slightly more meat than did American city dwellers in 1909, considerably more than they did in the war year of 1942, and a little less than they did in the peak year of 1965. Further, Early Republican New Yorkers ate about 10 percent more beef than did Americans in the early twentieth century, and only 15 percent less than those living in the affluent postwar era.

The records bespeak of an abundance of meat for purchase and consumption. Moreover, by linking market fees to the 1816 and 1818 slaugh-

TABLE 2.1. Per Capita Butcher's Meat Consumption in
New York City (lbs.), 1790–1818

Years	Beef	Veal	Lamb & Mutton	Pork	Total
1790	76.5	16.3	28.3	11.2	132.3
1795	96.3	20.5	35.7	14.1	166.5
1800	89.5	19.0	33.1	13.1	154.7
1805	93.2	19.8	34.5	13.6	161.2
1813	76.1	16.2	28.2	11.1	131.6
1816	92.1	19.6	34.1	13.5	159.3
1818	85.9	16.9	28.6	10.7	142.0

Sources: See text and appendix B.

ter estimates, while accounting for the excise applied on each of the four categories of butcher's meats, it is possible to convert fees into actual consumption rates for the twenty-five years before 1816.[14] Table 2.1 sums up the results, presenting annual per capita meat consumption estimates for New York City between 1790 and 1818. The data are far from perfect, but they provide important new insights into the dietary standards of Early Republican city dwellers. The figures show that per capita consumption of fresh red meat increased from 132.3 pounds in 1790 to amounts as high as 154.7 to 166.5 pounds between 1795 and 1816, excluding the war year of 1813, when the level of meat consumption fell temporarily. The corresponding rates of beef consumption increased from 76.5 pounds in 1790 to 89.5 and 96.3 pounds between 1795 and 1816. The 1818 figures indicate a decline of meat consumption compared to two years before. However, there is reason to believe that the 1818 records slightly underestimate the overall number of animals butchered in New York City, in which case the 1818 rates were probably closer to those of 1816 than the table suggests.[15]

How do these figures measure up to available estimates for the period? Table 2.2 presents comparable meat consumption rates in the Northeast from the mid-eighteenth to the early nineteenth century. The most consistent series comes from Sarah F. McMahon's meticulous research, based on a large sample of wills from rural Middlesex County in Massachusetts that recorded the annual meat allowance of widows. An annual meal allowance is not the same as per capita consumption but still serves as a useful indicator of societal definitions of a reasonable supply of meat.[16] As it turns out, the New York City average of about 160 pounds of butcher's meat between 1795 and 1816 compares well with McMahon's widow

TABLE 2.2. Meat Consumption in America (lbs.), 1740–1830

Period	Widow rate		Laborer Philadelphia (all meats)	Per capita New York City (butcher's meats)	Years
	Middlesex County, MA (all meats)	Southeast PA (all meats)			
1740–59	168.2	150.0	174.5		
1760–78	183.5				1772
1781–90	178.0			132.3	1790
1791–99				166.5	1795
				154.7	1800
				161.2	1805
1808–30	201.8			131.6	1813
				159.3	1816
				142.0	1818

Sources: Figures for Middlesex County, MA: McMahon, "A Comfortable Subsistence," 36–37, 56, table 4; for Southeast PA: Lemon, "Household Consumption," 61–63; for Philadelphia: Smith, "The Material Lives," 170, table 1; for NYC: Table 2.1, appendix B.

rates of 178 to 202 pounds from the late eighteenth to the early nineteenth century.[17] Similarly, it corresponds well with James T. Lemon's calculations of a slightly lower 150 pounds of widow's meat allowance in mid-eighteenth-century southeast Pennsylvania,[18] or Billy Smith's reconstruction of a Philadelphia laborer's diet of 174.5 pounds of meat in 1772.[19] It is, in fact, surprising that the New York City rates are only slightly below McMahon's figures, for they exclude preserved meats, as well as poultry, fowl, and game. If, on average, New Yorkers ate about 160 pounds of fresh red meat yearly, there had to be plenty more on their dinner table once those categories are also accounted for, adding up to an overall per capita meat consumption level well above rural averages.[20]

Quantities aside, these figures also help appreciate one profound difference between urban and rural diets. Horowitz notes that the widespread consumption of fresh meat, beef in particular, was a distinctive privilege of city dwellers.[21] Indeed, whereas almost all of McMahon's estimates derive from preserved meats (salt pork primarily, and to a lesser extent, salt beef), New Yorkers satisfied their appetite mostly with fresh meat. This distinction was the result of urban agglomeration effects, to be more precise, population size and density. Given their size, cities generated adequate and constant demand for fresh meat supplies, which had to be sourced from the countryside. Drovers herded livestock into urban markets, where butchers slaughtered the animals to prepare their meat for customers. The number of daily customers in any town beyond a certain size guaranteed that the hundreds of pounds of perishable fresh meat obtained would find ready purchasers in small quantities within hours. In rural areas, on the contrary, the same amount of beef had to be salted to avoid putrefaction, a key constraint on fresh meat consumption before the availability of modern refrigeration.

Extending comparisons beyond America helps further ground the discussion. For example, how did meat consumption in New York compare to that in other rapidly growing cities across the Atlantic? Source limitations abound, but Paris provides an unusually well-documented case. Thanks to the French capital's centralized and closely monitored system of municipal abattoirs, its records of the number of livestock slaughtered for consumption are exceptionally good. Table 2.3 compares the New York City estimates to calculations based on Armand Husson's documents from his *Les consommations de Paris* (1856).[22] Accordingly, in the late eighteenth and early nineteenth centuries, per capita annual consumption of fresh beef, veal, and lamb and mutton were strikingly similar in the two cities.

It is also true that Parisian meat consumption in the late eighteenth and early nineteenth century appears high compared to other European cities. Scholars have documented considerably lower rates, about two-thirds of the New York City figures, for London in 1837 and Berlin in 1845.[23] And these amounted to relatively abundant urban meat supplies in the European context. In Mediterranean cities, such as meticulously researched Barcelona, per capita butcher's meat consumption, excluding pork, amounted to as little as 20 to 30 percent of American standards.[24] Further, a closer look at the Parisian case in table 2.3 reveals that the difference between urban and rural diets was far more pronounced in France than in the United States. Whereas Parisians ate three times more meat than the average French citizen, according to Husson's records, per capita meat consumption in New York, as quantity was concerned, was not all that different from rural New England widow rates. The enormous discrepancy between Paris and the rest of the country resulted from generally more meat-oriented diets in urban than rural areas, coupled with a strong tradition of government involvement in the provisioning of the capital.[25] The French state directly and forcefully intervened to secure steady supplies of meat for Parisian consumers.[26]

In contrast, New York City had no jurisdiction outside of its municipal borders. No matter how tightly the Common Council regulated and monitored its provisioning system, supply chains linking urban consumers to farmers developed entirely on the basis of market transactions. Nor did

TABLE 2.3. Per Capita Butcher's Meat Consumption in New York City and Paris (lbs.), 1781–1818

Period		Beef		Veal		Lamb & Mutton		Total		Total meat consumption
NYC	Paris	NYC	Paris	NYC	Paris	NYC	Paris	NYC	Paris	France
1786–90	1781–86	80.4	88.3	17.1	12.6	29.8	24.0	127.3	124.8	42.1
1799–1807	1799–1808	88.8	89.0	18.9	20.1	32.9	26.9	140.6	136.0	43.2
1816 & 1818	1809–18	89.0	88.8	18.2	17.5	31.3	26.2	138.6	132.6	44.8

Sources: Figures for Paris: Husson, Les consommations de Paris, 142, 145, 148, 153–54, 157, 196; for France: Brantz, "Slaughter in the City," 138, table 2.3; for NYC: Table 2.1, appendix B.

New York State impose trade restrictions to divert specific sources of supply for New York City's benefit. Gotham's meat was obtained from autonomous drovers who collected herds from farmers in Westchester and Duchess Counties, from Upstate New York, like Mr. Lathrop and his two fat oxen from Danube, Herkimer County, more than two hundred miles distant, as well as from Long Island and New Jersey.[27] In other words, the high and steady meat consumption standards enjoyed by New Yorkers depended on the city's capacity to gain access to expanding and rich agricultural hinterlands. Furthermore, the same market forces determined the provisioning chains of other cities across America. On this ground, it is safe to suggest that meat consumption estimates for New York may be taken as representative of other major northeastern cities, like Philadelphia and Boston.[28]

The discussion comes full circle, for the evidence amassed at each step underscores the importance of stable supply conditions, supported by New Yorkers' relative economic well-being, to sustain these impressive consumption standards. The classic approach to the analysis of supply conditions, to study changes in food prices, only confirms this assessment. Since the standard price series for all types of commodities in the period are available for Philadelphia, wholesale meat prices are examined for both cities. Additionally, comparing meat and industrial commodities prices allows for tracing trends in relative prices, that is, changes in the terms of trade between agricultural imports and urban industrial exports. This is a relevant approach given American cities' dependence on market transactions with suppliers in the hinterland.[29] Figure 2.2 makes a strong case that Early Republican New Yorkers and Philadelphians did not witness any long-term rise or decline in their meat expenditures, even as prices fluctuated considerably. In particular, the wholesale prices of beef and pork in New York, and of all varieties of meat in Philadelphia, while certainly volatile, did not undergo any trend change over the three decades. Furthermore, the three price series are closely correlated, charting the same short-term fluctuations and one lasting inflationary period triggered by the War of 1812.[30] Last, meat and industrial commodities prices followed similar courses, that is, the relative price of meat to industrial goods remained largely unchanged.[31]

Put differently, the high meat consumption standards recorded for Early Republican New Yorkers were sustained by generally stable agricultural supply conditions and terms of trade between the city and the hinterlands. This should come as no surprise, for no major changes in farming production, animal husbandry, or transportation technologies occurred that would have significantly shifted the supply curve of provisions for urban residents. In fact, price trends charted for meat products closely mirrored those of other key provisions, such as fish or grain.[32] Overall,

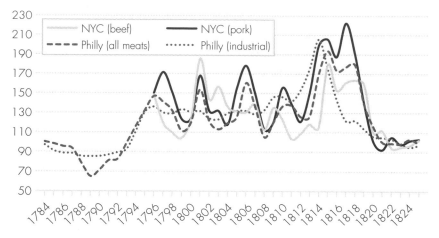

FIGURE 2.2. Wholesale price indexes (base years: 1821–25), 1784–1825. (*Sources*: See text and notes 30–31)

Early Republican city dwellers, while facing occasional but temporary price hikes, did not experience any sustained pressure to cut back on their food expenditures, nor did they have strong incentives to substitute meat with cheaper sources of protein, such as fish, or to shift to a less protein-based diet by consuming more grain.

In conclusion, based on a case study of meat, one of the more expensive but essential components of the American diet, New Yorkers in the late eighteenth and early nineteenth centuries ate remarkably well, both for their own time and compared to later periods. Their standard of living, insofar as food consumption was concerned, measured up to that of any recorded generation of Americans. This was the result of well-functioning supply chains that tapped into adequately expanding and abundant hinterlands. Importantly, New Yorkers depended entirely on market exchange to obtain their food supplies, for the municipal government had no jurisdiction outside of the city boundaries, while its tightly regulated market infrastructure only served to distribute provisions to residents. The analysis also reveals two unique qualities of urban provisioning. On the positive side, city dwellers not only consumed more meat than their rural counterparts who supplied them, but they also had the privilege of eating first and foremost fresh red meat, beef in particular. The "shoals of roast beef" that German economist and socialist Werner Sombart famously commented on one century later already represented a distinctive feature of their diet, thus defining an important aspect of urban American living standards.[33] On the negative side, given their dependence on resources beyond their control, in periods of crisis, like wars or epidemics, they were far more likely to experience temporary shortages than rural dwellers.

THE GEOGRAPHY OF THE PUBLIC MARKET SYSTEM

Up to this point, the analysis has centered on the question of supply. Even though the new estimates establish that New York City had gained access to abundant sources of butcher's meat, per capita consumption reveals little about their distribution to residents. One wonders if the impressive averages documented were reflective of the dietary conditions of most New Yorkers, or, what might be a better question based on available evidence, if the provisioning system ensured that inhabitants in all neighborhoods benefited from access. Urban provisioning is by definition a mediated process, structured by a city's political economy, regulatory framework, and corresponding infrastructure. Chapter 1 showed that Early Republican New York City was committed to managing food access as a public good, to be negotiated within the political arena rather than leaving it in the hands of unregulated markets. Gotham's regulation of access, then, warrants a closer study of the municipal market system's performance in fulfilling its mandate to ensure that all citizens find adequate quantity and quality of provisions at a convenient distance from home.

How successfully the public market system distributed the city's plentiful supplies is largely a matter of geography. From an administrative standpoint, the municipal model presented public officials with the responsibility of making three informed decisions about the spatial organization of the provisioning infrastructure: how many public markets the council should maintain, where these facilities should be located, and how much business each marketplace should accommodate. To appreciate the complexity of the issues, and to lay the ground for the spatial analysis, the discussion first turns to central-place theory. While the model is more commonly used to evaluate the urban system of a given territory, it has been widely adopted to study the spatial patterns of commercial activities within cities.[34]

To begin, food retailers sell what are considered par excellence convenience goods: typically relatively cheap goods, which are bought frequently, in the case of fresh food, maybe as often as each day. They are the opposite of so-called shopping or comparison goods: more expensive products, bought only occasionally. To predict the locational patterns of different types of market activities, central-place theory postulates their varying levels of centrality based on two countervailing variables. The first one is the economic reach of a given product, also called range, which refers to the maximum distance consumers are willing to travel to gain access to that good. The second is the condition of entry, or threshold requirement, describing the minimum demand needed to keep a specific trade profitable.[35] By extension of this logic, given their different levels of centrality, certain businesses supply goods for the whole city, while others cater to specific communities, neighborhoods, or customers from within a few blocks' radius.[36] At the same time, basic needs have to be met in all areas, whereas higher order demands are serviced at select locations.

These simple points help formulate predictions about the locational behavior of food vendors. First, in any city, one anticipates a relatively large number of food retailers compared to other types of businesses given food vendors' low threshold. Second, food vendors are expected to disperse, for they need to move near to their customers; how close largely depends on the means of the daily commute, which in a densely settled city usually falls within the range of a convenient walk.[37] Third, food vendors of the same goods seek out exclusive market areas to minimize competition and are therefore likely to disperse relatively evenly; how far from their nearest competitors depends on their threshold demand, that is, a function of local residential density and population characteristics.[38] Fourth, food vendors of different goods, selling complements not substitutes, may cluster together, for they attract a larger number of customers to the site thanks to external economies in shopping. Last, beyond a certain size, urban provision markets will generate institutions of higher centrality: public markets supply residents from an entire neighborhood, while wholesale markets service food purveyors from across the city.

Back to Early Republican New York City, the centerpiece of the theory concerns the mode and frequency of accessing provisions. On these points, the case is simple, since food shoppers purchased food almost exclusively by walking, and, given the technological constraints of food preservation, households purchased supplies on a daily basis.[39] New York was also a densely populated city that generated threshold demand across its entire urbanized area. On a third issue, however, the historical case bears no resemblance to the model. The central-place premise is that retailers operate in a free-market environment, unrestricted in their locational choices, with the only mechanism of spatial sorting being supply and demand. In contrast, the public market model provided a highly restricted landscape. Butchers were required to sell meat out of their stalls, country farmers were forced to bring their supplies into the marketplaces, and given these conditions, all the other vendors—fishmongers, fruit and vegetable vendors, sellers of milk and dairy, hucksters, even grocers—operated under strong incentives to seek out a location within or near the public markets.

Agglomeration economies derived from shopping externalities fueled such business concentration. Since residents had to frequent the local marketplace to buy their daily meat, it made sense that they purchased all other provisions during the same trip. Public markets offered the benefits of comparison shopping for price and quality. Here vendors of different goods served as complements, generating additional traffic for one another, while vendors of the same goods were not strictly competitors either, for the agglomeration economy of the entire marketplace, up to a certain point, boosted the sales of all participants. A simple regulatory framework, based on the right set of incentives and agglomeration effects, thus gave the council a commanding role in shaping the landscape of provisioning. This geography was not only subject to different spatial sorting than a free-market model but, in principle, reflected public priorities to ensure that all residents had access to adequate quantity and quality of provisions.

Agglomeration, however, was not the only geographic principle. The mandate that citizens in all areas should have convenient access to food supplies required the council to carefully deliberate where to locate its market-houses. From this viewpoint, central-place theory is again relevant. The theory predicts that public markets were evenly spaced as well, with distances between them being defined by the radius of a manageable walk. How many facilities were needed depended on this range and the city's built area. Surely, marketplaces had to be fewer and stand farther apart than independent shops in an unregulated environment: instead of serving customers from a few blocks' distance, they were par excellence neighborhood retail centers supplying a much larger catchment area. Besides, by adjusting their size and layout, marketplaces also offered the flexibility to respond to local residential density and population characteristics. Overall, for the municipal model to work well, it had to balance the competing principles of dispersal and agglomeration: public markets had to be opened across the city, while at the same time their capacity at individual sites needed to correspond to their catchment areas' demand.

Two additional factors should be considered. The first is New York City's natural geography. Manhattan is a long and narrow island, with a clear north-to-south orientation, situated at the confluence of the Hudson and East Rivers. For a mercantile city, access to water was the most critical transportation link and economic resource, hence, commercial activities concentrated along the rivers. A well-functioning public market system would similarly need to be anchored near the riverfronts to take advantage of transportation connections to supply hinterlands.

The second and more important factor is urban growth, a problem until this point omitted from the framework. Yet over the three decades between 1790 and 1820, Gotham's population quadrupled from 33,000 to 120,000 residents, while the city's densely built area doubled from around 620 to 1240 acres.[40] For central-place theory, the expansion of market activity is a direct product of urbanization.[41] As the city grows into hitherto nonurbanized areas, food purveyors are expected to follow as soon as threshold demand is met. Similarly, as older districts become more densely settled, new businesses are expected to appear to claim their share of a growing market. In spatial terms, urban growth is accommodated by the addition of new businesses and their denser spacing. By the same logic, food shops will be fewer and farther between in the lightly settled urban frontier than in densely populated central districts.

The public market model, however, presents a more complex case for two important reasons. On the one hand, the circumstance that the system's expansion required the approval of public officials, in response to petitions from interested citizens, introduced some conditionality to the process.[42] On the other, marketplaces were institutions of higher centrality, for even the smaller ones were attended by several independent vendors.[43] Correspondingly, their threshold demand was considerably higher, and the system's growth occurred in larger steps. One possible problem was that under the pressure of urban growth, some time lag would occur between the settling of frontier areas and the extension of market facilities there. If so, local residents would find their daily provisioning trips too taxing, at least until infrastructural growth could catch up. The alternative was to anticipate development by extending market facilities into frontier areas before there was adequate demand. Indeed, this was a common strategy, as documented in chapter 1, when property owners like Henry Rutgers organized local stakeholders and invested their own resources to acquire a new market-house. They treated public markets as anchor institutions to attract new populations and support urban development.[44] In an environment of growth, this was a safe bet. The only challenge was to channel growth to specific developments. Overall, given the politically mediated process of infrastructure growth and the agglomerated economy of the marketplace, both the expansion of the market system and the allocation of individual facilities relative to density and frontier growth are key issues for the empirical analysis.

Infrastructure expansion required the parallel investments of opening new public markets in urbanizing northern areas while also enlarging existing facilities in more densely settled southern and central districts. The process is best measured not by the number of public markets but by that of retail units, that is, market stalls within the system. Figure 2.3 traces how many residents there were for each butcher stall between 1790 and 1820, while also following the number of stalls for the period.[45] In

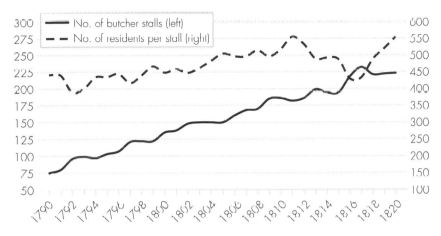

FIGURE 2.3. Number of butcher stalls and residents per butcher stall, 1790–1820. (*Sources*: See text and appendix B)

theory, there need not be a one-to-one relationship between the number of stalls and how many customers they could supply. Yet three structural constraints limited the scale of the butcher's trade. First, as already noted, food provisioning was a household chore to be conducted by walking in one's neighborhood. Butchers therefore could not expand their customer base beyond their market's catchment area. Second, the absence of proper refrigeration technologies, for both butchers and households, limited the scale of individual transactions. Customers would buy only as much meat as they planned to eat within a few days, while butchers would cut up only as much as they expected to sell on any given day. Third, even if a butcher could overcome these constraints, for example, by employing an apprentice, the modest size of his stall, mandated by statutes precisely to curb competition, posed practical limitations on how much merchandise he was able to handle. Insofar as the basic conditions of the butcher's trade remained unchanged, there was an upper bound to how many customers he could supply. In short, to meet New York's growing appetite for meat, the council needed to license more butchers and therefore add new stalls to the system.

Indeed, figure 2.3 documents that the number of butcher stalls in New York City increased consistently, almost year-to-year, from 75 in 1790 to a little over 220 by the late 1810s. The threefold expansion of the market system ensured that the number of consumers per stall rose only modestly: from around 430 in the 1790s to just below 500 in the first two decades of the nineteenth century.[46] In other words, even as the population grew nearly fourfold, the average butcher in the 1810s retailed meat to a clientele only about 15 percent larger than his predecessor one generation earlier, at most, a marginal increase. Evidently, greater demand was not met by more efficient business practices but by more butchers entering the trade, which, given the market laws' restrictions, required that the council add new facilities to the municipal infrastructure. These findings confirm chapter 1's analysis: in the Early Republican period, the council fulfilled its commitment to make the necessary investments for the public good of residents' access to food.

The council's decisions about opening new public markets—their location, capacity, layout, and architecture—or the enlargement of existing facilities depended on complex negotiations with local stakeholders, including property owners, residents, and market vendors. It is possible that even as the city government expanded its infrastructure at a sufficient rate, it allocated resources geographically ineffectively, and certain areas became oversupplied, while others were left undersupplied by market facilities. In order to study more carefully how successfully the municipal system distributed food supplies to all residents, seven maps (figure 2.4) are presented, documenting the spatial expansion of the public market infrastructure vis-à-vis the city's shifting population densities between 1790 and 1825. For each map, the size of the circles symbolizes the relative volume of trade of the individual marketplaces, relying on the best available measure. Population densities are calculated at the ward level, the smallest spatial unit available from the censuses.[47]

The first two maps from the turn of the eighteenth and nineteenth centuries depict a densely built walking city, where residents provisioned their households through a public market system dominated by Fly Market and complemented by smaller neighborhood markets, in order of size in 1792: Oswego, Bear, Exchange, Catharine, and Peck Slip. As predicted, marketplaces were spaced evenly, roughly, at equal distance from their neighbors, covering the entire urbanized area of the city. With the exception of Oswego Market, they were also situated by the waterfront, thus taking advantage of better transportation links to hinterlands.[48] All of them operated as retail markets: even Fly Market, despite concentrating no less than two-thirds of New York's entire food trade, did not acquire wholesale functions. This retail orientation was in part dictated by the market laws, which prohibited the resale of market goods for profit. Besides, for a relatively small city, such a centralized retail system made sense. Fly Market anchored the provisions trade at the city's most densely populated central districts, near the southern tip of the island along the East River. Distances remained small, and so even from the remotest parts, one could walk to Fly Market in just fifteen to twenty minutes. Agglomeration at such a scale presented many advantages: at Fly, customers were able to find all varieties of provisions, even as they also shopped for quality and price by comparing the same goods among different vendors. For those who considered this too long a walk, smaller local markets offered access to daily supplies. Over the next decade, the market system's geography remained largely unchanged, except that in order to meet rising demand in the rapidly developing northeastern districts, the council increased the capacity of Catharine Market, which by 1800 became the third largest after Fly and Bear.

This original market system, however, soon became overstretched. As new immigrants kept coming, and the city became ever more densely settled, while also relentlessly pushing northward, the geography of the market infrastructure also needed readjustment. The 1810, and especially the 1816, 1818, and 1822 maps, document the gradual development of a polycentric and two-tiered public market system. On the first point, the market system's spatial organization observed the central-place theorem in that public markets were distributed evenly, each serving as independent retail centers for their catchment areas, whose radius was defined by a convenient walking distance. Indeed, by the late 1810s, the maps show that the public markets were placed about equally far from one another, with an average distance of roughly 0.6 mile from any one marketplace to its three closest neighbors. Put differently, residents in all urbanized areas had access to a public market within a manageable ten-minute walk. Further, the distribution of the public markets closely mirrored the geographic features of Lower Manhattan, an island with the shape of an isosceles triangle, defined by the confluence of two rivers. In fact, by the late 1810s, all of the marketplaces were located near the waterfront, with the exception of Centre and Essex, which supplied the city's then northern districts, where the east to west distance was the widest to bridge.

On the second point about the hierarchy of the public markets, the maps reveal the consolidation of a two-tiered system. The central districts were supplied by the equally large Fly (replaced by Fulton in 1821), Washington, and Catharine Markets, while the newly urbanizing northern areas relied on the smaller Duane, Spring, Greenwich, Centre (replacing Collect in 1817), Essex, Grand Street (replacing Corlaers Hook in 1819), and Governeur Markets.[49] Differences between the sizes of the individual markets still did not reflect the separation of wholesale and retail functions, but they closely mirrored the distribution of the population. Indeed, when comparing the hierarchy of the public markets to the population density of their catchment areas' wards, a strong relationship is found between these indicators of supply and demand.[50] This is also confirmed by the number of hucksters, selling fruits, poultry, and dairy, at the five marketplaces where sources are available.

Overall, from the geographic analysis, it is evident that during the Early Republic, Gotham's provisioning infrastructure was spatially well allocated. The system was consistently expanded to keep up with urban

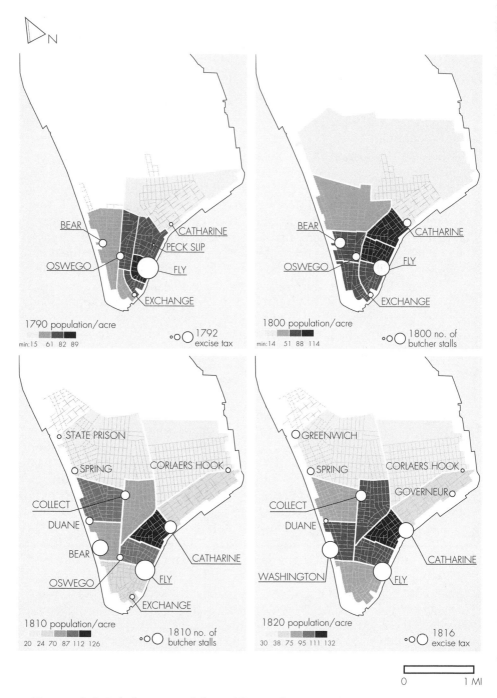

FIGURE 2.4. Development of the public market system, 1790–1825. (*Sources*: See text and appendix A)

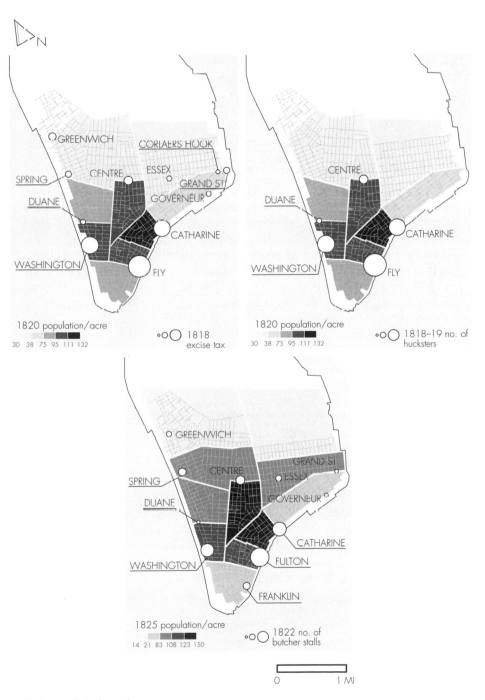

FIGURE 2.4. (*cont.*)

growth, and public marketplaces served all areas, providing residents in each neighborhood with convenient access to food supplies. The geography of the market system observed the central-place theorem, with facilities being distributed evenly across the city, each serving its district defined by the range of a convenient walk. It also mirrored the topography of Manhattan, taking advantage of water transportation to hinterlands. Moreover, the volume of trade of the individual marketplaces corresponded to their catchment areas' population size or demand. Put differently, the system balanced the countervailing principles of citywide dispersal and local agglomeration with considerable success, despite the intensifying pressures of accelerating population and spatial growth. Such an outcome required the council's sustained and skillful negotiations between the interests of different constituencies. Indeed, that the market system passed the test of distributing food supplies to all New Yorkers should be considered a real accomplishment of municipal governance. One should keep in mind that the process did not involve any master plan, but the location, layout, and size of every public market needed to be negotiated each step of the way. In conclusion, the geography of the public market system held up well precisely because it stood on the solid ground of hard-earned compromises among so many invested parties.

QUALITY CONTROL AND SOCIAL EQUITY

Two major points have been established so far. First, that in the Early Republic, New Yorkers enjoyed historically high living standards in terms of their food consumption. And second, that the public market system succeeded in distributing supplies to all neighborhoods, even as New York experienced accelerating growth to become the largest city of the Americas by the 1820s. It is important to note that neither of these points proves that the public market model was the most effective political economy and institutional framework to ensure the proper provisioning of residents. According to central-place theory, a free-market system of private retailers selling food out of shops across the city would have guaranteed that the spatial distribution of suppliers matched local demand, yet without any administrative intervention or cost to the public purse. To recall chapter 1, this was also the scheme proposed by the Commissioners' Plan of 1811. Even as they underestimated the city's future growth, the commissioners did mark up a vast public site for a centralized wholesale market, as well as endorse the emergence of a flexible retail geography dominated by private shops.[51] While the grid plan did not eventually provide for this vision of a new food economy, and the public market system survived for decades longer, it is worthwhile to note that a free-market retail alternative was deliberated at this early stage. How to draw the balance sheet of the public market system with this competing model in mind?

As for the subject of municipal expenditures on public markets, this did not present a major problem. In fact, as discussed in chapter 1, the system by and large paid for itself, and the council generated adequate revenues from its marketplaces. Levied in the form of an excise, collections rose year by year at the same rate as did the population. And even if similar fees could have been collected from private retailers in shops, tax collection was far more effective at a few marketplaces, where transactions occurred in plain sight of the market clerks, vendors, and customers, than it would have been at hundreds of dispersed locations. Nor did provisioning expenditures exceed revenues to the point of becoming an unfair tax burden on vendors and customers. While the sources do not allow for drawing an exact balance, it is safe to suggest that between 1790 and 1820, revenues slightly surpassed expenses, covering normal infrastructural costs and officials' salaries, as well as allowing for the system's periodic expansion until Fulton Market required public borrowing.

Still, what did New Yorkers gain in return for maintaining municipal control of the provision markets? The previous sections have argued that in terms of quantity and distribution, the public markets fulfilled their mandate to ensure access to food to all residents. This last section makes the case that, in comparison to the alternative of a free-market regime, the market system offered two regulatory advantages. First, it contributed positively to the city's public health. Second, it helped promote principles of fairness and equity by instituting mechanisms of redistribution between different groups of vendors, and between neighborhoods of different socioeconomic status.

On the first issue of public health, municipal markets exerted five mechanisms of quality control of the city's food supplies, most of which derived from their agglomeration effects.[52] First and most evident, market laws directly attended to public health matters. To shield against putrefaction, the council had traditionally restricted market trade from sunrise to midday, and prohibited the sale of highly perishable foodstuffs in certain seasons. For example, both custom and regulation forbade the sale of oysters in the summer spawning season, for in this period they were "milky, watery, poor, and considered unfit and unwholesome food."[53] In general, market laws instituted high penalties for selling unwholesome provisions, and assigned the clerks, deputy clerks, and later superintendents of markets to inspect and enforce quality standards. Market officials also monitored the accuracy of measures and weights, and were responsible for collecting revenues and fines. To be effective, they kept a close eye on the lawful occupancy and uses of market space, including stalls and other vending spaces within the market's boundaries and even the surrounding streets. They periodically prepared lists of vendors with their locations, issued or denied daily permits, and in cases of violations of the market laws, with an accompanying report, they had the right to suspend retail licenses. On a daily basis, they oversaw the general cleanliness of their respective marketplaces, employed sweepers for this purpose, and required butchers and other vendors to keep their stalls clean. In short, market officials, especially the deputy clerks, who attended their marketplaces daily, were granted extensive authority to uphold socially perceived norms of public health. What made their oversight effective was the circumstance that public markets concentrated the food trade at a manageable number of locations.

Municipal officials were one source of quality control; the internal agglomeration economy of the marketplace was another.[54] Even though market facilities, from building to stall, were city property, the business that took place inside and around the market-halls remained the domain of free trade. By concentrating the sale of all fresh food supplies into one location, the public market functioned much like today's supermarket. But whereas the supermarket is owned by one firm, the municipal market agglomerated hundreds of independent retailers, encouraging competition between vendors. In theory, competition promoted lower prices, greater selection, and better quality of goods. In other words, the public marketplace provided a balance between competitive business practice and strict government oversight. Given the market monopoly, residents had to frequent the neighborhood market to procure provisions.[55] There, however, they not only could purchase all of their supplies but were also able to compare prices and quality among vendors of the same goods.

The third source of quality control was peer pressure, another positive outcome of business agglomeration. Market vendors customarily monitored one another to prohibit violations of fair trade practices. As a principle, a butcher selling unwholesome meat would face formal and informal sanctions by fellow butchers. Numerous petitions by licensed butchers complained how shirk butchers, reselling meat in small pieces, violated the market laws.[56] The market law itself institutionalized oversight by peer pressure. If the deputy clerk suspected that a butcher sold unwholesome meat, he called on the authority of "any two butchers whom he may select for that purpose . . . (the said butchers being under oath) to determine whether such article or provision . . . is stale or unwholesome, or whether such meat is blown or stuffed, or whether such pork is measly, and their judgment shall be final and conclusive."[57] Market vendors had a vested interest not only in protecting themselves from unfair competition but also in upholding the reputation of their marketplace. In particular, the butchers, who sold meat every day in the same stall, were identified not only by the price, selection, or quality of their cuts but also by the general character of their marketplace.

Whereas the three mechanisms of quality control above derived from business concentration at the individual marketplaces, involving all vendors, the butcher's trade also had two characteristics that helped promote quality. The first aspect was craftsmanship.[58] Market laws granted a special trade privilege to the butchers, which critics may consider a form of rent-seeking. Yet the raison d'être behind strict limitations to open entry of trade was the recognition that butchers handled an essential but highly sensitive and perishable food product. Unlike other food purveyors, butchers were required to complete several years of apprenticeship before they could even apply for a license and vending space. Obtaining a market stall depended not only on availability but also on one's reputation. When a young butcher applied, he submitted a formal petition to the council, which was customarily endorsed by fellow butchers and residents, who testified to the sound business practice and flawless moral character of the novice. In general, butchers belonged to a well-organized and influential group of craftsman citizens.[59] Their high social status reflected their specialized skills in preparing and retailing animal flesh, safely and soundly, to Gotham's meat-loving citizens.[60]

The second aspect was that the butcher's trade fostered a lasting clientele base. For one thing, the lack of modern refrigeration technologies required households to visit the local marketplace frequently. For another, the butcher's business was spatially stable. Unlike other vendors, who occupied the marketplace on a first-come basis, butchers retailed meat in their individually assigned stalls, for which they paid certain taxes to the council.[61] Even as the stall remained municipal property, a butcher had exclusive rights of sale from this piece of market space. The point is that the market stall represented a butcher's largest investment. Since stalls were in limited supply, once a butcher obtained a vending space, he would hold on to this possession. If a butcher wished to relocate his business, he needed to wait until another stall became available either at his own marketplace or somewhere else.[62] The public market system thus not only restricted the sale of fresh meat to a handful of locations but also locked in butchers to specific slots of market space.[63] Consequently, the butcher's trade depended greatly on maintaining one's good reputation and serving a stable clientele. Considering that households bought meat several times a week, hundreds of transactions occurred between the same butcher and customer over the years. And for the consumer, repeated transactions were a guarantee that the regular butcher could be trusted with the merchandise. In fact, residents customarily endorsed their local butcher's petition to the council, testifying to the strong personal relations and mutual trust between the two parties.[64]

Overall, the municipal market system amassed fives lines of defense—government oversight, consumer choice, peer pressure, skilled craftsmanship, and sustained relations between vendors and customers—to create a formidable institution of food quality control at the level of retail. Alternatively, a free-market system of private meat shops and groceries would have been less effective in promoting quality standards. Strict government oversight of food retail transactions was possible because officials had to monitor only a handful of marketplaces as opposed to hundreds of dispersed locations. Customers could shop for quality and price since the public markets concentrated all available provisions at designated neighborhood centers. Peer pressure upheld basic standards of marketing because all transactions occurred under the watchful eye of other vendors and customers. And even if butchers at private shops could have mastered the same specialized skills, or built up a regular clientele, the public market put customer and vendor relations under persistent external scrutiny.

One caveat to this positive assessment concerns the practice of urban slaughtering. Public markets enforced food quality standards at the retail end of distribution, even as the other end of the provisioning chain, slaughtering and processing, was subjected to less municipal regulation. In 1789, the butchers managed to overhaul the colonial model of slaughter, in force since 1676, whereby the killing of animals was restricted to a single location, operated by a private individual under municipal contract. From the 1770s, this so-called Public Slaughter-House was situated at the outskirts near the Fresh Water Pond. Instead of having to drive their livestock to this one facility, after 1789 the butchers acquired the right to operate their killing sheds in principle anywhere in the city.[65] From a monopoly handed to a private contractor, the slaughter of livestock now fragmented into dozens of hands. It is not without irony that the butchers, who pushed hard to terminate this monopoly, half a century later fought even harder to protect the market monopoly of meat from outside competitors. The transition of slaughtering from a monopolistic concession to a decentralized practice represented a setback in the city's regulatory power over the meat supply. Anticipating possible public health risks, the council appointed inspectors to prevent nuisances, but those were typically recruited from among the butchers themselves. It is also true that terminating the slaughter monopoly was not without some logic. Lacking adequate capacity, the Public Slaughter-House became a nuisance itself, often creating overcrowding, traffic jams, and excessive wait times as butchers lined up with their animals outside from as early as 2:00 a.m. Granting butchers the right to slaughter animals and prepare their meat for market was both a matter of efficiency and an acknowledgment of their craftsman skills.

The outcome of the reform was the reorganization of the geography of slaughter, specifically, its decentralization into dozens of killing sheds. The Public Slaughter-House was hardly a modern building, but at least it isolated this nuisance at one place, whereas the butchers' scattered facilities, which were simple wooden structures, often poorly lit or ventilated and without adequate drainage, could bring public health risks closer to residents. In the late eighteenth and early nineteenth century, butchers typically bought livestock from independent drovers at the Bull's Head Tavern, located at the Bowery, only three blocks away from the Public Slaughter-House. Instead of driving the animals into this one facility, now they herded them along the streets into their slaughtering pens, more dispersed and across larger distances. Fresh meat then had to be carted from these places along the streets to the public markets before sunrise, when sales began. Furthermore, meat by-products—offal, bones, hides, skin, and blood—had to be disposed of by being either dumped into the rivers or sent off for processing by different noxious trades, including tanners, soap, and tallow makers.[66] At each step on the way, New Yorkers could come into contact within their neighborhoods, on the streets or other public spaces, with possible sources of disease, including livestock, animal excrement, exposed meat, and waste products. Urban slaughter was by necessity a messy process, but its unregulated and decentralized variety posed additional public health risks.

Looking at the records, however, reveals that decentralization remained rather limited: despite the absence of relevant regulations, slaughtering continued to concentrate in the most thinly populated northern areas, at least in the Early Republican period. The reason had to do with agglomeration effects on the supply side emerging from the daily routine of the butcher's trade, which consisted of two equally important sets of tasks, centered at two separate locations. Public markets structured the retail end of the trade. Before that, however, the butcher had to complete the labor of slaughtering and processing at another location. To minimize unnecessary commuting in their extremely busy mornings, it was imperative for the butchers to live adjacent to their killing sheds, as well as not too far from the Bull's Head Tavern, which remained at its Bowery location until 1825. Indeed, a closer look at the geography cautions against hurried assumptions that public health risks from slaughtering may have spread to the entire city.

While there are no systematic sources on the locations of killing sheds, the home addresses of butchers, listed in the city directories, serve as proxies for mapping the geography of slaughtering and meat processing in 1800 and 1818.[67] As the maps show (figure 2.5), the butchers continued to concentrate their operations around the Bowery, an area by and large

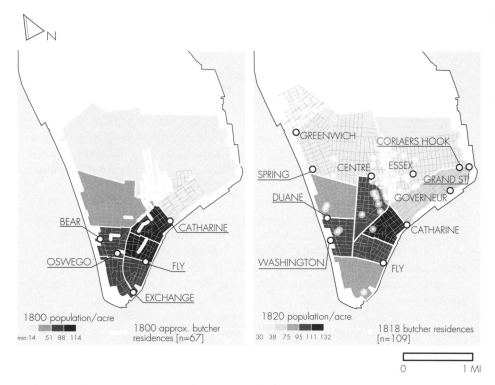

FIGURE 2.5. Approximate locations of slaughterhouses, 1800 and 1818. (*Sources*: See text and appendix A)

unpopulated in 1800, and still sparsely inhabited in 1818. Surely, residents in the vicinity had to put up with noxious odors, sounds, and sights resulting from the killing of livestock. Yet many of those living nearby were butchers themselves, or others whose livelihood depended on animal by-products, such as the tanners. To get the animals to the slaughterhouses, they had to be herded through the streets from the Bull's Head, but this did not disturb the more densely populated central and southern areas. Similarly, when carting meat to the markets, the butchers kept to specific routes, given the limited extent of decentralization. Besides, most of the work occurred before sunrise, when few New Yorkers were out in public. These qualifications are not meant to dismiss the adverse public health effects of unregulated slaughter. Still, it is important to note that even as the practice fragmented into dozens of facilities, it continued to concentrate in a sparsely populated area. The problem was urban growth. As the city expanded northward, and the streets around the Bowery began to fill in with houses, more and more inhabitants found themselves engulfed within this noxious geography. Considering the amount of capital butchers invested in their killing sheds, they had little incentive to move farther north. The 1818 map already signals a worrisome trend, even if the problem was not yet acute.

In fact, a well-functioning public market system, to some degree, helped offset the adverse public health effects of unregulated slaughtering. Most evident, public markets enforced quality standards at the end point of retail; in other words, they could compensate for problems that may have occurred at slaughtering, processing, or transport. They also helped contain the spread of nuisances, especially if compared to the alternative of a free-market regime of private shops. In a rapidly growing city, public markets solved the challenge of extending distribution chains into every neighborhood by concentrating food vendors into a handful of privileged sites. Instead of carting fresh meat into what would have been hundreds of meat shops and groceries scattered across the city's densely populated areas, the necessary traffic of perishable and noxious foodstuffs concentrated on a fewer number of routes, linking the butchers' district in the Bowery to a dozen marketing centers. Similarly, leftovers from the market trade, whether to be dumped or recycled, were collected at the same fewer locations. Surely, a centralized municipal slaughterhouse, complementing Gotham's tightly regulated food markets, would have been a more robust regulatory framework.[68] But insofar as slaughter was left in private hands, the marketplaces' countervailing agglomeration effects played an even more important role in protecting public health.

Earlier, a case was made about how the guild-like trade discipline of the butchers served to support food quality standards. Chapter 1 also documented how the butchers used their closely knit network and social status as an asset for political bargaining, ensuring that the council protected their privileges, sustained a robust public market system, and even granted them the right to slaughter animals in their own facilities. What the maps now add to the discussion is that the butchers' trade association was not only the product of professional but also of personal neighborly bounds. Virtually all regular-bred butchers lived within walking distance from one another. This mattered when an aspiring butcher sought an apprenticeship with a master, a novice applied for a license or stall to the council and needed others to vouch on his behalf, when words were passed around that a stall just opened up for occupancy, or when butchers had to take a collective stand on whether or not to enlarge a marketplace or where to erect a new one. Butchers certainly had a degree of loyalty to the marketplace, where they served customers daily. But they balanced this with a loyalty to their craft, where membership depended on both skills and personal bonds. One's reputation was tied both to the marketplace and this broader community, which granted favors to its members while also castigating those who failed to observe its rules. What the public market system helped with was to impose external checks on this guild-like organization, protecting the public against its potential abuses.

There can hardly be better testimony to this sentiment of neighborly bonds than an intriguing map drawn by a mysterious butcher from memory, looking back at his youth in the 1810s and 1820s from the distance of three decades later. Following up on each clue still leaves his identity uncertain. Nonetheless, a good guess is Ernest Keyser, who is first mentioned as a butcher living at 140 Bowery in the 1812 city directory, which is confirmed by the council's approval of his stall at Bear (Hudson) Market that year, and who is last mentioned as an active butcher at Washington Market still residing in the area according to the 1841 directory.[69] Whether Keyser or not, the butcher in his old age, around 1850, copied down from two published maps the streets of the meatpacking district, and then meticulously labeled on his sketch public buildings and natural landmarks, places of professional import, his neighbors and their slaughterhouses, and, most captivating, his personal narrative.[70] The process involved a small sketch first, which was later consolidated into a larger final version. The present redrawing of this mental map (figure 2.6) makes every effort to preserve the integrity of the author's perspective, which bespeaks volumes of a young butcher's personal experience of living and working in the neighborhood.[71]

Immediately evident from the map is how the butcher's retrospective blurs time, conflating landmarks from two different periods. The neighborhood is dotted by a little over sixty slaughterhouses, most of them located in two clusters a few blocks west of the Bowery below Houston Street, and a third one right northeast from where the two thoroughfares intersected. On the butcher's original map, they are marked with a reddish color, and more than half of them are labeled with the butchers' names, dating the map's central theme around the 1810s and early 1820s. A few uncolored footprints might mark some butchers' homes, while a feather-like pattern indicates animal sheds, especially near the Bull's Head. The Bull's Head, still in operation at the time, is not the only prominent site. Other landmarks—the Bridewell, Work House, Gaol, Bridge, Tea Water Pump, and Watch House—are also recovered either from memory or from the 1797 Taylor-Roberts map. More relevant, the Public Slaughter-House, marked with the date 1770, is diligently reconstructed, surrounded by the private killing sheds of a later generation of butchers. Other ghosts from the past include Bunker's Hill, which featured the city's bull-baiting arena after the Revolution, the Rope Walk, and the Fresh Water Pond, which had largely been drained by the author's youth. As the old butcher reconstructed his neighborhood, two separate geographies of slaughtering were assembled on the same map: one clustered around a centralized facility

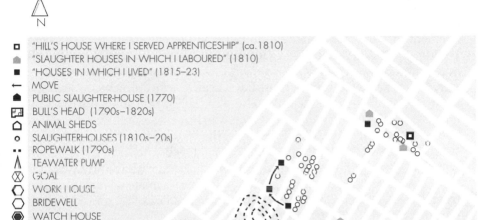

FIGURE 2.6. Mental map of unknown butcher, ca. 1805–23. (*Sources*: See text and appendix A)

nearby the Collect Pond, and another one defined by the private killing sheds of neighborly butchers.

This was a place the butcher intensely remembered. His symbols evoke the familiar streets and dense social networks that tied together people's lives personally and professionally. More often than not, he summons the butchers by names. In other cases, the map recalls his regular walks, as if passing by the fellow butchers' slaughterhouses. Onto this landscape, he inserts his personal narrative with remarks such as "slaughter houses in which I laboured" or "houses in which I lived." Most intriguing, one note identifies "Hills house where I served apprenticeship," also indicating the corresponding slaughtering pen across the street. The same setting of house with adjacent killing shed defined his working conditions for Hartell. By the early 1810s, but definitely no later than 1815, he must have established his own business, for he no longer identifies his home under another butcher's name. Instead, he labels three separate houses between 1815 and 1823, all located in close proximity to one another between Spring and Broome Streets, two or three blocks west of the Bowery. Presumably, his slaughterhouse must have been nearby, which confined his moves to the immediate vicinity. If he was indeed Ernest Keyser, his killing shed stood exactly equidistant from the three houses.

The map's narrative illustrates how the butcher's social and professional worlds were caught up within the narrow boundaries of the neighborhood. They defined where he lived and worked, with whom he associated, how he advanced in his trade, and how he made sense of his life from a few decades distance when trying to reassemble the pieces. Why he felt the need to draw the map, how he came to choose such an unusual medium, and to whom it was intended, one can only guess. The fact that except for some clues the map leaves the author's identity obscure suggests that his audience was himself: an exercise of memory rather than remembrance. In its unusual quality, the mental map testifies to the genuine experience of a closely knit community of craftsmen. This community oriented the butcher's trade: from the home, to the slaughterhouse where he labored, and the public market where he served customers. The map also indicates that the public market system was not simply a government service, at least not in the sense that the Croton system was to become a quarter century later; rather, it was an institutional framework embedded within public and private interests and responsibilities, with the butchers as one group of invested stakeholders.

The public market model, in fact, capitalized on the specific role of each group of stakeholders to promote fairness and equity in provisioning, a second aspect of the system's welfare benefits in addition to public health. In particular, the municipal model instituted two mechanisms of redistribution: one between the different types of food vendors and another across neighborhoods of different socioeconomic status. As for the first, before the 1822 revenue reforms, market fees were paid only by the butchers, whereas for the most part, fishmongers, farmers, and hucksters stood at the marketplace free of charge.[72] In effect, the excise tax was the price butchers paid for their privilege to sell fresh meat by their individual stalls. Additionally, it served as a form of transfer to incentivize the agglomeration of other vendors. Subsidizing farmers to bring their goods to the city made good economic sense: residents needed fresh farm provisions, and marketplaces offered a venue where producers and consumers could transact directly, bypassing the middlemen. Hucksters, typically elderly widows with prior affiliation to the markets, were granted retail licenses by the council on a case-by-case basis out of social welfare.[73]

Similar transfers to fishmongers, many of whom resided in the city, may have been less justifiable. It is also true that the butchers alone conducted steady year-round trade, and insofar as market fees were linked to the excise tax, only their line of business could guarantee stable revenues to support the market system.

The second redistributive mechanism connected the different neighborhoods. The geographic analysis has already made the case that thanks to negotiations between the interests of customers and vendors, public markets supplied all areas, while their scale and volume of trade reflected local population size, in effect, demand. One additional point has to be stressed: even as Gotham's neighborhoods increasingly varied in their levels of urbanization and socioeconomic status, the market infrastructure reached even the least developed northern zones. Extending food markets into the urbanizing frontier not only helped sustain growth but also supported poorer residents who tended to reside in these marginal districts. Butchers would have been more reluctant to open businesses there had the council not guided their decisions by the availability of stalls. And without the butchers' anchoring role in the market trade, fishmongers, farmers, hucksters, and others would have likely stayed away. Indeed, having been assigned stalls at the still peripheral Essex and Governeur Markets, the young butchers Ackly and Hyde strived to make a name for themselves and their public markets when they exhibited and offered their splendid pair of fat oxen for sale. A free-market system would have succeeded in linking up suppliers and consumers, and without taxes, transfers, political deliberation, or administrative oversight. The public market system's contribution was that it fostered spatial expansion and a geographically more egalitarian distribution of food supplies by making threshold investments in poorer, urbanizing districts.[74]

Illustrating this point, a last sequence of maps (figure 2.7) is included. The first pair shows the mean assessed wealth held by the residents of each ward in 1791 and 1826, while the second pair documents the ratio of merchant to artisan populations by ward, that is, the relative concentration of elite and laboring class citizens in those same years.[75] The maps reveal the increasing differentiation of urban space by wealth and social class in the Early Republic. In 1791, the most densely populated southeastern wards were the wealthiest parts of the city, where most of the merchants resided, whereas the less densely built and poorer western and northern wards gave homes to most of the artisans. By 1826, the maps show much greater socioeconomic stratification. The southern wards, even though no longer the most densely populated, remained the wealthiest, and merchants continued to live there. Some of the most densely inhabited central wards also held impressive amounts of wealth, and merchants began to move there. As a rule of thumb, as one walked northward,

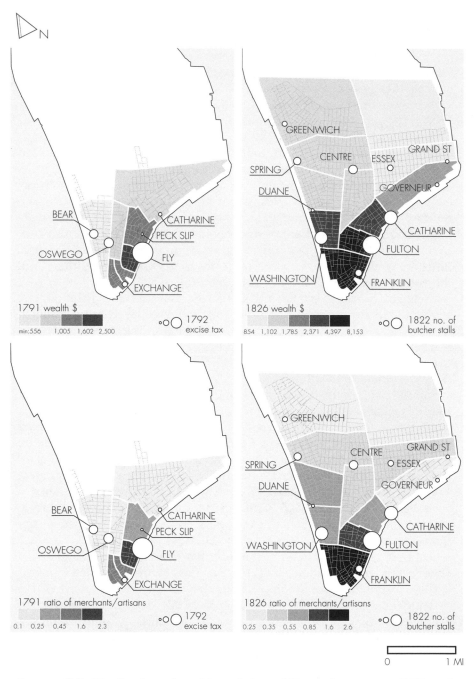

FIGURE 2.7. Distribution of wealth and the public market system, 1791 and 1826. (*Sources*: See text and appendix A)

the wards became less densely inhabited, far less affluent, and correspondingly more likely to be settled by artisans. The important insight is that no matter how poor or marginal a neighborhood was, residents still gained access to a public market. This is already notable in the maps of the walking city of the late eighteenth century, but it is clearly visible in the landscape of the rapidly expanding city of the 1820s. Overall, the public market system was not only responsive to local demand, but it also sustained, even anticipated, urban growth. It played a positive role by investing in and allocating resources to poorer frontier neighborhoods.

This last statement concludes the assessment and drives home the point that there were real social benefits to the public market system. In particular, the municipal model's role in sustaining basic food quality standards stands out at a time when there were no other institutions in place to serve this function. This was complemented by the system's redistributive effects, which helped support the urbanization of poorer frontier neighborhoods while also facilitating the diverse agglomeration of vendors who sold all varieties of food to the benefit of customers. Surely, the municipal model may have inconvenienced some, who lived too far from a public market, although the spatial analysis has found that, in the Early Republican period, the council succeeded in minimizing this problem by ensuring that virtually no residents needed to walk more than about ten minutes to buy provisions. Similarly, excise taxes may have driven up the retail prices of food, albeit market fees were by no means excessively high. Moreover, had food purveyors worked in private shops, they would have paid comparable sums for rents, which in turn would have been shifted to customers. This is not to argue that the public market system was the only appropriate or best way to organize the retail infrastructure of provisioning; rather, it is to acknowledge the model's social advantages, which were real in the case of New York City's well-ordered municipal markets.

Conclusion

This chapter set out to test how effectively the municipal market system fulfilled its political mandate to ensure the public good of citizens' access to food. The discussion followed three related subjects: the supply of food reaching the city, its distribution to residents, and the ways in which the municipal model contributed to the provisioning of New Yorkers. On all three accounts, the analysis presents new insights, reaching an overall positive assessment of the public market model. First, new evidence documents that New Yorkers enjoyed high living standards in terms of their food consumption by any historical comparison. Second, spatial analysis reveals that the city's public markets distributed abundant food supplies to residents in all vicinities. And third, further interpretation contends that the public market system played a critical role in enforcing quality while also promoting egalitarian principles.

Summarizing the chapter's conclusions more specifically, the meat consumption estimates shed new light on the living standards of Early Republican city dwellers. Between 1790 and 1820, New Yorkers ate an estimated 160 pounds of fresh red meat per capita yearly, an amount that measures up to the highest recorded figures in American history. Such plentiful consumption of meat, a relatively expensive food item, attests to their high dietary standards. The sources also detail some of the distinctive features of urban provisioning. City folk not only consumed more meat than those living in the countryside, but they also relied primarily on fresh red meat, which defined an important aspect of their living standards and set them apart from rural populations. The key element of the urban protein diet was fresh beef, complemented by veal, lamb and mutton, and pork. Sustaining their dietary needs, urban dwellers could count on generally favorable supply conditions in this period. Even as cities like New York grew at an accelerated rate, supply chains tapped into expanding and rich hinterlands to support booming urban populations. It is also true that the same supply chains were highly sensitive to external shocks such as a war or epidemics. In times of crises, urban dwellers, who did not produce their own food but depended on provisions from the countryside, endured considerable hardship.

Steadily expanding supplies were a necessary, but insufficient condition for the successful provisioning of New Yorkers. It mattered equally that market intermediaries functioned well to facilitate the distribution of foodstuffs to all residents. Under the municipal model, the market infrastructure had to be consistently upgraded and expanded to meet the changing needs of a growing city. The evidence shows that in the Early Republican era, the government was prepared to make the necessary investments to expand the provisioning system at the rate of population growth. Mediating between the disparate demands of neighborhoods, residents, and vendors, public officials determined the location, size, and capacity of market facilities with administrative competence. From a geographic perspective, the market system maintained adequate balance between the competing principles of agglomeration and dispersal, despite mounting pressure from urbanization. The city's markets reached every neighborhood, extending abundant and varied supplies to all residents. By the spatial criteria, they were successful and well-managed institutions.

The third set of conclusions examines the social benefits of the municipal model, identifying two critical areas. First, public markets helped sustain basic food quality standards by instituting five mechanisms of control deriving chiefly from their agglomeration effects. These were government oversight, consumer choice, peer pressure, skilled craftsmanship, and sustained relations between vendors and customers. Considering that Early American cities lacked other means to monitor quality, the significance of this role cannot be stressed enough. Second, the market laws established two channels of redistribution to promote social equity and fairness. They reallocated resources from the markets' elite class of butchers to the other vendors, as well as from the city's centrally located wealthier areas to its more marginal poorer districts. In this capacity, they contributed to urban development by extending threshold investments into frontier zones. Insofar as food quality and equity were worthy priorities of urban governance, the public markets of Early Republican New York played a positive role in organizing residents' food access.

CHAPTER 3

Constraints of Time

Public Market Schedule of Provisioning

A BUSY MORNING

"I had to rise with the dawn, make 3 fires, run to market, shave & get breakfast to be in my shop by half past nine," complained John Pintard to his daughter about his busy, but not that unusual, morning on November 14, 1816.[1] While his wife usually slept until nine, and his other daughter stayed in bed late, Pintard's days began as early as between 4:30 and 6:00 a.m., when he had to schedule a trip to the public market.[2] And such journeys were no rare commencements of a full day of work. Using conservative estimates, Pintard recorded in his household accounts 171 market trips in 1811 and 151 in 1814, while a decade later, even as his family increasingly relied on nearby grocers for daily provisions,[3] he noted purchases at the public market no less than 214 days in 1827, and 211 days in 1828.[4] In general, Pintard's market trips occurred, on average, three to four times a week during the 1810s and 1820s.

What made these frequent trips possible was that the Pintards lived on Fifty-Two Wall Street, only 900 feet away from Fly Market, the city's largest at the time. After 1821, when Fly was replaced by the more modern Fulton Market, the distances Pintard had to walk increased to about 2,000 feet. For quicker visits, however, he could consider the much smaller Franklin Market within an easy walk of 950 feet. In 1826, the Pintards moved to 429 Broome Street, where they lived at a convenient 700 feet away from one of the largest retail markets, Centre.[5] Besides, by the antebellum decades, the city's grocers, whose stores began to disperse across urban space, increasingly carried fresh food items, offering an alternative for the Pintards and thousands of other families to substitute the market journey with a quick visit to the store.[6]

The provisioning journey was structured not only by the distance one traveled to the public market but also by the conjunctures of time. Just as public markets distributed all varieties of foodstuffs to New Yorkers at a dozen privileged locations, their year-round business agglomerated food supplies of widely different seasonal cycles. Not surprisingly, seasonality first and foremost determined the frequency of residents' marketing visits. Whereas in the winter, Pintard ventured to the neighborhood marketplace only once or twice a week, in the summer and early fall, his marketing trips became part of his daily routine. His shopping rhythms reflected the availability and the perishability of fresh food supplies across the different months of the year. Virtually each and every food item served at the urban household's dinner table experienced seasonal variations. Driven chiefly by supply cycles, they represented the most profound temporal determinants of urban household provisioning. But natural time was complemented by patterns of social time: above all, the weekly cycle of urban marketing, which culminated in large-scale shopping on Saturdays, or the daily cycle, which made Pintard start the day so early in order to take advantage of the greatest variety and best quality of fresh food offered for sale at the local marketplace.

Time, along with space, thus functioned as a key structure for one of the most basic routines of urban life: procuring daily nourishment. In fact, public markets mediated between the agricultural and urban rhythms of food access, households' dependence on permanent supplies, and retailers' need of steady sales. The urban condition created a specific set of circumstances, imposing spatial and temporal constraints on provisioning. City dwellers, like the Pintards, depended on foodstuffs produced in the countryside, transported into the city, and distributed via mediating institutions, such as the public market, food shops, or vendors on the street. An essential task of managing one's household was to skillfully navigate the local food retail landscape. It is hardly an exaggeration that under the public market model, residents' walk to the neighborhood market was a routine as vital as their commute to work.[7]

For most New Yorkers, the marketing trip followed well-defined seasonal, weekly, and daily schedules of shopping. Moving on from chapter 2's spatial analysis, the objective of this chapter is to explore the temporal dynamics of public market provisioning. Specifically, probing what may be referred to as structural time,[8] a rhythm-analysis of New Yorkers' marketing journeys is presented.[9] Accordingly, this chapter reconstructs successively the seasonal, weekly, and daily rhythms of neighborhood food access, and, in the process, identifies how natural and social time determined Early Republican city dwellers' provisioning and consumption habits.

The core documentation for the analysis comes from two series of household account books, complemented by two sets of public market returns. The household accounts were generated by two prominent residents: Evert Bancker Jr. (1721–1803) and John Pintard (1759–1844).[10] Bancker was originally a New York merchant who later served as city surveyor.[11] As for Pintard, he began his career as one of New York's most prosperous merchants, but in 1792, he lost all of his fortune. Even though he never fully regained his wealth, he certainly remained a respectable and well-off citizen. He worked as secretary of the Mutual Assurance Company (1809–29) and the New York Chamber of Commerce (1819–29).[12]

Like most men in late colonial and early national cities, Evert Bancker Jr. and John Pintard assumed their responsibility as household heads to procure daily necessities for their families.[13] They also shared a peculiar habit: to meticulously register each and every purchase they made at the public market.[14] Bancker's household accounts survived for the years between 1772 and 1776, and between 1784 and 1788.[15] One generation later, Pintard produced a similar set of records running from 1811 through 1829.[16] All food purchases made by Pintard in the years 1811, 1814, and 1827, and by Bancker in 1787, were entered into a spreadsheet for the rhythm-analysis.[17] As pointed out, the Banckers and the Pintards belonged to the city's wealthier class of residents, hence, their food purchases may not be representative of the consumption habits of most New Yorkers. At the same time, the analysis concerns the seasonal, weekly, and daily rhythms of provisioning, and in this regard, one would expect less divergence across the social classes than in terms of the quantity and quality of food supplies procured.

On the retail end of the food distribution system, market clerks submitted monthly returns of the incomes earned on the City Corporation's market properties. As discussed earlier, until 1821, the council collected excise taxes on the amount of butcher's meat sold, requiring market clerks to register each head of cattle, calf, sheep, and hog slaughtered for sale at their respective public markets. The same returns that were used in chapter 2 to estimate annual meat consumption also allow for generating monthly estimates of meat sales for New York City in 1816. Complete records of monthly meat sales for Catharine Market in 1818, as well as daily counts for specific months at Washington Market between 1816 and 1819, are also available.[18] In addition, complete daily and weekly returns have survived for Clinton Market for 1847.[19] By this time, market clerks collected annual rents from the butchers paid in weekly sums, and daily fees from all the other vendors, including fishermen, hucksters, and farmers. Unlike butcher rents, whose amounts were fixed by the council and remained constant throughout the year, market fees varied with the number of vendors present at any given day, therefore reflecting seasonal and weekly cycles in household provisioning.

SEASONAL CYCLES

The best place to start the analysis is to explore seasonal variations in New Yorkers' provisioning routines. To this end, figure 3.1 charts the weekly frequencies of Bancker's and Pintard's marketing journeys, and the amount of weekly fees that were collected at Clinton Market. The data reveal a great deal of continuity in the seasonal cycles of residents' marketing habits over the sixty years covered. As Pintard's household accounts are consistently more reliable than those of Bancker's, they provide a benchmark for the first step of the rhythm-analysis.

Accordingly, at the beginning of the year, Pintard frequented Fly (1811, 1814) and later Centre Market (1827, 1828) twice a week on average. By the spring, the number of his provisioning journeys increased to three to four occasions, while in the summer and early fall, he made five to six trips each week. With the coming of late fall and early winter, his shopping schedule slowed down to return to two to three trips on average. Given that public markets were closed on Sundays, this means that in the peak season for food shopping, Pintard walked back and forth between his home and the local marketplace nearly each and every market-day.[20]

Bancker's accounts, while less consistent in recording his trips to the Oswego Market (1787), offer a useful comparison from one generation earlier.[21] They reveal comparable seasonal cycles in food shopping, albeit with a less pronounced increase from winter to spring, similarly frequent visits by the late summer and early fall, followed by a comparable drop at the end of the calendar year. Complementing the analysis, weekly revenues from Clinton Market (1847) represent the collective schedules of thousands of households residing in the market's catchment area. They further corroborate the patterns observed: that market trade was relatively slow in the winter, intensified gradually and progressively over the spring, peaked at volumes two to three times the level of the winter season from June through October, and then decelerated again toward the end of the year.[22]

While it is hardly surprising to identify strong seasonal variations in the intensity and volume of market trade, the sources make new interpretations possible. Above all, it is important to stress that public markets were year-round, permanent affairs, serving customers six days a week across the seasons. Despite their sales more than doubling between bottom and peak months, their baseline trade carried on evenly during the slowest periods. Seasonal cycles were essentially the result of agglomeration economies anchored by the market monopoly of meat, and determined by two important conditions. First, given that market vendors retailed primarily fresh food supplies, the selection of provisions offered for sale varied

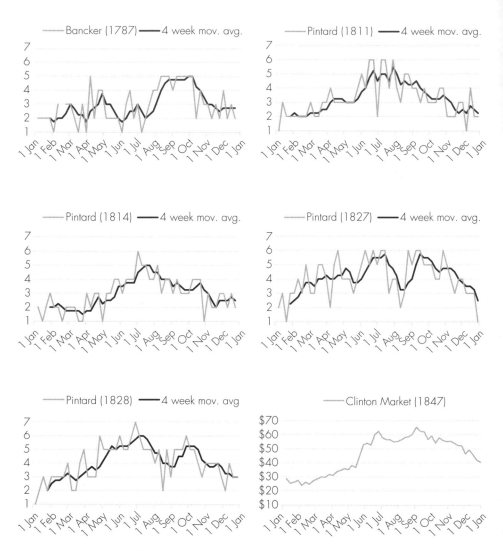

FIGURE 3.1. Weekly frequencies of provisioning, 1780s–1840s. (*Sources*: See notes 15–17 and appendix B)

Notes: Graphs 1 to 5 show the number of weekly provisioning trips made by Bancker (1787) and Pintard (1811, 1814, 1827, and 1828) to their respective neighborhood markets. Graph 6 documents the weekly amount of revenues (butcher rents and market fees combined) at Clinton Market (1847).

greatly with the seasons, enticing customers to different rates of shopping through the months of the year. Second, and more important, households had to worry about the preservation of perishable foodstuffs. The foremost limitation they faced was the lack of proper refrigeration. In fact, the technology of the time, the so-called refrigerator (an icebox consisting of two wooden boxes with insulating material in between), was not widely available until about the mid-nineteenth century. Even so, it was capable of storing food for only a short period.[23] Additionally, since ice was expensive to purchase until at least the 1830s, when technological improvements began to transform the industry, the use of iceboxes was limited to food purveyors and remained the privilege of better-off households in the antebellum era.

Moreover, constraints posed by the availability of supplies and the limitations of preservation technologies interacted to perpetuate seasonal cycles in urban provisioning. Public markets were slow in the winter, when business was largely confined to the baseline sales of butcher's meats, poultry and fowl by the farmers and hucksters, and shellfish, mostly oysters, by the fishmongers. Given the limited selection of food on display, families scheduled two trips per week to the neighborhood market. This was possible because in the cold weather, the decay of fresh food presented a lesser concern. With the arrival of spring, market trade gradually picked up, incorporating a wider array of provisions. In addition to the licensed butchers, fishermen, hucksters, and farmers ever more frequently attended the marketplace, as documented by the steady rise of revenues collected at Clinton Market. In the summer and early fall, as the different types of vegetables and fruits came into season, farmers and hucksters crowded the market stalls and the neighboring streets, fishermen hawked their impressive variety of catch, while the regular-bred butchers soldiered on with their year round sale of red meat. People not only had more fresh food supplies, but they also had to worry a great deal more about putrefaction, and thus the provisioning journeys of Bancker and Pintard became daily routines. In the peak seasons for food shopping, from around late spring through early fall, the public markets were beating faster: they pulled together all imaginable foodstuffs, attracting crowds of vendors and customers twice as large as during the winter, filling New York's teeming neighborhoods with a cacophony of sounds and smells while also clogging the surrounding streets with increased traffic and waste.

A more precise way to assess how the lack of reliable refrigeration influenced households' shopping schedules is to trace how much money was spent on each trip. If the main constraint was food preservation, one would expect that the highest frequency of marketing from spring through early fall was generally matched by lower expenses per trip. Conversely,

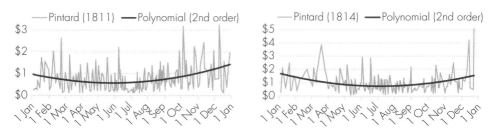

FIGURE 3.2. Market expenditures through the year, 1811 and 1814. (*Sources*: See notes 15–16 and 24)

Notes: The graphs show the amount of money Pintard spent on every one of his 171 and 151 marketing trips in 1811 and 1814, respectively.

in the winter, when residents made fewer visits to the neighborhood market, they also spent more per occasion. Figure 3.2 charts Pintard's expenses for each and every market trip in 1811 and 1814.[24] Just as predicted, it documents expenses twice as high in the winter than in the summer, while also showing greater volatility in Pintard's purchases in the colder months, indicating a shifting strategy of food shopping across the seasons. In the peak seasons, Pintard procured a wider selection of fresh foodstuffs, while also buying smaller quantities that lasted for only one or two days. Even if he came across a particularly enticing deal, the faster decay of provisions strictly limited the amounts he could safely store. In the colder months, when preservation posed less concern, Pintard could focus more on shopping for price and buying larger quantities from the narrower variety of supplies available. This strategy made good sense, for it allowed him to limit his marketing trips to as few occasions as possible. From the viewpoint of permanent market vendors, like the butchers, the inverse relationship between the frequency of residents' shopping trips and the amounts purchased, in turn, helped sustain year-round sales and incomes.

Having explored the seasonal schedules of provisioning, it is time to focus the analysis on the consumption cycles of important food items. A closer study of Bancker's and Pintard's monthly food budgets provides useful details. Figure 3.3 charts the two households' monthly expenses for six categories of fresh food supplies: vegetables and fruits on the one hand, and four sources of protein—specifically, butcher's meat, poultry and fowl, fish, and shellfish—on the other.[25] Again, Pintard's 1811 and 1814 account books offer a good starting point to discern the underlying seasonal rhythms.

Not unexpectedly, one finds strong seasonality in Pintard's purchases of vegetables and fruits, occurring mostly in the summer and early fall.

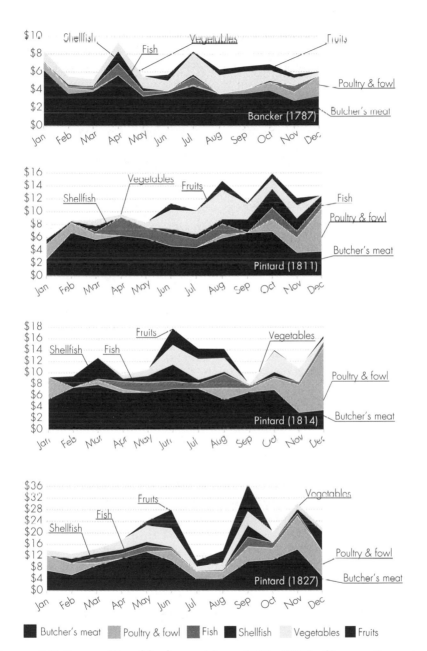

FIGURE 3.3. Seasonality of fresh provisions, 1780s–1820s. (*Sources*: See notes 15–16)

Notes: The graphs show Bancker's (1787) and Pintard's (1811, 1814, and 1827) monthly expenses on six categories of food supplies: butcher's meat (beef, veal, lamb and mutton, and pork), poultry and fowl, fish, shellfish, vegetables, and fruits.

The same seasonal cycles, as expected, may be observed in Bancker's budgets from a quarter of a century earlier, and Pintard's accounts from two decades later. More interesting, Pintard's 1811 and 1814 records testify to strong seasonal cycles in the family's supplies of fresh protein. One identifies the least seasonality in their expenses on the aggregate category of butcher's meats (beef, veal, lamb and mutton, and pork) representing a little less than 30 percent of the marketing budget. Conversely, their purchases of poultry and fowl, fish, and shellfish (8–10, 4–6, and 5–6 percent of the marketing budget, respectively) followed more pronounced seasonal variations.[26]

What is important to note is that seasonal rhythms in the consumption of the four sources of protein appear to be connected, contributing to a yearly cycle, altogether supporting a sustained year-round supply of protein for the family. The Pintards consumed first and foremost fresh red meat, which they ate in generous quantities all through the year. It is also true that a notable downturn occurred in their red meat consumption in the late fall and early winter, and to a lesser extent, in the summer. Compensating for these seasonal declines, the Pintards' dinner table was plentifully dressed with poultry and fowl in the late fall and early winter, especially during the months of November, December, and January. Similarly, the more modest summer downturn in the consumption of fresh meat was offset by the family's growing appetite for fish. As for shellfish, it is difficult to discern any consistent pattern across the two account books, other than the Pintards' general observance of the rule that oysters were not to be consumed during the summer.

Comparing Pintard's to Bancker's expenses from more than two decades before, one finds almost identical seasonal rhythms. For the Banckers, the consumption of red meat shows virtually no seasonality. The lack of even a slight dent in the late fall and early winter or the summer, however, likely reflects a source limitation: that in Bancker's case it is not possible to discount preserved meats from the analysis. Indeed, for poultry and fowl, one finds the same rhythm of concentrated consumption during the late fall and early winter, whereas for fish, the previously established pattern of late spring and early summer availability is again confirmed. While the Banckers expended a smaller share of their marketing budget on poultry and fowl and fish, the seasonal entry of these two alternative supplies of protein probably indicates that they also compensated for a modest downturn in the family's consumption of fresh red meat. Moving forward in time, Pintard's 1827 accounts further corroborate the familiar cycles of fresh protein consumption, especially the expected year-round dependence on fresh red meat, coupled with intensified poultry and fowl consumption in the fall and winter seasons. It is also true that the Pintards' fish purchases this year spread over a longer stretch of time, from spring through fall.

Overall, the components of the protein cycle persisted for two households at four points in time across four decades, thus indicating that the seasonal patterns observed were not specific to any given year but were structurally encoded in the urban schedule of marketing. The different seasonal cycles, agglomerated by the public markets, served to smooth fluctuations in households' yearly sources of protein. The fact that even well-off families such as the Banckers and Pintards observed these rhythms provides robust evidence that seasonal patterns in New Yorkers' protein consumption were primarily the function of the food supplies reaching the city markets, and insofar as agricultural conditions remained unchanged, these temporalities must have persisted.[27] Indeed, the Banckers and Pintards belonged to the class of New Yorkers who were relatively free to choose among the different butcher's meats, poultry and fowl, fish, and shellfish offered for sale at the public markets. Compared to most households, their sources of fresh protein were less constrained by their budgets than their own preferences and what the markets supplied at any given time of the year. In this sense, the Bancker and Pintard accounts underestimate seasonality: families with lower incomes must have experienced more marked seasonal variations in their protein diet depending on the relative prices of goods.

The discussion is yet incomplete, for the aggregated category of butcher's meats, by far the most important source of protein for city dwellers, may be hiding considerable seasonal variations. What happens if the category is decomposed into its four elements? Fortunately, in this case, the analysis no longer needs to be limited to the two families' expenses, but on the supply side, the market clerks' accounts provide complementary evidence. Figure 3.4 compares Pintard's and Bancker's monthly expenses on the four types of butcher's meats to per capita consumption estimates of the same in New York in 1816 and to their overall amount of sales at Catharine Market in 1818. Considering that the market returns register seasonal variations in meat consumption for all New Yorkers, reflecting the entire supply of meat reaching the city's markets, it makes sense to use these records as the starting point for the analysis.

Accordingly, the 1816 market returns reveal fairly small seasonal variations for the supply of beef, and conversely, pronounced seasonal cycles in the availability of veal, lamb and mutton, and fresh pork. Just as the aggregate supply of butcher's meats dominated residents' access to protein across the seasons, the supply of beef dominated the seasonal cycles of fresh meat consumption. Throughout the year, New Yorkers enjoyed plentiful supplies of beef, of which they ate anywhere between four to twelve

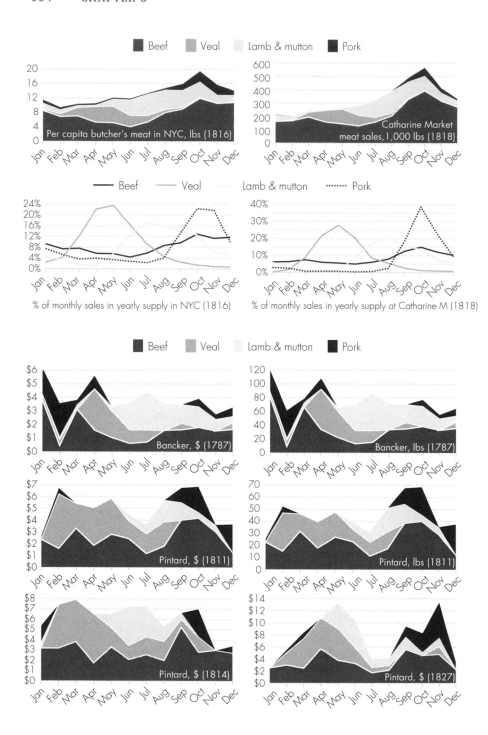

Beef Veal Lamb & mutton Pork

Per capita butcher's meat in NYC, lbs (1816)

Catharine Market
meat sales, 1,000 lbs (1818)

Beef Veal Lamb & mutton Pork

% of monthly sales in yearly supply in NYC (1816)

% of monthly sales in yearly supply at Catharine M (1818)

Beef Veal Lamb & mutton Pork

Bancker, $ (1787)

Bancker, lbs (1787)

Pintard, $ (1811)

Pintard, lbs (1811)

Pintard, $ (1814)

Pintard, $ (1827)

pounds per capita monthly, with the lowest amounts being consumed in the spring and the highest in the fall. They conceded some of their beef consumption once veal came into season from around late winter through early summer. When the supply of veal began to tail off, the beef diet was increasingly complemented by lamb and mutton from late spring through early fall. Last, from early fall through early winter, fresh pork entered the diet, matching the peak period of beef consumption.

These consumption cycles closely mirrored the agricultural seasons of meat production. Large livestock such as cattle and hogs were typically slaughtered in the fall and early winter, when farmers salted and barreled beef and pork to preserve supplies for the winter and spring. Increased consumption of beef and fresh pork in cities reflected the wider availability of large livestock in this period. Similarly, veal became available for urban consumers following the winter fattening season, while lamb was ready for slaughter from spring, four to six months after the fall breeding season. On the whole, the enormous size of New York City's food markets assured that these distinct seasonal production cycles integrated into a steady and diversified supply of fresh meat.[28]

The average New Yorker therefore could count on consuming an impressive ten to sixteen pounds of fresh red meat during each month of the year.[29] The urban standard of living, insofar as meat consumption was concerned, depended on these complementary seasonal cycles, which sustained an abundant and stable supply of butcher's meat over the months of the year and from one year into the next. Equally important, the butchers themselves depended on these connected seasonal cycles, which kept fluctuations of sales within reasonable bounds. By extension, without the butchers' permanent business there, the public markets would have fallen short of their mandate to serve as the primary sites of provisioning residents. In this sense, the butcher's trade fulfilled its anchoring function not only by spatially agglomerating the sales of different foodstuffs at the

FIGURE 3.4. Seasonality of butcher's meats, 1780s–1820s. (*Sources*: See notes 15–16 and appendix B)

Notes: The first graph presents per capita monthly consumption estimates for the four types of butcher's meats in New York (1816). The second shows the total volume of monthly meat sales at Catharine Market (1818). Using the same data, but to highlight seasonality more clearly, the third and fourth graphs show the percentage of monthly sales within the yearly total for each category of butcher's meat in New York (1816) and at Catharine Market (1818). The remaining six graphs illustrate the monthly expenses of the Banckers (1787) and Pintards (1811, 1814, and 1827) on the four kinds of butcher's meat. For the Bancker and 1811 Pintard accounts, monthly expenses are also converted into amounts consumed, using the retail prices of each type of meat as cited in their records.

public markets but also by temporally integrating the seasonal cycles of agricultural production into a year-round supply.

Going back to the sources, the fact that the market clerks' 1816 returns were aggregated from their daily counts of the head of animals slaughtered for sale at the public markets ensures that the data are robust and reliable. Importantly, the same results are confirmed by two additional sources. First, monthly meat sales at Catharine Market in 1818 document the same seasonal supply cycles, as shown by the second chart of figure 3.4.[30] Second, and on the demand side, the Bancker and Pintard marketing accounts, likewise charted, reveal the two households' close observance of the supply cycles of butcher's meat production.

The relatively less noticeable supply cycles of beef, with their spring and summer decline, followed by a peak in the fall, are observed in all household accounts.[31] Additionally, in Bancker's case, unusually strong fluctuations are found in the beginning of the year. Specifically, high amounts of beef consumption in January and March are interrupted by low consumption rates in February, which was compensated by the household's greater dependence on pork. This volatility most likely reflects that for the Banckers, as mentioned before, it is difficult to distinguish between expenses on preserved and fresh meats. Indeed, their exceptionally high amounts of purchases of beef and pork in the winter months coincided with the increased availability of barreled beef and pork following the fall and late winter slaughter season.

Moving on to veal, seasonal cycles in both households' purchases closely followed the availability of supplies at the New York markets.[32] One finds consistent patterns across all account books with low, but gradually increasing, veal consumption beginning in late winter, a peak in the spring and early summer, a gradual decline from midsummer until early fall, and finally, the general absence of fresh veal in the two households' diets in the fall and early winter seasons. One should note that even the Pintards, whose appetite for this comparatively more expensive meat well exceeded what most New Yorkers could afford, strictly observed the seasonal availability of veal. The case of lamb and mutton is similarly consistent between the market returns and the household accounts.[33] Lamb and mutton were absent in both families' diets in the winter and early spring, since their consumption cycle began in May, reached its peak in the summer, and petered out in the fall. Finally, the accounts confirm that fresh pork was eaten almost exclusively in the fall and early winter.[34] Only the Bancker accounts differ from the rest in that pork consumption reached its highest rates in January and February as opposed to the fall, reflecting that most of these purchases refer to preserved instead of fresh pork.

Evidently, both the market returns and the household accounts point to strong and persistent seasonal cycles in the consumption of beef, veal, lamb and mutton, and pork, urban Americans' main sources of fresh meat. Importantly, the data come from both the supply and demand sides of the provisioning chain. Moreover, the findings are even more conclusive if placed in the context of enduring and complementary seasonal cycles in the consumption of poultry and fowl, fish, and shellfish, New Yorkers' other main sources of protein. The highly seasonal character of vegetables and fruits is self-evident, and was observed as expected.

As a final note, a few words about bread, dairy products, and eggs. Bread was supplied by the city's bakers, and, as one would expect, it was eaten year-round. If there was any seasonality in its consumption, it is not possible to detect, since payments were usually settled on a monthly or bimonthly basis.[35] For milk, payments were made either in large sums or on a monthly basis, while for butter, the records document both case-by-case purchases and larger settlements, probably with the local grocer. In neither case do the accounts indicate any evident seasonality. Indeed, De Voe suggests that butter "is always to be found in great abundance in our markets, as well as in the grocery and other stores."[36] Eggs, on the contrary, "may be considered as being in season the year round, although in the spring months they are more plentiful and cheap."[37] While the marketing accounts are not consistent, they seem to confirm De Voe's claim that eggs were abundantly eaten in the spring.[38]

All in all, the evidence points to the primacy of agricultural production cycles in explaining seasonal variations in New Yorkers' diets. The fact that seasonality mattered is, of course, not unexpected. Rather, its pervasiveness and the extent to which it affected all varieties of fresh foodstuffs, even butcher's meats, are important insights. Further, what needs to be appreciated is the degree to which seasonal cycles, both between the four categories of butcher's meats and the different sources of protein, complemented each other to sustain stable and year-round supplies. The evidence points to a dietary system of integrated rhythms, where beef served as the baseline of meat consumption, even as other types of butcher's meats took a secondary role when they came into season. Complementing this dietary base, especially during slack periods of fresh red meat consumption, was a variety of other fresh sources of protein, above all, fish and shellfish, all drawn from Gotham's rich supply hinterlands. All of these supplies were assembled at the city's numerous and plentiful public markets. It was precisely this temporal agglomeration that ensured that the neighborhood market, whether beating slower or faster, continued to orient residents' shopping journeys throughout the year.

Of course, for contemporaries, seasonality was not so much a sophisticated system but the daily reality of household provisioning with which they needed to grapple. Indeed, De Voe's *The Market Assistant* (1867) regularly mentions the seasonal availability of specific fresh food items, while also commenting on some of the restrictions on the sale of game and fowl, or fish and shellfish, for specific months of the year, to better inform market customers. What is at first puzzling then about his notes on the subject is to find him asserting that "beef, mutton, lamb, veal, and pork, are usually found throughout the year, in its various seasonable preparations, in all the public markets, and they may be reasonably considered 'always in season.' "[39]

De Voe is, no doubt, the leading authority on nineteenth-century urban food markets. He also had the advantage of being a contemporary observer. However, the fact that his statement differs from the evidence mustered here does not prove that his comment or the conclusions reached in this chapter are wrong. Instead, the meat supply chains that sustained New York and other American cities underwent major transformations from the mid-nineteenth century onward. Technological changes in livestock production, stockyard practices, refrigeration and transportation, and, most important, an expanding railroad network, allowed northeastern cities to tap into vast new hinterlands for their meat supplies, which reached as far as the Midwest and beyond.[40] One less-appreciated aspect of this history has to do with the smoothing effects of nationally integrated livestock markets on the seasonality of urban meat supplies. There are unfortunately no comparable data available for New York City from the time of De Voe's publications to explore how much difference these changes made in the meat consumption cycles observed. Looking at monthly livestock counts from New Orleans' centralized slaughterhouse in 1875 offers some guidance. Insofar as these records can be taken as indicative, they reveal the general absence of seasonality in butcher's meats by the 1870s.[41] This leads to an intriguing question of chronology, left here for future research. The fresh red meat cycle, which satisfied the appetite of New Yorkers and city dwellers across America throughout the year, serving as the centerpiece of urban protein consumption from the colonial era through the 1840s at least, may have changed and gradually weakened with the advent of the railroad by the postbellum period.

Moreover, the pervasive seasonality of food supplies had important but little appreciated impacts on urban everyday life. Most immediately, it structured residents' daily routines of provisioning. Even as late as the middle of the nineteenth century, in spite of iceboxes becoming more common and enabling better-off New Yorkers to schedule fewer shopping trips, the Clinton Market returns document that for most households, the marketing journey remained a heavy chore. Besides, the seasonality of food supplies had indirect ramifications on the urban environment at various junctures, including traffic patterns, sanitation and public health, or even the sensual experience of the city, such as sounds and smells. Public markets represented one of the most seasonal aspects of urban life. They connected the city to its diverse hinterlands, inviting natural time to penetrate and structure residents' daily lives. In effect, they were a forceful reminder that despite the ever-more-complex transnational trade links and migration networks that sustained New York's rise and integration into a transatlantic web of cities, Gotham remained a local place, embedded in the second nature of agricultural production for its vital dependence on food supplies from the countryside.

Perhaps the most fascinating facet of this history is that seasonal supply cycles not only structured residents' provisioning habits, but the urban environment itself mediated, even amplified, their effects. Intriguingly, seasonality in the consumption of certain food items was more pronounced in the city than the countryside. This was most evidently the situation with butcher's meats. As discussed in chapter 2, one crucial difference between urban and rural diets was that the consumption of fresh meat, above all beef, was primarily the prerogative of city dwellers.[42] In fact, much of the seasonality in rural food consumption was based on the annual cycles of food preservation, including the practice to salt and barrel beef and pork as part of the fall and early winter slaughter season. New Yorkers, on the contrary, relied first and foremost on fresh red meat for their protein, which they ate year-round: a privilege derived from urban agglomeration effects. Beyond a certain size, cities generated sufficient and steady demand for fresh meat supplies, so that large livestock could be imported, slaughtered, and retailed for immediate sale throughout the year. The urban condition therefore presented a unique conjuncture: Early Republican urban dwellers could enjoy fresh meat year-round, yet the composition of their meat diet varied considerably with the agricultural production seasons.

WEEKLY SCHEDULES

Up to this point, the analysis has reconstructed the passing of seasons to trace how natural time, or, more accurately, the seasonality of agricultural production, influenced New Yorkers' provisioning and food consumption habits. Yet social time, above all, the weekly schedules of marketing, also played an important part in determining residents' shopping routines. Public markets were open six days a week, from Monday through Saturday. They closed on Sundays, with the exception of the fishmongers' trade, which was allowed to carry on in the morning. What were then the weekly schedules of provisioning? Addressing this issue, figure 3.5 charts the weekly cycles of market trade using the now familiar accounts of Bancker and Pintard, along with the daily returns of the clerk of Washington Market and the daily revenues collected at Clinton Market. As for the

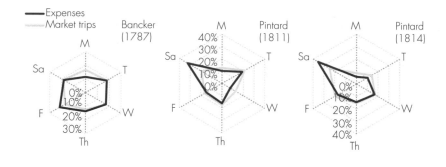

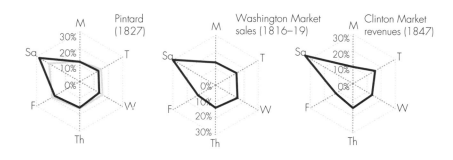

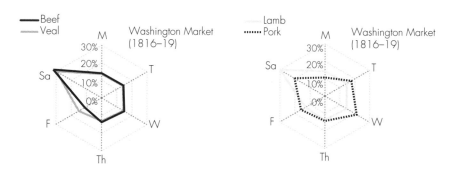

FIGURE 3.5. Weekly schedules of provisioning, 1780s–1840s. (*Sources*: See notes 15–16 and appendix B)

Notes: Graphs 1 to 4 show the distribution of Bancker's (1787) and Pintard's (1811, 1814, and 1827) marketing trips and expenses across the six market days of the week, from Monday through Saturday. Graph 5 depicts the same for the sales of butcher's meats (in pounds) at Washington Market (1816–19). Graph 6 looks at the weekly distribution of market fees collected at Clinton Market (1847). The two last graphs study the weekly distribution of sales between the four types of butcher's meats at Washington Market. In all cases, the data are expressed in percentages: the specific day's share within the weekly total.

household accounts, the graphs compare the allocation of both marketing journeys and expenses across the days of the week. In the case of Washington Market, the weekly distribution of sales for both the aggregate category and individual types of butcher's meats is also considered. Finally, the Clinton Market returns document how much revenue was generated on each market-day.

Starting with Bancker's and Pintard's marketing trips, only tentative patterns emerge from the records. In 1787, Bancker was equally prone to visiting Oswego Market on any market-day, except for Thursday, when he scheduled relatively fewer trips. In 1811, Pintard had a slight preference for going to Fly Market on Tuesdays, Thursdays, and Saturdays, whereas in 1814 and 1827, he was most likely to procure his supplies on Fridays and Saturdays, and the least likely to do so on Mondays. In general, and excepting Bancker's case, a notable preference is identifiable for food shopping on Saturdays. It is also true that in terms of the frequency of visits, the weekly cycle appears feeble at best: only one-fifth to one-fourth of the two families' marketing trips occurred on Saturdays.[43]

Far more telling is the alternative approach to examine how the two households distributed their marketing budgets between the six days of the week. In Bancker's case, one continues to find no apparent pattern. As for Pintard, all three years reveal a well-defined weekly schedule, in which Saturday consistently stands out as the most prominent day to buy provisions. Indeed, about one-third of Pintard's food expenses occurred on Saturdays.[44] And additional sources confirm that Pintard's schedules were more typical, while Bancker's case should be regarded as more exceptional. The predominance of Saturday shopping is evident in the Washington Market returns (1816–19), which document that nearly one-third of weekly meat sales took place on Saturdays. The same is true for Clinton Market (1847), where one-third of weekly market fees paid by farmers, fishmongers, and hucksters were collected on Saturdays.[45]

Given that market returns reflect the collective schedules of thousands of separate households and hundreds of independent vendors, their close correspondence to Pintard's accounts leaves no space for doubt that for New Yorkers, Saturday was by far the most important day of food shopping. The large volume of Saturday marketing was the direct result of the weekly work schedule, which allowed only one day of rest on Sundays, when the city's public markets also closed for business. The fact that Saturdays accounted for one-third of both the weekly purchases of Pintard and the sales at Washington and Clinton Markets is evidence that on Saturdays, customers bought at least two days' worth of supplies. The special status of Saturday shopping was encoded in the daily schedules of marketing. From Monday through Friday, the market-day commenced at daylight and lasted until early afternoon. On Saturdays, however, the public markets stayed open until much later, allowing vendors to carry on their trade into the night, as residents crowded into the neighborhood markets to purchase provisions in larger quantities, partly in preparation for their Sunday meals.[46]

One may inquire about the presence of subtler fluctuations in the weekly rhythms of marketing. On this point, the evidence is far from conclusive. The Washington Market and Clinton Market returns indicate an even distribution of trade from Monday through Friday. As for the two household accounts, no specific rhythms appear from the records, whether looking at the full year or season by season. For Pintard, at least some tentative patterns can be observed. Whereas in the summer months, Pintard's provisioning occurred almost every day, during the other seasons, his visits and expenses were paced in relation to each other. In the winter, spring, and fall of 1811, the combination of Tuesday, Thursday, and Saturday shopping appears quite frequently. The same sequence is often observed for the winter and spring of 1814. Other notable combinations include Monday, Thursday, and Saturday shopping in the winter and spring of 1827, and Wednesday and Saturday marketing in the fall of 1814.

Put differently, there were no particular days reserved in Pintard's schedule for food shopping. Whether he would visit the public market on any given day was largely determined by how long his supplies lasted from the previous trips. In turn, how many days he could skip between two market visits depended on the seasonally changing conditions of food preservation. The fact that similar rhythms cannot be traced in the aggregate market returns does not suggest that other households did not observe a similar approach in pacing their provisioning trips. On the contrary, since the market returns reflect the collective schedules of thousands of customers, at the aggregate level one would expect to find an even distribution of sales across the days of the week, with the exception of Saturdays, for there were as many schedules as there were households. Furthermore, the public market's thousands of customers gathered from a large enough area to represent a variety of social classes, with daily work routines as different as their occupations.

Last, were there any distinct weekly rhythms in the sales of the four categories of butcher's meat? The Washington Market data, as shown in the last two charts, suggest an interesting pattern. Accordingly, beef, veal, and lamb and mutton followed the exact same weekly cycles, characterized by a peak of sales on Saturdays. Pork, in contrast, behaved unlike these other three meats, with an even distribution of sales across the six market-days. Apparently, on Saturdays, when New Yorkers were most likely to visit the neighborhood market to procure butcher's meat and other provisions for their Sunday meals, pork was regarded as the least preferred option, probably even for lower-income families. It is also true that pork was not typically consumed fresh but as preserved and cured meat.

DAILY SCHEDULES

Social time not only determined the weekly cycles of marketing but also its daily rhythms. Lacking systematic evidence, daily rhythms are more elusive to reconstruct than seasonal or weekly schedules, yet they were critically important, for they played a crucial role in defining how socio-economic inequalities inscribed themselves onto the city's landscape of provisioning. To begin with, the public market laws instituted formal schedules of market trade. Concerns over public health, in particular, the spoiling of fresh food, not only found their way into the seasonal cycles of marketing (for example, by limiting the sale of specific food items to certain months) but also shaped the regular hours of the market-day. As already noted, the market-day commenced at break of day and continued until early afternoon: 2:00 p.m. in the summer (May 1–November 1) and 3:00 p.m. in the winter (November 1–May 1) season. Since they retailed a highly perishable food item, butchers had to conclude their sales one hour earlier. On Saturdays, public markets stayed open through the evening: according to the more detailed Fulton Market schedule, closing time could be as late as 11:00 p.m. This full-day schedule served to accommodate the increased volume of sales on Saturdays. On Sundays, public markets were closed, except for the fish stalls, which served customers until 9:00 a.m.[47]

Constrained within the formal schedules of the market laws, the rules of supply and demand nonetheless effectively determined the daily rhythms of marketing. In general, price signals influenced residents' shopping schedules along two main conditions: the selection of provisions available and their quality and freshness. Here again, the lack of reliable refrigeration exacerbated the impact of choice and quality on residents' marketing schedules. So how did prices and marketing schedules interact? As a rule of thumb, the earlier the hour, the greater the variety and the better the quality of the provisions, while as the day progressed, the selection and quality of the goods offered for sale gradually diminished. This, in turn, was reflected in the daily changes in prices, which tended to progressively decline from opening to closing hours. On their part, butchers tried to prepare as much meat as they expected to sell on any given day, and similarly, fishermen, farmers, and hucksters tried to bring a day's worth of fish or farm products to market. Prices did the rest, sorting out the selection and the quality of fresh food supplies to different social strata of customers corresponding to the times of the day. Residents, for their part, had to accommodate their own or their servants' shopping schedules to the appropriate hours of the market-day.

Like thousands of other residents, Pintard scheduled his provisioning trips early in the morning. In this period, according to De Voe, "it was the common custom for the thrifty 'old New Yorker,' when going to market, to start with the break of day, and carry along with him the large 'market-basket.' " The reason was that an "early visit gave him the desired opportunity to select the *cuts* of meat wanted from the best animals; to meet the farmer's choice productions, either poultry, vegetables, or fruit, and *catch* the lively, jumping fish, which, ten minutes before, were swimming in the fish-cars."[48] De Voe's use of the word "him" was not a gender-neutral reference, for he specifically meant gentlemen shoppers, just like Pintard. Indeed, until about the early nineteenth century, it remained common practice among middle-class men in cities to take care of food shopping for their families, in part because this involved a trip to the potentially raucous public space of the neighborhood market and the daily purchase of meat.[49]

By the antebellum period, however, food shopping fell entirely on the shoulders of women, in addition to all other household chores.[50] Wealthy and middle-class women could mitigate some of this increased burden with the help of domestics or by taking advantage of the wider availability of home delivery by upper-end food retailers. The same option was not available to working-class women who had to manage household provisioning on their own or with the help of their children. This does not mean, of course, that Pintard in the early nineteenth century did not already share the experience of marketing with women. In De Voe's version, shortly after the gentleman shopper's visit, "followed the 'good housewife,' who would not trust anybody but herself to select a fine young turkey, or a pair of chickens or ducks." She was also customarily accompanied by her "stout servant," who carried along with her the market basket as well as "a bright tin, covered kettle, ready to receive several nice rolls of *butter*."[51]

As shopping for choice products gradually tapered off, residents with more meager incomes began to schedule their marketing trips. And with the markets' customers becoming increasingly working-class, they also more typically consisted of women shoppers, especially by the antebellum era. Shoppers arriving at this second wave often found that they "had to take such as was left." In De Voe's judgment, already "by ten o'clock the market was considered through, although many poor persons and others, who were looking for bargains, would come after that hour."[52] At noon, the markets began to accommodate yet another rhythm, as street peddlers and other secondary traders joined in, finding their niche in reselling market leftovers at lower prices to the city's poorest customers. Despite complaints by butchers and other market vendors about unfair competition by unlicensed retailers, formal and informal trade, at least in this instance, complemented each other.

This secondary trade, being limited to past midday, was even acknowledged by the market laws, for it also served the interest of market vendors.[53] Each day by sunrise, the public markets assembled a vast amount of perishable food supplies that had to be disposed of in their entirety over the course of eight hours. Once closing time was approaching, and sales nearly halted, it made sense to facilitate the disassembly process by handing over the remnants at discounted prices to peddlers, who expanded market trade spatially to the surrounding streets, and temporally by carrying on their business late into the afternoon. De Voe's verdict on such street merchandise was hardly a ringing endorsement. He called it the "refuse of the markets, unfit to be offered by the respectable dealer," while he also accused street vendors of cheating by using "false-bottomed measures" and "short weights."[54] Still, he surely recognized the benefits of such an accommodation insofar as peddlers were prevented from directly competing with market vendors.

Last, Saturday markets present a special case, for sales continued all through the day into the night. Yet the daily rhythms of shopping were also similarly structured by income differentials. Specifically, on Saturdays, when public markets handled the largest volume of trade, late evening to night shopping was mainly dominated by working-class residents. One case frequently commented on by contemporaries is Catharine Market. In 1825, the reporter of the *American* described Catharine Market as a "great emporium for the mechanics and laborers on Saturday evening."[55] Similarly, De Voe notes that "Saturday night markets were . . . crowded, sometimes almost too overflowing" at Catharine Market in the early 1820s.[56] The most detailed description, however, comes a quarter century later from penny press writer George G. Foster, whose 1850 sketch portrays Saturday night shopping at Catharine Market in a vivid tone:

> Imagine all the coarseness, all the shameless filth, all the squalor and brutality from which you escaped, and then conceive, steeped to the lips in it, a population made reckless by ignorance, want and vice, and utterly regardless of public opinion, or even unconscious of its existence. Then you will have some faint idea of the many who frequent Catharine Market of a Saturday night.[57]

As Pintard's or Bancker's records clearly show, food provisioning on Saturdays involved all social strata of New Yorkers. At the same time, and disregarding Foster's sensational language, anecdotal evidence confirms that Saturday night marketing was first and foremost the terrain of laboring residents. On Saturday nights, working-class shoppers crowded into their neighborhood markets "to pick up the remnants," lending these public spaces a distinctively colorful, raw, and gritty character.[58]

In conclusion to the discussion on daily rhythms, two general points need to be apprehended. The first has to do with the underlying logic of unequal food access under the public market system, and the second with chronology. On the problem of inequality, chapter 2's spatial analysis argued that one of the municipal model's central contributions to the common good was to ensure the distribution of supplies to residents in all neighborhoods. In the Early Republican period, no particular area of New York appears to have been disadvantaged in this regard despite the city's relentless growth and northward expansion. The present temporal analysis modifies this earlier assessment. It brings attention to a different mechanism, not based on spatiality but on temporality, by which income disparities translated into unequal access to food supplies among households.

Insofar as the public market system dominated the city's political economy and geography of provisioning, it made relatively little difference in which neighborhood one lived. Certainly, public markets differed in size, and hence their agglomeration economies varied considerably. Yet even the smallest markets contained all types of provisions, with multiple vendors in each line of trade, an arrangement that ensured that customers were not disadvantaged in terms of food choice and quality between the vicinities. On the contrary, it mattered a lot more for the selection and quality of provisions at which time of the day one visited the local marketplace. Put differently, in early nineteenth-century New York, residential location imposed lesser constraint on access to abundant and healthy food supplies than did the daily rhythms of food shopping. Time and not space was the main dividing line, separating better-off customers from poorer ones at the urban marketplace. This also implies that even though public markets were among the city's most open public spaces for local residents to interact, to a degree, the daily rhythms of provisioning separated neighbors from one another as customers of different social status.

On the second question of chronology, it is worth stressing that the daily rhythms of marketing derived, in part, from the regulatory regime of the public market system and the lack of reliable refrigeration. By the time De Voe published his market books in the 1860s, these daily schedules had undergone considerable changes. First, more widely available refrigerator boxes restructured certain aspects of the retail butcher's trade.[59] Whereas the market butcher traditionally woke before daybreak to cut up as much meat as "could be profitably sold for the day," by mid-century, the "*modern* retail butcher" typically began his sales later, around eight o'clock, and stayed open until the evening. He was also less constrained in the amount of meat he could prepare for any given day, since refrigeration allowed him to keep some of his merchandise for the next day.[60] Second, improved refrigerator boxes allowed better-off households to schedule fewer market trips. Moreover, food vendors increasingly made the option of home delivery available to their regular customers.[61] Indeed, one of De Voe's motivations to write *The Market Assistant* was to revive the old custom of shopping regularly at the public markets, especially among the city's better-off citizens, who benefited the most from home delivery and the use of refrigerator boxes. The modern "marketer," according to De Voe, went less frequently, if at all, to the marketplace, and was less well versed in the art of food shopping than his or her predecessor.[62] His book was to serve both as inspiration and guidance for fellow New Yorkers to better navigate the city's public markets.[63]

Moreover, as will be examined in chapters 5 and 6, during the antebellum decades, public markets gradually ceased to be the privileged locations to buy provisions, just as private stores, including groceries and meat shops, and street vendors captured an increasing share of the retail food economy.[64] This general transition from public to private retail options had major ramifications for households' provisioning schedules. With the proliferation and dispersal of food vendors by midcentury, the well-defined daily rhythms of shopping that characterized the public market model fragmented into myriad competing and complementary schedules. Given the alternative points of food access, public markets imposed fewer constraints on customers' shopping routines. Groceries stayed open from morning until as late as 10:00 p.m. into the night, while shop butchers began the day early in the morning but often conducted their best business in the evening.[65] Street vendors, by definition, did not observe prescribed opening hours but could carry on their trade anytime. On the whole, as the variety of food vendors multiplied, New Yorkers' benefited from additional choices to determine when to conduct their individual provisioning trips. To be sure, changes in the daily schedules of food shopping were gradual and inconsistent. But the trend was, without any doubt, toward greater flexibility as shopkeepers tried to meet their local customers' needs in a free and unregulated retail food economy.

CONCLUSION

It is time to bring together the three distinct rhythms of seasonal, weekly, and daily schedules of household provisioning. One objective of this chapter has been to document the ubiquity and depth to which seasonality defined New Yorkers' food-shopping routines in the Early Republic. In fact, agricultural supply cycles determined the availability of all fresh food supplies, from fruits and vegetables, to fish and shellfish, and even butcher's meats. Equally important, the analysis highlights how the seasonal availability of various types of butcher's meats and other sources of protein was closely connected, contributing to a balanced dietary system that helped ensure urban Americans' high food-consumption standards. The prevalence of seasonality, while interesting, is hardly surprising. It is rather the interconnectedness of these rhythms and the vital role they played in sustaining robust diets that needs to be appreciated. New Yorkers could not only count on abundant supplies from expanding hinterlands but could benefit from seasonal consumption cycles that helped offset monthly variations in their sources of protein and other provisions. It may seem counterintuitive, but the city in fact amplified the effects of agricultural production seasons in residents' access to food supplies.[66] In particular, given city dwellers' expectation to eat fresh meat daily, the consumption of different sources of protein in general, and butcher's meat in particular, experienced stronger seasonal cycles in urban than rural diets.

Shifting focus to the supply side, the public market system itself hinged on these complementary cycles for stability. The municipal model could work insofar as public markets remained the uncontested centers of household provisioning for their respective areas. This required them to stay open each day of the week, each week of the month, and each month of the year. Without the butchers' anchoring role, which was sustained by their baseline sale of beef, complemented by the seasonal availability of secondary meats, the agglomeration economy of the marketplace would have been unattainable. At the same time, the butchers also depended on the agglomeration of complementary vendors, from the more consistent trade of fishmongers to the seasonal arrival of farmers, to make their market an indispensable neighborhood institution. Overall, the economy of the marketplace rested on a delicate balance between seasonality and permanence.

Moving on to weekly rhythms, the analysis presents three conclusions. First and foremost, the evidence clearly identifies Saturday as the most important day for households to buy provisions. Acknowledging this, official market schedules extended opening hours on Saturdays through late evening to accommodate the much-increased volume of sales. Market returns and household budgets consistently show that Saturday trade represented about one-third of the weekly total. This much-intensified traffic followed the logic of the workweek, which allowed most citizens one day of rest on Sundays. The second point has to do with residents' strategies to pace their marketing trips based on how much food was left from the previous visit. This, in turn, depended on the seasonally changing conditions of storing and preserving food supplies, which required more frequent visits in the warmer seasons. Even as pacing was central to all residents' food shopping, each and every household followed its own schedule, so at the aggregated level, one finds no evidence of additional weekly rhythms other than Saturday marketing. The last point concerns the interaction of weekly cycles with the hierarchy of meats. The records show that whereas the demand for fresh beef, veal, and lamb and mutton peaked on Saturdays, fresh pork was considered the least desirable option for Sunday meals. One should note that, despite the sources being fragmentary, weekly rhythms likely persisted through the mid-nineteenth century.

Finally, daily rhythms are the most difficult to nail down. They were also the most malleable and least enduring. Yet insofar as public markets remained the city's privileged centers to access food supplies, they imposed particular constraints on shopping, which also varied by customers' socioeconomic status. As a general rule, with the progress of the market-day, both the selection and the quality of provisions tended to fall, putting downward pressure on food prices, and, in turn, attracting progressively lower-income customers. Choice provisions were retailed at comparatively high prices at the commencement of the day, whereas by late morning the selection of goods significantly narrowed, and by midday leftovers were hawked at discounted prices to poor customers or resold to secondary dealers. Saturday sales followed a distinct schedule, yet, again, the same logic prevailed: by late evening and during the night, the markets catered to a predominantly working-class clientele.

What needs to be recognized is how the municipal model subjected all participants, vendors and customers alike, to a strict daily schedule of marketing. It was partly this temporal order that allowed public markets to assert their grip over most of the food supplies of their neighborhoods. In this instance again, the agglomeration of the food retail economy at the local marketplace was driven by mutually reinforcing spatial and temporal patterns. By the 1840s, however, next to the public markets, grocery stores, meat shops, and street vendors opened up competing and complementary schedules for residents. As they extended the hours of food retail to the entire day, giving customers greater flexibility and freedom to follow their individual preferences in food shopping, bit by bit they disaggregated the public markets' economy, both spatially and temporally.

In the overall assessment, the municipal market system gave rise to a strictly defined temporal order of urban household provisioning, integrating distinct seasonal, weekly, and daily rhythms. These temporalities were as important as the spatial configuration of the market system in defining the geography of food shopping in New York or other cities from the colonial era through the Early Republican period. They determined what kinds of provisions were sold in certain seasons; the rate at which the business of the public markets was beating through the months of the year or days of the week; how crowded, noisy, or smelly marketplaces and their surrounding streets were at any given day or time; how much higher or lower food prices were at specific hours; and what social strata of customers shopped at which time of the day at the neighborhood marketplace. In other words, seasonal, weekly, and daily schedules animated the urban landscape of provisioning. At the same time, their complex interactions lent stability and permanence to the market system. Next to space, time presented the other axis that defined residents' access to food supplies, shaping the provisioning routines of tens of thousands of households, like the Banckers and the Pintards.

CHAPTER 4

Catharine Market and Its Neighborhood

DANCING FOR EELS

At the crossroads of urban commercial exchange, Catharine Market served as one of Gotham's largest and most thriving food emporia by the early nineteenth century. It functioned as the regular meeting point for diverse participants in the provisions trade: neighborhood food vendors, including butchers, hucksters, and peddlers; Long Island and other New York region farmers; fishermen harvesting the city's plentiful coastal and inland waterways; and, of course, the area's booming and diverse population of merchants, artisans, and laborers shopping daily at this marketplace. Pulling hundreds of vendors and thousands of customers into its business magnet, Catharine Market, just like New York's other larger or smaller municipal marketplaces, created a vibrant neighborhood center, accommodating diverse, routine, and at times spontaneous social encounters in its public space.

Yet unlike any other place, Catharine Market was also a distinguished site of social and cultural exchange, regularly hosting the dancing performances of slaves and emancipated blacks at its improvised stage. In their dancing contests for eels or money, African Americans from Long Island, New Jersey, and New York attracted spectators from the neighborhood and across the city to this marketplace from the late eighteenth to the early nineteenth century. "Dancing for eels" was an ephemeral public spectacle captured for posterity by two fragmentary sources: one is a small and contemporaneous vernacular drawing of the performance from 1820, while the other is De Voe's reconstruction of the event in his chronicle of New York City food markets from the 1860s.[1]

Long Island slaves, De Voe recounts, introduced black public dancing into New York City. Whenever they crossed the East River to visit the city on their holidays, especially for Pinkster,[2] or when they brought in small skiffs to market their master's produce and whatever else they could sell (roots, berries, herbs, yellow or other birds, fish, clams, and oysters), they would spend the rest of the day engaging in extemporaneous dancing contests at Catharine Market to raise some money. There, he continues, they were

> hired by some joking butcher or individual to engage in a jig or break-down, as that was one of their pastimes . . . and those that could and would dance soon raised a collection; but some of them did more in "turning around and shying off" from the designated spot than keeping to the regular "shake-down," which caused them all to be confined to a "board," (or shingle, as they called it,) and not allowed off it; on this they must show their skill; and, being several together in parties, each had his particular "shingle" brought with him . . . Their music or time was usually given by one of their party, which was done by beating their hands on the sides of their legs and the noise of the heel.[3]

New Jersey slaves, on their tours to dispose of their masters' produce at Bear Market near the Hudson River, by taking full advantage of the late tide, would also "shin it" to Catharine Market across the city. Here they contended with the Long Islanders over the prize of a bunch of eels or some money, which the butchers and some spectators dropped in a hat.[4] As the contests gained renown and attracted audiences from across the city, New York City blacks, both slave and free, started to participate as well. Soon their numbers exceeded both Long Island and New Jersey African Americans, thus heightening the size and reputation of the Catharine Market public dancing contests.[5]

The drawing of the event by one spectator, and its illuminating reading by literary scholar W. T. Lhamon, contribute subtle details to De Voe's patchy narrative.[6] The image shows three African American men on the left side; two are dancing to the rhythm of the juba, which is being played by the third member of their party (figure 4.1).[7] In the background, by the harbor, a huge crowd watches the show. The audience has gathered through diverse paths and engagements: many are regular market vendors and neighborhood residents conducting their daily shopping exchanges; others are commuters and travelers, including passengers disembarking or waiting to board the Brooklyn ferry, country folk disposing of their goods at the marketplace, or sailors lodging in the many boardinghouses nearby; while others are casual passersby enjoying the open-air spectacle they chanced upon at this commonplace corner of the big city. Similarly, the spectators have assembled from distinct social worlds, forming a racially mixed crowd encompassing various ethnicities and the full spectrum of social classes.

On the right side of the image, next to the dancing team and level with them, near the fish market that serves as the incidental stage, a second trio, comprised of two butchers and behind them a third man of uncertain

FIGURE 4.1. "Dancing for Eels" at Catharine Market, 1820. (*Sources*: See note 7)

identity, perform their part of the public act. They amuse themselves in a highly theatrical fashion, shouting and joking with the dancers. They are depicted as assertive, even gratified with the spectacle and their own position at the marketplace. Oddly, for a sketch entitled "Dancing for Eels, 1820, Catharine Market," the foreground of the drawing is weighted equally between the two groups of black performers and their white hosts. Evidently, for the anonymous artist, the butchers orchestrating the spectacle stood just as much in the limelight as the dancers performing the show.

The artist's own vantage point is likewise telling, as he is appreciating the spectacle from the box seat of a comfortable stall, the wooden structure of which also serves as the frame of his drawing. According to De Voe, the customary place for the dancing contest was at the eastern side of the fish market, near Burnel Brown's Ship Chandlery. When the sketch is compared to an 1827 plan of Catharine Market, it appears that the artist worked from one of the fishermen's stalls. The tools he used, colored India ink and a draftsman's tracing cloth, were so common at the time that they do not reveal his identity. It is conceivable that he was a market vendor, a fishmonger, or a butcher, perhaps, with some disposition for the arts. The dancers, the butchers, and the artist form a circle. Interestingly, both groups turn their back to the spectator crowd and face the artist instead, as if they were putting on the show for his entertainment. And while this may be a matter of artistic convention, the butchers' seeming preoccupation with their own amusement rather than the audience's applause, despite their having sponsored the event, reveals their privileged status vis-à-vis the dancers and at the marketplace.

When the artist gave equal weight to the joking butchers and the dancers, he faithfully conveyed the social order of the public market. At the top of the hierarchy stood the regular-bred butchers, who, as De Voe explains, commanded the performances of the Catharine Market dancers for their own entertainment and to attract customers. The sketch conveys the same power relations when looking at the physical space that divides the two parties, which was by no means void of, but rich in, social context. Most suggestive are the butchers' body postures and gestures, as they assertively tease and challenge the dancers, and express their authority and supervision while also articulating their patronage. It is as if the dancers waited upon the butchers' whims rather than the audience's applause. Perhaps it was up to the butchers to judge which team won the contest? More important, the butchers acted out their social role as patriarchs of the marketplace and patrons of the dancers, some of whom may still have been slaves, while others had already escaped bondage. In the very counterpoise of the two parties, the drawing captures the complex social bonds that connected the butchers and the dancers: forged within the legacy of slavery, only slowly dissolving in New York State in the 1820s, while at the same time being refashioned by the emerging wage labor economy of the antebellum city.[8] From this viewpoint, the butchers took advantage of the subjugated and marginal social and economic status of the black dancers when they hired and promoted them to entertain Catharine Market's public.

It is also true that within the confines of the butchers' authority, dancers at Catharine Market commanded the attention of large audiences. A few could even establish their own name and reputation. Indeed, De Voe makes mention of the artistic triumphs of Jack, Francis (alias "Ned"), and Bob Rowley (known as "Bobolink Bob"), all three of them slaves owned by Long Island farmers, who became celebrities of citywide fame.[9] What happened when the institution of slavery was dismantled and no longer structured the social ties between the butchers and the dancers? In De Voe's version of a morality tale, Jack "was brought up by Mr. De Voo, who thought a good deal of him, and on the day when he was made free, he fitted him out in a new suit from 'top to toe,' and said to him: '*Jack*, if you go home with me, you shall never want; but if you leave me now, my home shall never more know you.'" Jack chose to be free; he "could not be persuaded to return home by many of the butchers and others, but would stay in the city." The last thing De Voe could gather was that when Jack "was set free by the laws, he became, after a time, a loafer, and died at this market."[10] Whether a biography or an urban legend, De Voe conveys the profound tragedy of Jack's personal narrative: even as he gained his freedom in the act of emancipation, he lost his status and position as a dancer at Catharine Market. More poignantly still, Jack's exercise of his new freedom by rejecting De Voo's continued patronage cost him his livelihood.[11] By the time De Voe made a field trip to Catharine Market in 1859 and inquired about these once legendary dancers, the spectacle was a long-gone matter of the past that left few traces in memory.[12]

Intriguing as this story may be, at first it seems to diverge from the core topic of provisioning New York City. It portrays the municipal marketplace from a different angle: as a neighborhood center and public space, no doubt an important and interesting subject, but arguably less central to the public market system's principal role to ensure access to food to all residents. Yet the story of black public dancing at Catharine Market also points to the more elusive neighborhood setting and social context of the market system. Thus far the book has explored three dynamics: the collective and private initiatives behind the public market model's political economy, the forces of agglomeration and dispersal that determined food access under its geography, and the complementary rhythms of supply and demand that animated its daily transactions between vendors and customers. The fourth dynamic of neighborhood ecology is harder to pin down than the triad of politics, space, and time, yet this is precisely how individual public markets acquired local legitimacy and the loyalty of all key participants in household provisioning. The anecdote of African American public dancing opens a path to disentangle these dynamics: how the local marketplace both oriented and was shaped by the daily demands and life of its community. Neighborhood and community, of course, are commonly used but difficult concepts for urbanists. What this chapter aims to do is to reconstruct, through a case study of Catharine Market, the social embeddedness of the marketplace within its vicinity. The analysis explores the negotiations that assembled Catharine Market, the formal and informal social and spatial order that sustained its daily congregation of vendors, and the pulls of demand that attracted local customers into its business magnet.[13]

ASSEMBLING CATHARINE MARKET

In 1786, several prominent inhabitants of New York's far-flung Catharine Street neighborhood petitioned the Common Council for "permission to erect a public market-house at Catharine Slip."[14] As was customary, both the ground and the construction costs were to be furnished by the interested parties. A committee was put in charge to determine the location, architecture, and building material, and in less than a month, Catharine Market opened for the accommodation of vendors. Butchers from the neighboring Peck Slip Market soon moved over there, and farmers from more distant Long Island and Westchester County began to transport their produce to Catharine Market. Lying next to the Catharine Slip terminal of the new Brooklyn ferry, the new marketplace joined the walking city with the flowing East River.[15] In this juncture of the city and its watery surrounds, the first fish stall was introduced in 1797, and soon thereafter several fishmongers began hawking their greatly varied catch from the bountiful Long Island waterways. Out of a heady blend of collective purpose and private ambitions, a new urban space opened up to anchor and serve the provisioning needs of a rising neighborhood. It directly connected Gotham's expanding northeastern districts to the city's diverse and rich hinterlands and anchored the food trade at a convenient location for residents in the vicinity.[16]

Catharine Market was brought into existence not only by the mobilization of neighborhood resources and business interests but, like all other marketplaces in New York, it also developed under the careful hand and close supervision of the city government. Matching the private funds that built the original market-house, while responding case by case to petitions by local residents and market vendors, the municipality opened the public purse to expand and rebuild the marketplace in the next three decades. Rapid population growth and booming trade required new facilities, and in satisfying the petition of prominent citizens, the council promptly erected a larger market-house in 1800, accommodating a total number of sixteen butcher stalls.[17] Similar requests impelled the building of a new fish market five years later, allowing market-boats to dock underneath and giving fishermen direct access from the water.[18] Again in 1816, as some residents complained about inadequate supplies of butcher's meats, the Market Committee answered by turning around the fish market to run parallel to the East River, thus freeing up space for a second, lower market-house on Catharine Street to accommodate more butchers and farmers. Thanks to this decision, the total number of butcher stalls increased to forty-eight, and thus Catharine Market could now claim its status as one of the city's largest emporia of food.[19] With this improvement the marketplace consolidated into its final shape, even as periodic complaints by market vendors and residents regarding the condition of facilities prompted the city to rebuild both market-houses in 1825 and 1831 as brick structures and with granite columns, while also adding eight more stalls to the lower market in 1837.[20]

Catharine Market was thus assembled from a patchwork of neighborhood demands that were sanctioned and sponsored by the city's entire political community. Additionally, the public market did not stand as an isolated infrastructure but was carefully integrated into its surrounding built environment, while anchoring a range of key services for the community. The marketplace directly communicated with the new ferry to Brooklyn, to which the only alternative was farther south at Fly Market. Then in 1810 the Common Council affixed a fire bell on top of the market-house, a vital utility in a highly inflammable city, for residents complained they lived too far from the nearest one, and "in case fire should break out in the vicinity a large amount of property must be destroyed before the alarm could be communicated to a distance and effectively assistance afforded."[21] Three years later a new pump was installed to provide fresh water and protect against fire, while in 1817, for its entire length, Catharine Street, the district's principal thoroughfare, acquired the prestigious urban fixture of gas lighting, reserved only to four other streets in the vicinity, including the Bowery.[22] Finally, the marketplace was furnished with a public scale in 1819 at the butchers' request, and in 1821 a permanent watchman was stationed nearby "in consequence of the many robberies that have been lately perpetrated in that vicinity."[23]

Overall, Catharine Market developed hand in hand with its neighborhood. By virtue of being the area's uncontested center of household provisioning, it also became a nucleus of valuable amenities and a privileged public space, orienting and giving identity to residents in the district. Insofar as Long Island slaves, coming to the city from across the East River, sought a stage to peddle their skills for some money, they could have hardly found a more convenient and bustling open air site, perhaps with the exception of the old Fly Market. And once the dancing contests became a regular fixture, involving African Americans from across the Hudson and the city, they were incorporated into Catharine Market's unique cultural landscape. In effect, the dancing contests grew out of and matured with the marketplace. It was hardly by chance that the previously mentioned drawing dates from 1820, precisely at the time when the spectacles were the liveliest and Catharine Market was thriving.

Indeed, serving one of the most rapidly developing neighborhoods of a booming commercial city, Catharine Market prospered in this period. Market trade grew each year, vendors made handsome profits, and local residents were amply supplied with provisions. What was in the 1790s a small and remote food market for a still sparsely settled urbanizing district, by the first decade of the nineteenth century became the third largest, exceeded only by the more established and centrally located Fly and Bear (later Washington) Markets.[24] In the 1810s Catharine Market gradually closed this still considerable gap: by 1816, in terms of the amount of meat sold and the revenues this generated, it nearly caught up with Washington, while its volume of trade reached a little more than two-thirds of that of Fly, the city's foremost provisioning center. Two years later, despite its small deficit in butcher stalls, Catharine Market meat sales overtook those of Washington, and produced only 20 percent less revenue than the old Fly Market.[25] Out of a total of eleven public markets, the still fledgling Catharine Market now controlled a little more than one-fourth of Gotham's entire meat trade. And in 1821, the first year that the council moved away from excise taxes to collecting rents from the butchers, Catharine Market earned more income than any other marketplace, while also commanding on average the highest rents for its stalls.[26] Even as Fulton Market, which replaced Fly in 1822, immediately upon its opening became the city's largest, Catharine preserved its second position until the mid-1820s. All in all, no other public market before or after experienced such a steady and dynamic growth than did Catharine Market in the first quarter of the nineteenth century.

The Market Committee was well aware of Catharine Market's importance for the neighborhood and its profitability for the city. In a matter-of-fact assessment from 1825, it concluded that

> the market establishment at Catharine Slip has become one of considerable importance; it is frequented by a great number of respectable Butchers, Country people, and Fishermen, and supplies a large proportion of the Inhabitants of the Eastern, and Northern Sections of the City. The publick derives from it a larger revenue in proportion to its cost than from any other Market.[27]

De Voe also confirms that in this period Catharine Market had a high reputation not only as a prime location to procure meat but also as one of the best markets for country produce and fish. Until the early 1820s, he claims, "it was the wholesale as well as the best retail fish market" in the entire city. " 'To get a bunch of fresh fish, you must go to the Catharine Market,' is an old saying," he adds.[28] And while by the mid-1820s Fulton Market began to draw away much of the wholesale fish trade, on the retail end, Catharine Market remained an outstanding fish market. Neighborhood residents in 1825 continued to proudly praise their marketplace "for the abundance and variety of its fish," which they asserted "is thought to surpass any of the kind of the United States."[29]

From its opening until the 1820s, Catharine Market's trajectory, it seems, can be summarized as a story of relentless growth, increasing diversity, and ever deeper integration into the built fabric and daily life of its neighborhood. Catharine Market and its vicinity not only developed in tandem but mutually depended on each other. The neighborhood was rapidly urbanizing, in part thanks to its affluent provisioning center, while steady population growth fueled the marketplace's ever larger and more diversified agglomeration of food purveyors: a virtuous circle driven by expansive economic growth. Keeping the process under check were, of course, the market laws, which ensured that retailers would cluster at

Catharine Market rather than disperse across the district. Additionally, each of the three constituent parties—local residents, market vendors, and city officials—participated in the decentralized democratic process to shape and manage the municipal marketplace, a critical neighborhood infrastructure. In this sense, Catharine Market was built by the public private partnership that was described in chapter 1. It was assembled step-by-step to satisfy a range of particularistic demands, and was sponsored through a balance of municipal funds and private contributions by interested citizens.

The emphasis, however, needs to be on the word "particularistic," for the above description highlights consensus and cooperation over disagreement and conflict. And while Catharine Market's trajectory was undoubtedly ascending, its development was by no means seamless, but was impeded by numerous detours as competing demands pulled the marketplace into different directions. Consensus about the development, layout, and daily operation of the neighborhood market was difficult to come by, and every so often the outcome left some groups unsatisfied. The laborious and quarrelsome politics of petitioning and local self-governance served precisely, to the extent possible, to negotiate the common good out of the many disparate and conflicting priorities and interests of the parties involved.

Take the case of the fish market, whose relocation to a separate facility in 1805, a sensible improvement for sure, followed several years of debate and bickering. The dispute arose in 1802 when the council endorsed the butchers' request for additional stalls, which would have required filling up the small and congested fish and produce sections. Soon hundreds of inhabitants mobilized to block the proposal, claiming that "unless some convenient place . . . can be provided for the accommodation of the Fishermen and Country people," such a plan "will prove a serious inconvenience to the petitioners and others residing in the said fifth and seventh wards."[30] Their stance resulted in a compromise by which additional vending space for the butchers was made available only after the new fish and produce market was built; hence, the interests of all parties, different groups of vendors and customers alike, were considered. Yet within a year some criticized the storing of fish and other provisions there as a "nuisance." In opposition, numerous residents and property owners filed a petition to defend the new facility, claiming that they "cannot conceive that any sickness or injury can arise from sound dry fish or provisions." They also questioned the legitimacy of the remonstrators, describing them as "a few individuals (one third of which reside at a distance from the place of which they complain)."[31] In sum, the fish market generated four years of continuous debates, and not because it was an exceptionally controversial issue. On the contrary, this was business as usual, for the marketplace was a shared asset of a large neighborhood with several communities and opposing claims.[32]

It was inevitable that the demands of different groups of vendors and customers would splinter in several directions. One may have valued the marketplace's vital services for the area while simultaneously objecting to some of its negative externalities. Similar to those who had protested the fish market before, residents living next to and regularly shopping at Catharine Market in 1817 complained about having "suffered great inconvenience from Market Wagons, which . . . are placed directly in front of our Houses." The farmers' "Horses taken out & fed," they continued, were "endangering the lives of our children and rendering our Habitations the receptacles of nauseous filth & dirt."[33] The remedy they proposed was not to impede the general business of Catharine Market but to push the wagons and horses to the "foot of Market Street," which should give them "more ample accommodation."[34] In all likelihood this meant to shove the same nuisance onto other residents or businesses farther down the street or to crowd more vendors into an already busy area. In a dense neighborhood, where public space was by definition tight, even as the marketplace attracted ever more vendors and customers, one group's benefit was often another group's inconvenience. This also points to Catharine Market's specific challenge, for being located on a narrow and busy thoroughfare, it lacked sufficient capacity to accommodate farmers and hucksters, who thus had to compete for space at the country market or adjacent streets.

The struggle to allocate adequate vending space for sellers of produce, milk products, poultry, and various edibles was in fact the most contentious issue at Catharine Market. While in principle a larger and more diverse marketplace was to everyone's advantage, in practice, which group—the butchers, fishermen, or ferry passengers—should cede the necessary space, and which buildings' occupants or owners should bear the inconvenience of the farmers' and hucksters' raucous trade, was the stuff of political bargaining, fueling proposals and endless debates. One radical solution to remedy "the present confined situation of Catharine Market" and "the want of accommodation to the country people" was put forth by a dozen or so property owners in 1824, who proposed to replace the food market with another one on a "more extensive plan" just above Catharine Street, between Water and South. This would have consisted of a single facility with two wings on a conventional rectangular plan. "Catharine Street will then be one of the avenues leading to the Market," while the plan would free up the passage to the Brooklyn ferry, which is "frequently obstructed with carts, by reason of the street being too narrow."[35]

Instantly, about seventy-five petitioners—including owners, leaseholders, and occupants of lots, houses, and businesses—objected: "we are satisfied with the present location of the Catharine Market, & we believe it has all the conveniences for Butchers, Fishermen, Country People & Hucksters."[36] While the petitioners clearly understood that this was not the case, from their viewpoint more was at stake than easy access to provisions. In its area a marketplace boosted real estate values and generated increased turnover for businesses. The relocation, they argued, "would injure a great many others who have bought Property in the vicinity of the present Market. And we believe that your Honorable Body would not decrease the property of Individuals, & increase the property of other Individuals, without great Public necessity."[37] Still, recognizing that lacking adequate space, the country people might "leave the said market and dispose of their produce throughout the city," local inhabitants and market vendors, including the butchers, who also opposed the market's removal, joined together in 1828 to convince the council to return to the original practice of allowing farmers and hucksters to occupy the sidewalks around the market-houses.[38] Apparently, crowded and untidy streets were more tolerable than plunging sales of produce, a drag on the business of all other vendors.

It should come as little surprise though that just within two years the same dispute reignited, for others objected to this resolution. They insisted that the country market was adequate and that the streets must be kept unobstructed.[39] The previous plan to relocate Catharine Market was also reintroduced, this time endorsed by a much larger number of petitioners: the surviving forms alone contain more than two hundred signatures.[40] But then again, this costly development was stopped by the all-too-familiar arguments: the marketplace was sufficient to accommodate all vendors, the interests of nearby property holders must be protected, and the financial burden on the taxpayers was unjustified.[41] Overall, even as the debate came full circle again and again, with the main lines of disagreement solidly established, the general layout of the marketplace remained largely unchanged.[42] Evidently, with all of its imperfections, Catharine Market was a workable compromise for the various competing and particularistic interests of neighborhood provisioning.

In the end, Catharine Market was assembled piece by piece over several decades. Its location, spatial layout, and structure were the physical manifestation of countless inputs deriving from the complementary and competing agendas of various stakeholders: municipal officials, market vendors, and customers; local property holders, business owners, and residents; and regular patrons, visitors, and commuters. Building a marketplace to everyone's satisfaction was close to impossible. In this sense, the public market was more of an institution of contentious compromise than of general consensus. Its measure of success was the degree to which it accommodated the various needs of several communities in one neighborhood.

Catharine Market, it appears, was a success story on most accounts, at least in the period from the late 1790s to the early 1830s. Its business thrived and continued to expand every year, and its collection of vendors increased both in size and variety, while its roots in the built environment and daily life of the area grew ever deeper. It is also true that intensifying disagreements over the accommodation of farmers and hucksters foreshadowed potential problems about the long-term viability of this marketplace as the predominant site of provisioning in the neighborhood.

What the petitions clearly document, however, is that the most fought-over asset at Catharine Market was space itself. The challenge was how to allocate adequate spaces to all market vendors, thereby maximizing the benefits of business agglomeration while at the same time ensuring that the market was accessible to everyone, that goods and people moved around freely, and that nuisances from the sale of provisions did not spill over into the immediate surroundings. The negotiations were complex and involved multiple parties and priorities, and those participating had differing leverage. The point is that Catharine Market was not only assembled piecemeal from numerous disparate interests, but it also embodied the unequal bargaining power of the constituent parties. Consequently, its spatial organization, from the formal spaces of the market-houses to the informal spaces of the nearby streets, closely mirrored the market's social structure. Unraveling this sociospatial hierarchy holds the key to understanding Catharine Market's everyday order and functioning. Further, it provides the physical and social contexts within which to situate the fascinating spectacle of African American public dancing contests.

Vendors: Catharine Market's Spatial Order

The spatial organization of the public market cannot be understood outside of its social production, in particular, the main participants involved, their relative social hierarchy, physical location, daily use, and management of the marketplace. It should come as no surprise that at Catharine Market, as at other public markets in Early American cities, the butchers were the most influential group. Sometimes in concert with and at other times in conflict with the council, they ran the show.[43] Butchers earned their social status as the marketplace elite by virtue of serving as gatekeepers to a critically important and highly perishable food item. As discussed earlier, the central role of fresh meat in the American urban diet warranted their dominant position, while their daily labor required highly specialized skills. Being skilled artisans, butchers were able to form tight and exclusive trade organizations, much like traditional guilds, which gave them substantial leverage over the political process and daily conduct of neighborhood provisioning.

Unlike the other vendors, who dealt in foodstuffs subject to stronger seasonal cycles, butchers also served customers in their individually assigned stalls every day. In fact, no other group identified with the market place, or invested as much into its long-term viability and reputation, as did the butchers. Fishmongers, even though regularly present, were not necessarily residents of the city, nor were they as well organized or as embedded in municipal politics. Hucksters, nearly all of whom were women, many of them elderly widows, received permits to sell vegetables, fruits, milk and dairy products, poultry, and various edibles from the Common Council out of public generosity.[44] And farmers, many of whom were well respected by the butchers, transported all varieties of farm products to the marketplace only periodically on the ferries, in their own boats, or by their carts: in this sense, they were frequent visitors rather than permanent occupants of the marketplace.[45] In general, butchers provided the anchor trade for the city's municipal markets. Without their orderly stalls, year-round sales, and daily attendance, Catharine Market would never have acquired the scale and diversity of business to become the dominant site of household provisioning in its neighborhood. The public market was no doubt an agglomeration of independent food vendors, but this process originated from and was sustained by the regular trade of licensed market butchers.

Accordingly, in every detail, from the arrangement of stalls to the layout of the public market, the butchers' dominant position relative to the other vendors was evident.[46] What distinguished the butchers first and foremost was that they retailed from personally assigned stalls, which were numbered, with their occupants' names visibly posted (figure 4.2).[47] At Catharine Market, butcher stalls were arranged in pairs, lined up in an orderly fashion along both sides of the two principal market-houses.[48] In contrast, fishmongers annually drew their respective stands between each other within the fish market's shed, while further down the hierarchy, farmers and hucksters occupied vending spaces on a first come, first served basis.[49] As the boundary line between farmers and hucksters was blurred, they normally competed for the same marginal spaces at Catharine Market, crowding inside the small country section of the lower market, standing outside of the two market-halls, or spilling out onto the nearby streets. As a general scheme, the status of the various groups translated directly into their differential access to vending spaces, varying by their central or peripheral locations and individual or collective management.

The butchers' ability to control individual retail locations derived in part from the established methods of market revenue collection. As a re-

FIGURE 4.2. Thomas F. De Voe at his Jefferson
Market stall, mid-nineteenth century.
(*Sources*: See note 47)

minder, until 1821, the council collected excise taxes on the amount of
butcher's meat sold, freeing all other vendors, for the most part, from
having to pay taxes. Under this tax regime, individually assigned and permanent stalls gave the butchers a prominent place at the public market
while also guaranteeing the council a reliable source of income. After the
overhaul of the revenue system, butchers were charged annual rents for
their stalls in weekly sums, while all the other vendors had to pay daily
fees for the right to stand and sell at the market.[50] The collection of market
revenues hence became directly tied to the individual occupancy of
butcher stalls and the communal use of retail spaces by the other vendors.
In addition, between 1822 and 1835, the council sought to maximize revenues by leasing out stalls to the highest bidder. Despite fierce protests
from the butchers against the so-called premium system, one-third of the
city's stalls, but only about 10 percent at Catharine Market, were allocated
in this competitive fashion. In effect, this policy turned municipally owned
market space into stalls that the butchers considered their own property.[51]
In general, rents and premiums amounted to a considerable investment.
In turn, they gave a degree of rootedness to the butcher's trade. Fees, on
the contrary, reflected the greater irregularities that characterized the
sales of the other vendors. Further, since butcher stalls came with exclusive rights over pieces of market space, the Market Committee set annual
rents according to their estimated values. In this sense, butchers obtained
their stalls through a tightly regulated real estate market, governed by
individual titles and obligations, while fishmongers, and especially hucksters and farmers, occupied vending spaces based on temporary arrangements, custom, and informal rules.

In an effort to visually represent the spatial structure of Catharine Market at its best period of the 1820s and early 1830s, three maps are intro-

duced (figure 4.3).[52] Importantly, nearly all of New York's public markets were organized in the same tripartite division of separate meat, fish, and produce sections, with their layout varying considerably according to their footprint and the kind of land they occupied: public space on the street or lots inside of the block. Catharine Market was the largest example of the street market type, standing in the middle of Catharine Slip, where the neighborhood's main thoroughfare widened for a two-block stretch to enter the East River docks. One distinctive feature of Catharine Market was that being situated on a narrow strip of public space, it consisted of three separate buildings to accommodate its many vendors and customers. The three facilities included the original upper market-house between Cherry and Water Streets, filled exclusively with butcher stalls; the lower market between Water and South, containing butcher stalls and a modestly sized produce section; and the fish market's shed, which ran perpendicular to the street facing the East River. All other street markets (Spring Street, Duane, Governeur, Greenwich, Grand Street, Essex, Franklin, Manhattan, Tompkins, and Jefferson) remained smaller single structures.[53] Due to its dynamic growth and limited space, Catharine Market developed much like the old Fly Market, which had consisted of three buildings on Maiden Lane. In contrast, larger public markets from the 1810s were typically built on lots within blocks, such as Washington, Centre, Fulton, and Clinton Markets. Catharine Market, however, predated this new and more expensive construction standard, and preserved the layout of more traditional eighteenth-century municipal markets.

Looking at the maps, the sheer dominance of the meat trade and the butchers in the spatial layout of Catharine Market is evident. Butcher stalls occupied nearly two-thirds of all available indoor market space, including the entire upper and more than half of the lower market-house. Additionally, in the early 1830s butcher rents generated between two-thirds and three-fourths of all revenues, by far the highest ratio for any of the city's markets, demonstrating the butchers' powerful presence there. This lucrative rent collection not only reflected the butchers' use of the greatest amount of vending space, but that they were also able to sustain relatively higher taxation. In 1832, for instance, the council earned on average half a dollar per square feet from the butchers compared to less than half that amount from all the other vendors on its Catharine Market properties.[54] Unfortunately, the data do not allow for separating fees paid by fishermen, hucksters, or farmers, and thus the relative rental value of the country and fish markets cannot be assessed. Furthermore, farmers and hucksters, whether or not they held daily permits, also occupied the sidewalks and streets around the market-houses, where they still had to pay fees insofar as the market clerk managed to collect them. In other words, the relatively smaller amount of market fees were earned from a

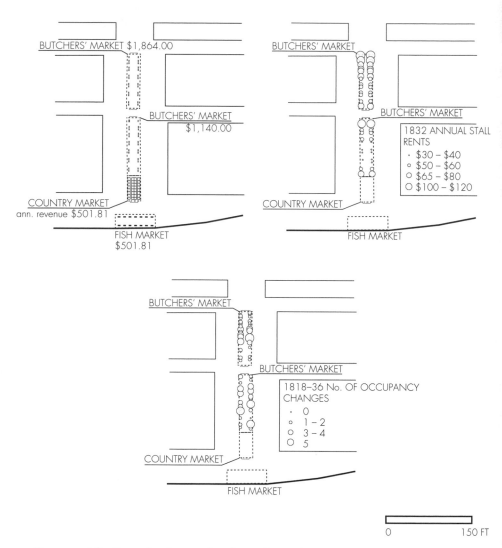

FIGURE 4.3. Organization and value of retail space at Catharine Market, 1820s–30s. (*Sources*: See text, notes 54–55, and appendix A)

far larger area than the actual produce market, underlining how Catharine Market's business agglomeration also encompassed the informal landscape of surrounding public spaces.

A closer analysis of the rental value of butcher stalls reveals another, subtler hierarchy within the internal spatial organization of the marketplace. As the second map documents (figure 4.3), butcher rents varied considerably at Catharine Market: from the cheapest and least desirable stalls to the most expensive and sought-after ones, there was a large, fourfold surge in yearly rents.[55] Considering that butcher stalls were standardized in material and size, these price variations reflected the willingness of some butchers to invest much greater capital in obtaining an advantageous vending place. Importantly, stall rents were not determined by a competitive bidding process but were set by the Market Committee according to a best estimate of their relative value within and across the marketplaces. In general, rents were set higher in the upper than the lower Catharine Market, and this pattern was further altered by the accessibility of the stalls, whereby those located closer to the entrances commanded higher, and those in the middle section lower, rents.

The real estate value of market space, in other words, was a function of customer circulation as judged by the Market Committee. Catharine Street served as the main corridor linking the heavily trafficked Bowery, Chatham, and Division Streets and their surrounding areas to the bustling East River docks. As the majority of residents from ward 4, the western half of ward 7, and the southern parts of ward 6 and 10 reached the marketplace from the direction of the city via Catharine Street, their provisioning rounds usually led them first to the upper, then to the lower, and finally to the fish market section. Similarly, as shoppers entered one of the two market-houses, many favored the more readily available stalls near the entrances. One can easily imagine the daily traffic of Catharine Market, with the numerous butchers attending their stalls, hawking their merchandise to arrest the flow of customers as they pushed through the market-halls from either end of the buildings.

These real estate patterns were not specific to Catharine Market's distinctive layout, which consisted of three facilities. Two comparisons demonstrate the wider relevance of the case. At first, Catharine Market's two halls are compared to nine other markets in a diagram (figure 4.4), depicting the rental value of stalls.[56] Only one side of the market-halls is considered: for the street market type, rents were identical on both sides of the hallways, while for those standing on lots inside the block, such as Centre or Clinton Market, the street side was more prominent and accommodated more stalls, and hence it better serves the analysis. The data clearly show that for all street markets, rents were most expensive at the two ends, where the entrances were located, while they fell considerably in the mid-sections. Catharine Market was distinctive only in that it was larger than the other street markets, and therefore its rents varied more within and between the two buildings. A similar, albeit more complex pattern is found with Centre and Clinton Market: rents were highest in the midsection, where the main entrances were situated, and where both markets turned at right angles alongside their blocks; they tended to be relatively high at the two ends as well, where the side entrances were and where the butchers' market connected to the fish section; and, finally, they were the lowest between these areas of increased accessibility.

In addition, the city's two largest public markets of Fulton and Washington occupied entire city blocks, and were arranged on a more complex ground plan, with more than just two or three entrances. A second comparison between Catharine and the larger, more modern, and expensively built Fulton Market further confirms that circulation and accessibility were the key factors behind the valuation of retail space (figure 4.5).[57] Here, as well, a considerable threefold gap separated the cheapest and the costliest stalls, and again, without an exception, the highest rates were charged for those closer to one of five entrances. Additionally, butchers tended to pay more along the intersection of Front Street and Fulton, the area's principal avenue and approach to Fulton Market, while rents tended to be lower on the less heavily trafficked Beekman Street side, or near the riverfront access at South Street, a pattern analogous to the diverging rates of the upper and lower Catharine Market. Overall, even as public markets widely varied in layout and building history, the underlying logic by which the assessment of vending space worked was much the same. The premium spots were always near the gates, especially the most heavily used ones, which served to channel and filter the traffic and liveliness of the adjacent streets and sidewalks into the market-halls' narrow and orderly passageways.

As the long and narrow corridors of Catharine Market filled with the cacophony of sounds produced by butchers and shoppers, cutting and chopping, selling and buying, gossiping and arguing, some voices echoed more prominently than others. Just as some stalls were better positioned to take advantage of market traffic than their neighbors, some butchers had established deeper ties to the marketplace than their peers. One would expect that the geography of stalls and the hierarchy of the butchers were connected, whereby retail spaces that leased for higher sums, in turn, earned greater profits and stability for the vendors. The third map of the Catharine Market sequence (see figure 4.3) gives some credence to this point. Between 1818 and 1836, a total number of 133 butchers occupied Catharine Market's forty-seven stalls, and, on average, they stayed in business for a little over five years, a considerable degree of stability in food retailing.[58] Tellingly, stalls located closer to the entryways of either

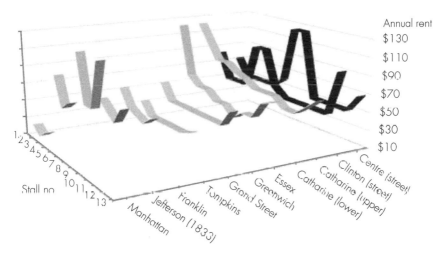

FIGURE 4.4. Value of retail space at public markets, 1832. (*Sources*: See text, note 56, and appendix A)

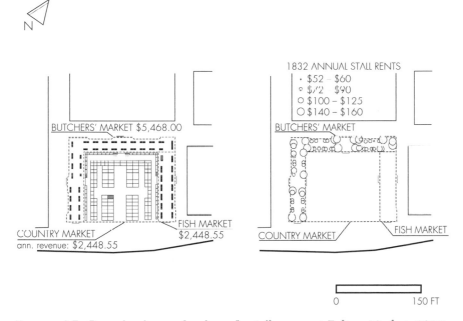

FIGURE 4.5. Organization and value of retail space at Fulton Market, 1832. (*Sources*: See text and appendix A)

market-houses changed occupancy less frequently than those in the center, and, as expected, the upper market tended to provide more permanent locations. When focusing on the twenty-one butchers who worked at Catharine Market for a period of at least ten years, one finds that twelve of them occupied stalls close to the entrances, three upgraded from cheaper stalls in the middle of the hallways to more expensive ones closer to the gates, and only six occupied centrally located and less accessible stalls over their entire career.

Stability in business also helped foster social bonds via collegial or kinship relations. Whereas nearly half of the market's 133 butchers had a family member (on the evidence of their names) work at some point at Catharine Market, the same ratio for those veteran butchers who stayed there for more than ten years and held stalls by the entrances was about 80 percent.[59] It seems that beneficial location provided support for the butcher's socioeconomic status: those with more accessible stalls ran more reliable businesses, which enabled them to assist kin (son, brother, or other relative) in obtaining a vending space that had just opened up for occupation, or pass down their own to a family member. The causality, of course, may have worked the other way around, since those who could afford to lease choice stalls were more likely to be the better established butchers with more access to capital in the first place. Indeed, like all other marketplaces in New York, Catharine Market had its fair share of butcher dynasties, including the Martins, Tiers, Valentines, and, above all, the Varians.[60] Overall, butchers indisputably dominated Catharine Market, forming a tightly knit group of craftsman vendors whose formal control over market space and informal authority over its daily use reigned supreme. At the same time, within their ranks a subtler hierarchy also existed, with some butchers more firmly grounded in the physical and social fabric of the marketplace.

One incident will demonstrate forcefully how the butchers' eminent position at the marketplace translated into informal control over its daily life and social order. De Voe jotted down an account of a punishment for an 1820 theft that happened in Catharine Market:

> A few days ago I was a witness to a very novel scene which occurred in *Catharine Market.* A man was detected in stealing. He had his choice either to go to Bridewell or else to run through the market three times and be subjected to the cuffs and kicks of the numerous Butchers attending this market: he chose the latter and the operation was performed to the no small gratification of many: when it was done he decamped with the greatest speed, no doubt, thinking that he might yet have to undergo the punishment of the Law.[61]

Such instances of private order law enforcement by the butchers were hardly exceptional, as one drawing of a similar episode at a marketplace at York, Pennsylvania, suggests.[62] The same "joking butchers" who staged the Catharine Market dances were equally ready to take matters into their own hands and turn to collective violence to enforce societal norms. As the dominant group, they played a crucial informal role in upholding the moral order of the marketplace, to which the formal sanction of the state, in the guise of the Bridewell penitentiary, represented an alternative authority. From this perspective, then, the governance of Catharine Market belonged to two coexisting spheres: the municipality, represented by the market clerk, who oversaw formal laws and regulations, and the local community of the marketplace, led by the butchers, whose right to exercise power was legitimized by customs and social norms. In Catharine Market's small and densely knit social world of collegial, kinship, and neighborly bonds, the butchers made use of their eminent position to enact corporal punishment in the public eye. In this highly ritualized and theatrical fashion, they helped maintain and restore the moral equilibrium of their community, or so they thought.

The public display of punishment and the butchers' prominent role in its execution returns this chapter to Catharine Market's hosting of the African American public dances, while the spatial analysis here helps reconstruct the physical stage and social setting of the performances. Surely, the two events were distinct as for content, yet they shared fundamental similarities in terms of the power relations, social dynamics, and spatial context involved in their production. To take the question of power first, where the parallels are more evident, the anonymous sketch and De Voe's account likewise stress how the dancing contests were situated within the public market's strictly defined status hierarchy, with the butchers standing on one side and the dancers on the other.[63] Among the Catharine Market vendors, the butchers were by far the best positioned to temporarily transpose the farmers' control over their slaves or to regularly hire free blacks in order to orchestrate public dancing contests.

The dancing performances also encompassed the two ends of the spectrum of goods on sale: at one end, the indispensable merchandise of fresh meat, sold exclusively by regular-bred butchers, at the other, the random assortment of items brought to market by the marginalized groups of African American peddlers, including their skills in dance. This is not to deny any agency on the dancers' part, or to suggest that some did not enjoy the contests, upon which they built their reputation. Still, the power dynamics were clear, and dancers like Jack, one of the celebrated performers, could be displaced from Catharine Market at the butchers' whim. Since the peddlers' sales were deemed irrelevant, and their presence kept marginal, their own position hinged on the protection of others, in particular the butchers. In the public market's strictly defined hierarchy, where the butcher's vital trade claimed the top seats, the fishmongers' formally recognized occupation came second, the farmers' much-needed seasonal arrivals held useful bargaining chips, and the sales of licensed hucksters received the public's benevolence, unlicensed peddlers without any formal affiliation, such as the black dancers, found themselves on the fringes. Because social status and spatial order were closely intertwined, with butchers working at personal stalls, fishmongers occupying a communal shed, and farmers and hucksters negotiating daily for spots at the country market or nearby streets, the precarious position of peddlers manifested in their perilous claims for space. Even as they performed for hundreds of spectators at the fish market's improvised stage, the dancers laid out their shingles on quicksand, for they were treated as celebrated guests at their own performances.

That the competitions took place at the fish market section is equally telling. True, when considering the alternatives, there were not that many options. Around the market-houses on either side of Catharine Slip, streets and sidewalks were overflowing with business: farmers and hucksters occupied every nook of space, hawking their sales from wagons, carts, and baskets; shoppers meandered through the thick crowd of vendors as they completed their daily rounds; goods were hauled from one place to another; and pedestrian and vehicular traffic traversed the adjacent public spaces. Inside, the market-houses were fully devoted to the butchers' commerce, whose stalls, tools, and merchandise occupied both sides of the hallways, leaving only a narrow passage in the middle for customers. There was hardly any space left for dancers to perform and an audience to enjoy the show. The same market-halls may have served as an effective backdrop to carry out an intimidating and ad hoc collective punishment, but to stage regular dancing contests for large audiences, these spaces were utterly inadequate.

If the dancers were to put on a show, it had to be at a place more spacious and less disruptive to commerce. Arguably, a spectator crowd near the fish market interfered with the fishmongers' trade, even as massed onlookers impeded access to the waterfront, a potential inconvenience for both them and the Brooklyn ferry's passengers. The fishmongers and the ferry company may not have been too eager to concede some of their domains to host the performances. Space was a highly contested resource in this section as well, dragging the fishermen and the ferry company into battles over access to the wharf.[64] At the same time, the public market as a whole must have benefited from the spectacle of African American public dancing, for it attracted large crowds and produced positive agglomeration effects. The issue was which group should accommodate the event and to what extent it benefited their business rather than being an inconvenience. That the contests were located at Catharine Market's waterfront edge makes sense, for this was the only open space available. What lays bare the unequal power of the different groups of vendors over Catharine Market, however, is that in spite of the fish market serving as the stage, the butchers, not the fishermen, acted as masters of ceremony for the performances.

Customers: The Neighborhood Magnet

As hitherto documented, Catharine Market was a neighborhood institution, assembled piecemeal from the complementary and competing demands of local stakeholders: officials, vendors, and residents. A massive agglomeration of independent retailers, it was a privileged site of household provisioning, occupying a distinctive, compartmentalized, and hierarchically structured piece of public land. Its edifice was cemented together by the well-defined sociospatial order of its vendors, which reflected customary privileges, rights, and responsibilities. At the same time, stable and orderly arrangements were incongruous to the public market's own thrust of trade agglomeration, which, in a dynamic neighborhood, pulled ever more shoppers and vendors into its business magnet. As new vendors sought to gain a foothold in this closely parceled setting, they inevitably challenged prior arrangements, lending a degree of volatility to Catharine Market's sociospatial boundaries. Furthermore, seemingly endless quarrels over space were more than anything the mark of a thriving business environment, fueled by booming demand and an expanding customer base.

But who were the regular customers of Catharine Market? From what distance, and at what numbers did they gravitate there? What was the scale and scope of the marketplace's agglomeration economy, accounting for customers, vendors, and provisions? Also, what was the meaning of "neighborhood," or to use a more contemporary term, "vicinity," in the context of household provisioning, arguably the most routine daily encounter in public space among local residents?[65] Moreover, space was animated by time, so how did seasonal, weekly, and daily rhythms of shopping manifest at Catharine Market, which served both as its neighborhood's dominant provisioning center and defining public space?

Establishing the range, catchment area, and size of the customer base provisioned by Catharine Market is not without its methodological problems, and the results can only be approximate. The value of the effort is to provide some sense of the experience of business agglomeration from the perspectives of both vendors and customers. The catchment area drawn here for Catharine Market (figure 4.6) borrows from a comprehensive method, developed in chapter 5, to project gravity areas for all public markets in New York City in the mid-nineteenth century. It makes use of an 1849 customer list for Jefferson Market, which is then used as a reference to estimate the catchment areas of all other public markets between 1840 and 1855, using the simple but reasonable assumption that larger marketplaces would attract customers from proportionately larger areas and vice versa.[66] Given that Catharine Market's overall size and layout changed little after 1816, even as local residents continued to walk for their marketing journeys, the catchment area projected for 1840 should also be valid for this earlier period. One concern may be the reliability of the original projection, for the method makes use of a single reference market. Fortunately, two petitions by Catharine Market customers from 1839 and 1844, listing their home addresses, confirm the soundness of the estimation, for the great majority of the addresses fall well within the projected area, as is evident on the map.[67] Overall, two distinct approaches have yielded consistent results, indicating that Catharine Market pulled customers from the entire ward 4, roughly half of wards 6 and 7, and about one-fifth of ward 10. Under these assumptions, it served an area of a little over 28,000 residents in 1820, which, accounting for population change, corresponds to about 25,000 people in the well-documented year of 1818: an impressive customer base by any measure.[68]

One immediate benefit of this figure is that it helps appreciate the massive scale of Catharine Market's economy. To take stock, in 1818, Catharine Market accommodated forty-seven regular butchers, many of whom were assisted by a young apprentice, whose numbers must have reached a few dozen.[69] A list from 1818 also documents the presence of forty-eight licensed huckster women. The number of regular fishmongers is harder to pin down, but according to an 1840 list, twenty-five fish vendors worked here at the time. Considering that until the early 1820s Catharine Market was the city's prime fish market, their number probably exceeded twenty-five in this earlier period.[70] Additionally, farmers or their agents arrived regularly from the countryside to attend the marketplace. They were not registered, but in a petition from 1828, no less than sixty-one farmers voiced their concern over the lack of space to dispose of their goods.[71] Then, as both the narrative of the African American dancers and the endless quarrels over space show, Catharine Market's economy included dozens of informal vendors, who sold leftover foodstuffs in small measures from marginal spots, even after official market hours. Moreover, shopping externalities extended to neighborhood grocers, even to shopkeepers in other sectors, thus contributing to the consolidation of retail trade on Catharine Street. Overall, about 300 food vendors made their living directly out of Catharine Market, provisioning an area with a population of

FIGURE 4.6. Catharine Market's catchment area, 1820–40s. (*Sources*: See text and appendix A)

about 25,000 inhabitants. By way of comparison, Catharine Market's capacity in 1818 would have been adequate to supply most of the population of New York City thirty years earlier. Under the regulatory structure that fresh meat and most of fresh food supplies had to be sold at public markets, Catharine Market was the center of an enormous agglomeration of food vendors and customers.

One may wonder how well Catharine Market customers were provisioned compared to most New Yorkers. Table 4.1 presents some figures for this question.[72] Given that the census does not provide any information about the socioeconomic status of New Yorkers at the time, such an approach also offers a chance to peek into local residents' living stan-

TABLE 4.1. Sales at Catharine Market and New York City, 1818

	New York City	Catharine Market
Population	107,625	24,756* (23%)
Number of occupied butcher stalls	208	47 (22.6%)
Number of residents per butcher stall	517	527
Number of hucksters	193**	48 (24.9%)
Number of residents per huckster	558	516
Market fees	$9,490.70	$2,470.06 (26%)
Number of residents per $1.00 tax	11.3	10
Per capita sales of beef, lbs.	85.9	105.8
Per capita sales of veal, lbs.	16.9	16.2
Per capita sales of lamb and mutton, lbs.	28.6	31.7
Per capita sales of pork, lbs.	10.7	6.6

Notes: *The population figure may be slightly underestimated; ** the total number of hucksters in the city is somewhat undercounted, since the lists do not include the smaller Spring, Essex, Corlaers Hook, Governeur, Grand Street, and Greenwich Markets.
Sources: See text, notes 68 and 70, and appendix B.

dards. To begin with, in 1818 there were 517 residents for each occupied butcher stall in New York City, while the corresponding figure at Catharine Market was remarkably close at 527. The same ratios for hucksters were 558 and 516, respectively, a slight discrepancy, probably due to the lack of huckster lists for several small markets, which leaves the city's tally slightly overestimated. Turning to market fees, that is, the excise collected on the sale of butcher's meats, the data are again convincing, for it took about the same number of inhabitants, eleven for the city and ten for Catharine Market, to generate one dollar of municipal revenue annually. To explain the small difference, besides possible inaccuracies with the estimation, it is feasible that Catharine Market customers had a slightly greater appetite for meat in general, or had some preference for the more heavily taxed varieties.[73] The composition of the meat sales gives some credence to the latter point, for Catharine Market customers appear to have eaten somewhat more of relatively expensive fresh beef and less of cheaper fresh pork than the average New Yorker.[74] Overall, it is evident that Catharine Market in the late 1810s was thriving, just as its vicinity boomed. Its customers could afford to purchase about as much, or even slightly more and higher quality butcher's meats and other provisions, than their fellow citizens.

TABLE 4.2. Number of Customers at Catharine Market, 1818

	Weekly		Daily (M–F)		Saturday		Hourly (M–F)	
	At market	Per butcher	Market	Butcher	Market	Butcher	Market	Butcher
Winter	14,120	184	2,086	27	3,690	48	298	4
Spring	19,621	255	2,920	38	5,023	65	417	5
Summer	27,626	360	4,583	60	4,709	61	655	9
Fall	22,058	287	3,459	45	4,761	62	494	6
Average	20,856	271	3,263	42	4,543	59	466	6

Sources: See text and note 75.

So how bustling was Catharine Market? And what did it mean that it was the neighborhood's most crowded and busiest public space? Knowing that close to 25,000 residents depended regularly on Catharine Market for their provisions in 1818 still leaves one uncertain about what kind of crowd and sociability this massive population generated on a daily basis over the year. In order to give a sense of the proverbial urban experience of "rubbing shoulders with one's neighbors," tables 4.2–4.4 present an effort to estimate the "typical" traffic of customers and goods at Catharine Market. The estimation relies on sensible assumptions.[75] Still, one should bear in mind that these are rough figures: their purpose is to offer an experiential interpretation of Catharine Market as a busy neighborhood market and public space.

Turning to table 4.2, Catharine Market accommodated more than 20,000 individual shopping trips weekly. This average, of course, varied greatly across the seasons, and it also includes repeated trips by the same shoppers, for households had to procure provisions more than three times a week. Not all shopping rounds led to a butcher, despite meat's centrality in provisioning. Accordingly, the typical butcher at Catharine Market served an estimated 271 customers weekly, with most households visiting his stall about twice a week. Expressing customer traffic in daily rates, Catharine Market must have received well over 3,000 shoppers on a regular weekday, which corresponded to 42 clients per butcher. Adding seasonality to the picture, the marketplace was teeming with more than 4,500 customers on a summer workday, compared to less than half of this crowd in the winter. Saturday traffic was on average 50 percent larger, yet, as expected, it also varied less seasonally. Households could rarely miss out on a Saturday shopping, yet in the leaner and colder months, they could get away with one additional visit sometime between Monday and Friday. In the more plentiful and warmer months, on the contrary,

TABLE 4.3. Meat Sales at Catharine Market, 1818

| | Weekly | | Daily (M–F) | | Saturday | | Hourly (M–F) |
	At market (head of animals)	Per butcher (head)	Market (head)	Butcher (lbs.)	Market (head)	Butcher (lbs.)	Butcher (lbs.)
Beef	111.8	2.4	15.1	144.8	36.2	346.3	20.7
Veal	102.1	2.2	14.3	22.8	30.8	49.1	3.3
Lamb	375.9	8.0	52.4	44.6	113.8	96.9	6.4
Pork	23.6	0.5	3.7	10.6	5.0	14.1	1.5
Total	613.5	13.1	85.6	222.7	185.7	506.3	31.8

Sources: See text and note 77.

they typically had to schedule three more weekday trips. Perhaps the most tangible measure to consider is hourly traffic, by which rate an estimated 466 shoppers passed through Catharine Market, among whom six patronized any single butcher. Of course, market traffic ebbed and flowed across the business day: Catharine Market was packed with shoppers early morning, then sales slowed down considerably by ten o'clock, leaving a trickle of shoppers for the closing hours to hunt for leftovers.[76]

The marketplace, however, was not just crowded with people, vendors and buyers, engaging in daily transactions, but also with a vast amount of merchandise offered for sale every day: fresh meat, hung up or laid out neatly on the butcher stalls; fish and shellfish retailed from stalls, boats, and buckets; poultry, produce, and milk and dairy hawked by stands, carts, and wagons; in general, all varieties of foodstuffs sold and hauled around at different parts of the marketplace. And while it is impossible to document the volume of supplies disposed of at any given market-day, at least for butcher's meats, the amount can be reconstructed with considerable accuracy, as it is attempted in tables 4.3–4.4.[77]

To take stock, Catharine Market processed more than six hundred animals per week, of which roughly 112 were beef cattle, the most preferred variety of fresh meat. In other words, a typical Catharine Market butcher slaughtered, prepared, and retailed to his customers thirteen head of livestock, including two or three head of cattle weekly. In more tangible terms, he handled about 223 pounds of fresh meat, including 145 pounds of beef, on an average weekday, and more than twice that amount on Saturdays. This corresponded to the sale of 32 pounds of butcher's meat, including 21 pounds of beef at every tick of the hour. Of course, one should remember that focusing on averages obscures the picture, for Cath-

TABLE 4.4. Daily Volume of Meat Sales per Butcher at Catharine Market (lbs.), 1818

	Winter		Spring		Summer		Fall	
	M–F	Saturday	M–F	Saturday	M–F	Saturday	M–F	Saturday
Beef	141.6	279.3	104.1	282.8	113.9	226.2	219.4	596.8
Veal	2.5	4.1	51.3	125.0	32.6	59.6	4.7	7.5
Lamb	27.3	51.5	5.4	12.2	82.2	173.6	63.7	150.1
Pork	6.6	6.4	0.9	1.3	1.4	1.9	33.3	46.6
Total	178.1	341.4	161.7	421.3	230.0	461.5	321.0	801.0

Sources: See text and note 77.

arine Market was beating at different rhythms and offered different selections of butcher's meats seasonally, especially outside the year-round supply of beef. Even in this least seasonally dependent supply chain then, the volume of sales a typical butcher handled more than doubled between the leanest late winter to early spring months and the most beef-plentiful fall season. Additionally, besides their continuous preparation of beef, Catharine Market butchers also processed different livestock from slaughter to retail through the year's progression.

The sheer volume of merchandise should impress, especially at around opening hours, when each of the butcher stalls, neatly but compactly lined up on both sides of the market-halls, were stocked with hundreds of pounds of butcher's meat. Well before dawn, this vast amount of food had to be transported to and unloaded at Catharine Market. It must have been a ghastly sight, intensified by the lack of sunlight, as Catharine Market's forty-seven butchers and their apprentices descended daily to the marketplace from their private killing sheds, pushing their cartloads of freshly slaughtered meat along the Bowery and Division and Catharine Streets. Only a few hours prior, they had been slaughtering and dressing livestock for the market-day. Their meat was still warm as it arrived at Catharine Market, where butchers had to navigate through the wagons and horses of farmers who had been camping outside overnight. The marketplace was not yet open, the city was barely awake, but Catharine Market's streets, sidewalks, and hallways were overflowing with vendors and goods. To agglomerate the provisions of an entire neighborhood, Catharine Market reached beyond its immediate boundaries every break of day: it tapped into the slaughterhouses of the butchers' district near the Bowery, crowded the Brooklyn ferry with passengers and supplies, and congested the neighboring streets with the hauling of foodstuffs.

Once all goods were assembled, the daily routine of the marketplace set in, and transactions became more localized. As outlined before, the disassembly process followed the schedules and incomes of local customers, determined by the triad of declining selection, deteriorating quality, and falling prices of goods from sunrise to midday. Small quantities of provisions, meant to last for only a few days, were hastily carried back by thousands of shoppers into their houses, tenements, and boarding rooms. Just before the marketplace officially closed, another, more marginal geography also surfaced, as leftovers were picked up by peddlers for resale past market hours and across the wider area. In principle, Catharine Market was then swept and cleaned under the market clerk's supervision, waste was removed to be disposed of (some of it being recycled, the rest to be dumped into the East River), vendors left their retail spots, and farmers departed the city, while the surrounding public spaces were given back to regular traffic. By the afternoon, there was little evidence that for nearly half of the day, and much of it before sunrise, Catharine Market animated a vast and dynamic landscape of food provisioning. One should remember that Catharine Market was only one of many public markets in New York. The dynamism and energy pulsating out of this vast food emporium was generated by marketplaces across the city.

CONCLUSION

Surely, Catharine Market in the 1810s and 1820s dazzled with its vast volume and panoply of merchandise, its daily gathering of vendors from the vicinity, the butchers' district farther north and even beyond the city boundaries, and its crowd of neighborhood patrons, fleeting commuters, and strolling visitors. In its quotidian grip over the lives of thousands of residents, the marketplace exhibited the affluence of America's leading port city. Many records document how local customers were as well provisioned as New Yorkers in general, even though the city's geography still bore the imprints of a commercial economy, with wealthy merchant households occupying the southern and central areas and more humble artisan and laboring populations settling into booming northern wards. This is not to deny that significant inequalities existed between the consumption habits of poorer and wealthier households. Yet such disparities did not manifest in observable spatial patterns, with average consumption rates differing between merchant and artisan districts. In early New York, even Catharine Market's more humble customer base consumed an impressive amount of meat, a quantity that residents of any European city would have envied. Admittedly, this average hides as much as it reveals, for the temporal analysis of chapter 3 showed that under the public market model, time and not space was the key determinant of unequal access to food supplies.

A general impression of plentiful provisions would be hard to deny in light of the evidence. The same was also acknowledged by contempo raries, perhaps most intriguingly by a reporter of the *American*, who in 1825 called Catharine Market "the great emporium for the mechanics and laborers on Saturday evening."[78] To obtain irrefutable evidence, the shrewd journalist set up a social science experiment of sorts. In assessing the financial conditions of Catharine Market's customers, he visited the place on a Saturday evening on April 6 and stood by the market-houses "to offer a 'joint and trimmings' to any one who appeared to be in want." Over a period of two hours, the undercover reporter tallied 870 men and women shopping at the public market, a figure that matches closely the hourly traffic estimated earlier.[79] Concluding his research, he asserted that "I observed but one individual whose external appearance warranted my offering the boon." Catharine Market customers apparently were not tempted by his meager offerings. Tellingly, the journalist titled his field report of Catharine Market "Proof of the Comfortable Situation of the Working Classes in our City."

The vicinity thus supported a thriving center of commerce and a bus-tling public space, whose economy penetrated deep into the homes of local residents. In its capacity to supply 25,000 people, Catharine Market tied together a far larger area, and at much greater intensity than any other public space, except for the other municipal markets. The public market had a comparative advantage of fostering open-ended sociability, for it was not a weekly affair like the church, of which there were about a dozen in the area, nor was it as limited in its geographic pull as the poor man's saloon at the corner. Here customers recognized familiar faces from larger distances and several times a week. Besides, nobody was excluded, for the market's strict sociospatial order prescribed everyone's place: where certain groups of vendors conducted their business, or at which hour different social strata of customers made their purchases. Overall, Catharine Market was at the center of the largest geographic definition of the neighborhood, and with the greatest level of accessibility. It was by no means an egalitarian place, precisely because every aspect of its built and social fabric reflected the power relations that made and sustained the marketplace.

Yet it took an open public place such as Catharine Market to host a spectacle as complex and fleeting as the black dancing contests. Perhaps the spontaneous emergence of these dances required at first a small and flimsy marketplace in a humble district just being settled for such an ac-tivity to be tolerated. Once the dances took root, Catharine Market's for-tune of becoming one of Gotham's leading centers of commerce helped the performances gain citywide reputation. Over time the dancers became an enduring presence here: members of Catharine Market's eclectic community of vendors, local patrons, and visitors. The dancers' position remained marginal for sure: the shows' existence hinged on the butchers' goodwill and the audience's ovation, and, tellingly, emancipation, instead of propelling the performers to greater visibility, pushed them entirely offstage. Their disappearance from Catharine Market's limelight, of course, did not mean that the dances ceased to exist. Instead they dispersed across the city's laboring districts, relocating underground and reinvigorating a lively cultural scene that had long flourished in Gotham's famous black dancing cellars—another story.[80] Yet the presence of these spectacles at one of Early New York's busiest, most accessible, and humblest of public spaces captures the dense web of social bonds from which the public market was constantly made and remade to sustain an urban neighborhood.

PART III

Free-Market System of Provisioning, 1830s–50s

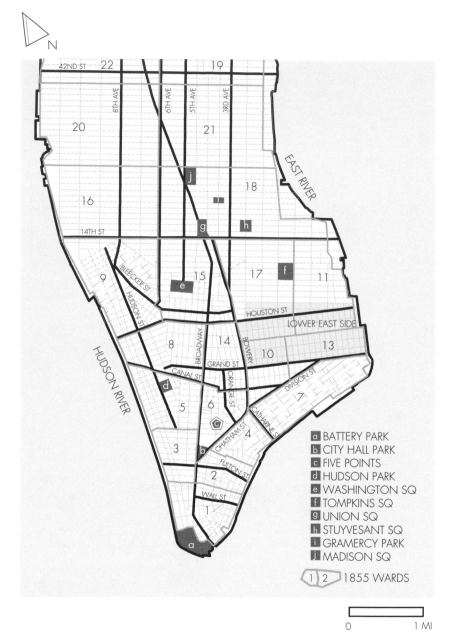

Orientation map, ca. 1855

CHAPTER 5

Withdraw the Bungling Hand of Government

Free-Market Geography of Provisioning

Purely a Business Matter

Ten years had passed since the city had decided to deregulate the public market system. Still, the debate that had erupted in the 1830s about the balance of government agency and private enterprise in provisioning, resulting in the market laws' repeal in 1843, continued into the 1850s. As chapter 1 established, the market model came under attack from all sides, including from residents, who claimed that their provisioning needs were unmet; informal vendors, who protested that they were unfairly cast aside; and municipal officials, who found the system administratively too burdensome and financially much too unproductive of taxes. To be sure, aligning with the sentiments of the time, a free-market ideology permeated all these critiques. Nonetheless, whether or not food provisioning was to be left entirely to private enterprise was not an obvious matter. Much of the public market system survived liberalization, even if decades of disinvestment left the infrastructure greatly diminished in its reach and generally in tatters. In the meantime, municipal investments expanded robustly in other vital domains of urban life, above all, the provisioning of the water supply and the expansion of the street system, demonstrating that the balance of public and private goods was a subject of case-by-case negotiations.

The question of food access was tackled head-on by the comptroller, A. C. Flagg, in a lengthy communication on the city's market property in May 1854. By then self-regulating food markets had been granted a decade to restructure household provisioning. The legitimacy of "opening the market privileges to all," Flagg reminded the Common Council, was a foregone conclusion, the natural evolution of things.[1] Moving his agenda further, he deemed it timely to propose the idea that the city should lease out its existing public markets to private investors for a fixed annual rent, thereby "leaving all the market arrangements to be made on enlightened, liberal and simple business principles."[2] He also ventured to ground the discussion within a broader liberal political economy credo. "The supply of this city with eatables, through the markets, is a business of great importance; but it is purely a business matter," he ascertained. By way of discrediting the place of government in food provisioning, he declared categorically: "Does not our security, after all, rest on the *business man*, rather than on the government official? Why, then, not withdraw the bungling hand of government . . . and in this, as in other matters, let trade regulate itself?"[3]

Flagg well understood that the proof of the pudding was in the eating, and he was confident that evidence was on his side. If the municipal model foreclosed hundreds of aspiring food purveyors from pursuing their occupation, even as it fell short of the demand of a growing metropolis, now that this "restricted system . . . was measurably broken up and scattered by the ordinance of 1843," the free-market model should boast a robustly expanding supplier base.[4] Indeed, he tallied 312 shop butchers compared to 266 market butchers in 1853, an excess of 46 private sector retailers, which, he added, was part of an upward trend. Quoting from the 1851 "Annual Report of the Commissioner of Streets and Lamps," he also asserted that "the Fifteenth, Sixteenth and Eighteenth Wards, with a population of one hundred and seven thousand . . . have not a public market, and are satisfied to let the marketing regulate itself."[5] Flagg's choice of words—"restricted system," "broken up," and "scattered"—along with his supporting evidence of healthy industry growth, and his endorsement of self-regulating markets, were carefully calibrated. Insofar as the free market had maintained food access to all inhabitants through the laws of supply and demand, and without any government meddling, the proof had to be a geographic one. The landscape he envisioned was one of open entry, where privileged public markets were challenged or replaced entirely by thousands of small businesses scattered across urban space. His vision was a dynamic yet orderly environment of food access, sculpted by the invisible hand of unregulated markets.

The document reads like a lecture, conveying a single-minded message about the virtues of self-regulating trade. Conveniently, Flagg skirted around some sensitive issues. Take his flagship figure of 312 licensed shop butchers. In reality, the number was far greater: according to the 1854 city directory, which surveyed the population based on self-declaration, no less than 821 separate meat shops, or private markets, as they were often called, operated in the city, and this is after subtracting all double counts of multiple butchers working at the same location.[6] In comparison, only 338 market butchers were counted by the surveyors, corresponding well with Flagg's numbers, considering that a few stalls were shared by several butchers. In passing, Flagg noted that his figures may "not include the whole number who are actually selling meats in shops out of the regular markets," and it likely would have made him happy to discover that private sector trade was more than two and a half times greater.[7] As the man in charge of city finances, he nonetheless should have worried about the loss of license fees, worth about $5,000 annually, from this vast unlicensed trade. More significant, the lack of registration reflected the city's diminished police power to oversee private provision markets, precisely as critiques of deregulation had warned ten years earlier.

For Flagg, who wished government out of food or other markets, even as he paid lip service to the municipality's role "to enforce such wholesome regulations as are required for the preservation of the public health," it seemed wiser to avoid the subject.[8] Besides, the presence of meat shops paled in comparison to that of groceries, of which roughly 3,250 operated across the city.[9] In an unregulated environment, these nonspecialist retailers were increasingly capable of capturing the fresh provisions trade, formerly limited to public markets. The splintering of food retail into thousands of locations not only added to revenue loss, but, more important, altered the geography of provisioning by placing it further beyond the sight of government. For Flagg this was in all likelihood a welcome development, for it promised greater convenience as suppliers moved closer to customers. How public market vendors fared in this sprawling and competitive landscape despite having invested substantial capital into their stalls was another matter.[10]

In general, this new geography surely was "broken up" and "scattered," with vendors dispersing across Gotham's vastly expanding built environment. "Opening" up the former "restricted" system of public markets undoubtedly helped infuse the food economy with renewed vitality. Flagg was accurate in asserting that deregulation ushered in a new terrain of provisioning, and he was eager to see liberalization run its transformative course. It is plausible that, by the 1830s, as the numerous petitions in chapter 1 have suggested, the public market system suffered from a degree of inertia, in which case deregulation in 1843 was a sensible strategy to promote food access for citizens in all areas. Just because Gotham could boast a well-ordered public market system in the century's first quarter, there was no guarantee that this would last through the antebellum era.

It is equally true that Flagg's vision of a dynamic, self-regulating, and well-ordered provisioning landscape was an oversimplification, an artifact of liberal ideology more than the reality on the ground. The invisible hand may have reconfigured food access, matching up suppliers and customers with ease, but more subtle patterns also emerged as an unregulated food economy mapped onto the city's rapidly changing geography. Past investments held on, for public markets survived even as they were weakened; the city's economic base broadened from commerce to manufacturing, reorganizing land-use patterns; the population swelled and became more differentiated by demographic and socioeconomic background, restructuring entire neighborhoods, reshuffling residents between them, and generally moving the city's population center northward; and a vastly expanding built fabric settled onto Manhattan's ambitious grid in newly urbanizing districts. The purpose of this chapter is to study more closely the geography of food access under the new free-market regime. Did the public market model suffer from inertia as critiques proclaimed, thereby warranting liberal reforms? How did the food economy develop at a time when New York secured its position as America's first metropolis? What were the spatial patterns of provisioning that emerged in mid-nineteenth-century New York City? And beyond this specific case, what do they reveal about the geography of food access under a liberal political economy?

DECLINE OF THE PUBLIC MARKET SYSTEM

In assessing the first question, whether or not the public market system fell behind urbanization prior to deregulation, the discussion follows a familiar path. The approach developed in chapter 2, to measure the retail capacity of the municipal infrastructure by its number of butcher stalls and how many residents an average stall supplied, is extended to the second quarter of the nineteenth century by figure 5.1.[11] The same set of constraints, including a pedestrian customer base, inadequate refrigeration, and the tight spatial dimension of the market stall, continued to limit a butcher's ability to augment the scale of his operation. Under these circumstances, industry growth within the formal public markets continued to depend on public investments rather than efficiency gains; increasing the system's capacity followed from building new or enlarging existing facilities through the process of political bargaining.

Clearly, after the mid-1820s, and especially after the 1830s, the commitment of city officials to the provisioning infrastructure gradually weakened. Following decades of persistent and sufficient investments, the municipal market system's expansion failed to keep up with accelerating urban growth. The recession of 1837–43, coupled with changing municipal priorities to construct the Croton aqueduct, crowded out all government investments on provisioning. Even after the recession, when municipal expenses rebounded to expand the street, water, and sewer networks, and, most notably, Central Park, the decline of the market infrastructure continued, well past the Civil War. Accordingly, the number of residents per stall began to soar, passing the threshold of 500 by the mid-1820s, moving beyond 700 by the 1830s, and reaching 877 by 1843, the year of deregulation. Even though butchers may have increased their volume of

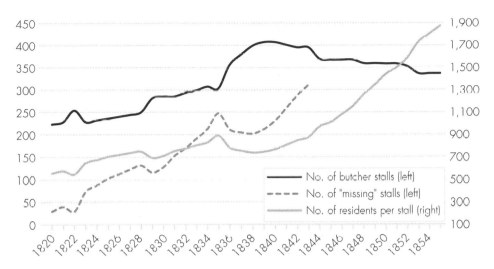

FIGURE 5.1. Number of butcher stalls, residents per stall, and missing stalls, 1820–55. (*Sources*: See text, note 12, and appendix B)

sales within the margins possible, this could hardly have compensated for the pressing lack of retail capacity. In a reasonable estimate, by the decade before deregulation, the public market system needed two hundred stalls, that is, it fell short of demand by 30 to 40 percent.[12] Easily one-fourth of New York City's meat retail must have occurred outside of the formal system.

It is hardly surprising then that butchers, burdened by considerable rents, complained ever more often to the council about the proliferation of unlicensed meat and other food sales, as recounted in chapter 1. Similarly, the petitions of customers who spoke up on behalf of unlicensed vendors, as well as residents' intensifying complaints about lacking easy access to a public market, appear more grounded, in light of the evidence. It seems that deregulation addressed a real deficit of municipal provisioning capacity, thus inviting a resurgent informal economy to meet soaring demand by lifting the barriers to open trade. Flagg would have attributed this shortfall to the "bungling hand of government" in an industry where, by his lights, it never belonged in the first place.

But before hastily accepting the comptroller's conclusions, a closer analysis of the geography of the public market system is warranted. Were problems with inadequate capacity exacerbated by a spatially poorly designed infrastructure? Or was the reverse the case? Did the location of facilities mitigate possible food distribution problems arising from shifting population densities and accelerating growth from 120,000 to 800,000 people between 1820 and the Civil War? The cartographic analysis of chapter 2 is continued here until 1855, with the size of the circles in the maps again representing the relative volume of trade of the individual marketplaces, which are, in turn, overlaid on ward-level population density maps.[13] This is a bird's-eye view of the process of market system expansion, inevitably overlooking subtle but important variations of density, land use, economic activity, or social composition, pertinent even at the block level. The utility of the approach resides in its capacity to grasp the entirety of the city and its municipal provisioning system by a standard measure, comparing food sales across market centers to local demand. Enhancing the comparison, relative catchment areas for retail marketplaces are also projected for the period between 1840 and 1855.

By the evidence of the first six maps in figure 5.2, the verdict of a feebly expanding public market system is compounded by that of a geographically ineffective one. Until the mid-1830s, additional marketplaces, specifically, Tompkins and Jefferson, at least were opened in developing and thinly populated northern districts, just as older facilities were retired in favor of newer ones, including Clinton, Weehawken, Union, and Monroe. Yet after 1836, this already timid development came to a complete halt, and despite Gotham's relentless march northward, not a single new market was opened to supply frontier areas. By the early 1840s, a fissure emerged within the geography of provisioning, whereby households in rapidly urbanizing areas north of Fourteenth Street were left without convenient access to public markets. Perhaps not by coincidence, this split mirrored the boundary line where the highly regimented street grid of the 1811 Commissioners' Plan gained full command over Manhattan's geography and development.

Turning one's gaze from north and south to east and west, another shortfall emerges, more closely associated with retail activity and shifting residential densities. This pattern is more subtle, yet it is also more telling, for it directly speaks of local customers' access to daily provisions. In the central wards, where public markets continued to supply residents, their capacity and level of trade generally declined moving from west to east, a trend that emerged and gradually deepened from the mid-1830s. Importantly, this did not correspond to residential distribution, but, on the contrary, some of the most crowded central-eastern wards were left with the smallest facilities.

Comparing the average yearly rents butchers paid for their stalls across the different marketplaces makes this observation more salient (maps 7–10 in figure 5.2). The logic is that the amount of capital any butcher was willing to invest into having a legitimate retail space mirrored his business expectations and earnings. Indeed, the relative value of retail space in 1828 corresponded to the centrality of a market's location and

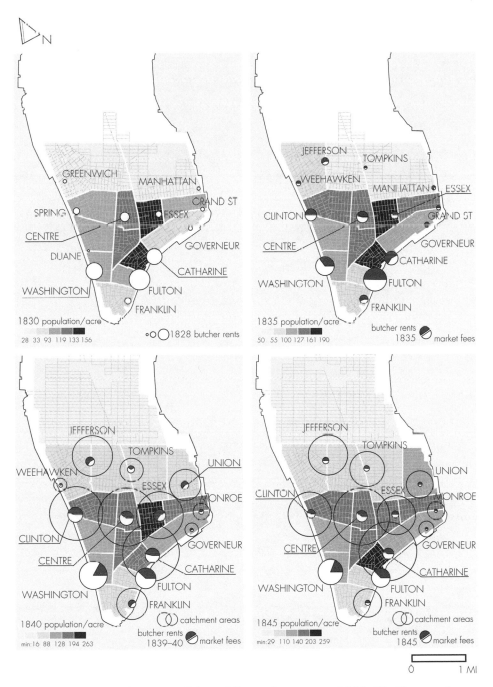

FIGURE 5.2. Development of the public market system, 1828–55. (*Sources*: See text and appendix A)

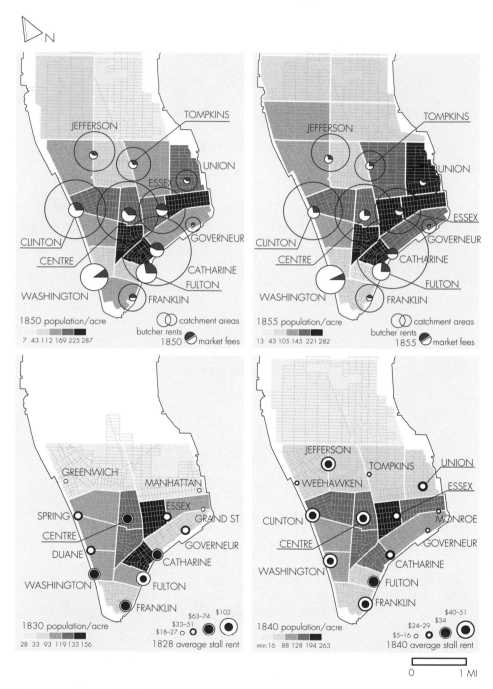

FIGURE 5.2. (*cont.*)

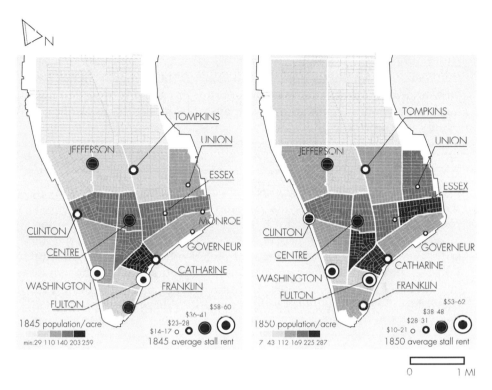

FIGURE 5.2. (*cont.*)

local population densities. By the 1840s this relationship vanished entirely, with rents varying by a ratio of one-to-three between eastern and western markets, even as the former served areas with much larger populations. Evidently, butchers at Jefferson or Tompkins Markets were prepared to expend more capital than their fellow tradesmen at Union, Essex, or Governeur, despite a potentially smaller customer base.[14] Similarly, Catharine Market, which only two decades earlier commanded some of the highest sales and rents, now leased stalls for lesser amounts than the smaller Jefferson Market. It is improbable that food consumption would have dropped by such enormous margins. Instead, market vendors in these densely settled districts faced sharper competition from outside retailers, whether these newcomers were selling informally or acquiring retail licenses after liberalization.

But before examining the sprawling landscape of an unregulated food economy, a discussion of the consolidation of wholesale and retail hierarchy is in order. The maps document an enormous surge in market fees, notable by 1835 and unmistakable by the 1840s, at Washington Market and to a lesser extent Fulton Market, evidence of their increasing reorientation to wholesale activities.[15] These had long been the two largest markets in the city, yet by the 1840s, their surrounding areas were largely emptied of inhabitants, leaving their oversized retail capacity far from the center of the population. The division of labor between the two wholesale markets remained somewhat arbitrary, albeit Washington handled far greater volume in every imaginable foodstuff, while Fulton mainly specialized in the wholesale fish trade.[16] In 1855, Washington Market alone, with its sprawling western extensions to the docks, earned no less than 60 percent of all market fees compared to Fulton's respectable 17 percent share.[17]

The reorientation of Washington and Fulton Markets to wholesaling by the antebellum era was a logical development that also served to repurpose their existing infrastructures. Several factors powered this transition. Most important, the city's size, now exceeding a population of a quarter million, necessitated the emergence of higher-order provisioning institutions, supplying retailers over a much-expanded urban area. The market laws traditionally kept the separation of wholesale and retail at bay, for they generally prohibited the resale of provisions for profit. With the market laws' grip weakening by the 1830s, and their repeal in 1843, such vertical integration was no longer inhibited by government regulation. Further, liberalization meant that retail points could multiply indefinitely, creating a more differentiated geography of provisioning, with food purveyors of various kinds working out of shops and more commonly depending on wholesalers. Unlike market butchers, who traditionally purchased and slaughtered their own livestock, meat shop butchers and grocers obtained their supplies from wholesale merchants. Similarly, as the sale of fish, shellfish, produce, and other foodstuffs gradually relocated from public markets to freestanding stores, fishermen and farmers, or their agents, no longer vended their goods directly to consumers.

There were other factors as well, more distinctive of the geography of New York City. As the lower wards gradually emptied of population, Washington and Fulton Markets lost much of their regular customer base of local residents. This was, however, amply compensated by their new line of business to supply food retailers and other nonresidential clients, in particular, hotels and restaurants, the largest concentrations of which were located at the emerging central business district in Lower Manhattan.[18] By midcentury, the major hotels clustered along Broadway nearby City Hall, while restaurants mushroomed in the commercial downtown, serving a new generation of middle- and upper-class customers, who commuted daily to the center for office work from uptown residential districts.

The concentration of wholesale trade at the southern end of Manhattan also reflected historical developments in the city's transportation connections. Wholesaling required the centralization of transport networks, whether anchored by railroad depots, port facilities, or their combination. The legacy of New York City's water-oriented commercial economy held sway for the provisioning industry even in the railroad era. Indeed, both wholesale markets were nested within a historical geography of water transport, engulfed by bustling and noisy docks canopied under a forest of masts. Public markets had long depended on riverfront access, ferries, and boats, and Washington and Fulton Markets obtained their preeminent positions by taking advantage of their dense nodes of water connections. The main reason that Washington outgrew Fulton in importance was that by midcentury commercial traffic across the Hudson River far surpassed the volume of cargo traversing the East River.[19] In general, the provisions trade benefited greatly from exploiting this natural geography, as foodstuff continued to pour into the city through the numerous docks of the two wholesale markets. Further, ferries and boats also linked up with railroad heads across the two rivers in New Jersey, Brooklyn, and Long Island, thus aggregating goods for a rising metropolis.[20]

This wholesale geography, however, remained one-sided, favorably positioned to take advantage of water transport but situated too far down south to fully tap into the new economies offered by railroads. Neither one of the two wholesale markets benefited from direct railway connections, even though by the mid-1850s three railroad companies (New York & Harlem, New York & New Haven, and Hudson River) already brought passengers and freight traffic directly into Manhattan.[21] Steam engines were banned south of Thirty-Second Street entirely, yet even below this boundary, tracks supporting horse-drawn carriages by the three companies did not run all the way to Washington and Fulton Markets. Merchandise arriving by land thus had to be unloaded and hauled to both wholesale centers by horse-drawn wagons and carts, traversing busy streets—hardly an optimal arrangement. Traffic was particularly heavy around Washington Market, leaving the surrounding streets grid-locked and the sidewalks virtually impassable, thus adding considerable costs.[22]

Furthermore, the southern slant of the wholesale market system introduced novel transportation inefficiencies by reason of being anchored too far down the island from the center of population growth. This was in part the outcome of Manhattan's natural geography, being a long and narrow island, where the only direction to expand was to the north. By midcentury, wholesalers stocked provisions for thousands of food purveyors, whose shops dispersed across the city, supplying their local customer bases. With wholesalers being anchored down south, even as the population progressively moved northward, distribution chains became ever more stretched. Hauling foodstuff between the two wholesale centers and the myriad retail locations was, of course, inevitable. But the persistent lengthening of distribution chains imposed considerable inefficiencies, even as the continued reliance on horse-drawn wagons and carts required their pushing their way through Manhattan's crowded streets. Adding to the challenges, suppliers working out of the two wholesale centers found their daily commutes increasingly taxing. Unlike retail food vendors, who typically resided at or nearby their work premises, whether shops or stalls, wholesalers working in or around Washington and Fulton Markets threaded long journeys to work.[23] The most burdened were wholesale butchers, who had to negotiate multiplying distances between their homes, slaughter-houses, and stalls, even as they carted ever larger amounts of merchandise down south to the wholesale markets.

All in all, the analysis outlines an infrastructure weighed down by in-sufficient investments relative to rapidly growing demand. Looking from south to north, in effect, trailing Manhattan's development over time, it becomes evident how a once essential neighborhood utility gradually dis-appeared from the built environment. By 1855 no less than 170,000 New Yorkers, one-fourth of the population and rapidly growing, lived in vicini-ties without access to a public market. If facilities were entirely lacking in the urbanizing north, they were overextended in the historic south, in districts that had shed most of their residents. Here Washington and Ful-ton Markets had shifted to wholesale trade. Yet they were not ideally located to serve this function, since they were too far south of the vast majority of the population; nor did they fully benefit from modern trans-portation, because they lacked direct access to railroads. Instead, their rise as wholesale centers was the result of historical contingencies, in particu-lar, the combination of infrastructural capacity built a quarter century before, and their preexisting agglomeration of supply chains based on water-transit centered at the port facilities. Shifting the focus to east-to-west patterns, even where public markets remained available to residents in the southern and central wards, those in the east underwent consider-able decline. Some, like Union, Monroe, or Governeur, withered into vir-tual irrelevance, and the once celebrated Catharine Market struggled to stay afloat, even as Jefferson prospered and earned decent revenues for the city and its vendors. The public market system, robust, comprehen-sive, and tightly organized only a few decades earlier, after the 1830s underwent fragmentation. The cartographic analysis not only corrobo-rates but even accentuates the earlier verdict of a system in decline during the second quarter of the century.

Contemporaries, of course, were not blind to these imbalances. The absence of adequate facilities up north was most evident. It motivated many of the petitions cited in chapter 1 by citizens complaining about their lack of access to a public market. It was also made manifest in oc-casional concessions to the market laws, such as the granting of temporary licenses on a case-by-case basis to butchers in frontier areas, or the periodic extension of the market laws' spatial boundaries.[24] The lack of facilities up north was even featured in Flagg's communiqué, when he boasted that more than one hundred thousand people resided in rapidly urbanizing wards beyond the reach of public markets, who, he assured, were perfectly content with the new free-market arrangement.[25] In comparison, the east-to-west pattern was less evident, and as a trend it escaped the attention of both contemporary observers and scholars. Even De Voe only touches on this issue when he complains about how Union Market lay nearly deserted by 1845 due to the licensing of meat shops, or laments the sorry state of Catharine Market in the 1850s.[26]

In general, whether one defended the public markets or agreed with Flagg in wishing them farewell, by the 1850s, municipal documents conveyed a general sense of malaise with the entire system. The last major effort to upgrade the infrastructure by rebuilding Washington Market in 1851, after successive debates, design planning, and appropriation of funds, was ultimately abandoned.[27] The project was ditched despite a consensus by all parties that Washington was New York City's, even the nation's, uncontested food emporium, yet it lacked adequate capacity to handle its vastly expanding trade, while it was also in a dilapidated state. The arguments presented convey all sides' recognition of a well-consolidated wholesale and retail hierarchy, and the essential role that Washington Market played in supplying the metropolis. Conflicting views about the market's specific location vis-à-vis the river, the streets, the center of population growth, and its distribution chains were voiced. Still, the attempt failed, not because of specific planning disagreements but due to the lack of funding or, rather, the triumph of a free-market ideology in food provisioning. Needless to say, business continued to swell, causing Washington Market facilities to further deteriorate. By 1860, city inspector D. T. Valentine dismissed any discussion about the possibility of renovating Washington or Fulton Markets, stating that "they cannot be repaired, for there is nothing to repair, while their demolition would give satisfaction to all."[28] He did not spare passing an equally harsh judgment on the public market system as a whole, which he declared "a disgrace to the city."[29]

In short, the state of affairs was a poor one. Contemporaries, just as scholars more recently, noticed and commented on the decline of the public market system in the antebellum era.[30] Moving from a patchwork of petitions, reports, and market biographies, the geographic analysis has rendered this process visible in a comprehensive fashion, preparing the ground for a comparison with the more thinly documented landscape of unregulated provisioning.[31] But before applauding Flagg and his precursors for having paved the way for a private sector takeover after 1843, one should bear in mind that infrastructural decline was the product of inadequate social investments due to shifting municipal priorities. It should not be mistaken for the inherent failure of government provisions. In fact, the municipal model's former success cautions that under adequate public investment and proper management, it could supply residents well, even as it sustained urban growth. It is also true that under the pressure of accelerating urbanization, which propelled New York into the rank of world cities, inadequate public market expansion was to a degree understandable. The balance of public and private goods was a highly contested and open-ended question. Where to allocate municipal funds and focus regulatory power, whether to the infrastructure of food or to the supply of water, another vital resource that the private sector was less readily available to provision, was a legitimate matter of urban policy and governance.

Contours of an Unregulated Geography

As a reminder, threshold and range are key variables of central-place theory, providing an analytical framework to assess the spatial organization of urban retail.[32] In a free-market environment, these variables allow for predicting the size and locational patterns of various industries. Examining the spatial organization of the public market system, these two terms were applied in chapter 2 to situate the food trade within a broader discussion of urban retail geography. In particular, the analysis highlighted how food vendors represent an industry with low threshold demand, where a relatively small pool of customers is adequate to sustain a profitable business, for they sell basic necessities required by all residents. Similarly, since customers need to purchase provisions on a daily basis, they normally commute from a narrow range of easy walking distances. Given these two conditions, one expects food shops to be among the city's most numerous businesses, dispersing across the entire urbanized area. As a rule of thumb, they seek out mutually exclusive catchment areas vis-à-vis their competitors, even as they coexist with stores nearby that carry complementary provisions. These predictions are hardly surprising, and experience suggests that unless mandated otherwise, as in the case of the market laws, food purveyors are copious and geographically dispersed in a walking city, leaving little to ponder over about their geography. Yet to make sense of food access under a deregulated economy, a closer look is warranted. By what measure should one speak of low threshold and range in the food economy of mid-nineteenth-century New York? What were the specific patterns of dispersion in food distribution? And how did those arrangements map onto the broader geography of a rapidly growing and changing metropolis?

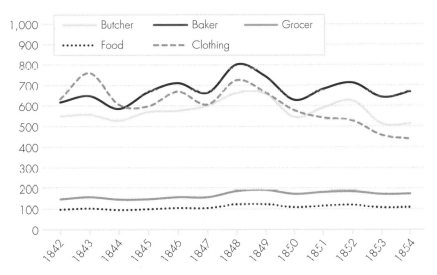

FIGURE 5.3. Number of residents per food and clothing shops, 1842/43–1854/55. (*Sources*: See text and note 33)

In an effort to measure threshold demand, figure 5.3 expands on the previous approach of counting the number of residents per retail unit to include all types of food vendors listed in the city directories from 1842 until 1854.[33] As expected, the food trade operated under very low threshold requirements, with as few as one hundred residents per retail location. This figure takes into account all varieties of food purveyors, ranging from grocers, butchers, and bakers to less central and hence less numerous vendors of oysters, fish, vegetables, fruits, and milk and dairy. As a point of reference, another basic necessity, clothing, is added to the chart, including in that category boots and/or shoes and hats to cover all common attire. While a basic good for sure, clothing presented an occasional and not a daily purchase, explaining why threshold demand was about five times higher in this sector than in the provisions trade. It is also true that the threshold for clothing was on a downward trend, from around six hundred to five hundred, indicating a historical transition away from home production to the purchase of ready-made and secondhand clothing after the mid-nineteenth century. In comparison, no trend of any sort can be observed for provisions: as theory predicts, industry expansion was endogenous to population growth, following the simple rule that every additional one hundred inhabitants created adequate demand for another food retailer to set up business.

Certainly, the food trade consisted of different types of businesses, with threshold demands varying significantly. Not surprisingly, the generalist trade of grocers—traditionally centered on dry food, yet with the demise of the public market system ever more commonly incorporating the retail of fresh provisions—had the lowest threshold of about 170 inhabitants.[34] Bakers, in comparison, required a threshold population of 670, while butchers, counting both market vendors and meat shops, needed about 580 residents. Moving to less essential foodstuff, seldom or less uniformly consumed, there could be as many as several thousand residents for each fish or oyster dealer. One point to stress, as evident from the chart, is the remarkable persistence of threshold numbers for the three essential trades of grocers, butchers, and bakers. Even as the population nearly doubled between 1842 and 1854 to pass 600,000 people, all three key sectors of the food industry expanded at a commensurate rate to match growing demand. This is especially remarkable in the case of butchery, where immediately after deregulation the ratio of residents per retail unit reverted rather close to the figure of 500, where it had been in the early nineteenth century under a robust and well-functioning municipal market system.[35]

The concept of threshold leads one step closer to appreciating the massive scale of the food industry, the relative importance of its essential trades, the robust growth of the sector fueled by urbanization, and the profound shift that occurred with the transition from a public to a free-market economy of provisioning. Flagg himself turned to the number of meat shops relative to market stalls along with the notion of a "broken-up" system to describe how quantitative change heralded a qualitatively new and distinct environment of food access. Setting aside his vast underestimation of this more visible dimension of the process, he did have the evidence to make a plausible case for an emerging and thriving private sector food economy, which, he hoped, would eventually prove the public market system obsolete.

Moving to range, however, his vision of a "scattered" landscape sounds less satisfying. What did it mean, for instance, that residents in the northern wards, with no access to public markets, were content with the new geography of self-regulating food markets? "Scattered" is an elusive standard, and the theorized dispersion of food shops leaves one uncertain about the specific patterns. A more precise analysis requires plotting the actual distribution of all food retailers while taking into account changing residential patterns, the pressure of intensifying urban growth, and the short walking distance that defined households' provisioning trips. Such an approach presents a more solid platform to assess the emerging landscape of an unregulated food economy, expanding on the earlier analysis of the public market system. Further, it situates the subject of food access within the city's broader economic geography with regard to both residential and commercial patterns.

As for residential patterns, land-use maps at the level of blocks offer a holistic yet detailed approach to study the underlying spatial organization of Manhattan's built environment, including the geographic extent of its inhabited areas, where the problem of food access is directly relevant. Relying on building-footprint level land-use designations from the Perris Fire Insurance Atlas of 1852–54, color plate 1 depicts the intensity of each of three basic land-use types (commercial, industrial, and residential) by the block below Forty-Second Street.[36] The maps outline the spatial order of mid-nineteenth-century New York, rendering visible the city's distinctive functional zones, including its single-use and mixed-use districts, even as they capture some of the economic change that propelled the rise of America's first metropolis. Exploiting this data set on the built environment, the maps provide a snapshot of New York's economic geography and urban development, establishing the spatial context within which the subject of food access should be situated.

To begin with, it is evident that by the mid-nineteenth century, Lower Manhattan, below City Hall, became a commercial center, almost completely void of residential population.[37] As ward-level population density maps earlier outlined, this process of residential displacement had been unfolding since the 1830s. Only west of Broadway and east of the Hudson River did commercial structures continue to mix with residential uses in a ribbon of densely developed blocks. In addition, commercial land use expanded northward along the two principal axes of Broadway and the Bowery. Offices, hotels, theaters, and all varieties of stores settled along these thoroughfares, linking the commercial center to expanding residential districts. The historical waterfront sustained its original maritime orientation to become America's leading port, with docks and piers along both rivers, accommodating all types of commercial and passenger ships, barges, ferries, and boats. Merchant houses and wholesalers competed for waterfront access, which explains why commercial uses dominated the shore farther north. It was in the midst of this bustling commercial waterfront that the two wholesale markets, built in an earlier era, were still located. Lacking residents who depended on daily supplies, independent food shops most likely stayed away from downtown, unless they participated in the wholesale provision trade centered at Washington and Fulton Markets.

Moving on to the city's expanding industrial geography, what catches the eye is the widespread dispersal of industrial facilities across the entire built-up area, mixing in with residential and, to a lesser extent, commercial uses. One should note that the map falls short of accounting for a range of industrial uses, especially the proliferation of small workshops, including infamous sweatshops, inside of residential buildings.[38] New York became a city of myriad workshops, producing every type of industrial goods imaginable. Jostling for space in a densely built environment, they stood side-by-side, occupied back lots, or penetrated residential structures. Larger facilities like breweries or distilleries here and there implanted themselves into this hodgepodge, mixed-use environment of homes, workshops, and stores, especially in working-class districts.[39] It is also true that certain industries, already organized into factory production, such as ironworks, gasworks, or foundries, settled along the shore, where they could benefit from direct access to water-based freight transit. The intensity of industrial use thus increased alongside the rivers, pushing out residential buildings in a narrow rim of blocks inland. The maps reveal how the historic commercial waterfront yielded to this new industrial geography, reflecting New York City's shifting and broadening economy. More to the point, central-place theory would suggest the general absence of retail food purveyors along these developing industrial zones.[40]

It comes as no surprise that residential structures dominated the built environment. Among the slightly more than sixty thousand buildings below Forty-Second Street, about 77 percent of them were devoted to housing. Commercial land use paled in comparison, representing 5 percent of the building stock, while industry's share comprised another 17 percent, not counting the various sweatshops overlooked by the Perris Atlas.[41] Besides, these percentages also underestimate the extent of commercial space, for three out of ten residential buildings included stores at their ground floor, generating mixed-use streets to be surveyed shortly. What is important to note is the degree to which residential use encompassed the entire urbanized area, with the exception of downtown and the immediate environs of the waterfront. Its intensity varied block by block, depending on the amount of land taken up by workshops and factories, commercial buildings, and ground-floor stores. Additionally, churches, schools, and other public buildings interspersed in this densely built fabric of residence and work. In assessing the geography of food access, the extent of residential use serves as the base of comparison for the theorized dispersal of provision shops. Unlike public markets, whose larger economies supplied entire neighborhoods, private food retailers, including grocers, meat shops, bakers, and others, set up their businesses in close proximity to customers: down to the short range of one block.

Another dimension of this bird's-eye view of nineteenth-century urban land use concerns the geography of residential buildings with ground-floor trade. This was by far the most common mixed-use arrangement, and it played a central role in determining the hierarchy of the street system. For most of Manhattan's urbanized area, except for downtown, Broadway, and, to a lesser extent, the Bowery, land prices did not systematically price out residential use. At the same time, residential buildings on select streets, benefiting from greater accessibility, generated higher rents, incentivizing landlords to accommodate stores at the street level. Food retailers almost without exception set up their businesses in such mixed-use structures, given their low threshold and range. Whereas blocks provide an appropriate spatial unit to study the customer base of food retailers, understanding where these businesses were located within Manhattan's built environment calls for a street-level analysis.

A complete view of ground-floor retail is presented by the first map of color plate 2, representing all residential buildings with stores beneath.[42] It complements the previous block-level map for a comprehensive geography of commercial use, rendering visible the spread of businesses across the city, their patterns of clustering and dispersal along the street system, and their uneven settlement within residential districts.[43] It documents how the distribution of stores contributed to a street hierarchy. Broadway's position as the most illustrious boulevard was indisputable, albeit the Bowery presented a competing axis of a more working-class character, with storefronts lining both sides. A collection of secondary retail streets—including Chatham, Division, Grand, and Houston on the eastern, and Canal, Hudson, and Bleecker on the western halves of the city—is also visible. There were other smaller retail centers as well, in particular, Orange Street, running through the Five Points, and Catharine Street, leading from Chatham Square to Catharine Market by the East River. Finally, retail shops also penetrated into the heart of residential neighborhoods, especially in the most densely populated central eastern wards.

Farther north, where the grid asserted its grip over Manhattan's built environment, businesses settled along the avenues, away from the residential cross-streets. The sheer power of the grid to reshape Gotham's commercial geography is astounding. Certainly, as others have argued, the grid plan facilitated urban development by creating a more rational and efficient real estate market.[44] What the discussion has not stressed enough is how much it also reconfigured land-use patterns, reinforcing Manhattan's natural geography to create a straitjacket of south-to-north orientation, foreclosing the possibility of commercial development along east-west arteries. Whereas below the grid plan, secondary retail corridors, such as Houston or Canal, emerged on crosstown axes, the metropolis laid out by the Commissioners' Plan had a more predictable order. On avenues, commerce was incorporated into the ground floor of residential buildings, forming mixed-use commercial arteries. On cross-streets, ground-floor stores opened more sparsely, and instead rows of houses were interspersed by workshops and factories. There were exceptions to these patterns, especially in some new areas of residential development, or clustered industrial zones. But by and large, this logic held sway, rolling out a new geography of commercial development for the metropolis.[45]

So where did different categories of commercial businesses belong in this wider geography of mid-nineteenth-century urban land use and trade? To nail down the specifics of food access in an unregulated economy, the subsequent three maps of color plate 2 explore four separate industries with different degrees of centrality, in effect, disaggregating the previous maps of commercial land use and ground-floor retail.[46] At the highest level, the two sectors of banking and hotels display highly clustered geographies. Banks concentrated in downtown locations, specifically on Wall Street, a few blocks nearby, and close to City Hall, thus offering customers, from the city or elsewhere, a central district where they could obtain financial services. The few banks not in Lower Manhattan, even though on prominent streets, were typically savings banks serving residents from the vicinities. Hotels present a different pattern of clustering: they typically settled along Broadway, from downtown to Union Square and around City Hall. This does not include the many boardinghouses located near the docks and in dense working-class areas. For hotels, catering to an elite clientele, Manhattan's main promenade and the southern edge of City Hall were the most viable locations. These geographies were reinforced by the recent articulation of mass transit. Accounting for the intensity of omnibus traffic on each street, the map documents how residential areas up north connected to downtown south, with omnibus lines following avenues and major streets to eventually merge on Broadway and, to a lesser extent, the Bowery. Higher order commercial establishments, like hotels or banks, sought out these more accessible locations.

Clothing stores present a more directly relevant comparison to food shops. Their businesses spanned the entire city, yet they also sought out commercial corridors. Their largest concentration was in a shopping district downtown, south of City Hall. Additionally, clothiers lined Broadway, and even more so Chatham Street through the Bowery. Other retail streets, including Grand, Houston, Canal, and Hudson, and north on the grid plan, Third and Eighth Avenues, also served as centers for the clothing trade. Finally, the small Catharine and Orange Streets, the latter especially focusing on secondhand trade, should be added to the list. Evidently, the geography of clothing mirrored the commercial arteries identified for ground-floor retail. Equally notable is how among the grid's numbered avenues, clothing only concentrated on Third and Eighth. It was the relative centrality of the two avenues, and their tapping into the largest potential customer base on the city's eastern and western halves, respectively, that explain why these were more desirable business addresses. Clothiers also settled along the omnibus lines, seeking out more accessible locations in general. Indeed, clothing stores sold par excellence comparison goods, benefiting from a clustered geography that pulled together a larger customer base from greater distances. Whether they served commuters from the whole city, such as those in downtown, or relied on

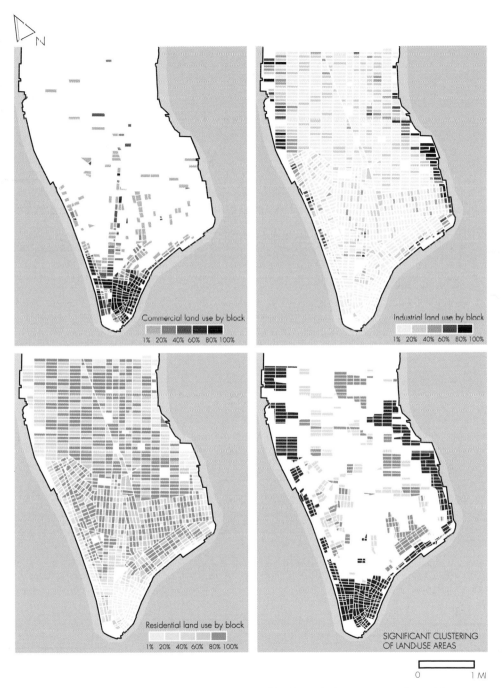

PLATE 1. Intensity of land-use types by block and their areas of significant clustering, 1854. (*Sources*: See text and appendix A)

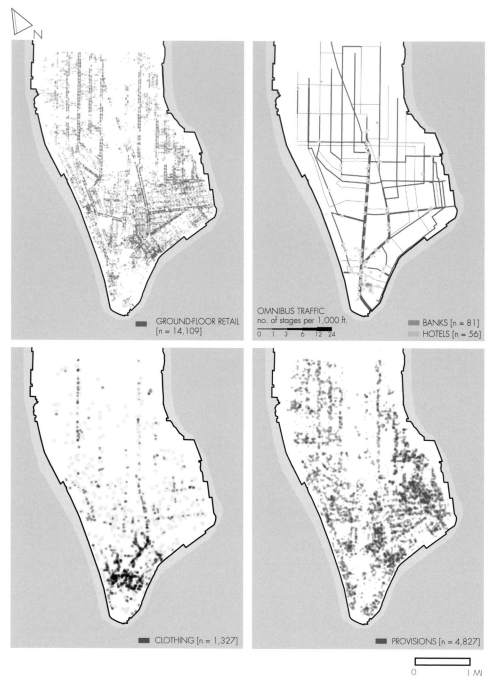

PLATE 2. Geography of commerce, 1854. (*Sources*: See text and appendix A)

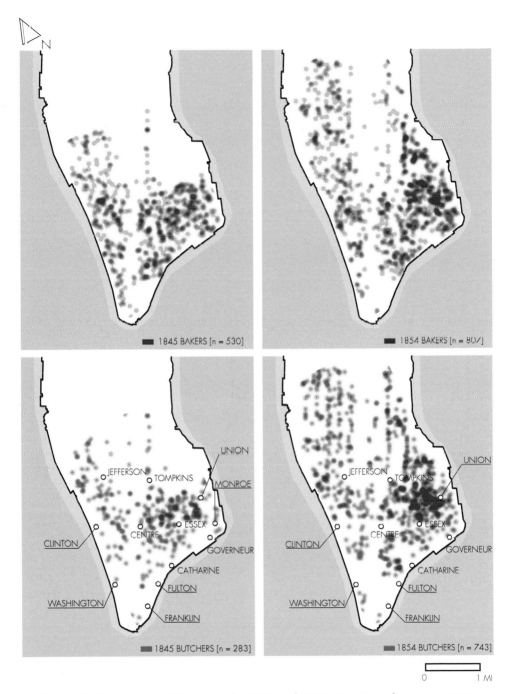

PLATE 3. Geography of food retail, 1845 and 1854. Continued on next page.
(*Sources*: See text and appendix A)

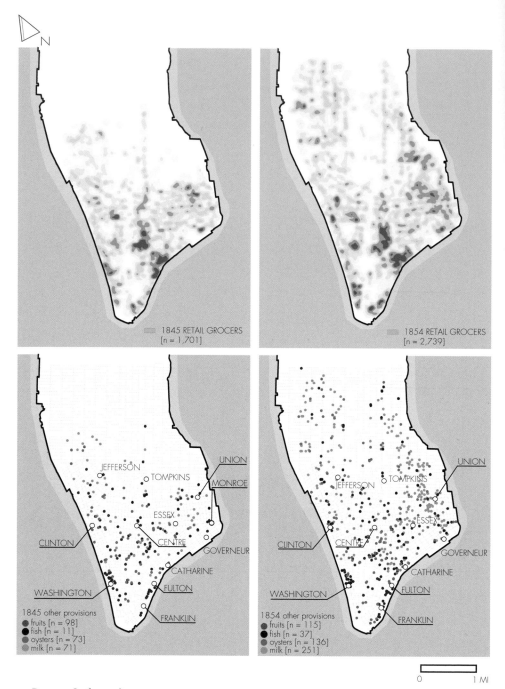

1845 RETAIL GROCERS
[n = 1,701]

1854 RETAIL GROCERS
[n = 2,739]

UNION
JEFFERSON
TOMPKINS
MONROE
ESSEX
CLINTON
CENTRE
GOVERNEUR
CATHARINE
WASHINGTON
FULTON
FRANKLIN

1845 other provisions
● fruits [n = 98]
● fish [n = 11]
● oysters [n = 73]
● milk [n = 71]

UNION
JEFFERSON
TOMPKINS
ESSEX
CLINTON
CENTRE
GOVERNEUR
CATHARINE
WASHINGTON
FULTON
FRANKLIN

1854 other provisions
● fruits [n = 115]
● fish [n = 37]
● oysters [n = 136]
● milk [n = 251]

0   1 MI

PLATE 3. (cont.)

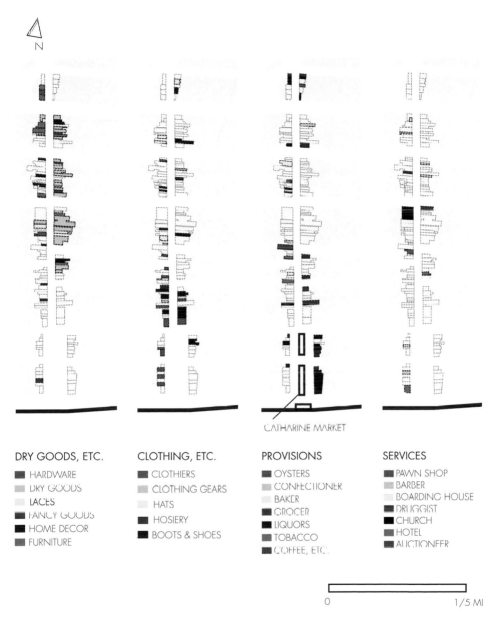

N

CATHARINE MARKET

DRY GOODS, ETC.	CLOTHING, ETC.	PROVISIONS	SERVICES
HARDWARE	CLOTHIERS	OYSTERS	PAWN SHOP
DRY GOODS	CLOTHING GEARS	CONFECTIONER	BARBER
LACES	HATS	BAKER	BOARDING HOUSE
FANCY GOODS	HOSIERY	GROCER	DRUGGIST
HOME DECOR	BOOTS & SHOES	LIQUORS	CHURCH
FURNITURE		TOBACCO	HOTEL
		COFFEE, ETC.	AUCTIONEER

0   1/5 MI

PLATE 4. Catharine Street retail shops, 1851. (*Sources*: See text and appendix A)

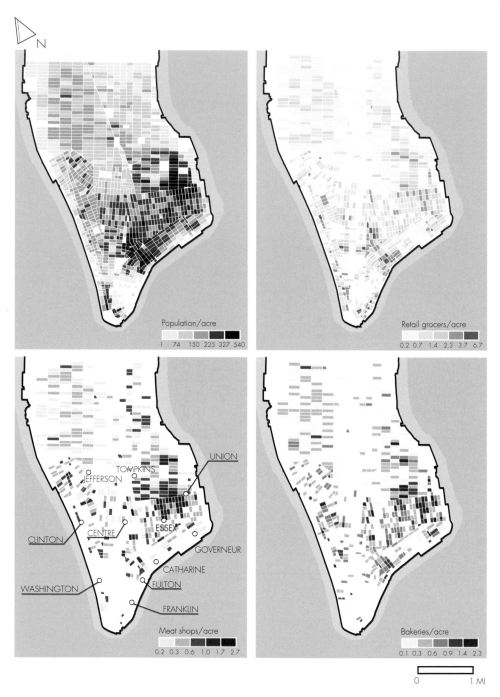

PLATE 5. Population and food retail density, 1854. (*Sources*: See text and appendix A)

PLATE 6. Residential patterns by class and food retail density, 1854. (*Sources*: See text and appendix A)

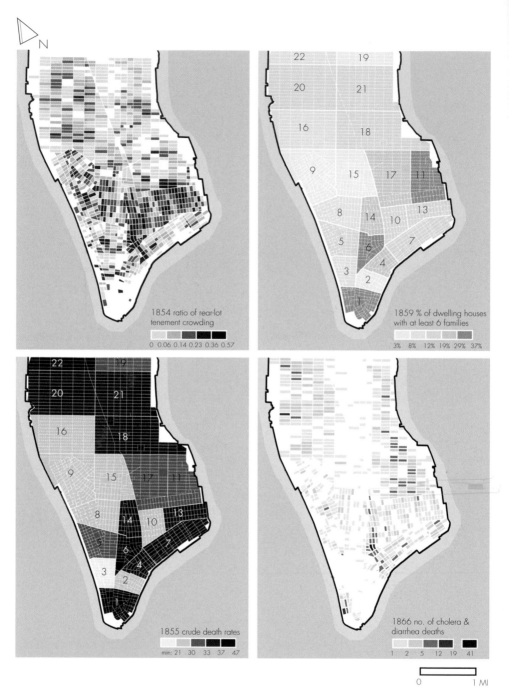

PLATE 7. Housing conditions and disease environments, 1854–66. (*Sources*: See text and appendix A)

shoppers from the vicinity, like those on Catharine Street, depended on their relative centrality within the sector.

It is in comparison to these patterns of distribution and clustering that the idea of a dispersed geography of food access should be appreciated. The last of the four maps plots several thousands of food purveyors, including grocers, butchers, and bakers, as well as fish, oyster, fruit, vegetable, and milk vendors.[47] Immediately, the map shows what dispersal in reality meant relative to the more agglomerated geographies of higher-order businesses. And there was more to this geography than just dispersal. In the area where one finds the greatest concentration of clothiers, right below City Hall Park, there was a general absence of food purveyors. In fact, the central business district virtually lacked any retail food shops, except for the narrow stretch of blocks between Broadway and the Hudson River, where commercial uses did not entirely price out residential buildings. Additionally, the industrial waterfront, roughly one block inland from the rivers, did not support food shops either. In an unregulated economy, as predicted, food retailers opened shops right next to their customers. Indeed, the maps of residential land use and food provisioning closely mirror each other.

In another way as well, provisioning and clothing produced inverse geographies. Whereas clothiers sought out principal thoroughfares, food shops generally stayed away from such choice locations. Only a few occupied addresses on Broadway and the Bowery. Even some secondary retail corridors like Grand or Canal Streets were largely avoided. They did settle on other commercial streets like Houston, Division, Hudson, and Bleecker, or Orange and Catharine Streets, but by and large below the grid, retail centers were more likely than not bypassed by food shops. Orange and Catharine Streets offer instructive cases, for many of the neighboring side streets in these densely packed working-class districts teemed with grocers, butchers, and bakers. On the two streets, however, food shops remained less numerous due to competition from retailers of higher order goods. In addition, retail streets were mixed-use locations, and thus could not accommodate the same number of inhabitants. In an economy where catchment areas were as narrowly defined as blocks, streets, and corners, accessing the heart of residential zones was the key locational incentive, not to mention the lower rents commanded by such addresses.

Up north, however, where the grid reconfigured land-use patterns, food shops were likewise pushed onto the north-south avenues. This is the strongest proof of the grid's control of Manhattan's commercial geography, for provisioning was the only trade that in theory could ignore this locational pressure. To be sure, food shops often moved into the interior of blocks, carving out their necessary customer base of a few hundred residents. Indeed, the vast majority of ground-floor retail that located on streets and not avenues was one type of provision store or another, while the exclusivity of avenue location was far more pronounced for clothiers. Still, the avenue effect was robust even for food vendors despite their industry's low threshold and range. The real difference between the avenues was the degree to which they became veritable business corridors, attracting customers from larger distances to stroll and comparison shop. By this measure only Third or Eighth Avenues qualified, whereas the other north-south axes were mainly focused on the sale of convenience goods—above all, daily provisions—to residents from their vicinities.

Furthermore, even as they dispersed, retail food shops clustered in certain areas more than others. Most noticeably, ward 6, situated between Broadway and the Bowery south of Grand Street and north of City Hall, and the blocks on either side of Catharine Street, were teeming with provision shops. Likewise, on the Lower East Side, within a few blocks' distance from Houston, a significant cluster of food retailers emerged. These were all densely populated, working-class, immigrant districts: Gotham's emerging tenement neighborhoods. The mechanisms by which food access corresponded with class, immigration, or living conditions will be studied in chapter 6. What matters here is to recall that it was precisely in these eastern wards that public markets, including Union, Essex, Governeur, and even Catharine, underwent rapid decline in both their volume of trade and profitability, regardless of their dense populations. Evidently, public markets in these areas faced especially sharp competition from nonmarket vendors, a subject to be explored shortly.

Equally important, there were a few residential districts where food purveyors were conspicuously absent, all of them situated in Manhattan's upper half between Third and Sixth Avenues. These enclaves centered around prestigious avenues and squares, including Fifth Avenue, from Washington Square up north passing by Madison Square; Madison Avenue; Union Square; and Gramercy Park, with Irving Place and Lexington Avenue traversing it. Whereas most New Yorkers could find food shops on their own block, street, or nearest corner, residents in these districts were at least one block away from such businesses. Opportunely, these were also the wealthiest neighborhoods, where households could rely on domestic help or home delivery.[48] Indeed, the absence of commerce on these elegant avenues and their adjacent streets was often the product of restrictive covenants, designed to preserve their exclusive residential character. The best-known example is Gramercy Park, where the developer Samuel B. Ruggles imposed deeds on his lots requiring that only dwelling houses of brick or stone, at least three stories, could be built around this private park.[49] At an aggregate scale, these private initiatives of zoning succeeded in minimizing undesirable uses, such as industries or nuisance trades. They also served to reduce intrusion by nonresidents, maintaining self-contained public spaces for elite New Yorkers. A stroll on Fifth Avenue was an elegant affair, in part because it was undisturbed by the crowds and noises of commerce, especially the noxious practices and smells associated with the food trades.

It should be evident by now that the dispersal of food purveyors in an unregulated economy produced a more complicated and patterned development than theory alone would suggest, especially when situated within the broader context of land-use and retail geography. In the last step of the analysis, it serves to disaggregate the geography of food retail and trace its evolution over time, comparing the two years 1845 and 1854 (see maps in color plate 3).[50] Responding to residential growth, the food sector expanded dynamically and uniformly across all trades, from bakers, butchers, and grocers to more specialized retailers like fish, oyster, fruit, or milk dealers. In addition, the grid realigned the geography of food provisioning. In this regard, bakers obeyed the avenue pattern the least, most likely because of their distinctive practice of combining retail activity with quasi-industrial uses in the same facility. Butchery had even more demanding spatial constraints, yet slaughtering was done at separate sites, away from customers.[51] Insofar as the retail component dominated locational choices, the avenue alignment of the grid held sway.

There were, however, considerable differences in the spatial distribution of individual trades. Proving central-place theory right, bakers dispersed across the city most uniformly.[52] In contrast, meat shops followed a more patterned geography. Their locations reflected their positioning vis-à-vis the closest marketplace. Focusing only on residential areas, some public markets—including Jefferson, Tompkins, and, to a lesser degree, Catharine—managed to fend off the competition of private meat shops. The reverse was the case in the working-class, immigrant Lower East Side, north of Grand Street and east of the Bowery, where butcher shops dotted every block and street, encroaching upon the original catchment areas of Union, Essex, Monroe, and Governeur Markets.[53]

The geography of groceries presents a third pattern. To a remarkable extent, they followed their customers to each block, street, and corner. In fact, with the exception of elite uptown enclaves, New Yorkers could hardly reside at an address without having access to at least one grocery within a distance of three hundred feet; in practical terms, a little more than a one-minute walk. At the same time, their dispersal was not even, but groceries significantly clustered in wards 4 and 6, Gotham's other contiguous immigrant and working-class tenement districts.[54] Accordingly, vendors at Catharine and, to a lesser extent, Centre Market faced especially sharp competition from grocers, who captured an ever larger share of the local food trade. These findings about the geographies of meat shops and groceries explain the earlier noted pattern about the public markets' declining business and profitability moving from west to east.

At last, a look at the more specialized and less central trades of fish, oyster, fruit, and milk vendors provides additional details. The notable concentration of fruit vendors around Washington and Fulton Markets confirms the agglomerative power of the two wholesale markets, while the increasing dispersal of fish and oyster dealers between 1845 and 1854 conveys the general process by which retail public markets lost ground to a mushrooming free-market economy of food provisioning. Milk vendors were generally dispersed, but they also appear somewhat concentrated a few blocks inland from the East River, in close proximity to industrial uses, and near the Lower East Side, where many slaughterhouses were located, suggesting the presence of cow stables in these generally working-class districts.

Overall, having focused on threshold and range, the key variables for central-place theory, the mapping analysis has revealed a profoundly altered geography of provisioning by midcentury. From the original configuration of agglomerated public markets, the geography of provisioning transformed into a complex and highly differentiated system of food distribution. Dispersal, or "scattering" in Flagg's words, was no doubt the main dynamic for this unregulated geography. Yet it is just as important to appreciate how at once patterned and fragmented this emerging landscape was, taking into consideration the particular circumstances under which deregulation occurred.

First, the dispersal of provision shops was determined both by urban growth and changing patterns of land use, thrusting Manhattan's population center northward, while at the same time emptying older areas of inhabitants. Additionally, the street network, with its consolidating hierarchy of key thoroughfares, mixed-use corridors, and residential streets, also realigned by the grid's uniform and expanding layout, guided the locational choices of food vendors. Second, the old public market system survived: even though its expansion completely halted, and facilities were being left to decay, Washington and Fulton Markets amassed ever greater shares of the wholesale trade, while neighborhood retail markets continued to supply local customers. Consequently, in the city's southern half, the new geography of food shops grafted onto an existing municipal order, with the two models competing and complementing each other, whereas north of Fourteenth Street, food access was entirely subjected to the reign of free markets. Third, different areas acquired their unique geographies of provisioning. At one end of the spectrum, wealthy uptown areas excluded provision stores and other undesirable businesses from their immediate vicinities. At the other end, centrally located working-class areas were teeming with groceries, meat shops, and other food vendors.

It was precisely the local articulations of these dynamics that produced a far more differentiated and fragmented geography of provisioning than in the Early Republican era. The bird's-eye view of mapping rendered the general arrangements and their underlying spatial production legible for a booming and heterogeneous city. Still, the daily experience of food shopping was grounded at the pedestrian scale of blocks, streets, and corners. It is time to resolve this picture more finely by examining four neighborhoods, corresponding to four distinctive environments of food access.

PEDESTRIAN SCALE: FOOD SHOPPING IN FOUR NEIGHBORHOODS

A good place to start a walking tour of mid-nineteenth-century food shopping is one northern district, where public markets were entirely absent, and thus the new geography of private provision shops dominated the landscape.[55] Focusing on the district between Seventeenth and Twenty-Seventh Streets and Fifth and Ninth Avenues (figure 5.4), a food system governed solely by free-market incentives and the grid plan is observed. The prominent pattern was dispersal, whereby independent food shops—grocers, butchers, bakers, and others—located at the ground floor of mixed-use buildings dotted the landscape. To avoid competition, they sought out small, individual catchment areas. Insofar as clustering occurred, this was limited to avenues and street corners, giving the most accessibility to residents. A fair number of grocers, bakers, and butchers also had businesses on cross-streets, especially in more densely developed blocks, where they could count on adequate customer traffic. But by and large, the food geography was defined by avenues and corners, except for Fifth Avenue, which did not have a single provision shop.

This was a straightforward landscape for customers to navigate, where the key consideration was proximity. No matter where one resided, there were a few groceries, and at least one baker and butcher shop, available within one block's distance. Assembling the basic necessities of daily life could be completed in one quick round with stops only a few minutes apart. Another benefit was that private provision shops were not restricted in their business hours like public markets, hence, customers could schedule their visits more flexibly throughout the day: grocers, for instance, often carried on their sales into the night.[56] In terms of proximity and flexibility, therefore, this new geography offered much convenience to local residents. At the same time, the new landscape was less conducive to comparison shopping for quality or price than the public markets. A walk along a four-block stretch of Seventh Avenue would deliver three to four meat shops, hardly a match for Jefferson Market's sixteen butcher

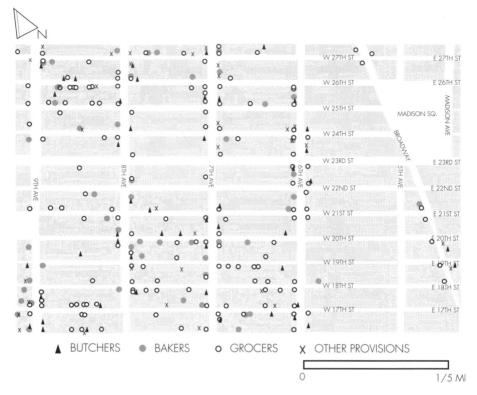

FIGURE 5.4. Provisioning north of Fourteenth Street, 1854. (*Sources*: See text and appendix A)

stalls. And even if there were a handful of groceries near one's home, their selection of produce, fish, or meat paled in comparison to the public market's agglomeration of foodstuff. The new free-market geography offered easy access and temporal flexibility, significant advantages no doubt. Yet this more sprawling geography also demanded extra effort from those who sought to compare supplies for quality or price. Conveniently for wealthy households, like those living on Fifth Avenue or nearby, domestics could complete such taxing rounds.

Continuing south on Sixth Avenue all the way down to Washington Square, a different provisioning landscape, defined by the cohabitation of a public market and private food shops, emerged (figure 5.5). At the intersection of Sixth and Greenwich Avenues, the medium-sized and vibrant Jefferson Market supplied local residents. Despite deregulation, between 1843 and 1855, market business here remained robust and profitable, with stall rents among the highest, even growing, and market fees dy-

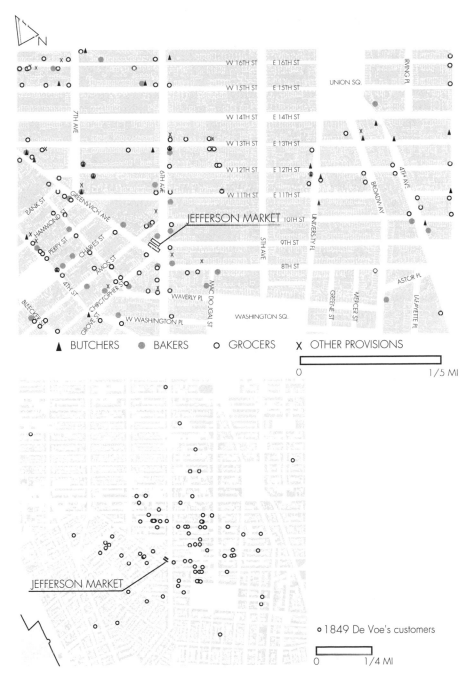

FIGURE 5.5. Provisioning north of Washington Square, 1854. (*Sources*: See text and appendix A)

namically increasing.[57] Meat shops did operate in the area, but they were kept at bay from directly interfering with the market's traffic. Groceries, bakers, and other provision shops speckled the landscape, especially to the west of Jefferson Market. Nonetheless, the persistent rise of market revenues suggests that many of these businesses complemented rather than competed with market vendors.

Notably, Manhattan's elite class of citizens continued to patronize Jefferson Market. Indeed, De Voe's customer list, reconstructed from an 1849 petition to the council on his behalf, finds a large share of his loyal clients residing on the elegant addresses surrounding Fifth Avenue. It is telling how Jefferson Market's catchment area stretched so far north, especially on the tranquil residential streets between Fifth and Sixth. For better-off New Yorkers, the old tradition of provisioning via regular-bred butchers and other market vendors remained a valued choice. In addition to relying on domestics, they could take advantage of the growing custom of home delivery from the public markets, organized by the butchers and their apprentices, to help overcome larger distances.[58]

The reverse situation was found in the Lower East Side's densely populated, working-class, immigrant neighborhoods.[59] These sprawling tenement blocks east of the Bowery between Grand and Houston Streets were home to Essex and Union Markets (figure 5.6). After deregulation, both suffered from greatly diminished rents and stagnating market fees, seeing only a modest recovery in the 1850s.[60] The close-up reveals intense competition on the ground, whereby meat shops and groceries occupied each block, street, and corner, directly penetrating the markets' catchment areas, significantly reducing their trade. If there was any pattern beyond the omnipresence of food vendors, it was their seeming preference for corner locations.

Residents on their part found themselves in a greatly transformed environment of food access. Certainly, the transition from a public to a free-market-based geography had its antecedents, for unlicensed sales had sprung up here already in the 1830s.[61] But even if deregulation mainly formalized an already changing food economy, the vigorous takeover by private meat shops had no parallel elsewhere. Household provisioning became a genuinely localized affair, confined to one's narrowly defined home turf. With provision shops staying away from retail corridors, the daily chore of food shopping did not drag people out from their own block or street. Nor did food purveyors cluster as they once had at the public market or along the avenues under the grid plan. If one had access to multiple shops of the same type within a stone's throw distance, it was the product of dense neighborhood living: with more than a thousand people on a typical block, there was adequate customer traffic to support several businesses.

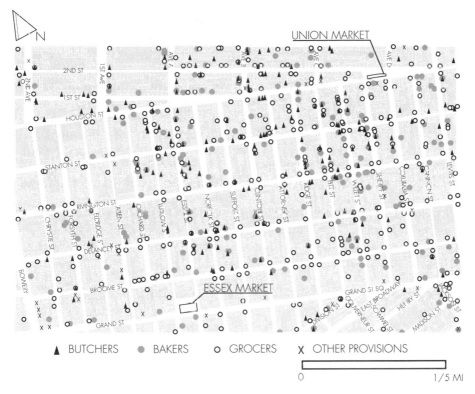

FIGURE 5.6. Provisioning in the Lower East Side, 1854. (*Sources*: See text and appendix A)

In one last step, revisiting the area of Catharine Market from chapter 4, one finds a situation halfway between Jefferson Market's complementary and the Lower East Side's competitive relations (figure 5.7). Following its history through the first quarter of the century, Catharine Market was described as a thriving business environment, one of Gotham's largest and most lucrative food emporia. The picture was not this rosy by midcentury. From one of the city's proudest marketplaces, it underwent a sharp downturn starting in the mid-1830s. Despite its numerous vendors, overall butcher rents and market fees declined to the level of medium-sized markets, while its formerly priciest stalls became relatively cheap to rent.[62] Other markets also struggled from competition in a liberalized food economy, and Catharine Market certainly did not fade into irrelevance. But whereas before it was a match to Fulton and Washington Markets, now it did not do much better than Essex, while in its profitability it also underperformed the significantly smaller Jefferson Market. Its fall from grace was lamented by De Voe himself, who, upon his 1859 visit, found the place a shadow of its past glory days and much too abandoned.[63]

What De Voe witnessed was a marketplace that struggled to stay afloat despite its vicinity's growing population, a sure sign that much of this new demand was being captured by independent retailers. The map reveals a landscape conquered by private food purveyors not unlike on the Lower East Side, although with intermittent absences in commercial blocks, especially near City Hall, Chatham Street, and the Bowery, and along the industrial waterfront stretching from Market Street north. Everywhere else, independent food shops proliferated, reconfiguring the daily routine of food shopping to the most narrowly defined neighborhood experience limited to one's block, street, and corner.

There was an important difference, however, between the two emerging working-class, immigrant districts; specifically, here groceries rather than meat shops dominated the landscape. Surely, dozens of private butcher shops opened in Catharine Market's area as well, yet their presence was not nearly as overwhelming as for the Lower East Side markets. Catharine Market managed to fend off some of the competition from its immediate environs, albeit not to the same effect as Jefferson. Nor did it lose as many of its vendors as did Essex or Union Markets, even if its sales were reduced considerably. Encroached upon by all types of provision shops, above all, hundreds of generalist grocers, competition undermined Catharine Market's formerly vast and vibrant agglomeration economy. Once a dominant marketplace that oriented the daily routines of food shopping for an area comprised of 25,000 residents, it gradually subsided into a more limited role as one of several, yet still important, places to buy provisions.[64]

In all fairness, Catharine Market's decline was a gradual development, not so much triggered but exacerbated by deregulation in 1843. As discussed in chapter 5, countless small battles, mostly about space, were occasioned here by different groups of vendors to gain or improve their access to customers, or by residents and property holders to protect themselves from the market's negative externalities.[65] The distinctive layout of Catharine Market, being confined to a narrow and crowded slip, fueled many of these debates, for space was by definition scarce, and one group's access often implied another's exclusion, just as one neighbor's convenience could be another's nuisance. Yet the same battles that through the 1820s led to workable compromises, by the late 1830s produced a stalemate. A recurring complaint about the dearth of vending space, especially for farmers and hucksters, eventually hurt Catharine Market's entire economy and made it less buoyant by the time of deregulation.[66]

Catharine Market may have rebounded had the ground around it not shifted so much. However, its problems multiplied. Groceries, dispersing

FIGURE 5.7. Provisioning near Catharine Market, 1854. (*Sources*: See text and appendix A)

across the vicinity, played an increasingly competitive role, picking up a large share of the market's trade in all foodstuffs, ranging from produce to fish and meat. Local butchers as early as the 1820s complained about unlicensed meat sales nearby.[67] Having found that "a great number of persons from the country resort with their waggons to the Bowery to dispose of mutton, veal, pork, poultry & etc.," the council back then bolstered its market laws.[68] Yet by 1841, when unlicensed meat sales were again frequent, officials no longer had the wherewithal to act.[69] Even fishmongers the next year fought in vain against "the practice heretofore of allowing persons, otherwise than Regular Fishermen, to stand in the street outside of the market for the sale of shad."[70] The patchwork of petitions available can hardly do justice to the extent to which the marketplace's monopolistic trade was already disintegrating before 1843. Deregulation accelerated and broadened this process, and while Catharine Market managed to withstand the competition from a few blocks' range, farther afield, its sales were gradually being chipped away. By 1854, the map testifies to an uneasy settlement between a still significant but retreating public market and a surging free-market economy that had its roots in informal trade.

Overall, the neighborhood close-ups presented four districts with four different environments of food access. In general, they confirmed Flagg's vision of a scattered food economy or central-place theory's premise of dispersal under low threshold and range. At the same time, in a booming and increasingly complex city, the reality on the ground became far more nuanced. The specific articulation of food retail options in each area reflected a range of intervening local conditions, including land-use patterns and residential settlement, the street layout and the grid, and the prior installment of public markets, in particular, their vitality and effectiveness in offsetting competition from a rising free-market sector with complementary business relations. The composite picture that emerges by mid-century is a fragmented and differentiated geography, in which residential location by and large determined one's options of daily food access. This was a profoundly different framework from one generation before, when New Yorkers across the city shared a common experience of provisioning their households at the local public market.

There were considerable advantages to this new geography, to be sure. Under a free-market regime, food purveyors moved closer to their customers, reducing the average distance of provisioning. Whereas earlier Pintard had walked three to four blocks to the public market, now residents could find provision shops on their own blocks or streets. Unlike Pintard, who had to observe the public market's rigid daily schedules, customers also enjoyed greater flexibility in procuring life's necessities, whether in the morning, during the day, or in the evening after work.

Further, a more differentiated food economy allowed greater specialization, whether in terms of goods, such as the city's sprawling oyster shops or the prevalence of meat shops in the Lower East Side, or in services, like the widespread practice of home delivery, more commonly available in wealthier districts.

What was sacrificed in this transition, however, was that private food shops, even if customers shopped from one store to the next, could not compare to the variety and volume of foodstuff available under the public market's agglomeration economy. In part because of its spatial and temporal constraints, the municipal model was more conducive to foster comparison shopping for price and quality. Not unrelated, but even more critical, as the food economy relocated from public to private spaces, it increasingly escaped the oversight of participating groups, especially the municipal government. Indeed, as Flagg's communiqué reveals, one decade after deregulation, more than 60 percent of private meat shops escaped registration, which does not even include street vendors and others not listed in the city directories. In other words, the new free-market economy was not only more accessible, flexible, and differentiated but was also wholly unregulated and unmonitored. It is left to chapter 6 to study the consequences.

CONCLUSION: "THE MYSTERIES OF SHOPPING" ON CATHARINE STREET

De Voe may have ended his visit to Catharine Market on a gloomy note, reminiscing about its once bustling trade and the "merry laugh, song and dance" of its celebrated black performers.[71] Yet his single-minded concern over the sorry state of Gotham's public markets, colored by his distrust of nonmarket vendors, made him miss the deeper structural forces that transformed the city's entire commercial geography, of which food vendors represented one-third of all businesses. Clearly, a burgeoning informal economy and deregulation were the key factors that propelled food retailers outside of the public markets' trade agglomerations. But this chapter has looked deeper by asking how this unregulated food economy was incorporated into New York City's broader commercial geography, in the context of accelerating urban growth, a vastly expanded and reconfigured street network, changing patterns of land use, and dynamic population movements.

What the maps have shown is that mid-nineteenth-century Gotham boasted a well-defined commercial geography with a central business district, two prominent thoroughfares, a fair number of mixed-use retail corridors, and a vast number of residential streets. All hierarchies of businesses, from banks and hotels to clothing and food shops, had to find their economically viable places within this dynamic landscape. The sale of ready-made clothing, a trade that a few decades prior did not exist, now proliferated into hundreds of stores, clustered along veritable retail streets to facilitate shopping.[72] Conversely, the main pattern for food shops was to disperse and follow customers into the heart of neighborhoods, in effect, to withdraw from Gotham's public markets and retail centers, except for the grid's avenues. When De Voe lamented the lackluster daytime traffic of Catharine Market, recalling its formerly jam-packed streets, hustle and bustle, and noise, best captured by the 1820 sketch of African American dancing contests, he made a misleading comparison, for not only had the food economy itself splintered but the center of urban public life had moved away from the marketplaces to the streets.[73]

Accounts of antebellum New York City's main thoroughfares, its vibrant street life through day and night, became common tropes for contemporaries and historians.[74] Broadway and the Bowery, the two principal avenues, are the most evoked places to illustrate the urban spectacle of promenading and shopping. Yet a metropolis like New York was furnished with different varieties and standards of public street life at different locations, some of which are less visible through descriptive sources. The earlier map in color plate 2, showing the clustering of clothing stores on Manhattan's streets, from Broadway's elegant boulevard to Orange Street's narrow path across the Five Points, conveys in one composite image the city's wide spectrum of busy pedestrian life with its differentiated consumer cultures. The map also reveals that had De Voe allowed himself a leisurely walk along Catharine Street, from the public market all the way up to Chatham Square, he would have experienced the excitement that in this neighborhood three decades earlier was Catharine Market's prerogative. This new spectacle of public street life was no longer anchored by the local food economy but thrived on Catharine Street's vibrant retail trade of dry goods.

"Is this Catharine street?" asked impatiently "a fair daughter of Erin" of her companion in the opening scene of the seductively titled sketch, *A Peep into Catharine Street, or the Mysteries of Shopping*, penned by the anonymous "late retailer" in 1846.[75] The tour began at the street's entrance from the city center as the two shoppers "turned down from Chatham square into this avenue of furniture shops, shoe shops, tin shops, cloak shops, meat shops, bread shops, candy shops, crockery shops, pawnbroker's shops, segar shops, hat shops, dry-goods shops, groceries, and markets."[76] Tellingly, Catharine Market was not explicitly featured; only chance remarks hinted at its existence. At the same time, the author took every opportunity to exhibit the frenzy of shopping on Catharine Street. "It is no wonder that the lady was astonished," he noted, "for such a conglomeration of merchandise of every sort and description cannot be found jumbled together in the same space any where else in this great metropolis."[77]

Speaking of trade agglomeration, the late retailer explained how "the crowd that is continually passing, jostling, dodging, and buffeting, is fully answerable to the vast mass of wares and goods crammed into every building, and oozing out of every window, crevice, loophole, and door . . . to the seekers after bargains that perpetually haunt this quarter."[78] He used the same hyperbolic language when referring to Catharine Street shoppers, whom he described as

> specimens of every kindred, tribe, tongue and people, on the face of the earth. . . . The Esquimaux and the Hottentot, the Arab and the Mexican, the Tuscarora and the Tartar, the European and the Alleghanian, the Jew and the Greek, may all be found, from time to time, loitering and bantering, jabbering and bargaining, with a degree of ardor and enthusiasm . . . in the mysteries of this chaos of merchandise.[79]

This was, no doubt, highly inflated prose, for Catharine Street was not by any measure New York's most vibrant retail center. Its business agglomeration, both in breadth and depth, paled in comparison to the nearby Bowery, for example. Nor did the majority of shoppers come here from all over the city. If their looks, accents, and customs revealed their diverse backgrounds, mocked by the author in a set of prejudiced anecdotes about different ethnicities of shoppers, it was because New York by then had embarked on a new age of mass immigration, and the area around Catharine Street had one of the city's highest number of immigrants. By all accounts, Catharine Street was primarily a neighborhood center, frequented mainly by shoppers living in the surrounding wards. It had a dynamic economy with an impressive number and array of shops, yet it was also quite local and average in character, which makes the comparison to Catharine Market all the more appropriate.

To be fair, the late retailer's boasting of all kinds of trade on Catharine Street was more grounded in reality.[80] For its entire length of 1,800 feet, the 1851 street directory tallied an impressive 137 stores and services, nearly all of them occupying the ground floor of two- to three-story brick or frame residential buildings.[81] With its continuous storefronts, paved sidewalks, gas lighting, and one omnibus line, it offered an accessible and suitable place for strolling and comparison shopping.[82] Approaching from the center (color plate 4), the late retailer's fictitious shoppers chanced upon a three-block stretch of dry goods stores, Catharine Street's most copious businesses, selling all kinds of fabric. Furniture and other homeware shops, extending from Chatham Street's concentration in that industry, also spilled over here. Stores selling all types of ready-made clothing were available along the street, but especially on its lower section near Catharine Market. This still important public market continued to dominate Catharine Slip all the way down to the ferry. Additionally, private provision shops, more limited in number, were spread evenly, and hotels, boardinghouses, or services, including a pawnshop and a barbershop, were similarly dispersed. The overall effect was a par excellence retail corridor that pulled together all varieties of stores, even specializing in certain trades, albeit at a modest scale and quality, thereby reflecting the social composition of its surroundings.

Perhaps most intriguing is how new this geography was, a point not lost to the late retailer. "Twenty years ago, before Catharine street came in vogue, Chatham square was the head-quarters of dry goods at retail in the eastern portion of the metropolis, from which the Bowery, Division, Catharine and Pearl streets radiated with their modicum of trade," he stated matter-of-factly.[83] Back then, Catharine Street was little more than a residential address, except for Catharine Market, of course, where the commercial life of the area concentrated. In fact, the whole endeavor of wandering from shop to shop would have been foreign to the late retailer's customers from just one generation earlier. "Then there was very little . . . of what is termed shopping and *cheapening* goods. Every dealer had his customers, who sent their orders or came to him as regularly . . . as to their butcher or baker."[84] This was a simpler time, when "the merchant knew his customers as his friends, and the feeling was reciprocal."[85]

About his present circumstances, the late retailer felt more conflicted. His guide switched back and forth between the excitements of shopping on Catharine Street and the deceitful practices he believed this new spectacle fostered. Much to his amazement, built environment and social customs both had changed to accommodate strolling and shopping. To his anxiety, the new landscape generated cutthroat competition, pushing prices down to cost-levels and dragging businesses into a whirlpool of quick returns and fraudulent credits, in general undermining "the morale of shopping."[86] Above all, he moaned how the retailer no longer could count on "regular customers" but relied entirely on "shoppers," requiring him to compete for a "portion of the fluctuating current of trade, upon which alone his bark must ride or be for ever wrecked."[87] To catch customers, a whole compendium of "baits" were being deployed, such as the "tasteful display of the windows, the exhibition of cheap articles at the doors, and the pressing invitations to walk in; being practiced by all."[88]

Inside the store, the adventure continued. Again, the late retailer spared no verbal flourishes when likening shopping to a "contest of knavery between buyer and seller, in which the greater quantity of villainous acuteness is certain to triumph."[89] He was wary of "the one price system," which, in reality, he claimed, meant that retailers charged a different price with each customer, depending on what they thought he or she could afford.[90] Shopping on Catharine Street resembled a game, with the buyer and seller trying to outsmart each other. Illustrating the point, he offered several catchy anecdotes: that of the "Stocking Hunter," who kept taxing his patience for four months, probing his entire stock of hosiery daily, to finally make a purchase just a week before passing away; that of "the bevy of Hibernians numbering three fine athletic fellows," who in their pursuit of a black cloth for a coat, and insisting on "the best," rejected every sensible choice, only to be subjected to the storekeeper's hoax of being offered an inferior piece at excessive price, which they seized upon, "for an Irishman's idea of the value of any article of merchandise is suggested by the price demanded alone"; or that of a "dashing young gentleman," who having journeyed to New York to acquire "his nuptial outfit," and lacking a vest, refused every "shown silks and satins, marseilles and embroideries, velvets and cashmeres," eventually to leave the store with "a yard of Russia Diaper, worth *one shilling*."[91]

Each step along the way, moves and countermoves were made in the exploits of shopping, at least in the late retailer's account. The merchant was challenged by shoppers who combed through his entire stock of goods, evoking the lower prices, higher quality, or wider selection of neighboring stores. In turn, he took advantage of green customers by selling them items at inflated prices or at short measure. To be sure, this was a highly opinionated picture, more a hyperbole than an accurate portrayal. When painted with a lighter tone, it conveyed a genuine sense of the excitement that permeated this working-class promenade, whether people came here to shop or to enjoy the spectacle. When it leaned toward criticism and mockery, it revealed the narrator's own discomfort with a new world of trade defined by intense competition, probing shoppers, and cunning sales practices. Much of this uneasiness derived from the author's fixation on competition. In fact, he generally overlooked the street's many complementarities, whereby each and every store generated additional traffic to its neighbors by virtue of their agglomeration.

On this last point, Catharine Street closely mirrored Catharine Market in its heyday, when in an earlier time that public market anchored the vibrant commercial and public life of its neighborhood, attracting thousands daily into its business magnet. Admittedly, the specifics were less similar, for Catharine Street focused on different sectors, largely bypassing the food trade. Moreover, it was the product of a free-market economy, whereas Catharine Market had prospered under the guiding hand of the municipal government. Besides, it presented a different geography in its physical layout by virtue of being a street on which to stroll rather than a plaza on which to congregate. Overall, Catharine Street was the neighborhood variant of New York City's evolving geography of public life, increasingly more centered on the various commercial streets. By all means, it was a humble and quotidian place, where each store played its small part to constitute a vibrant public space of local commerce and shopping. And just as "dancing for eels" at Catharine Market had vanished as the defining public performance of one generation ago, so Catharine Street attracted residents and customers from beyond the area to participate in its new spectacle of the "mysteries of shopping."

CHAPTER 6

The Price of Deregulation

Food Access and Living Standards

UNFIT FOR HUMAN SUSTENANCE

After nine months of arduous research, in January 1865, the Council of Hygiene and Public Health of the Citizens' Association of New York published its landmark report on the sanitary condition of the city.[1] Regarded by many as the most important public health document of the period, the report ushered in a momentum of reform in the postbellum era, setting New York on a new course of municipal activism in public health. The survey was a product of its time. Like its parallels in America or abroad, it was overly concerned with environmental conditions and fixated on tenement housing and sanitation, and even in these areas, its proposed reforms were limited to regulating housing markets and land use while boosting municipal investments and oversight of sanitary infrastructures.[2]

Still, the document was a tremendous intellectual achievement, representing the culmination of decades of public health thinking and the consolidation of a reform agenda that eventually made a difference in reversing soaring mortality. The report also provides an entry point to situate the geography of an unregulated food economy within broader issues of urban living standards. Two themes stand out. First, the report followed an analytical process that was fundamentally spatial. Second, it treated food access tangentially and as a matter of nuisance only, revealing how by the 1860s provisioning had been marginalized by housing and sanitation from the key areas of urban public policy.[3]

Take first the point about a geographic approach. The sanitary report represents a systematic application of what may be called "data-driven mapping" in terms of its method and reasoning. The physicians involved did not break new ground but stood on the shoulders of an earlier generation of "sanitarians," who had fielded similar surveys of this and other cities, compiling, charting, and comparing environmental data to establish correlations between sanitary conditions and disease. Where the

1865 sanitary report stood out was in the scale, comprehensiveness, and detail in which it sought to canvass Gotham's sprawling and unintelligible landscape.

At the outset, the entire research design centered on finding a balance between the mandates of a "thorough and systematic sanitary inspection."[4] While the main objective was to collect "accurate information concerning the sanitary condition of every portion of the city," the report was also "to leave no cause of unhealthiness and no existing disease undiscovered and uninvestigated."[5] Accordingly, Manhattan's built-up territory was divided into twenty-nine roughly equal-sized areas, each assigned to a sanitary inspector with a medical degree.[6] They were to survey their districts from one end to the other, moving ahead systematically block by block.[7]

Blocks, or "squares" as they were called, were singled out as the elemental units of spatial analysis.[8] "Streets, courts and alleys" were not to be neglected either, and constituted a second layer.[9] Zooming onto the site of residence, the "house" layer represented a third spatial unit, to be inspected much like the block, by moving progressively inward: from the lot, to the specific buildings, their interior spaces, even by individual floors and homes if warranted.[10] The public health risks to be surveyed were then tied to the specific locations, ascertaining that they were to a large degree preventable if only the residents and the municipal government would clean up these places.[11]

The intuition to clean up the mess Gotham had become was well founded, even if the underlying medical reasoning was flawed. Chasing effluvia and miasmas across the city pushed inspectors to focus on a compendium of interrelated issues.[12] Not surprisingly, anything linked to drainage and sanitation was to be scrutinized.[13] Housing conditions were to be surveyed meticulously, with special attention to tenements, the main culprit of the era.[14] Further, a whole variety of nuisances were to be recorded, from liquor shops to factories and food-related trades, including stores and markets, and slaughterhouses in particular.[15] These massive data were then to be cross-examined against local population characteristics, treating the built, social, and moral environments as inseparable.

The entire enterprise, of course, was by definition overambitious in both design and execution. Inasmuch as the survey sought to expose extreme sanitary hazards, the inspectors delivered such finds in profusion.[16] Yet no matter how much the survey design tried to control for the potential pitfall of generating massive amounts of disparate data, many months of fieldwork conducted by thirty-one physicians, with varying levels of competence and dedication, produced an eclectic report.[17] This becomes evident when comparing its two tomes. The first part, which made general observations about the whole city, spoke with a unified voice, hammering home the familiar points about Gotham's excessive and uneven mortality and the preventable causes of disease and their environmental origins, followed by policy recommendations centering on one message: to clean up the city.[18] The second part, presenting the bulk of the empirical evidence, is a much longer compilation of district-level surveys containing some impressively detailed studies,[19] and more hastily produced ones.[20]

More pertinent to the book, the report's environmentalist premise sidelined the subject of food access, which was relegated to the category of nuisance, arguably the only way in which urban policy by the mid-nineteenth century could recognize the issue. Certainly, the inspectors were asked to survey markets, groceries, and slaughterhouses, and register when these presented sanitary hazards. But this was a halfhearted effort, except for the council's assault on private slaughtering, which revived an older tradition of nuisance laws and decades of complaints by health officials.[21]

A handful of comments communicate some awareness that the sanitary report overlooked an important area. In its account of "special nuisances," the report complained about the lack of any regulation, and called upon the "faithful inspection of . . . food articles previous to their being offered in market."[22] Two decades past the deregulation of the 1840s, sanitarians finally asked for a "reform of the whole system of supplying animal food," and for the government "to regulate the butcheries and the market system."[23] Yet in the same breath the council excused itself from further assertions, for it "is not called upon to give the details relating to the gross impositions and the sources of evil that are inflicted by . . . the absence of control of the sanitary condition of slaughtered animals and food articles."[24] The omission is telling since the report concedes "that animals variously diseased, and meats variously injured for use as food, are sold daily to the unsuspecting multitudes who purchase in the established markets of the city, and to the still greater numbers who depend upon the thousand minor shambles that are found in all populous districts."[25] Apparently, food provisioning had fallen into the blind spot of municipal governance.

Some of the inspectors found it frustrating to leave such an important health issue inadequately treated. Fourth District inspector Ezra R. Pulling set the tone when he complained that "the quality of the food sold at the corner groceries and butchers' shops in this neighborhood deserves a more extended notice than it can receive here." He then bluntly stated that "a casual examination shows much of it to be unfit for human sustenance."[26] His concerns were echoed by others, including Twentieth District inspector E. H. Janes, who warned that "another cause of disease which deserves particular attention from our authorities, is the inferior quality of food used by the poor."[27] Likewise, Seventeenth District inspector Guido Furman fretted about "the ill-effects which followed the use of such articles of diet," then swiftly referred to the observations of Twenty-Fifth District inspector J. Lewis Smith.[28] Smith, in turn, mainly remarked on the survey's neglect of this "subject which has not received the attention it deserves; but enough is known to lead to the belief that improper or insufficient food is a cause of impaired health and of disease among the poor."[29]

Maybe enough was known casually. Yet the report that fashioned itself as the first systematic and exhaustive account of Gotham's public health environment left the subject of food access to an incomplete survey of "nuisances." Nor has historical scholarship made a concerted effort to expand our knowledge of unequal housing and sanitary conditions to the third basic necessity of food supplies in a rapidly changing city. The purpose of this chapter is to write food access in an unregulated environment back into our understanding of mid-nineteenth-century urban living standards.[30] Fieldwork and social geography were the approaches pursued by public health experts. The method here is to exploit new resources with digital mapping. The central question is how did food access shape living standards in a metropolis experiencing rapid growth, rising inequalities, and intensifying segregation? Further, how did unequal access to provisions map onto the more familiar inequalities of housing, sanitation, and disease conditions? The subject is complex, and at each intersection, from issues of quantity to distribution and quality, the historical record is patchy. But posing a new set of questions and proposing new answers is a step in the right direction.

SUPPLY CONDITIONS

The best place to start the discussion is to assess how the city's supply conditions changed, thus bringing the earlier analysis of this subject into the middle of the nineteenth century. In chapter 2, new meat consumption estimates were introduced to document the abundant food supplies of New Yorkers in the Early Republic. The objective here is similar, but taking the same approach is not possible given the context of an unregulated food economy and the fewer sources on meat consumption available. Fortunately, national-level estimates, generated by the rich economic historical literature concerned with the antebellum puzzle, offer points of reference.

It will be convenient to offer a brief outline of the antebellum puzzle. The term refers to a fascinating debate about the period's surprising combination of economic growth and rising per capita income on the one hand and deteriorating biological standards of living, specifically declining physical stature and rising mortality, on the other.[31] Thirty years of scholarship by economic historians has produced a general consensus about the phenomenon, with two principal lines of explanation. First, the nutritional thesis pioneered by John Komlos asserts that dietary standards, above all, the amount of protein consumed at early ages, have a significant influence on adult physical stature.[32] Komlos's discovery was that "after 1839, average calorie and protein intake declined and did not reach its earlier level again until the 1870s."[33] Additional data on food consumption have corroborated the discovery that nutritional conditions generally worsened in antebellum America in all varieties of foodstuff.[34] This negative trend is by now firmly established and widely regarded as one key explanation of declining stature.

A second line of reasoning pursued by Michael Haines and others grounded this original discussion more broadly within the context of mortality and disease environments. On this point, the approach is more akin to the conversations of nineteenth-century sanitarians. Most important, worsening mortality rates have been convincingly linked to intensifying urbanization.[35] Additionally, urbanization and increasing mortality themselves were found to contribute to declining stature, demonstrating the accumulating challenges to citizens' biological well-being by a variety of structural factors, ranging from nutrition to the urban transition.[36] The "antebellum puzzle," Haines and his coauthors declare, "resulted from a complex set of factors, including urbanization, increased population mobility, worsening mortality conditions, greater contact via improved transport infrastructure, and deteriorating nutrition."[37]

While the individual causal mechanisms merit careful attention, they are not the subject of this book. What matters here is the recognition that urban dwellers faced twin pressures from deteriorating disease environments and generally worsening conditions of food access. The relationship between the two is most relevant. Consumption estimates by Komlos and others help extend the previous analysis of Early Republican supply conditions to this later, more sparsely documented period. Soaring mortality was by no means unknown to contemporaries, as the sanitary report attests. Likewise, a rich body of scholarship has shown that population concentration in cities adversely affected life expectancy until public health reform was able to reverse the trends from the latter half of the nineteenth century.[38] What remains to be explored more closely is how food access and urban environments interacted to put residents' living standards under strain.

Do the sources on antebellum New Yorkers confirm the consensus of economic historians on nationally declining meat consumption rates? One challenge is that the council's decision to shift tax collection from excise to rents, coupled with the deregulation of municipal provisioning markets, resulted in generally lesser documentation of Gotham's meat supplies. Table 6.1 pulls together all relevant sources, comparing average per

TABLE 6.1. Per Capita Butcher's Meat Consumption in New York City and the United States (lbs.), 1790–1859

Years	NYC Butcher's meats					USA (Komlos) Production				Consumption	USA (Floud et al.) Production			
	Beef	Veal	Lamb & Mutton	Fresh Pork	Total	Beef	Mutton	All Pork	Total	Total	Beef & Veal	Mutton	All Pork	Total
1790–1818	89.4	18.9	32.9	13.0	154.3									
1836	88.2													
1837	69.9													
1838	62.4													
1839						79	18	142	239	213	78.70	1.17	130.25	210.12
1842	69.9	12.3	20.9	7.8	111.0									
1849						72	14	121	207	194	71.09	1.42	116.91	189.42
1859						73	11	99	183	181	73.07	1.82	106.93	181.82

Sources: Figures for NYC: Table 2.1, appendix B, and note 39; for USA: Komlos, "The Height and Weight," 913, table 9; Floud et al., 310, table 6.4.

capita consumption rates for the three decades between 1790 and 1818 to the sporadic data points available until deregulation did away with reliable recording of local meat sales and slaughter rates. Additionally, national-level estimates from the federal censuses are included, with the caveat that these refer to the entire nation, not only New York City.[39]

The table confirms that New Yorkers' meat consumption standards underwent a declining trajectory in the antebellum period, indicating a considerable drop of 20–30 percent between the Early Republican figures and the 1842 rates. Importantly, 1842 was also the final year of a severe recessionary cycle, which began in 1837. Looking at beef specifically, one finds evidence that households forsook a significant portion of their customary consumption standards, with rates dipping from an estimated 88.2 pounds in 1836, to 62.4 pounds in 1838, and still remaining at 69.9 pounds in 1842.[40] The decline appears slightly higher for the other butcher's meats of fresh veal, mutton, and pork, which is understandable, for beef was a staple of urban diets. While Komlos had no prerecessionary data, he nonetheless hinted at some degree of causation, suggesting that the recession may have triggered, or at least exacerbated, declining dietary standards.[41]

Assessing the role of the recession is not easy, given the fragmentary nature of the evidence. On the one hand, beef consumption rates for New York City give credence to the view that the recession was to blame for declining meat consumption. Further corroborating this, annual rents collected from the market butchers underwent a parallel downward trend between 1835 and 1842, as shown in figure 6.1.[42] That butchers became more unwilling or unable to pay their regular stall rents to the council strongly suggests that the industry was struggling as a consequence of plunging sales in a recessionary period. With slightly different chronology, the two sources point to the same conclusion that the recession of 1837–43 must have exerted a significant downward pressure on New Yorkers' provisioning standards.[43]

On the other hand, it is highly unlikely that the recession alone was to blame for worsening dietary standards, since in that case consumption rates should have rebounded. As table 6.1 shows, that did not happen. The discussion here needs to turn to Komlos's research for national-level data, which more recently have been substantiated by similar estimates by Roderick Floud et al. Importantly, the New York City figures line up well with both sets of meat consumption figures.[44] Comparing the New York and national data shows that consumption standards shifted to lower equilibria across all species of meat after the recession. Indeed, total consumption appears to have declined by another 15 percent in the next two decades relative to its already low point in 1839.[45] Overall, the records indicate that Early Republican city dwellers ate about 20 to 30 percent

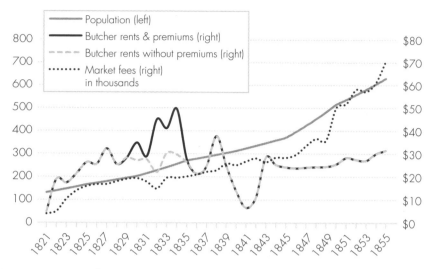

FIGURE 6.1. Market revenues, 1821–55. (*Sources*: See text, note 42, and appendix B)

more meat than the antebellum generations. This was no doubt a substantial decline, further aggravated by the recession. However, its persistence after 1843, a period when the American economy experienced an expansionary cycle for nearly two decades, points to a long-term shift in the supply curve, rather than falling demand as the main culprit for deteriorating nutritional standards.[46]

The logical place to turn for clarification on suspected supply pressures is price data, reminiscent of the approach taken in figure 2.2.[47] Looking at figure 6.2, two periods punctuated by the recession of 1837–43 can be distinguished. First, from the 1820s until the early 1830s, meat prices were generally stable, while industrial prices declined modestly, with the result that the relative price of meat to industrial goods climbed moderately. This stability came to an end by the mid-1830s, when meat prices soared to reach a plateau early in the recession, even as industrial prices remained mostly unchanged, resulting in rapidly appreciating relative meat prices. Finally, as the recession deepened, meat prices nose-dived to stabilize again for a few years in 1842. In the second period, from the mid-1840s to the Civil War, two trends already imminent before the recession became prominent. Relatively stable industrial prices were now coupled with persistently rising meat prices until 1857, that is, the start of another recession. The resulting rise in the relative price of meat was the continuation of the earlier trajectory from the mid-1830s, interrupted only temporarily by the recession. Extending the analysis to grains and fish, figure 6.3 points to parallel trends, only with lesser volatility, sug-

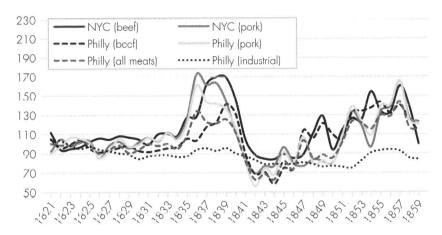

FIGURE 6.2. Wholesale price indexes, part 1 (base years: 1821–25), 1821–59. (*Sources*: See text and note 47)

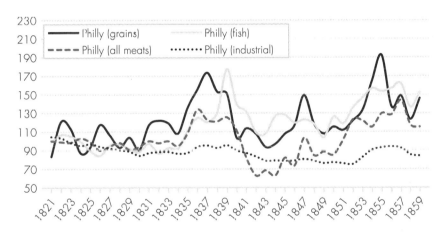

FIGURE 6.3. Wholesale price indexes, part 2 (base years: 1821–25), 1821–59. (*Sources*: See text and note 47)

gesting that the main development of appreciating real and relative food prices from the mid-1830s to the Civil War was prominent for all commodities.

The two figures substantiate the earlier points about intensifying pressures on the nutritional standards of city dwellers. They show that the recession did not trigger but rather exacerbated an already declining trend in meat consumption, which was, in turn, driven mainly by unfavorable supply conditions. Market officials in New York City shared this view when in December 1839, in the middle of the recession, they still blamed the "late high prices of beef" on "the scarcity of the supply."[48] The recession surely did its part, requiring households to cut back significantly on their food expenses, most likely by substituting cheaper carbohydrates or fish for meat, as indicated by the lesser drop in those prices. With weakening demand, prices eventually had to fall, but this could last only until the recovery took hold. At that point, the same supply pressures asserted themselves, pushing up both real and relative food prices. In sum, meat consumption was dragged down on the demand side during the recession. More important, it was squeezed by structural factors from the supply side with long-lasting effects.

Assessing the evidence leads to the conclusion that from the 1830s through the Civil War, urban demand for meat and other foodstuff in New York and elsewhere outpaced the supplies available. Even as new transportation technologies, in particular, canals and railroads, linked cities to expanding hinterlands, agricultural output failed to keep up with urbanization. At a time when mass immigration pushed New York City's population over 800,000 and Philadelphia's close to 600,000, it was inevitable that urban provision markets came under supply pressures. As Floud et al. conclude, "rapid population growth by urbanization and immigration had fettered food supplies per capita for major foodstuffs."[49] Yet there is no need to exaggerate the impact of this shift in the supply curve, for per capita meat consumption remained high by any international standard, since its decline occurred from a historically high base.[50] Even so, the key point remains that, judged against the favorable conditions of the Early Republican period, antebellum New Yorkers found it more challenging to sustain their provisioning standards.

LAYERS OF INEQUALITY

Establishing that supply conditions became generally less favorable provides basic context. Yet this point needs further scrutiny on two closely related grounds: food distribution and quality. After all, what did it mean that New Yorkers on average experienced mounting pressures in their consumption standards at a period when income disparities were rising, and urban expansion was producing increasingly segregated housing markets and disease environments?[51] In a deregulated economy, in which government oversight was fading, access to food acquired widely different circumstances depending on one's neighborhood and social status. Supply pressures did not affect all areas and residents to the same extent. Interrogating how food access mapped onto Gotham's deeply stratified social geography moves the analysis toward a more nuanced evaluation of the role of provisioning in mid nineteenth century living standards.

The following discussion completes the mapping analyses of chapters 2 and 5 both chronologically and thematically. A range of issues are examined, in particular, local demand and population density, residential segregation by class, housing and disease environments, and immigration and ethnic clustering. The analysis proceeds through the layering of spatial patterns, seeking out similarities between local conditions of food access and the surrounding socioeconomic and built environments. The assumption is that finding geographic association between two distinct phenomena may indicate their significant connections, possibly even causal relations. It is left to informed interpretation to uncover the mechanisms at work, avoiding the pitfall of spurious correlations. Still, mapping analysis presents the only systematic approach to situate food access within its thick socioeconomic context in order to reveal a key but understudied source of urban inequality.

To appreciate the weight of the matter, one should consider as a point of reference that working-class families in the second half of the nineteenth century devoted a much greater share—easily one-half of their income—to food than they did to any other basic necessity, including housing.[52] Certainly, New York was, and has ever been, a distinctive place, for in America's largest, densest, and fastest growing city, rents were exceptionally high, and, just as in the case of prices, they increased robustly after the recovery in 1843.[53] Yet no matter how much working-class New Yorkers felt squeezed by soaring rents, expenditures on food amounted to a greater portion of their budgets. This point is not meant to dispute contemporaries' or scholars' insistence on the centrality of housing, for that condition was inextricably tied to the most basic inequalities of urban life, above all, to uneven exposure to health risks. The objective here is rather to incorporate food access into the broader conversation about nineteenth-century urban living standards.

Further, the analysis is reminiscent of the sanitary report's ambition to canvass the entire city for its complex interplay of living and public health conditions. Mapping analysis presents the advantages of a comprehensive and bird's-eye view, which the surveyors themselves could not have. Complementing this picture of broad strokes and patterns with details from the ground, the discussion draws on the surveyors' comments on food-related issues, even if their inquiry into the subject remained fragmentary and fixated on matters of nuisance. Still, the two accounts of data-driven mapping and fieldwork-based anecdotes allow for cross-examining findings.

Moving from one layer to another, a population density map offers a good starting point for the analysis. Density provides an indirect measure of local demand while also serving as a proxy for socioeconomic status. Chapter 5 established that in the antebellum decades, the public market system not only lost ground to private food shops but also became inadequate in distributing supplies to residents. The once strong association between the municipal markets' volume of trade and their catchment areas' population density gradually vanished by the mid-nineteenth century. The flipside was that more private sector retailers moved into those areas where public markets were now lacking or retreating. In effect, the period witnessed a general but uneven transition from public to private sector provisioning. It remains to be seen how the proliferation of food shops reflected local population densities. Considering the smaller catchment areas of grocers, butchers, or bakers, density also has to be reexamined at the smaller spatial unit of blocks instead of wards. Fortunately, the Perris Atlas of 1852–54 makes it possible to derive block-level population estimates, and to develop a residential density map of Manhattan in fine detail for this early period.

Color plate 5 compares block-level population densities to the concentration of food retailers, including grocers, meat shops, and bakers, in 1854.[54] Given their small range, one expects a close association between the distribution of suppliers and local demand, albeit this does not need to be perfect since individual shops may have handled different volumes of sales. Indeed, such a relationship appears on the maps. Specifically, peaks in the concentration of groceries correspond to the most densely inhabited districts, above all, wards 4 and 6 and to a lesser degree the Lower East Side. Another area with a large number of retail grocers coincides with downtown's single surviving residential zone by the western rim of ward 1. As for smaller pockets where groceries are more numerous than residential density would imply, along the commercial waterfront or nearby industrial plants farther north, local agglomeration effects likely derived from wholesale trade linkages.

The relationship between density and the distribution of meat shops is less evident. It manifests clearly for the Lower East Side, but barely at all for the equally densely inhabited blocks of wards 4 and 6. Elsewhere the association holds, although it is interrupted by the public markets. Specifically, west of the Bowery, market butchers managed to fend off some of the competition from meat shops in the adjacent blocks. For bakeries the situation falls in between, prevalent in the Lower East Side but less so in wards 4 and 6. Tellingly, there is one uniform pattern across all three maps: the absence of provision shops in one large and contiguous area, north of Washington Square between Third and Sixth Avenues. Population densities were among the lowest here. Yet these were also some of the most clustered single-use residential districts, and other areas with similar densities warranted the presence of many food vendors.

At first look, population density appears to be a reasonably good predictor of the geography of food access. In an unregulated food economy, it seems, market mechanisms by and large allocated supplies to where there was demand, and without the "bungling hand of government." At the same time, discrepancies in how density and suppliers were aligned are equally suggestive. For instance, how to explain the complete lack of food shops in one large area inhabited by more than a hundred thousand people? Likewise, how to account for different geographies between the three key sectors of the provision trade? In chapter 5, the analysis approached the subject from the supply side, probing the local equilibria of competitive and complementary relations. The focus here is on differential demand, and on this point density alone is a rigid yardstick, for consumption standards, whether considering quantity, quality, affordability, or the types of provisions purchased, varied by the socioeconomic, ethnic, or cultural backgrounds of local residents.

Take first the issue of class, or more accurately, income differentials. A population density map provides an appraisal of the socioeconomic geography of antebellum New York. In a mid-nineteenth-century city, density was among the strongest indicators of unequal health risks. With building heights not exceeding four to five stories, high density by necessity meant crowded living conditions, typically in tenement-type dwellings with scanty to nonexistent sanitary installations. More than a quarter century had passed since elite New Yorkers had sought out densely developed downtown districts for their residences. By the 1830s and especially in the postrecession boom, they relocated north, favoring exclusive residential enclaves with better-quality dwellings and modern amenities, leaving behind the city's central districts with their jumble of older decaying housing and purpose-built tenements.[55] The resulting bifurcation of housing markets is well known to historians.[56] Similarly, how crowding was closely tied to public health risks was self-evident to contemporary sanitarians. The density map offers a quick systematic grasp of this geography.[57]

In an effort to associate density more closely with class, color plate 6 compares the distribution of all provision shops to the residential patterns of different occupational groups.[58] Given New York's widening mortality gap, one's best health insurance policy was to reside in an exclusive neighborhood, with less density and crowding, superior housing stock furnished with modern water and sewer connections, situated on land with good drainage, and at a safe distance from nuisances.[59] At least, this was the wisdom of the time and the premise of the sanitary report, and, for the most part, has been confirmed by scholarship. Clearly, the price to be paid for healthier accommodation was homeownership or higher rents. Looking at the distribution of different occupations of residents provides a picture of New York City's intensifying class divisions of space.

At a glimpse, the degree of residential segregation between upper-, lower-middle, and working-class citizens is strikingly clear. More to the point, the strong association between these residential patterns and density is evident. Elite New Yorkers, represented here by bankers, merchants, lawyers, and brokers, overwhelmingly lived in the city's north-central districts. Below them in the social hierarchy, clerks and shopkeepers, including tailors and food vendors, generally dispersed but by and large remained underrepresented in the most exclusive areas, which they could seldom afford, or conversely, the most densely populated or industrial ones, which they tried to avoid. Finally, laborers mostly resided in tenement areas developing around low-lying industrial zones along the riverfronts, as well as central and Lower Manhattan's densely packed neighborhoods, in particular, large parts of wards 4, 6, and 7, the Lower East Side, and the western rim of ward 1. It is in fact remarkable how much working-class status corresponded to living in high-density or in mixed-use areas near industrial plants, and, conversely, how elite status warranted low-density living in single-use residential enclaves.

Back to provisioning, chapter 5's interpretation of the absence of food purveyors between Third and Sixth Avenues north of Washington Square is now corroborated by the maps. Elite New Yorkers did not tolerate industrial facilities and retail shops amid their elegant dwellings, especially if the factories and shops represented a potential nuisance. The lack of food retailers in these exclusive enclaves did not imply poorly supplied households. For one extra block of distance, easily overcome by the labor of domestics and the burgeoning custom of home delivery from Jefferson and Tompkins Markets or similar upscale shops, all nuisances related to the food industry were effectively zoned out. Residents did not have to put up with the transport and unloading of supplies, their storage and preparation, the removal of garbage and waste from the premises, or the presence of offensive odors that often accompanied these activities, especially in the case of perishable food like fresh meat or fish. To what extent local provisioning conditions amounted to a public health advantage is difficult to determine. But it must have made some difference that restrictive covenants excluded nearly all nuisances, yet without jeopardizing food access. Indeed, sanitary inspectors seldom recorded "special nuisances," food related or otherwise, in these wealthy areas.

Nor should the opposite situation of intense concentrations of food retailers in high-density areas be interpreted as evidence of access to plentiful and healthy food supplies. In a city deeply divided by class, omnipresent food shops lining the ground floor of crowded tenement blocks were less the evidence of well-working provision markets than of highly segmented ones, whereby environmentally disadvantaged neighborhoods were also relegated to the risky terrain of low-end, low-quality food options. The density of stores offers an inadequate indicator of the local availability of supplies, for it does not account for differences in the stores' volume and quality of sales. The proliferation of food purveyors in these crowded districts was driven by a combination of two factors: booming populations that generated greater demand and lower incomes that pushed local food markets to the bottom end of the scale.

Working-class areas were ripe for the small-scale operations of typically immigrant entrepreneurs who took advantage of the low-capital threshold needed to open a store in the industry. Intense competition transformed local provisioning landscapes by undercutting trade, such as at Catharine Market, or drastically diminishing it, such as at Union or Essex Markets. Elsewhere, small shops mushroomed in the midst of newly emerging tenement blocks. Selling cheaply, in smaller quantities and at lower quality, was a common strategy among food purveyors in these low-income areas, because prices mattered so much more to their customers. Local residents may have found several provision shops at a stone's throw, but the selection and quality of their goods paled in comparison to those of Jefferson Market and other upscale stores serving wealthier uptown citizens. Besides, as both contemporaries and scholars have pointed out, some of the groceries operating out of tenement buildings were, more than anything, liquor shops, selling provisions on the side.[60]

To what extent food consumption standards differed by income is hard to tell with precision, but this could only manifest in two principal ways. On the one hand, poorer New Yorkers could afford to eat lesser amounts. Soaring food prices that depressed city dwellers' per capita consumption standards in the antebellum decades by necessity exerted a much heavier downward pressure on the food budgets of low-income households.[61] In other words, the caloric intake of working-class New Yorkers must have compared unfavorably, not only to better-off citizens at the time but also to laboring people from a generation earlier.

On the other hand, lower-income residents could stretch their food budgets by buying cheaper, lower-quality provisions. Quality is a complex subject, with at least two different meanings. It can refer to customers' preferences for certain goods versus others, a standard that may have little to do with more objective criteria related to health. Butcher's meat provides a useful example, where a clear hierarchy between different qualities of cuts set wealthier and poorer consumers apart. De Voe's *The Market Assistant* attests to the strict status ranking of the different cuts of beef, New Yorkers' main source of protein.[62] Leaving details aside, the general rule of thumb was that better-off New Yorkers were more likely to purchase boneless, tender, and more flavorful cuts, which they usually ate as roasts or steaks, whereas poorer residents depended on tougher, leaner, bonier pieces prepared mostly in stews and soups. The same logic applied to other butcher's meats as well, including veal, mutton and lamb, or fresh pork. These distinctions, while certainly meaningful, had little to do with the health standards of citizens.

The other meaning of quality, frequently commented upon and more pertinent to the discussion, refers to the wholesomeness of provisions. This was at the heart of the traditional market laws, which established the market monopoly of meat along with other less-intrusive quality enforcements and fair trade regulations, in an effort to uphold the public good of citizens' access to food. This was also the central theme of the butchers' protests against deregulation. Whether or not their resistance was motivated by rent-seeking or a principled protection of basic food standards, the notion that public markets were the central pillar of public health, the only line of defense safeguarding customers from the health risks of unwholesome supplies, was a widely used argument.

Never shy to exploit hyperbolic language, in February 1840, for example, the butchers accused deregulators with aiming "to break down every barrier, and destroy every guard that the law has erected for the preservation of peace, health and morality."[63] In a more sober tone, but arguing the same point, the Market Committee endorsed their petition: "It is unnecessary to enter into a full discussion of the effect of an unregulated pursuit of the business of butchers upon the public health and convenience." Only if police regulations are fully carried out, "slaughter houses be removed entirely out of the populated parts of the city," and "all meats offered for sale undergo a proper supervision, as in other large cities in Europe," they reasoned, could the market laws be abolished without harmful consequences to public health.[64]

To the critics' credit, deregulation was not complemented by any reform to rein in potential health risks from unwholesome supplies or insalubrious retail practices. Instead, caveat emptor—"let the buyer beware"—and the invisible hand had their ways. Even as provision stores multiplied, the council lacked the additional police power to keep track of them, not to mention to monitor their sales. The same authorities that had earlier overseen a dozen public markets now were tasked to monitor sanitary regulations over thousands of sites, yet the council did not even manage to register half of the meat shops that had opened a decade beyond deregulation.[65] Worries about unwholesome provisions were voiced ever more often by a third constituency: the city's health officials. Like butchers and the Market Committee before them, they warned about the dangers of leaving the food system entirely in the hands of self-regulating markets. One case in point is city inspector George W. Morton, who in his 1855 report warned that the "sale of diseased meats is carried on to an alarming extent in this city." He further reasoned that the health risks disproportionately affected the poor, since their "inducement ... is cheapness of price, and this temptation in our poorer neighborhoods is irresistible."[66]

In its remarks on food access, the sanitary report thus trod a familiar path, but without elevating those comments into a systematic survey like for housing and sanitation. However, its observations were tied to specific areas and populations, substantiating the findings of the mapping analysis. Indeed, the inspectors provided a handful of case studies that complement the mapping analysis in establishing the association of working-class status, high-density residence, and low-quality food shops. Not only did Fourth District inspector Pulling express his concern about leaving the subject inadequately treated, but he also recorded specific details. His survey of Gotham Court, his area's most notorious tenement, included an account of its ground-floor grocery, in which were "retailed a variety of articles of food, including partially-decayed vegetables, rather suspicious looking solids, bearing respectively the names of butter and cheese, and a decidedly suspicious fluid bearing the name milk."[67] In depicting provisioning in his district, he portrayed a veritable food jungle of groceries and meat shops. "Unwholesome meat, particularly *slunk* veal, is constantly vended and consumed. Piles of pickled herrings are exposed to the air till the mass approaches a condition of putridity; and this slimy food, with wilted and decayed vegetables, sausages not above suspicion, and horrible pies, composed of stale and unripe fruits, whose digestion no human stomach can accomplish, all find ready purchasers."[68] Inflated rhetoric aside, Pulling makes a cogent point: in a poor neighborhood, absent of any municipal oversight, there was no lower bound to the quality of food consumed. From this he made a jump to health outcomes. "These decaying animal and vegetable remains are daily entombed in the protuberant stomachs of thousands of children, whose pallid, expressionless faces and shrunken limbs are the familiar attributes of childhood in these localities," he averred.[69]

Similar observations about substandard supplies in other poor districts abound. Farther north on the West Side, Seventeenth District inspector Furman warned "in connection with the overcrowded condition of tenant-houses" that "the diet of many families occupying this class of houses is insufficient in quantity and quality. To meat, fresh vegetables, and fruits, they are almost strangers, and subsist on inferior farinaceous products." Inferring causality, he claimed that "this mode of living with their surroundings produces a low standard of health, and oftentimes disease." Specifically, "the sale of stale vegetables, fish, and unripe fruit by street-hawkers to the poor, is a most potent cause in producing cholera morbus, diarrhoea, and dysentery."[70] In discussing the tenant populations of the adjacent Twentieth District, Inspector Janes similarly observed that "the food of these people consists principally of the cheap meats and groceries purchased in the immediate neighborhood, and the half-wilted vegetables furnished by the street-hawkers."[71] He linked inadequate nutritional standards to the compounding health risks of crowded, unsanitary living. More generally, he forewarned about the dangers of "the inferior quality of food used by the poor."[72] Along the same lines, Inspector Smith, in charge of the city's northern fringes, inferred that "the practice of rigid economy among the poor induces them to purchase cheap and tainted meats and unripe or stale vegetables, and, in the summer season, the effect of this diet is apparent in the production of such diseases as cholera morbus."[73] To cite one last example from a tenement district a few blocks north of Tompkins Square, Inspector H. M. Field highlighted the link between poor-quality housing and ubiquitous, low-end food shops: "if it is not, indeed, impeaching the honesty of the word *shop*, to apply it to these nondescript cabbage and potato stores."[74]

Despite the inspectors' fragmentary observations and hurried conclusions about the adverse health effects of deficient provisioning, their grasp of the connection between poor residence and inadequate food supplies closely accords with the mapping analysis's findings of high-density and/ or low-income districts and proliferating low-quality food shops. This good fit between inspectors' reports and mapping analysis provides a forceful demonstration of the multilayered and cumulative environmental challenges that confronted poor residents. One would wish to ascertain if deregulation and the resulting spread of low-end food shops did in fact lead to increased food-borne diseases, as the inspectors assumed. Death rates skyrocketed and peaked in New York from the mid-1840s through the 1860s, but deteriorating food supplies were only one of several factors contributing to the city's severely compromised public health environments, along with mass immigration, rising poverty, escalating density, and deficient sanitation.[75]

Considering mortality from diseases more likely related to food, such as diarrhea or dysentery, leaves the issue still unresolved.[76] One finds that mortality caused by diarrhea rose by a factor of two to three from the mid-1840s, and the surge of dysentery-related deaths was even higher. Yet again, it is unclear how much of this derived from contaminated water supply and deficient sewage disposal.[77] What is certain, however, is that the city's huge investments in its water supply system had limited public health benefits in this period, for landlords were not required to subscribe to the service, thus reserving access to Croton water mainly to better-off New Yorkers.[78] Further, increased water consumption put additional pressure on the patchwork of sewers, and not until the 1850s did the city begin to expand the network systematically.[79]

It was precisely in the midst of this enduring public health crisis that Gotham transitioned to an unregulated and highly differentiated food supply system. The increased risks of food-borne diseases and deficient nutrition produced by this environment must have played their part in escalating mortality. In pursuing the analysis further, the discussion needs to delve deeper into the interactions of food access and local sanitary and living conditions, introducing additional layers to the mapping analysis. One circumstance to account for is tenement housing, the main culprit of worsening public health, according to nineteenth-century sanitary experts. Crowding by necessity increased exposure to a variety of deadly diseases, and in an unregulated housing market, landlords packed as many people in as little space as possible. Water and sewer connections were not mandated by municipal regulation, consequently, more often than not, tenement residents had limited or no access to clean water or sewage disposal. In short, tenements are a strong indicator not only of crowded and poor residence but also of unsanitary living, all of which brought greater vulnerability to health risks. This is a well-known history. It is also well understood which wards and districts were the most affected by an excess of overcrowded and unsanitary tenements, or "fever-nests," as the sanitary report called them.

What matters here is the extent to which sprawling and low-quality provision shops dominated such vicinities. Adding precision to the comparison, color plate 7 presents a map of tenement crowding in mid-nineteenth-century Manhattan at the block level, focusing specifically on the dreaded category of rear-lot tenements, deprived of air and sunlight. In addition, an 1859 tenement density map by ward is also included.[80] Comparing the geography of rear-tenement crowding to the earlier food retail density maps reveals important similarities.[81] Two by now familiar clusters, one running across wards 4 and 6, and another one at the southern ends of wards 11 and 17, stand out. It is, in fact, quite striking how closely the association between small groceries and jam-packed tenements holds in both vicinities. The same relationship for bakeries, and especially meat shops, is more evident for the Lower East Side than the other area. Elsewhere, it is hard to discern patterns, but this reflects the situation that north of Houston Street, blocks had not yet been fully developed. In this case, rear-lot tenements are a less useful proxy to capture poor and crowded dwellings. For Manhattan's northern half, the inspectors' comments, indicating a general association between tenement living and deficient access to provisions, offer guidance. It is reassuring of the validity of these observations that, among others, Pulling's ward 4, a veritable food jungle by his account, also emerged as one of Gotham's most crowded tenement areas, or that Field's remarks about the bare-bones food shops north of Tompkins Square coincided with the highest concentration of laboring people residing in tenements.

Another approach is to compare mortality rates across different areas, which can be determined at the ward level. Crude death rates are not a particularly sensitive measure; besides, by now it is evident that wards are too large of an area to appreciate fully spatial patterns of social inequality.[82] Still, the next map of ward-level mortality (color plate 7) documents rates nearly twice as high for the densely packed and poor ward 6, consisting of the infamous Five Points, than for the more thinly populated and elegant ward 15, with Washington Square at its center. In general, wards east of Broadway and the Bowery suffered from higher mortality, consistent with their greater density and tenement crowding, as well as messier and more sprawling landscapes of food access.

One solution is to zoom closer to the block level, which is possible for two important diseases, but only by stretching the chronology a bit. In 1866, New York City endured its last major cholera epidemic, and this time, health officials recorded the residences of each of the victims along with those perishing from "diarrhea."[83] There is no reason to believe that the city's geography of housing, sanitation, or food access changed in any appreciable way during this decade. The cholera map (color plate 7) reveals an alarmingly familiar pattern, with the same clusters of peak mortality in the most destitute parts of wards 4 and 6, the southern tip of wards 11 and 17, and a stretch of blocks north of Tompkins Square, whose deficient food supplies were noted by Inspector Field. Smaller centers of cholera deaths are also found in the crowded residential section of ward 1 in Lower Manhattan, and north in the seventeenth and twentieth sanitary districts, where Inspectors Furman and Janes, being alarmed by deficient food supplies, implied their potential contribution to diarrhea and cholera mortality.

It is not the contention here that inferior-quality provisions were directly to blame for excessive cholera and diarrhea mortality in these vicinities. Cholera is a water- and food-borne disease, and it is most commonly related to inadequate sanitation: contaminated water supply and deficient sewerage, two hazardous infrastructural conditions that prevailed in tenement zones or low-lying, flood-prone districts.[84] The same is true for what sanitarians at the time classified as "diarrhea," which, to be accurate, was not an illness per se but a symptom of typically intestinal diseases like cholera. That the 1866 cholera map closely corresponds to that of population density and rear-lot tenement crowding from a decade before is an important finding, but not an unexpected one. It would have rung familiar to contemporary health experts, and even the wider public appreciated the health benefits of living in an exclusive uptown neighborhood.[85] In antebellum New York, or other major cities, where one lived was a matter of life and death. The maps only make strikingly visible what the experience of laboring New Yorkers so dreadfully confirmed.

Rather than positing a direct causality between inferior provisions and food-borne diseases, the argument presented here is that unequal access to provisions mapped closely onto this crowded and hazardous terrain as another layer of structural inequality. Residents of impoverished areas not only suffered from deficient housing and sanitation, but their food supplies were also compromised both in quantity and quality. The critical point is that there was a pattern to this, just as there were patterns to those better-appreciated resources beyond the occasional warnings of sanitarians or such blanket statements that laboring citizens had less income to procure provisions. More accurately, one should think of food access as an element of the urban environment: a structural condition produced by the rules of supply and demand in an unregulated system. Without any government oversight to enforce quality standards, the food economy of antebellum New York had become much like its housing market, producing profoundly unequal outcomes for different segments of the population. At one end, wealthier New Yorkers enjoyed high-end food suppliers and premium services such as home delivery, even as they resided in modern dwellings with sanitary fixtures, in low-density and healthy neighborhoods. At the other end, poor New Yorkers experienced worsening options of food access, even as they lived in crowded and unsanitary dwellings in densely packed and high-mortality areas.

While the actual negative health effects are beyond the reach of sources, one should consider the different ways in which inadequate food supplies could exacerbate already worsening mortality conditions.[86] The issue was not so much that occasional incidents of food poisoning occurred,[87] but that deficient nutritional standards could leave poor residents' bodies weaker and more susceptible to illnesses, even as they lived in overcrowded, disease-ridden districts. Allocating calories to fight off diseases, for example, meant that children may have not grown into their full potential, whether in terms of stature, body mass, or brain development. In fact, this was the distressing conclusion recently reached by UNICEF to explain excessive rates of malnourishment among present-day children in India, highlighting the ways in which poor sanitation interacts with nutritional standards to aggravate negative health outcomes.[88] Similarly, intestinal diseases prevent the body from fully absorbing calories and nutrients, just as frequent diarrhea leaves bodies smaller and generally less resilient to diseases, again, a major disadvantage for those living in high disease-risk environments.

Furthermore, while it would be a stretch to blame high cholera or diarrhea mortality on insalubrious provisions, the spoiled and decaying foodstuff sold profusely from small tenement shops must have aggravated the risks of infection, whether it was consumed during a cholera year or just a "normal" period of mortality. Persistently high rates of diarrhea indicate widespread intestinal diseases, and while ingesting infected food may have not been the direct source of death, it could weaken one's immune system in an environment where deadly diseases prevailed. The retail of fresh food by definition generated some nuisances. It was not without reason that elite areas intuitively "zoned" provision shops out. And such nuisances were far more likely to prevail in areas with already low sanitary conditions, leaving foodstuff unwashed and contaminated or food-related waste dumped on the streets, back alleys, and courtyards. Absent of any municipally enforced standards of food distribution and quality, there was no lower bound to how bad conditions could get other than what customers tolerated, a dismal threshold in impoverished neighborhoods.

Through this analysis, inadequate food access appears as one crucial but underappreciated component of a gruesome mix of poor living conditions in mid-nineteenth-century cities. From the three most basic necessities of housing, sanitation, and food supplies, what was unique about provisioning was its trajectory. Housing, hitherto completely unregulated, became defined as a central domain of public policy to be gradually if only timidly regulated from the late 1860s. Water and sanitation warranted antebellum New York's greatest public works with the Croton aqueduct, despite that individual buildings were, for a long time, not required to link up to water and sewer mains.[89] Provisioning, however, experienced the opposite development of near-complete deregulation.[90] Sanitarians were puzzled about the consequences. Even as they felt confident about the need to tame the tenement evil and address Gotham's deficient sanitary conditions, they did not understand how to assess or respond to an unregulated environment of food access.

An obvious tradition to turn to was police regulations of nuisances, which is what the sanitary report reasserted. Yet experts like Pulling understood that something more systematic was needed to address the junglelike food economy that had sprung up in the ruins of the former public market system in his district and elsewhere. On the whole, in antebellum New York, even the most limited housing reforms were yet to come, and the new public waterworks had barely reached those who lived in tenement-type dwellings, while local food supplies were no longer regulated and monitored by any government entity. If there was a time when New Yorkers were left on their own to provision their most basic needs, this was it. And for those with the least resources, this meant that on all three essential fronts, their living environments posed significant and compounding challenges to their living standards, health, and physical well-being.

In effect, precious little stood between residents and a risky terrain of household provisioning. Antebellum deregulation of provisions shifted the management of risk away from the public domain toward the private consumer. And privately enforced quality control by necessity left the poor more vulnerable to the dangers of nutritional shortfalls. In an earlier era of regulated provisioning, personal relations and trust provided vital protection. The public market system had fostered tight social relations between vendors and customers through repeated transactions over the years, serving to sustain food quality. In contrast, the unregulated food economy of the 1840s and beyond experienced much greater volatility, with small shops seldom staying in business for several years, not to mention peddlers who roamed the streets of poor districts. Adding to the instability of vendor and customer relations was the enormous mobility and turnover of poor tenant populations.[91] Other advantages of the public markets, like comparison shopping between adjacent stands selling the same types of goods or peer pressure from competing vendors, went missing. In theory, customers could choose between different food shops nearby, but this hardly compared to the massive agglomeration economy and tightly managed competition of a place like Catharine Market at its heyday. Nor were food vendors typically craftsmen in this brave new world where anyone at anyplace could open a shop, even in such a delicate business of highly perishable foodstuff as the meat trade.[92]

This leads to the last remaining issue: the distinctive features that sprawling food economies assumed in the city's densest and most crowded areas. Whereas in the working-class districts stretching across wards 4, 6, and 7, small and generalist groceries dominated the food economy, in the Lower East Side, specifically at the junctures of wards 10, 11, 13, and 17, their slightly lower density was compensated by more specialized shops, in particular butchers, but also bakers. Income does not explain this pattern since both areas had similar concentrations of laboring people living in tenements. It is also true that there were more cholera victims in the former cluster, and, generally, mortality rates were persistently higher there. Food distribution probably played some part in explaining this difference. Referring back to the earlier point on the benefits of craftsmanship, even in the poorest parts of the Lower East Side, residents were more likely to procure meat from specialized butchers than at ward 4, for example. Presumably, training and experience in handling time-sensitive and perishable food products should have made some contribution to quality.

A more pertinent and related issue is immigration. On this point, the two districts differed significantly, as shown by the maps of figure 6.4.[93] In general, wards 4 and 6, as well as wards 11 and 17, were the two areas with the highest concentration of immigrants. In the former cluster, more than two-thirds of the population was born abroad, while in the latter, the share of the foreign-born was more than one-half by 1855, with probably similar rates in the adjacent sections of the neighboring wards. These were much higher rates than in elite areas, despite the fact that in antebellum New York even the most native ward was one-third immigrant. The key difference between the two zones had to do with their ethnicity. Whereas wards 4 and 6 and the neighboring sections of 7 and 14 were predominantly Irish, the Lower East Side comprised the heart of the German settlement. And it is well documented that between antebellum New York's two largest immigrant groups, Germans fared better on nearly all dimensions of their material and health conditions.[94] Whereas both areas were solidly working class, poverty was more concentrated and widespread in the Irish neighborhoods.

Some differences in income thus were part of the story. But ethnicity played a more important role. It was not accidental that butcher shops, and to a lesser extent bakeries, proliferated in Klein Deutschland. In fact, as Robert Ernst has shown, Germans had a unique proclivity for the food industry, opening small groceries, and especially entering the butchering trade or baking more frequently than any other ethnicity. Capitalizing on their Old World skills as food purveyors and supplying a traditionally meat-eating ethnic clientele, German butchers became successful small entrepreneurs. Already in 1846, about one-half of New York butchers were immigrants, mostly of German, but also of Irish and English, origin. By 1855, no less than two-thirds of the foreign-born butchers were German, even though they comprised only 29.5 percent of all immigrants.[95] What the maps document is in effect the emergence of an ethnic food economy, possibly the earliest manifestation of such a key neighborhood institution that has since shaped and defined the economies and identities of countless ethnic and racial enclaves in American cities.

The success of meat shops in Klein Deutschland helps explain why traditional public markets in that area, specifically Union, Essex, and Monroe, were much diminished by outside competition after the 1840s. Further, German butchers' advance serves to reinterpret deregulation from the vantage point of immigration. A considerable ethnic divide prevailed between market and shop butchers, whether they still worked informally or had obtained a municipal license. As earlier detailed, market butchers belonged to a closed group of craftsmen, with an apprenticeship system and tight trade organization, whereby setting up a business and obtaining a stall required an arduous petitioning process and personal connections. In short, market laws shielded native-born butchers from the competition of newcomers. Deregulation in 1843 opened the floodgates of immigrants entering the trade, and Germans seized the opportunity. Newcomers in general must have found opening a small provision

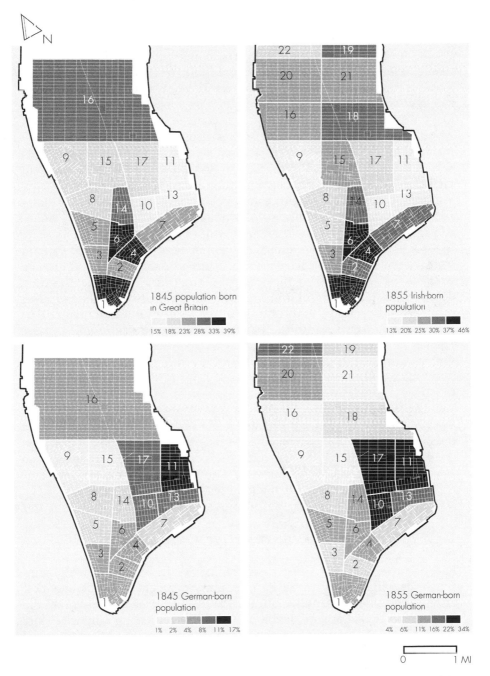

FIGURE 6.4. Residential concentration of Irish and German immigrants, 1845 and 1855. (*Sources*: See text and appendix A)

shop significantly easier than penetrating the closed circles of public market vendors.[96]

The most pertinent issue about this immigrant food economy is that ethnic ties helped foster personal relations and trust, which in an unregulated environment served as an informal layer of protection against substandard provisions. In this context, one may consider ethnic loyalty an institution of privately enforced quality control, much akin to the mechanisms of peer pressure or comparison shopping facilitated by the public markets. In general, personal relations based on ethnic bonds structured food-related transactions in the Lower East Side more than in the Irish vicinities. German-born residents in Klein Deutschland, themselves coming from meat-eating societies and hence relatively more skilled in meat shopping, purchased supplies from local butchers who were their compatriots, and who prepared and sold them more familiar products.

Conversely, in wards 4 and 6, poor Irish residents could not rely on similar ethnic ties with food purveyors, just as they had less experience with buying and preparing meat. Lacking the Old World skills, the Irish did not make it in the meat trade at any similar rate. Nor did they succeed in other food-related enterprises. Even the ownership of groceries commonly passed from Irish to German hands by the 1850s. Insofar as they worked in food retail, they typically engaged in more marginal trades, such as fish and oyster dealers, fruit and produce vendors, or peddlers.[97] How much difference ethnic loyalty and prior skill-sets made is difficult to judge. Certainly, neither of these two sprawling food landscapes measured up to the standards of De Voe's neatly kept stall at Jefferson Market. Yet in a food economy where government played virtually no role, while discounted price was an irresistible "inducement" for working-class residents, any mechanism that shielded the poor from possible abuses was relevant. The ethnic bond between vendors and customers in Klein Deutschland was precisely such a vital institutional arrangement.

THE SLAUGHTERHOUSE NUISANCE

Food distribution and access were pivotal issues for health and living standards. Importantly, just as provisioning was handed over to free and unregulated markets, it also fell outside the remit of municipal policy. One exception was private slaughtering, in which area the sanitary report was more vocal about the urgency of reforms needed, declaring the practice a "special nuisance."[98] This was an issue in which deregulation occurred more than half a century prior, when in 1789 butchers earned the right to kill animals at their facilities.[99] The impetus to re-regulate slaughter derived partly from the liberalization of the retail end of food distribution. Gotham's accelerating growth also made the practice more intolerable.

Approaching the issue from the standpoint of nuisances, the sanitary report treated slaughtering primarily as an environmental hazard and only secondarily as a matter of food policy. Slaughterhouses were to be surveyed by the inspectors, with attention to their sanitary conditions and surrounding built, social, and disease environments.[100] Tallying up how many such facilities there were, then locating and inspecting them in systematic fashion, was in itself an accomplishment. Compared to its hesitant approach to food policy, the sanitary report declared that "the 173 slaughter houses in this city are too offensive to health and decency to be longer permitted in their present localities. These establishments are now thrust into the midst of the most crowded districts, and it is to be observed that a loathsome train of dependent nuisances is found grouped in the same neighborhoods."[101]

On their part, the surveyors did not disappoint in unearthing horrific details. Take the appalling conditions found by Seventh District inspector F. Nolan when surveying six large slaughterhouses west of the Bowery between Houston and Spring,

> all of which are necessarily very filthy, and, of course, injurious to the public health, owing to the large collections of offal which is allowed to accumulate before its removal, and which is constantly undergoing decomposition; also the continued flow of blood, and with urine and faecal matters into the gutters, commingling with the refuse of the streets, have a most deleterious effect on the atmosphere.[102]

Such conditions prevailed in a cluster of blocks affecting five thousand residents. Thousands of others traversing the Bowery were also "daily exposed to the foul emanations."[103] Further, a public school adjacent to one of the slaughterhouses subjected children to dreadful scenes of animal cruelty. Nolan prepared a map, along with a sketch, of the mean streetscape, depicting the school, the slaughterhouse encircled by spectators, a cattle herd overrunning pedestrians, and a large manure heap, illustrating the multiple threats to safety, health, and morality.[104]

This was the westernmost side of four centrally located districts with copious slaughtering. East of the Bowery, Inspector Robert Newman counted no less than thirty-eight facilities in his Thirteenth District, one-fifth of which he classified as "filthy" and a perpetual nuisance.[105] He demanded reforms: restricting slaughter pens to certain areas, requiring their connections to sewers, limiting the driving of cattle to specific hours, hiding the killing from public view, and removing all waste.[106] Farther east, Inspector Edward D. Derby of the Fourteenth District found a dozen killing sheds, all of which he pronounced nuisances, "always to be found in a filthy condition, exhaling the most offensive odors, reeking with decomposing offal, and offensive alike to morality and senses." When examining their direct effects on health, however, he conceded that "they are not in themselves . . . productive of disease," rather they "add their full share to the many provocative influences which are so indigenous to a tenement neighborhood."[107] That private slaughtering compounded the public health risks of tenement areas became the consensus view. Fifteenth District inspector James Ross warned that "the worst class of these slaughter-pens is found in rear buildings amidst the most densely-packed tenant-houses."[108]

Slaughterhouses penetrated other neighborhoods as well, warranting analogous remarks.[109] There is no point in reciting further comments reiterating the opinion that unregulated slaughter was generally offensive and unsanitary, and the denser an area was, the more nuisances it created. More revealing is Derby's cautious point that there was no clear evidence that slaughterhouses directly increased local mortality. The miasmatic theory offered a shorthand notion of the connection, for insofar as people were thought to inhale deadly diseases, the offensive odors of slaughterhouses justified their closure on public health grounds. In reality, slaughterhouses were not that different from other nuisances, for they principally aggravated dismal public health conditions in tenement areas, for example, by allowing runoff from blood, offal, and waste to pollute water supplies. Undeniably, they were especially invasive to the senses. Yet they were also less widespread than public discourse would have it.

In a sequence of three maps, figure 6.5 depicts the geography of slaughter in late antebellum New York.[110] Compared to the well-defined butchering zone of the early nineteenth century, by the 1850s private slaughterhouses were found in multiple areas, generally moving northward. They largely disappeared from the most central wards west of the Bowery between City Hall and Houston, and were entirely absent south of Spring and Rivington Streets. Notably, they did not disperse indiscriminately, nor did they penetrate the most densely populated blocks. Such claims were the products of public health treatises and the optical illusion of aggregating nuisances at the levels of wards and districts. Instead, dispersion was balanced by clustering, since there were economies to be gained from better access to supply chains.

The most notorious cluster was situated directly north of the old butchering zone spanning the four sanitary districts noted above. In fact, it was confined to one narrow ribbon of blocks between Houston and Rivington. This was a major nuisance for residents and those crossing the area. For the record, these did not belong to the most densely populated blocks but fell in between the two peak-density tenement zones of wards 4 and 6 and

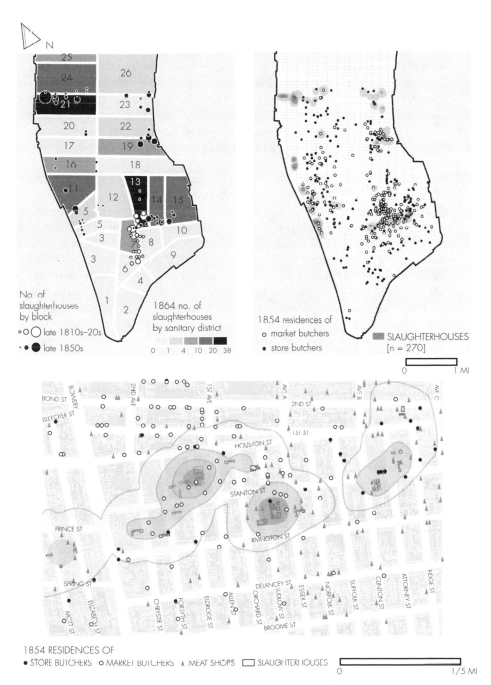

FIGURE 6.5. Geography of slaughter, late 1850s. (*Sources*: See text and appendix A)

the Lower East Side. All the other clusters were situated along the rivers and up north in developing industrial districts, exploiting transportation links and the greater availability of space.[111] By and large, slaughterhouses were located in working-class areas, many of them near insalubrious quarters, where they aggravated local health problems. Still, the vast majority of working-class areas were not directly affected. While invasive and in need of reform, the slaughterhouse nuisance was not nearly as omnipresent as contemporaries suggested.[112] As nuisances they were especially offensive, which explains why they became the prime target of sanitarians. Focusing on them, however, diverted attention from deeper structural problems with food distribution, which concerned far more neighborhoods and residents.

A closer look reveals that the geography of slaughter was also undergoing transition. Small killing sheds, owned mostly by market butchers, comprised the Houston and Rivington Streets cluster and other lesser pockets, while slaughtering became consolidated in industrial-size plants along the riverfronts and the outskirts. This is corroborated by the distinct residential patterns of market and shop butchers. Whereas the former group continued to live in proximity of their killing sheds, from which they supplied their stalls daily, the second group dispersed more evenly, residing next to their shops, obtaining their supplies from slaughtering plants or Washington and Fulton Market wholesalers. The maps capture this transition from an artisan to an industrial model. Market butchers sustained an older tradition, where the entire process of slaughtering, dressing, and retailing was conducted by one craftsman. Deregulation facilitated the separation of wholesaling from retailing, with hundreds of shop butchers and thousands of grocers focusing only on the latter.

Preoccupied with local nuisances, sanitary experts missed these broader industry developments. Their reform agenda targeted primarily the removal of killing sheds from densely populated central districts, which typically belonged to market butchers. Paradoxically, their campaigns helped accelerate the separation of slaughter from retail, a process that undermined the butchers' ability to monitor meat supplies on behalf of their customers. And just as the presence of private killing sheds amid tenement houses was a nuisance, the reorganization of slaughter at industrial-scale sites out of the hands of skilled butchers or any government oversight posed considerable risks to food quality.

Indeed, by the 1850s, well over half of Gotham's livestock derived from distant midwestern markets. At the same time, the vast majority of food vendors never saw the animals alive, nor did officials have any capacity to monitor their conditions of slaughter. Vague plans about a system of municipal abattoirs—essentially centralized, industrial-scale slaughtering facilities, typically located at the outskirts and with railroad connection—

on the European model had been floating around for about a decade. Such ideas also surfaced in the sanitary report, pointing to "a growing necessity for a faithful inspection of slaughtered animals." The reformers mentioned "a practical scheme of *abattoirs* that shall be adapted to the wants of this populous and growing metropolis," for which "the great *abattoir* system of Paris" is cited as reference.[113] Still, what is more notable about the report is not the presence of such claims but their elusiveness. Abating the slaughterhouse nuisance was given greater weight and urgency than creating a public abattoir infrastructure.

The report's fervent antinuisance stand and references to public abattoirs reflected ongoing conversations since the early 1840s, following the deregulation of public markets. They were also in sync with European sanitary discourses. The first health official to discuss the matter was John H. Griscom, an American disciple of internationally known sanitarians Edwin Chadwick of London and Alexandre Jean-Baptiste Parent-Duchâtelet of Paris.[114] In his 1842 annual report as city inspector, he pressed for the relocation of slaughterhouses from the center into one or two large facilities up north by the rivers "under the eye of an inspector."[115] He mustered the familiar arguments, from sanitary considerations to claims about public decency or safety issues about herding livestock on the streets. Notably, he focused chiefly on abating nuisances and less on meat inspection and quality.

Three years later, city inspector Cornelius B. Archer expanded on Griscom's points, also shifting the discussion more to food policy.[116] He recalled an 1842 case of smoked beef poisoning to highlight the threat of infection. He warned against "*the introduction in our city of cattle that are diseased,* or have been attacked with diseases vitiating their flesh; an evil which cannot, when dressed and offered for sale, be detected by the buyer."[117] This was especially alarming in light of Gotham's dependence on western markets for livestock. The solution he recommended was to build public abattoirs, "in the vicinity of Fortieth-street, and immediately upon the rivers."[118] As a model, he advocated "the adoption of the plan in operation in similar establishments in Paris, where in 1809, Bonaparte caused the erection of five public *Abattoirs* or Slaughter-houses in the suburbs."[119] Significantly, "all animals slaughtered at these places, should be subjected to a rigorous inspection, condemning all that are unsound, and that no meat should be offered for sale in our market that had not been inspected and approved of."[120]

The most detailed plan for public abattoirs was proposed by a civic-minded citizen, Joseph L. Frame, who, in 1850, petitioned the council on behalf of a large constituency of residents. His cause emerged out of a public debate following the 1849 cholera epidemic, with the grand jury of New York calling for an end to private slaughter and that the "Common

Council appropriate certain lands, contiguous to either river, and beyond the densely populated districts, for the killing of animals."[121] The butchers fought back, defending their property and right to keep their killing sheds, denying any evidence of disease risks, and stating that existing sanitary measures offered adequate protection.[122] Among the signatories was Gotham's most learned butcher, De Voe himself. The Special Committee entrusted with the subject sided with the butchers, arguing that a slaughterhouse was not a nuisance per se, unless kept in an unsanitary condition.[123] The decision pushed Frame to press his case.[124] He prepared a plan for a public abattoir system with two large facilities, addressing all details.[125] Should the butchers deny that their slaughterhouses were health risks, he retorted that "according to this theory . . . it will be well for the City, to have an increased number of Slaughter Houses dispersed throughout the City for the preservation of health; and even convert them into Hospitals."[126] To the claims that abattoirs should be left to private enterprise, he responded that this approach would "defeat the very design, which of all others, is most important, as to its success: that of organization and concentration."[127]

Predictably, Frame's petition was shelved, and the Special Committee's judgment to leave private slaughtering undisturbed prevailed. The grand jury's stand and Frame's plan were in fact the closest antebellum New York had gotten to a municipal abattoir system. Over the next decade, in report after report, city inspectors voiced the same concerns about unregulated slaughtering.[128] If they devoted fewer pages to the subject, this likely reflected their growing frustration with having to repeat the same arguments to no avail.

The sanitary report thus echoed decades of public health debates about New York's outdated model of private slaughterhouses, expressing a heightened sense of alarm about nuisances but less clarity on systemic reforms to food inspection at municipal abattoirs. It also encountered the infrastructure at its most chaotic period due to prolonged municipal inaction. The challenge to remove all animal waste, including bones, offal, hide, and blood, illustrates the case.[129] The job was contracted to outside firms, and even with the greatest care, this was a line of business fraught with difficulties. Incompetence and corruption made matters worse, when the council assigned a five-year contract to Reynolds & Company. By the spring of 1853, the private interests of some city officials in the firm became exposed, and the comptroller refused to pay the bill. As the investigation dragged on for more than a year, even this poor service came to a standstill. The nauseating sights and odors from slaughterhouses prompted newspapers to launch another campaign to push the noxious trade into the outskirts. Again, no reforms materialized and the nuisances kept piling on.[130]

Less visible, but more important, the lack of government oversight of the entire provisioning system posed a systemic public health problem. As livestock markets spanned ever greater distances, large private slaughtering plants entered the landscape, and provision shops proliferated, government control was urgently needed.[131] The council not only failed to erect municipal abattoirs, but even its more modest scheme to modernize Washington Market, which would have asserted some oversight at the wholesale level, was abandoned, as discussed earlier.[132] At the retail end, public markets were already in tatters, while private provision shops and street vendors escaped any municipal inspection.[133] The landscape of meat provisioning from slaughter to retail—in fact, Gotham's entire food system—was given over to private interests, leaving no space to accommodate the public good. In this context, nuisances like the private killing sheds of market butchers were only the most noticeable yet less consequential hazards of a generally defunct infrastructure whose failures spread across the city, especially affecting poor, underprivileged neighborhoods.

In closing, one should note that the sanitary report stands apart from previous public health documents in that it prepared the ground for reforms shortly after the Civil War. The details exceed the book's time frame, but it is fitting to end the discussion with a reference to their content as concerns slaughterhouses. After the report's publication in 1865, and amid news of another cholera epidemic, the state legislature passed a new public health law, setting up the Metropolitan Board of Health, the first relevant government agency of any American city. Relying on experts and an army of inspectors, the board proved its worth by reducing cholera deaths in 1866. In the following years, it made important headway in abating nuisances following the sanitary report's agenda. Among other achievements, the board ended private slaughtering in the center. Just as important, its reforms did not extend to creating a public abattoir system; nor did they systematically enhance municipal food inspection.

The board's efforts to expel slaughterhouses from the more populous areas did not advance without a fight. The butchers, as they did for decades, stood their ground, defending their private property and rights.[134] They mustered all the familiar arguments, denying that their slaughterhouses were nuisances.[135] This time, however, the reformers managed to implement reforms. Benefiting from overwhelming public support by citizens' petitions and newspaper editorials, the board passed legislation to end slaughter below Fortieth Street in 1867. With the last legal hurdles clearing, all slaughterhouses were expelled below that boundary within two years.[136] This was a long-overdue regulation for a dense metropolis approaching one million. At the same time, it only concerned the geography of slaughter, pushing it up north and outside of Manhattan, thus accelerating an ongoing process. Further, as the city continued to expand, what was still a thinly populated district in 1867 soon became urbanized. Butchers, residents, and officials clashed again in 1874 about the same issue of fifty-four private killing sheds clustering at various points between Fortieth and 110th Streets.[137]

More critically, the council or board did not take control of slaughtering but left the industry to private enterprise, which facilitated its concentration into large private abattoirs, with questionable public health outcomes. "Having no authority to erect such abattoirs, the board could only encourage individuals to construct proper buildings for the business of slaughtering, at suitable distances from the built-up portions of the district."[138] By 1869 four abattoirs served New York City: one in Harlem at 106th Street by the East River; another one at Forty-Fourth Street, also by the East River; and two others in New Jersey at Communipaw and between Hoboken and Jersey City along the Hudson River.[139] The board was initially optimistic about the prospects of large modern abattoirs. De Voe was more skeptical and described the Communipaw and Harlem facilities as scams: massive, dilapidated wooden structures, abattoirs only in name, sharing nothing but size with their Parisian models.[140] It appears he had a point, for by the mid-1870s the press endlessly reported how some of the abattoirs became nuisances of colossal proportions themselves, requiring sweeping reforms.[141] Frame's point, that abattoirs left to private interests were an inadequate solution, rings a bell. As the critics well understood, without strong government oversight, private abattoirs could become enormous public health risks from both the standpoints of nuisances and food inspection.

Conclusion

The central question of this final chapter was how food access shaped urban living standards in the antebellum period in America's first metropolis. The analysis has shown that access to provisions experienced three structural changes. First, supply conditions generally worsened. One component of this transition was the falling consumption levels for meat and other basic foodstuff that resulted from supply pressures after the 1830s in New York City and elsewhere. Urban dwellers found their food budgets squeezed relative to previous generations, despite vastly expanding and nationally integrating markets enabled by improved transportation networks. In other words, rising demand from urbanization outpaced the availability of agricultural supplies, leading to declining consumption standards, a condition especially pressing in major urban centers like New York.

A second component of supply challenges stemmed from the city's foodshed expanding from regional to national markets, a development that made New Yorkers ever more dependent on impersonal supply chains that were increasingly beyond their control. In an earlier era, supply chains consisted of a series of transactions embedded in personal relations. As the story of butchers Ackly and Hyde in chapter 2 testifies, residents bought meat from their regular butchers, whose supplies of livestock derived from the butchers' customary drovers, who in turn assembled the herds from regional farmers personally known to the drovers. Now supply markets spanned beyond the reach of such informal networks. Butchers knew precious little about the origin, conditions of production, and transport of the predominantly western livestock supplied to customers. Consequently, the food supplies of antebellum New Yorkers not only experienced a measurable decline in quantity but, just as important, came under pressure from the aspect of quality as well.

Second, the political economy of provisioning in New York City transformed structurally. The responsibility of residents' access to food was pushed from the public to the private domain, leaving the matter in the hands of free and unregulated markets. This was a historical departure from the Early Republican consensus that access to food was a public good to be organized and managed by a system of public markets. Now retail food markets were wholly liberalized; Gotham's once famous marketplaces, including the wholesale Washington and Fulton Markets, were inadequate and also generally in tatters; the slaughter of livestock fragmented into hundreds of sites, escaping government oversight; and whatever regulations remained on the books were a dead letter. Across the urban food system, the municipality played no role in ensuring that market intermediaries functioned properly to supply residents with wholesome provisions. The case of meat was emblematic of this process by which access to food became a private good.

Health officials expressed their concerns about the city's loss of oversight of its food supplies, yet they were unprepared to advocate meaningful reforms. The public market system was deficient and outdated by midcentury, not least because of decades of inadequate investments. Asserting control higher up in the provisioning system, at the levels of wholesale and slaughter, would have provided plausible remedies, as some European examples showed.[142] City inspectors or the sanitary report recognized the benefits of such arrangements, usually citing Paris as the model. Still, on food-related matters, experts lacked the clarity and resolve that they demonstrated in their campaign for sanitary systems and tenement regulations, or in their frontal attack on nuisances. Nuisances provided a framework to address specific issues about provisioning, such as the menace of private slaughterhouses. But this was a limited, even misguided, approach, for it diverted attention from the systemic failures of an unregulated and defunct provisioning infrastructure, serving a city of one million without any institutional guarantee to sustain the public good.

A third structural change was the city's development. By the Civil War, New York became not only America's most populous city but also the Western world's third-largest, experiencing an unprecedented pace of urbanization. Its commercially oriented economy grew and diversified into industrial activities, providing a magnet for immigrants from vast distances. Antebellum New York was a metropolis in the making, with a diverse population, whether by occupation, socioeconomic status, or ethnic origin. Accommodating such intense economic and demographic pressures put the city's physical and social geography under strain, with urban growth running apace, competing demands on land use transforming entire districts, and intensifying segregation splintering residents into distinct neighborhoods.

New York remained a compact city, but huge socioeconomic distances, reflecting unequal living conditions, separated one neighborhood from another. The most pressing issues included housing conditions, levels of crowding, and access to basic amenities like sanitation. Importantly, unequal living conditions contributed to vastly disparate health outcomes. This chapter's premise was that residents' access to food supplies, just like their access to other basic resources—above all housing and sanitation— had its specific and dynamic geography, subject to changing historical conditions. As the evidence reveals, under the conjunctures of deteriorating supply conditions and laissez-faire provision markets, fragmenting and uneven food access became another defining layer of sociospatial inequality in the urban environment.

One way to appreciate the impact of these three structural changes on New Yorkers' provisioning standards is to take the perspective of individual customers or households. By and large, antebellum residents had to negotiate a far more complex, uneven, and riskier terrain of provisioning than those in the Early Republican period. Whereas before public markets served to agglomerate the sale of all types of foodstuff at privileged locations, facilitating comparison shopping as well as instituting basic mechanisms of quality control, in this new differentiated and unregulated food economy, the logic of caveat emptor held sway. New Yorkers were left to their own devices to monitor price and quality. And private-order quality control was by necessity a problematic arrangement, especially for those lacking the resources.

To begin with, each and every transaction was burdened by asymmetric information, where the vendor knew more about the goods than the buyer. At the same time, sales were not subject to systematic third-party control, whether from municipal officials or competing vendors, to protect customers from potential abuses. With supply markets reaching ever farther across the continent, oversight shrank across ever more links of the supply chain, leaving even retailers less informed. Repeated transactions and personal trust could compensate for some of the perils. In principle, customers could choose to leave one food vendor for another if sold substandard provisions, or suffered incidents of food poisoning. Upscale food purveyors like De Voe and others in his area had their reputation to protect if they wished to sustain a wealthy customer base. The same pressure, however, did not apply to any comparable extent to vendors in working-class districts. In the German Lower East Side, an ethnic food economy could at least mitigate the risks stemming from poverty and the lack of third-party oversight. In most poor neighborhoods, like the Irish Five Points, such informal institutions of quality control were generally absent.

The segmentation of food access by income was an inevitable outcome of a liberal economy. The real problem was that with deregulation, the city lost its baseline of provisioning standard, which public markets had before served to sustain. As sanitary inspectors noted, for laboring New Yorkers, the only factor to consider was the price of provisions. With food budgets tightening, and the ranks of laboring-class New Yorkers widening, there was virtually no lower bound to the quality of supplies that found ready purchasers. Privately enforced quality control worked for those who could protect themselves thanks to their income, personal relations, or experience. Yet it left those without the necessary resources having to negotiate a perilous landscape of provisioning. For better-off New Yorkers residing in more desirable and healthier residential zones, the widening range of food provisioning options could offer greater flexibility and convenience. In impoverished parts of the city, veritable food jungles emerged, posing considerable risks to residents' health standards.

That poor residents were especially at risk was a point generally not lost to city inspectors and the authors of the sanitary report. By their lights as mid-nineteenth-century reformers, who perceived urban problems through an environmentalist lens, the connection between residence and nutrition was a logical one. Moreover, they observed the connection at close hand and recorded their findings in sometimes penetrating testimony. Such claims, however, were not sustained by comprehensive fieldwork like those devoted to housing or sanitation. Nor have historians examined closely how food access fit into antebellum New York's profoundly changing geography. The central thesis of this chapter is that unequal access to food supplies, one of three basic necessities of urban life, next to shelter and sanitation, became a structural condition of inequality, part of the nineteenth-century city's increasingly segregated social and built environments. The evidence has documented how this segmented geography of food access developed, and how it became closely tied to other fundamental layers of sociospatial inequalities.

The statement that New Yorkers' provisioning standards not only became more differentiated but that such inequalities were spatially mediated and layered makes an important difference of interpretation, for it highlights the accumulating perils of living in impoverished neighborhoods. Residents in working-class districts already paid a penalty for having to reside in densely built blocks and crowded tenements with inadequate sanitation. As if these burdens were not enough, they also experienced concentrated deterioration in the quality of food supplies available to them. Layer by layer, poor New Yorkers found their most basic living conditions compromised, with significant negative health effects. This was the abyss of Gotham's public health crisis, and the evidence shows that declining nutritional standards played a major part, not only by way of the amount of food consumed but also in terms of its quality.

Conclusion

Chapter 6 ended on a somber note, perhaps giving the impression that the deregulation of food markets helped unleash a full-scale environmental assault on poor residents' living standards. Such a conclusion would be unbalanced and exaggerated. Yet there are elements of truth to this distressing picture. Consider the several layers of environmental risks endured by working-class immigrant New Yorkers, for example, in the vicinity of the once prosperous Catharine Market. It is hardly an overstatement that circumstances had never been this unfavorable, compromising their most vital living standards of health and life expectancy. Indeed, for tens of thousands of residents, living conditions were alarmingly unsanitary and overcrowded, reaching levels of density that had no precedent. Remedies were as yet slow to come: as of the 1850s, the Croton water, an infrastructural marvel and excellent in quality, barely reached the tenement population; sewer connections, despite considerable investments, were patchy at best, and more often than not clogged and overflowing; and housing reforms, while gathering momentum, still only existed in the debates and treatises of a small circle of social reformers. The deregulation of food markets exacerbated existing environmental hazards by introducing another layer of structural inequality in residents' access to basic resources. From this perspective, the historical account presented reads like a cautionary tale, confirming widely held beliefs about the social costs of untamed free markets in life's necessities.

It is equally true, however, that by the 1830s New York City's public market system became an inadequate model of food access. There was certainly ground to the critics' view that it upheld a premodern vision of a just food economy, which may have served a small city well, but it fell short of the needs of a rising metropolis. By the antebellum period, the municipal model inconvenienced tens of thousands of customers who lived too far from a marketplace, while many believed that by limiting competition, it caused the retail prices of food to rise. Further, government control was achieved through a system of trade privileges, which disadvantaged, even excluded from the retail food sector, those who were not licensed market vendors. Lacking the personal ties that held the public market system together, a new generation of immigrant entrepreneurs, trying to gain a foothold in the city's lucrative food economy, faced considerable obstacles to entry, which pushed many to pursue their businesses outside of the formal system. With infrastructural development lagging behind urban growth, the ranks of dissatisfied customers and unlicensed vendors were rapidly increasing, contributing to a parallel informal economy. This was far from an ideal arrangement to address the vital challenge of feeding an enormous city. Whether or not deregulation in 1843 was the right policy choice, one should keep in perspective that the context had shifted from Gotham's once celebrated public markets to a declining municipal infrastructure coupled with unyielding informal sector growth.

In taking stock, therefore, this book does not wish to give the false impression that free-market reforms were an inherently bad option. Under the conditions of accelerating urbanization and lacking market infrastructure, deregulation was in many ways a reasonable strategy to open up and reenergize the food economy. In fact, it was the solution that the majority of New Yorkers, especially working-class residents, nonmarket retailers, and aspiring immigrant entrepreneurs demanded. While there was considerable opposition to the market laws' repeal, this mainly derived from a privileged class of vendors, above all, the butchers, and some city officials, in particular, members of the Market Committee. What constituted one group's protected status under the market laws amounted to another group's exclusion by the market monopoly. And just the reverse, what represented the leveling of the playing field for all food retailers under a free-market regime, threatened the traditional business practices of licensed suppliers, undermining a social pact that for generations bound the food economy together.

On this point, contemporary parallels abound. To cite just two current examples pertinent to New York and other cities, similar debates have erupted about the costs and benefits of transportation network companies such as Uber or online hospitality companies like Airbnb. Mobilizing the resources of the sharing economy, Uber has directly confronted New York's historically tightly regulated taxi medallion system, while Airbnb has shaken up the hospitality industry. By comparison, one may argue that just as sprawling food shops and street vendors reconfigured food access in mid-nineteenth-century New York, so has Uber shifted the supply curve for taxicabs, and Airbnb has done the same for tourist accommodations. Furthermore, similar to market butchers who complained about declining sales and lost investments on their stalls, traditional New York taxicabs face a shortfall of business traffic, while those owning a medallion have witnessed the value of their assets plummet. If the engine of a free-market economy is creative destruction fueled by innovation, at each juncture there are winners and losers: the question is how to negotiate the competing interests of the different parties for the greater public good. From this perspective, Gotham's transition from a municipal to a liberal provisioning system may be interpreted as a history of retail revolution with contradictory outcomes: on the one hand, a more dynamic food economy, with more access points, offering customers shorter trips and greater flexibility of schedules; on the other, a wholly unmonitored provisioning system, with adverse outcomes to food quality, contributing to greater inequality in food access among residents of different socioeconomic status.

When drawing the final balance, the foremost concern with deregulation was that it resulted in the municipal government's complete surrender of its oversight of the food supplies at a critical stage of urban development. In assessing the historical outcome, considering the alternatives offers a baseline for comparison. Take the critique that the public market system was archaic and inadequate to support a major city. As a matter of fact, market systems beyond the scale of New York's were not unheard of. Several major cities, mostly in Southern and Central Europe, pursued the policy to invest both in the wholesale and retail functions of their market-halls in the second half of the long nineteenth century.[1] In principle, city officials in New York could have decided to revoke antiquated trade privileges while at the same time expanding robustly on the public market infrastructure, preserving a significant degree of control over the food supplies. Such a policy could have bolstered government oversight of the entire food system while also taking advantage of the markets' centralizing and regulatory powers to complement independent provision shops.

The most effective and enduring case of a public market system arguably belongs to Barcelona. For nearly two centuries, market halls have fulfilled a vital role in provisioning residents, with one generation of municipal officials after another improving the infrastructure, a progress not even disrupted by Spain's tumultuous twentieth-century political history. Barcelona's commitment to its public market model dates back to the 1830s, but especially after the 1870s, paralleling the timeline when New York City left its own infrastructure abandoned. By the turn of the twentieth century, no less than sixteen, while by the 1980s, a remarkable forty-one market-halls served a growing population, attracting the majority of all food purchases. Not even the recent rise of megastores could undermine the popularity of neighborhood public markets. In current estimates, the market halls retain more than 40 percent of the total amount of fresh food supplies sold, while, thanks to their agglomeration economies, more than 90 percent of all food purchases take place in one's neighborhood of residence.[2]

The point is not so much to applaud the wisdom of city officials in Barcelona as to suggest the realm of possibilities. In other words, the public market system's demise in mid-nineteenth-century New York or other

American cities was not an inevitable outcome but the result of specific policy choices, whether conscious or unconscious. Insofar as the public market system was archaic and inadequate by 1843, this was not an inherent attribute of the institution, but rather it reflected the lack of social investments and regulatory reforms to build a comprehensive municipal provisioning infrastructure. Indeed, less ambitious and piecemeal improvements failed to materialize as well. For instance, New York could have modernized its wholesale markets while leaving the retail sector largely to its own devices, yet its halfhearted attempt to rebuild Washington Market did not make it beyond the drawing board. At the least, it could have constructed municipal abattoirs, another widely discussed possibility, but on this question administrative deliberations did not even yield operable plans. The single achievement of food policy, to push slaughterhouses beyond Fortieth Street following decades of heated public debates, the proverbial case of an elephant giving birth to a mouse, is symbolic of the level of inaction in this domain.

In a world of limited resources and contested policy choices, problems that were considered more urgent, such as sanitation, Central Park, or tenement house reform, took priority, while food provisioning fell out of the agenda. To be sure, city officials had to consider opportunity costs, and a public water supply was certainly a legitimate priority over provisioning infrastructures. Whether or not the same was true for Central Park is more ambiguous. Rather than weighing the importance of one area of public policy versus another, what matters for this book is the long-term consequence: access to food, unlike access to water, did not develop into a modern public good in the nineteenth-century American city. This statement leads to two larger lessons from the case study, namely, that political economy choices about the balance of public and private goods are historically contingent, and that policy decisions can have profound social impacts.

Where to draw the boundaries between the domains of public and private goods is arguably the defining dilemma of any free-market-based democratic society. Understanding the historical circumstances involved, and the specific societal responses given at each juncture, is most relevant to urban history, for cities, more than other places, need to come to terms with rapidly changing human conditions. Antebellum cities, among them New York especially, faced unprecedented economic, demographic, and social transformations that demanded a range of administrative and infrastructural solutions, questioning and redefining established public and private distinctions. The liberalization of food markets, even as Gotham asserted control of its water supplies, expanded investments into sanitary networks, and laid down the intellectual foundations of future housing reforms, warns about the highly contested nature of such policy decisions.

It is, in fact, instructive of our understanding of antebellum political economy to fully appreciate these contradictory outcomes. The lesson is not to accept too readily convenient narratives, such as the expansion of a market society in Jacksonian America, or, conversely, the widening field of public goods and services in nineteenth-century cities. Recognizing the open-ended and contested nature of these and other policy choices helps recover their specific historical contexts and the stakes involved.

Considering the stakes, the book documents the profound consequences that the deregulation of food markets had on the built environment of the city, and the daily lives and living standards of its residents. Specifically, it outlines the complex interplay of political economy, urban geography, and the material conditions and social inequalities of New Yorkers. With the dissolution and formal repeal of traditionally tightly controlling market laws, the full power of free-market forces was unleashed to restructure the geography and daily routine of provisioning. Similarly, the lack of government oversight across the entire provisioning chain allowed, even accelerated, the fragmentation and polarization of residents' food access. A wholly new geography emerged, whereby residential location determined one's options of food access, corresponding to each neighborhood's class and ethnic divisions of space. In a city with ever deeper socioeconomic disparities, the liberalization of food markets propelled a formerly more egalitarian resource to become another structural layer of inequality, much like housing and sanitation. In Gotham's mosaic of uneven resources, the landscape of provisioning fragmented between areas of privately enforced food order and veritable food jungles. The problem was not so much with deregulation but rather with the failure to impose any institutional measure to offset its negative outcomes. Giving full rein to market forces compounded the adverse effects of resource deprivation—encompassing all three necessities of housing, sanitation, and food supplies—on underprivileged neighborhoods.

Taking the long-term perspective, this study reveals the emergence of a world of food access in certain ways familiar to our own experience of the city. Today's language of food justice worries less about what is described here as food jungles than food deserts: areas without ready access to fresh, healthy, and affordable food supplies, an environmental factor found to contribute to higher rates of diet-related health conditions, including obesity, diabetes, or heart disease.[3] Instead of the chaotic proliferation of substandard food vendors in working-class immigrant neighborhoods, current debates center on residents' lack of access to supermarkets and groceries that carry fresh foodstuffs as opposed to highly processed, unhealthy items. By recent Department of City Planning estimates, no less than three million New Yorkers reside in areas of "high need for fresh food purveyors," to be found in all five boroughs, but especially in low-income neighborhoods across the Bronx, large sections of Brooklyn, and the northern parts of Manhattan.[4] To be sure, "high-need" areas are not the same as food deserts, yet they still indicate a significant dearth of food access, correlating with diet-related health problems. At the other end of the spectrum, healthy and organic food options are an obligatory attribute of any smart and gentrifying neighborhood. The form of inadequate food access discovered in this book, captured by the metaphor of the jungle, and that of present-day New York, epitomized by the notion of a desert, differ in innumerous ways. But in essence, they represent the mirror articulations of the same critical issue of inadequate and substandard access to food supplies, typically coinciding with other forms of resource deprivation based on residential segregation. This book has reconstructed how the first iteration of a spatially unequal landscape of food access came about by the mid-nineteenth century to become a defining and enduring feature of the American urban environment.

Abbreviations

ARCI	New York (N.Y.). City Inspector, *Annual Report of the City Inspector of New-York* (New York: 1804–60) (with modification of titles through the years)
BA Documents	New York (N.Y.). Board of Aldermen, *Documents of the Board of Aldermen of the City of New-York* (New York: 1834–68)
BAA Documents	New York (N.Y.). Board of Assistant Aldermen, *Documents of the Board of Assistant Aldermen of the City of New-York* (New York: 1834–68)
CCAP	City Clerk Approved Papers, New York City Municipal Archives
CCFP	City Clerk Filed Papers, New York City Municipal Archives
CCMD	Common Council Microfilm Database, New York City Municipal Archives
MCC	New York (N.Y.). Common Council, *Minutes of the Common Council of the City of New York, 1784–1831*, 19 vols. (New York: M. B. Brown Printing & Binding, 1917)
NYHS-MD	New-York Historical Society, Manuscript Division
NYPL	New York Public Library

Appendix A

Maps

(A) The several maps in the book are the product of a comprehensive geographic information system (GIS) analysis. With few exceptions, the book's GIS data, including the ArcGIS shapefiles and the corresponding excel spreadsheets, were produced by the author. As for shapefiles, the process included the creation of four main sets: specifically, (1) *Manhattan streets shapefiles* (1797, 1817, 1831, 1849); (2) *ward boundaries shapefiles* (1790–1855); (3) *public markets shapefiles* (1790–1855); and (4) *business and home addresses shapefiles* for various occupations (1845, 1854; for butchers also 1800, 1818).

Other shapefiles for (5) the anonymous butcher's mental map (ca. 1805–23); (6) Catharine and Fulton Market stalls (1828–40); (7) home addresses of customers at Catharine (1839, 1844) and Jefferson Markets (1849); (8) building footprints on Catharine Street (1852); (9) Manhattan omnibus lines (1854); and (10) the Citizens' Association's sanitary district boundaries (1864) were also created.

In tracing the relevant features for the shapefiles, several historical base-maps were georeferenced and consulted. These include: Benjamin Taylor and John Roberts, *A New & Accurate Plan of the City of New York in the State of New York in North America* (New York: 1797); Thomas H. Poppleton, *Plan of the City of New-York: The Greater Part from Actual Survey Made Expressly for the Purpose, the Rest from Authentic Documents* (New York: Prior & Dunning, 1817); Humphrey Phelps and William Hooker, *Map of the City of New York: With the Latest Improvements* (New York: H. Phelps, 1831); William Perris, *Map of the City of New York* (New York: Perris & Hutchinson, 1849); John F. Harrison, M. Dripps, and Kollner's Lithographic Establishment, *Map of the City of New-York Extending Northward to Fiftieth St* (New York: M. Dripps, 1857).

Additionally, the georeferenced Perris Fire Insurance Atlases of 1852–54 and 1857–62 from the New York Public Library's (NYPL) Lionel Pincus and Princess Firyal Map Division were used: William Perris, *Maps of the City of New York, Surveyed under Directions of Insurance Companies of Said City* (New York: Perris & Browne, 1852–54); William Perris, *Maps of the City of New York, Surveyed under Directions of Insurance Companies of Said*

City (New York: Perris & Browne, 1857–62). The Perris Atlases were georeferenced through crowdsourcing by the NYPL. They can be accessed as Web Map Service (WMS) servers via the NYPL's Map Warper website: http://maps.nypl.org/warper/.

The process of pulling large numbers of home and business addresses for specific occupations from the city directories was made infinitely easier by the New-York Historical Society's (N-YHS) recent initiative to make their rich collection of directories electronically searchable. Onsite access to their collection of EBSCO's "Gateway to North America" digital database was critical for developing the book's geospatial data.

(B) In addition to the shapefiles created by the author, the public availability of other shapefiles was also important. First and foremost, the NYPL's crowdsourced production of a historic building footprints shapefile, based on the 1852–54 Perris Fire Insurance Atlas, including all data embedded in the ninety-eight map sheets, was essential for the book's GIS analysis, especially in chapters 5–6. The original *Perris buildings shapefile* was edited for block- and street-level analyses of land use and density in mid-nineteenth-century New York as part of ongoing research with Leah Meisterlin. In the book, the edited shapefile was used. The *Perris buildings shapefile* was also used to build the address locator needed for the batch geocoding of home and business addresses. The original *Perris buildings shapefile* can be downloaded from the NYPL's Map Warper website: http://maps.nypl.org/warper/.

Second, the *1852–54 street network* and corresponding *city blocks shapefiles*, used in several maps in chapters 5–6, were also created in collaboration with Leah Meisterlin by altering the *Manhattan street centerlines (ca. 1930) shapefile*, originally produced and made available by the Historical Urban Ecological GIS Data Portal (HUE) of the Center for Population Economics (CPE) at the University of Chicago Booth School of Business. Likewise, to create a *Manhattan shoreline shapefile*, HUE's original *Manhattan ward boundaries (1863–1930) shapefile* was used. The *Manhattan street centerlines (ca. 1930)* and *Manhattan ward boundaries (1863–1930) shapefiles* are publicly available from the HUE data portal: http://hue.uadata.org/gis/.

(C) Several people contributed to the process of creating the book's GIS maps. Collaboration with Leah Meisterlin was essential in the creation of important shapefiles, as earlier noted, and in their analysis (see later). Meisterlin also provided invaluable guidance about potential GIS techniques. For details on the analysis of the Perris buildings footprints data, see the forthcoming article: Gergely Baics and Leah Meisterlin, "Zoning before Zoning: Land Use and Density in Mid-Nineteenth-Century New York City," *Annals of the American Association of Geographers* (2016).

Research assistants have provided crucial help at various stages. A for-

mer Barnard student, Gabrielle Lewis, assisted with the process of entering home and business addresses from city directories into spreadsheets.
This laborious work was later carried on diligently and with precision for
more than a year by Erzsébet Kertesi. Another Barnard student, Somala
Diby, assisted with the geocoding of thousands of addresses: despite using
an address locator, about one-fourth of the addresses required careful
manual checking. All of the maps were originally created in ArcGIS 10.3
software by the author. For their final format, they were redesigned with
care and creativity in Adobe InDesign and Illustrator software by Rachael
Dottle, another student at Barnard. I am thankful for the excellent and
hard work of all these assistants in contributing to the mapping analysis.
Additionally, the font type used for the maps, called Geo Sans Light, was
designed by Manfred Kline; it is available for free from http://manfred
-klein.ina-mar.com/.

In what follows, further details about methodology and sources (in addition to the shapefiles already described) are provided for each set of
maps in the book, moving chapter by chapter.

CHAPTER 2

Figure 2.1: Development of the public market system, 1790–1825

The maps show the relative volume of trade of the public markets (sym-
bolized by proportionate circles), overlaid on population density by ward.
For 1792, 1816, and 1818, the data come from excise taxes paid by the
butchers. For 1792, excise data are available as aggregate sums for Oswego, Exchange, and Hudson/Bear Markets, collected by one market
clerk, and for Fly, Peck Slip, and Catharine Markets, collected by another.
These two aggregate amounts were distributed between the individual
markets, knowing their numbers of stalls and the estimated average rental
value of those stalls. For 1816, excise tax data are available (incompletely)
for Fly, Washington, Catharine, Spring, and Duane Markets; for 1818,
they are also available for Centre Market. For the missing markets, excise
data were estimated assuming a one-to-one relationship between the
number of stalls and the volume of trade (see further discussion in appendix B). For 1800, 1810, and 1822, the number of butcher stalls serves as
an indicator. For 1818–19, the number of hucksters at Fly, Washington,
Catharine, Centre, and Duane Markets, where data are available, are also
included. For sources on market data (excise taxes and butcher stalls), see
appendix B. For huckster lists, see Common Council Microfilm Database,
New York City Municipal Archives (CCMD), Market Committee (1818),
66:1535; Market Committee (1819), 72:1595.

For ward-level population data, the federal and state census figures were used. For sources, see Ira Rosenwaike, *Population History of New York City* (Syracuse, NY: Syracuse University Press, 1972), 18; Robert Ernst, *Immigrant Life in New York City, 1825–1863* (New York: King's Crown Press, 1949), appendix 3, 191; United States Census Office, *Census for 1820, Published by Authority of an Act of Congress, under the Direction of the Secretary of State* (Washington, DC: Printed by Gales & Seaton, 1821), xxiv, 62, 102–18, 236–37.

Figure 2.5: Approximate locations of slaughterhouses, 1800 and 1818

In addition to the relevant map layers of figure 2.4, home addresses of butchers were obtained from the 1800 and the 1818 Longworth directories. For sources, see David Longworth and Abraham Shoemaker, *Longworth's American Almanack, New-York Register, and City Directory: For the Twenty-Fifth Year of American Independence* (New-York: D. Longworth, 1800); David Longworth, *Longworth's New York Register, and City Directory, for the Forty Third Year of American Independence* (New-York: For Thos. Longworth, 1818).

Figure 2.6: Mental map of unknown butcher, ca. 1805–23

In redrawing the mental map of the anonymous butcher, the various features of his original maps (including his first smaller sketch and the larger final map), along with their explanatory notes, were traced and reproduced as shapefiles. For sources, see New-York Historical Society, Manuscript Division (NYHS-MD), "Map of the Area Later Bounded by 4th Street, Pitt Street, Madison Street, Park Row and Broadway, Manhattan, New York (N.Y.)" (between 1853 and 1880).

Figure 2.7: Distribution of wealth and the public market system, 1791 and 1826

In addition to the relevant map layers of figure 2.4, data on ward-level mean assessed wealth (the mean value of taxable real and personal wealth), and the ratio of merchants to artisans within a ward's population in 1791 and 1826 come from the tables of Eric Hilt and Jacqueline Valentine, based on their extensive research on the wealth and status of New York City households in the Early Republic. The authors also provide ward-level data on the rate of stockholding and the distribution of retailers in 1791 and 1826, and for the rate of slaveholding in 1791. Using any one of these measures as an indicator of the social differentiation of urban space does not significantly alter the maps' results. Eric Hilt and Jacqueline Valentine, "Democratic Dividends: Stockholding, Wealth, and Politics in New York, 1791–1826," *Journal of Economic History* 72, no. 2 (2012), 332–63; for tables, 340, 347; for maps, 342.

CHAPTER 4

Figure 4.3: Organization and value of retail space at Catharine Market,
1820s–30s
Figure 4.5: Organization and value of retail space at Fulton Market,
1832

De Voe's manuscript records include ground plans for all public markets, dating from 1827, 1833, 1835, and 1838. For tracing the footprints of Catharine and Fulton Markets as accurately as possible, including their stalls, the 1835 ground plans were consulted, complemented by De Voe's published histories. De Voe's records on stall rents were then linked to the maps for the retail space analyses. For the diagram on the value of retail space at the public markets in 1832 (figure 4.4), the same sources were used as for these maps. For sources, see NYHS-MD, De Voe, *Manuscripts*, "The Butchers' Stands in the Twelve Markets in the City"; "Ground Plans of the Thirteen Markets in the City of New York, 1694–1866"; "New York City Markets Collection, ca. 1817–ca. 1878," 1–2; Thomas F. De Voe, *The Market Book: A History of the Public Markets of the City of New York* (New York: A. M. Kelley, 1970 [1862]).

Figure 4.6: Catharine Market's catchment area, 1820–40s

In addition to the relevant map layers of figure 2.4, the estimated catchment area of Catharine Market in 1840 is included (for a discussion of the methodology, see figure 5.2), along with the home addresses of Catharine Market petitioners in 1839 and 1844. For the petitions, see City Clerk Filed Papers, New York City Municipal Archives (CCFP), Markets (1839); Markets (1844).

CHAPTER 5

Figure 5.2: Development of the public market system, 1828–55

Like in figure 2.4, the ten maps in the series document the development and changing internal hierarchy of the public market system between 1828 and 1855, and are overlaid on population density maps by ward. For each map, the size of the circles represents the public market's relative importance. Three different indicators are utilized: for 1828 butcher rents are used; for 1835, 1839–40, 1845, 1850, and 1855, butcher rents and market fees (daily fees collected from all the other vendors) are combined into one indicator; and for 1828, 1840, 1845, and 1850, the average annual rents butchers paid for their stalls are also included. For sources on market data (butcher rents and market fees), see appendix B.

In addition, for the period between 1840 and 1855, relative catchment areas were estimated for the individual retail markets, thus excluding Washington and Fulton. For projecting catchment areas, an 1849 petition on behalf of Thomas F. De Voe, then butcher at Jefferson Market, was used to locate the residences of eighty-seven of his customers. Catchment areas at one or two standard distances from the center point of these locations were projected, comprising about 68 percent or 95 percent of the home addresses. The Jefferson Market catchment area was then used as a reference to estimate catchment areas for all the other markets. Two assumptions were made: first, larger markets drew customers from proportionately larger distances, yet within their areas, they generated the same density of exchanges; and second, the reverse, all markets relied on an equally large territory, yet within their areas, larger markets generated more trade. The reality was in between the two assumptions. Here, only catchment areas using the first method are presented. For a more detailed discussion, see Gergely Baics, "Feeding Gotham: A Social History of Urban Provisioning, 1780–1860" (PhD dissertation, Northwestern University, 2009), 142–72, especially 162–72. For Jefferson Market customers list, see NYHS-MD, De Voe, *Manuscripts*, "New York City Markets Collection, ca. 1817–ca. 1878," 1.

For ward-level population data, the federal and state census figures were used. For sources, see Rosenwaike, *Population History of New York City*, 36; United States Census Office, United States Department of State, *Fifth Census: or, Enumeration of the Inhabitants of the United States, 1830; To Which Is Prefixed, a Schedule of the Whole Number of Persons within the Several Districts of the United States, Taken According to the Acts of 1790, 1800, 1810, 1820* (Washington, DC: Duff Green, 1832), 50–51; New York (State), Secretary's Office, *Census of the State of New York for 1835; Containing an Enumeration of the Inhabitants of the State, with Other Statistical Information* (Albany, NY: Croswell, Van Benthuysen & Burt, 1836); United States Census Office, *Sixth Census or Enumeration of the Inhabitants of the United States, as Corrected at the Department of State, in 1840* (Washington, DC: Blair and Rives, 1841), 114–15; New York (State), Secretary's Office, *Census of the State of New York for 1845; Containing an Enumeration of the Inhabitants of the State, with Other Statistical Information* (Albany, NY: Carroll & Cook, 1846); United States Census Office, United States Department of State, *The Seventh Census of the United States: 1850* (Washington, DC: Robert Armstrong, 1853), 102; New York (State), State Secretary, *Census of the State of New York for 1855; Prepared from the Original Returns* (Albany, NY: C. Von Benthuysen, 1857).

Figure 5.4: Provisioning north of Fourteenth Street, 1854
Figure 5.5: Provisioning north of Washington Square, 1854
Figure 5.6: Provisioning in the Lower East Side, 1854
Figure 5.7: Provisioning near Catharine Market, 1854

This series of maps presents neighborhood-level close-ups of the provision store maps in color plate 3. At this larger scale, the edited *Perris buildings* and *city blocks shapefiles* are included as layers to provide a sense of the urban fabric. Further, maps showing home addresses of Jefferson (1849) and Catharine Market (1839, 1844) customers, on the basis of resident petitions, are also included to give a sense of the two markets' catchment areas. For lists of Catharine and Jefferson Market petitioners, see figures 4.6 and 5.2, respectively.

CHAPTER 6

Figure 6.4: Residential concentration of Irish and German immigrants, 1845 and 1855

For the percentage of foreign-born populations by ward—specifically, those born in Germany (1845, 1855), and in Great Britain (1845) and Ireland (1855)—the state census figures were used. For sources, see New York (State), *Census of the State of New York for 1845*; New York (State), *Census of the State of New York for 1855*.

Figure 6.5: Geography of slaughter, late 1850s

Figure 6.5 includes three maps on the geography of slaughter in late antebellum New York. The locations of slaughterhouses were identified with the help of the Perris Fire Insurance Atlases. The 1852–54 Perris Atlas, for which the *Perris buildings shapefile* is available, marks only some of the city's slaughterhouses, typically the larger facilities. In comparison, the subsequent 1857–62 Perris Atlas is more systematic, and also registers the smaller killing sheds. The attempt was to combine the two resources to create a slaughtering map of Manhattan in the mid- to late 1850s up to Forty-Second Street, the boundaries of the *Perris buildings shapefile* and the city's more densely built areas. Slaughterhouses farther north, about twenty, a relatively small number, are thus not included. In locating the slaughterhouses, all ninety-eight sheets of the 1852–54 atlases, and all 123 sheets of the 1857–62 atlases, were consulted block by block. The location of each slaughterhouse was then recorded on the *Perris buildings shapefile* footprints. Perris, *Maps of the City of New York* (1852–54); Perris, *Maps of the City of New York* (1857–62).

On the first map, the slaughterhouses of the late 1850s, based on the Perris Atlases, are aggregated to the block. For chronological comparison, the same aggregation was done with the anonymous butcher's map of slaughterhouses in the 1810s and early 1820s (see figure 2.6). These block layers were then overlaid on the Citizens' Association's sanitary district boundaries, showing the number of slaughterhouses by district in 1864. The second map presents the precise location of slaughterhouses in the late 1850s, also performing a Kernell density analysis. In addition, the geocoded home addresses of market and shop butchers from the 1854 city directory are included. The third map presents a close-up of the second, including meat shops as well, and adding the *Perris buildings shapefile* layer to give a sense of the urban fabric at this larger scale. For slaughterhouses by sanitary districts, see Citizens' Association of New York, Council of Hygiene and Public Health, *Report of the Council of Hygiene and Public Health of the Citizens' Association of New York upon the Sanitary Condition of the City* (New York: D. Appleton, 1865). For home and business addresses, see Charles R. Rode, *The New-York City Directory, for 1854–1855* (New York: Charles R. Rode, 1854).

COLOR INSERT MAPS

Color plate 1: Intensity of land-use types by block and their areas of significant clustering, 1854

This set of land-use maps, showing the percentage of the total built area devoted to one of three basic land-use categories (commercial, industrial, and residential) by block, and their areas of significant clustering, was developed in collaboration with Leah Meisterlin. The original data for the analysis come from the NYPL's *Perris buildings shapefile*. The edited shapefile, containing more than sixty thousand building footprints, was aggregated to the block level, the most appropriate spatial unit to study urban land use, by using the *city blocks shapefile*. For further details on the land use maps, their methodology and analysis, see Baics and Meisterlin, "Zoning before Zoning."

Color plate 2: Geography of commerce, 1854

This set of maps complements the first map in color plate 1 in showing mid-nineteenth-century Manhattan's commercial geography. The first map, representing all mixed-use residential structures with ground-floor retail, was also developed in collaboration with Leah Meisterlin. For this map, the *Perris buildings shapefile* had to be recoded, designating all "residential" buildings "with store under" as "mixed-use" structures with ground-floor retail. For details, see Baics and Meisterlin, "Zoning before Zoning.".

For the other three maps, business addresses of banks, clothing shops (clothiers, boots and/or shoes, and hats), and all varieties of provision stores (bakers, butchers, grocers, and fish, oyster, fruit, and milk vendors) were obtained from the 1854 city directory and entered into spreadsheets. The addresses were geocoded with the address locator built from the *Perris buildings shapefile*. The locations of hotels were available in the original shapefile. For each group, Kernell density analyses were performed and overlaid, using the center points of building footprints. As an additional layer, the intensity of omnibus traffic (number of stages per 1,000 feet) was included in the map on banks and hotels using the 1854 city directory's listing of omnibus lines and their number of stages. For business addresses and a listing of omnibus lines, see Rode, *The New-York City Directory, for 1854–1855,* appendix, 30–31.

Color plate 3: Geography of food retail, 1845 and 1854

These eight maps document the locations of food vendors in 1845 and 1854. Store addresses of all types of food vendors (bakers, butchers, grocers, and fish, oyster, fruit, and milk vendors) were obtained from the 1845 and 1854 city directories and entered into spreadsheets. These were geocoded with the address locator built from the *Perris buildings shapefile*. For bakers, butchers, and grocers, Kernell density analyses were also performed and overlaid. For the maps on butchers, and for those on other provisions, the locations of public markets, as in figure 5.2, were included as well. For addresses, see John Doggett Jr., *Doggett's New York City Directory, for 1845 & 1846* (New-York: John Doggett, 1844); Rode, *The New-York City Directory, for 1854–1855.*

Color plate 4: Catharine Street retail shops, 1851

Data for Catharine Street shops were obtained from the 1851 Doggett street directory. For tracing the building footprints on Catharine Street, the Perris Fire Insurance Atlas of 1852–54 was used. For business addresses, see John Doggett Jr., *Doggett's New York City Street Directory, for 1851* (New York: John Doggett Jr., 1851).

Color plate 5: Population and food retail density, 1854

The maps of color plate 5 compare the block-level concentration of three types of food retailers (grocers, meat shops, and bakers) in 1854 to population density by block. In aggregating food retail shops to the block, the same set of *provision store business addresses shapefiles* were used as in color plate 3 and figures 5.4–5.7.

The map, showing population density by block in 1852–54, was developed in collaboration with Leah Meisterlin. It uses a dasymetric approach: ward-level population data from the 1855 state census was disaggregated to the level of blocks, using the total area of residential building footprints. These were obtained from the *Perris buildings shapefile* by selecting those buildings that were coded for residential use, measuring their footprint areas, and then aggregating them by the block. The method has certain problems. One concern is that residential buildings with the same footprint may be home to one or several households. This problem, however, mainly affects density estimates within the wards and not between them, since ward-level census figures already compensate for much of the variation. Second, the *Perris buildings shapefile* does not contain information about building heights, which could in theory impact the total area of living space by block. Yet building heights were generally limited to four to five stories, so this should not pose a major problem. Probably, the results slightly underestimate peak densities, and hence the differences between high- and low-density blocks are on the conservative side. Crowding on some blocks therefore may have been higher than the map estimates. For a discussion of the map and its methodology, see Baics and Meisterlin, "Zoning before Zoning." For ward-level population figures, see New York (State), *Census of the State of New York for 1855*.

Color plate 6: Residential patterns by class and food retail density, 1854

This series of maps compares the block-level concentration of all provision shops to the residential patterns of different occupational groups by block. The first map presents a combination of the previous food retail density maps, aggregating butchers, bakers, grocers, and fish, oyster, fruit, and milk vendors to the block, using the same set of shapefiles as in color plate 3 and figures 5.4–5.7.

The next three maps, showing the residential patterns of different occupational groups by block, provide a detailed and comprehensive view of class segregation in mid-nineteenth-century Manhattan. For this, the home addresses of about 4,500 individuals listed in the 1854 city directory were geocoded, using the address locator based on the *Perris buildings shapefile*. For upper-class New Yorkers, the addresses of all bankers, merchants, lawyers, and brokers were obtained. Well over 90 percent of the home addresses below Forty-Second Street were matched and geocoded, yielding a total of 1,519 residential addresses (bankers n = 52; merchants n = 299; lawyers n = 750; brokers n = 418). The addresses were then aggregated at the block level and divided by the estimated population of each block from the population density map (color plate 5). Additionally, to outline more clearly the specific residential patterns of elite occupations, standard deviational ellipses comprising about 68 percent of residences by category were also drawn. The same process was followed for the other groups. For lower-middle-class occupations, clerks, tailors, and food shopkeepers (shop butchers and bakers) were selected. The geocoding resulted in a similar success rate, yielding a total of 1,223 home addresses (clerks n = 479; tailors n = 373; food retailers n = 371). For laborers, a slightly different approach was taken, for in their cases the directory usually does not register separate work addresses. Here using the only address available, a random sample of 2,000 was pulled from the roughly 6,500 laborers listed, resulting in a total of 1,766 geocoded addresses. For addresses, see Rode, *The New York City Directory, for 1854–1855*.

To be noted, the ratios obtained from dividing the number of residents belonging to upper-class, lower-middle-class, and laboring groups do not represent their total share within the block's population, for the data come from a select number of representative occupations; besides, the directories themselves are incomplete, especially moving down the socioeconomic ladder. Instead, these ratios indicate the relative distributions of the three classes.

Color plate 7: Housing conditions and disease environments, 1854–66

The first map of the sequence, estimating tenement crowding by block, was developed in collaboration with Leah Meisterlin, making use of the *Perris buildings shapefile*. The conceptual approach was to rely on the sanitary report's idea of the tenement evil, specifically, map the intensity of rear-lot tenement crowding. The technical solution was to select out dwellings in the blocks' interior (without direct street frontage, generally deprived of adequate air and sunlight), aggregate their total footprint area per block, and divide this figure by the block's unbuilt interior area. The resulting ratio provides a measure of the intensity of rear-lot residential crowding, additionally capturing the issue of inadequate ventilation. Importantly, the map does not cover all tenements in Manhattan, because the Perris Atlas does not distinguish between dwelling types. Instead, it identifies those footprints that in all likelihood were rear-lot tenements, presenting the most alarming housing type for health reformers. In principle, the method serves to locate tenement crowding across the city. One caveat is that lower ratios in urbanizing northern areas may reflect that these blocks, despite their containing tenements, had not yet been developed into their interior. For a discussion of the map and its methodology, see Baics and Meisterlin, "Zoning before Zoning."

The second map shows the percentage of dwelling houses with at least six families (which thereby can be categorized as tenements) within the residential housing stock of each ward. For data on the number of dwelling houses by the number of families living in them, see New York (N.Y.). City Inspector, *Annual Report of the City Inspector of New York for the Year Ending December 31, 1860 (ARCI)* (New York: 1804–60), 202–3.

The third map shows crude death rates (number of deaths per 1,000 people) by ward in 1855. These were calculated by using the total number of registered deaths in each ward, discounting from them those deaths that occurred in public institutions like hospitals therein located. For data, see ARCI, New York (N.Y.). 148, 220.

The last map of the set shows the number of cholera- and diarrhea-related deaths by block in 1866. The data were obtained from the Metropolitan Board of Health's map of the same subject. The map provides exceptionally good data about the geography of the two diseases. In creating their map, the board registered each and every fatal case for its exact location. Further, it revisited each case where the victim died in a hospital to record the location from which the patient was moved. Cholera- and diarrhea-related deaths were marked up on a map with a circle or cross, respectively, each symbol representing one case and its exact location. In redrawing the map, the numbers of cholera and diarrhea-related deaths were counted down by block. At times, where a large number of cases occurred in close proximity, it was challenging to count each circle and/or cross, given the original map's quality. For data, see New York (State), Metropolitan Board of Health, *Second Annual Report of the Metropolitan Board of Health of the State of New York* (Albany, NY: Charles Van Benthuysen & Sons, 1868), map between 274–75.

Appendix B

Public Market Data

The book's research builds on a systematic collection of public market data, entered in spreadsheets, from published and archival municipal records on the one hand and Thomas F. De Voe's published books and manuscript research on the other. The sources pertain to two series of market data: butcher stalls and revenues. Public market data provided the basis for a variety of the book's analyses, as detailed below. In addition, revenue data were also used to generate meat consumption estimates.

BUTCHER STALLS DATA

The Common Council's published and archival sources, and De Voe's books and manuscript records, contain counts and/or lists of butcher stalls for the individual public markets for specific years. To create annual time series data on butcher stalls for covering the entire period (1790–1860), careful estimates were made for the missing years, drawing on De Voe's detailed histories of the individual public markets. Additionally, all butchers' names and stall information for those years when available were entered into a spreadsheet to allow tracing butchers over a longer period, or to follow changes in the occupancy of stalls.

Published Common Council records: New York (N.Y.). Common Council, *Minutes of the Common Council of the City of New York, 1784–1831* (*MCC*) (New York: M. B. Brown Printing & Binding, 1917); David M. Matteson and New York (N.Y.). Common Council, *Minutes of the Common Council of the City of New York, 1784–1831: Analytical Index* (New York: M. B. Brown Printing & Binding, 1930). Manuscript Council documents: from the New York Municipal Archives, the full extent of the Market Committee files in the Common Council Microfilm Database (CCMD), and after 1831 the Common Council Filed Papers (CCFP) were also consulted. For stall counts, CCMD, Market Committee (1818), 66:1535; CCFP, Returns of Different Markets, 1847, 1848, 1855, 1867. Additional source: New York (N.Y.), *List of the Constables, Marshals, Butchers, Cartmen, and Porters, for the City and County of New-York, in the Mayoralty of De Witt Clinton, esq.* (New-York: H. C. Southwick, 1809). De Voe's published book: Thomas F. De Voe, *The Market Book: A History of the Public Markets of the City of New*

York (New York: A. M. Kelley, 1970 [1862]). De Voe's archival records are available at the New-York Historical Society, Manuscript Division (NYHS-MD): Thomas F. De Voe, *Manuscript Records*, "Ground Plans of the Public Markets in New York City, 1694–1866"; "List of Butchers in N.Y.C. 1656–1844, with some Biographical Notes"; "New York City Markets Collection, ca. 1817–ca. 1878," 1–2.

Figures 1.1, 2.3, 5.1, and table 4.1 make use of the annual series on butcher stalls. In figures 2.3 and 5.1, and in table 4.1, the number of residents per butcher stall is also shown, which was calculated from yearly population estimates. For these, all available census figures were consulted (1790, 1800, 1805, 1810, 1814, 1816, 1820, 1825, 1830, 1835, 1840, 1845, 1850, and 1855), assuming a constant rate of growth between the two closest observations; for sources on census data, see appendix A, figures 2.4 and 5.2. Further, in studying the stability of the butchers' trade and the frequency of stall occupancy changes, tables A and B in note 63 of chapter 2 rely on De Voe's individual level data on butchers and their stalls.

MARKET REVENUE DATA

As discussed in chapter 1, until 1821 the Common Council levied *excise taxes* (called market fees) on the head of animals slaughtered for sale at the public markets. After 1822, the council overhauled this system, shifting from excises to rental incomes comprised of three sources of revenue: (1) butchers paid annual *market rents*, fixed by the Market Committee, in monthly and later weekly sums; (2) all other vendors paid *market fees*, collected daily by the market clerks; (3) premium butcher stalls (in reality, stalls that just opened up for occupation) were auctioned for the highest bidder for a *premium* until 1835. These were the standard market incomes, discounting fines charged for the violations of the market laws.

(A) *Annual excise taxes (1786–1818)*: As part of the municipal model of provisioning, market clerks were required to register and collect fees on all cattle, calves, sheep, and hogs slaughtered for sale at their respective public markets. Incomplete records of the aggregate amount of market fees collected from the butchers are available from the *MCC* between 1786 and 1818.

Specifically, for 1786–89, 1791–1800, and 1813, the *Minutes of the Common Council* report the total annual market fees. For 1801–2, the records combine fees for the two years. For 1804–6, documents refer to the fiscal year (beginning Nov. 1). For 1804, the treasurer's share of 50 percent was reported. For 1807, fees refer to fourteen months (including Nov. and Dec. of 1806). For some of the years the net amount is given, which does not include the market clerk's salary (10 percent) or expenses on sweeping, which can be reconstructed. For each year, the full amount of market fees was calculated, since this directly reflected the number of animals slaughtered for consumption in New York. For 1816 and 1818, market fees were calculated based on the market clerks' original returns (see next section).

(B) *Excise taxes from original returns (1816–18)*: In addition to yearly excise tax data, a critical amount of the market clerks' manuscript returns of monthly sales in 1816 and 1818 have survived for the three principal markets of Fly, Washington, and Catharine. Additionally, De Voe quotes figures from the same sources for some of the missing months. Specifically, manuscript monthly returns are available from the CCMD collection for Fly (1816: May–Oct.), Washington (1816: May–Oct., Dec.; 1818: Mar., Oct.–Dec.; 1819: Jan.–Apr.) and Catharine Markets (1816: May–Oct.; 1818: each month). De Voe's *The Market Book* contains complementary monthly counts for Fly, Washington, and Catharine Markets (1816: Jan.–Apr.). Notably, for certain months, the original Washington Market returns include daily counts as well. Furthermore, Washington Market returns usually include animal counts for the small Spring and Duane Markets. Finally, De Voe cites aggregated totals for Fly, Washington, Catharine, and Centre Markets (1818: Jan.–Sept.). For sources, see CCMD, Market Committee (1816), 59:1416; Market Committee (1818), 66:1535; Market Committee: Stalls & Licenses (July–Dec. 1818), 66:1537; Market Committee (1819), 72:1595; De Voe, *The Market Book*, 234–35, 351, 411.

For establishing monthly meat sales (of head of livestock) in 1816 and 1818 for all public markets (from which figures annual per capita meat consumption and yearly excise taxes are also estimated), first, all available data were used to fill the gaps in Fly, Washington, and Catharine Markets' monthly returns. The more complete 1816 returns were used as reference data to make estimates for the missing months of 1818. Second, animal counts were estimated for those public markets where data were missing. In 1816, Fly Market had 63, Washington 55, and Catharine 24 (later 48) occupied butcher stalls. The other markets were smaller. In 1816, Collect had 12, Greenwich 6, Spring 5, Governeur 3, Duane 2, and Corlaers Hook 1 butcher stalls. In 1818, Fly had 64, Washington 55, Catharine 47, Centre 14, Essex 8, Greenwich 6, Spring 5, Grand 3, Governeur 3, Duane 2, and Corlaers Hook 1 butcher stalls. To estimate the volume of sales at those markets where no data were available, a one-to-one relationship was assumed between the number of stalls and the volume of meat sales. The respective trades of Fly, Washington, and Catharine Markets do bear out such a linear relationship.

Once livestock counts were estimated for all public markets, applying the excise rates on the different animals allowed for calculating the total amount of market fees in 1816 and 1818. In 1790, the council decided on the following excise rates: it charged 2 shillings for each head of cattle, 4 pence per calf and sheep, and 6 pence per hog. Subsequent market laws, such as the one from 1793, upheld the same taxes, while the 1812 and 1814 market laws used the same respective rates but in dollar-cents. For converting pence into cents, the council's rate of 0.96 penny to a cent was used. By 1812 and 1814, there were minor exceptions to this taxation, but the rates remained the same until 1821. Reassuringly, incomplete annual excise tax data for 1816 and 1818 from the council minutes indicate that the conversion from animal counts to market fees produced reliable results. For sources, see *MCC*, 1:534; New York (N.Y.), *Laws and Ordinances Ordained and Established by the Mayor, Aldermen and Commonalty of the City of New-York* (New York: Hugh Gaine, 1793), 6–10; New York (N.Y.), *Laws and Ordinances Ordained and Established by the Mayor, Aldermen and Commonalty of the City of New-York* (New York: Pelsue and Gould, 1812), 154–64; New York (N.Y.), *A Law to Regulate the Public Markets* (New-York: J. Hardcastle, 1815).

Figure 2.1 charts the yearly excise tax data along with the estimated population (on census figures, see section on stalls). Similarly, table 4.1 draws on these estimates for New York City and the Catharine Market neighborhood in 1818. Figure 3.5 uses the daily returns, available for Washington Market, to chart its weekly rhythms of sales.

(C) *Rents, fees, premiums (1821–60)*: For annual market revenues and expenditures between 1821 and 1830, all volumes of the council minutes were consulted. Further, De Voe's manuscripts provide additional detailed records on rents and stalls, at the level of individual butchers, for much of the period. For sources, see *MCC*; NYHS-MD, De Voe, *Manuscripts*, "Ground Plans of the Public Markets in New York City, 1694–1866"; "List of Butchers in N.Y.C. 1656–1844, with some Biographical Notes"; "New York City Markets Collection, ca. 1817–ca. 1878," 1–2.

Between 1831 and 1860, data on yearly market revenues are available from the comptroller's annual reports. The 1853 and 1858 reports also tabulate market rents and fees, covering the entire period. Unfortunately, they do not provide information on premiums. For all missing or incomplete data, including premiums, the original reports between 1830 and 1860 were used. To save space, only two comptroller reports are cited here, specifically the 1853 and 1858 summary reports: New York (N.Y.), *Annual Report of the Comptroller, of the City of New York, of the Receipts and Expenditures of the Corporation, for the Year 1853* (New York: McSpedon and Baker, 1854), 742; New York (N.Y.), *Annual Report of the Comptroller of the City and County of New York, Exhibiting the Receipts and Expenditures of the City and County; Also, the Loans, Receipts and Reimbursements upon the Various Trust and Special Accounts for and during the Fiscal Year Ending December 31st, 1858* (New York: Charles W. Baker, 1859), 46–61.

Additionally, complete daily and weekly returns, pertaining to market rents and fees, have survived for Clinton Market for 1847. CCFP, Returns of Different Markets, 1847, 1848, 1855, and 1867.

Figures 1.2, 1.3, and 6.1 rely on these annual market revenue data. Additionally, for figure 1.3, data on City Corporation and sinking fund incomes are obtained from the same set of sources, specifically, the council minutes and comptroller reports. For figure 6.1, population data is based on the census figures (see section on stalls). Finally, for figures 3.1 and 3.5, data on weekly revenues and schedules of shopping at Clinton Market (1847) are obtained from its daily and weekly returns.

MEAT CONSUMPTION ESTIMATES

Estimating per capita butcher's meat consumption (fresh beef, veal, lamb and mutton, and pork) from market revenue data was a two-step process, as explained in chapter 2. First, it involved the calculation of per capita meat consumption figures from the 1816 and 1818 original market clerk returns. Second, it involved converting annual excise taxes for the years between 1790 and 1813 into meat consumption figures.

As for the first step: returning to the earlier section on original market returns, the estimation process yielded the total number of head of livestock slaughtered for sale at the city's public markets. In 1816 for a population of 93,634, an estimated 19,165 head of cattle, 24,450 calves, 79,852 sheep, and 9,491 hogs were slaughtered in New York City. In 1818, the corresponding figures were 20,535 cattle, 24,190 calves, 76,900 sheep, and 8,645 hogs for a population of 107,625.

To translate head of animals into per capita butcher's meat consumption (fresh beef, veal, lamb and mutton, and pork), Komlos's conversion rates were used: 450 pounds of dressed weight for "Northern cattle," 40 pounds for sheep, 133 pounds for hogs. For lack of better data, the average dressed weight of a calf was set at 75 pounds, corresponding to the relative amount of excise taxes collected on calves relative to cattle (4 versus 24 cents). For sources, see John Komlos, "The Height and Weight of West Point Cadets: Dietary Change in Antebellum America," *Journal of Economic History* 47, no. 4 (1987); John Komlos, "Anomalies in Economic History: Toward a Resolution of the 'Antebellum Puzzle,'" *Journal of Economic History* 56, no. 1 (1996), 202–14; Robert E. Gallman, "Dietary Change in Antebellum America," *Journal of Economic History* 56, no. 1 (1996), 193–201. On population figures, see section on stalls.

As for the second step: knowing the excise rates applied on each of the four species of livestock makes it possible to convert excise taxes for the years between 1790 and 1813 into head of animals, and thereby into per capita meat consumption figures. For such a conversion, one needs to know the relative distribution of the four types of butcher's meats. Lacking such data, the estimations made a reasonable but not unproblematic assumption: that the 1816 ratios between the sales of fresh beef, veal, lamb and mutton, and pork reflected stable consumption patterns for the period between 1790 and 1818.

For beef and pork, two sets of data validate this method. First, the only comparable estimates for the composition of Early American urban meat diets, calculated by Billy Smith, yield nearly identical consumption ratios for the two meats (for the precise figures, see note 19 in chapter 2). Second, wholesale prices in Philadelphia and New York City reveal a strong association between the prices of barreled beef and pork (see figure 2.2, including notes 30–31 in chapter 2). Even as beef and pork prices show much volatility, these changes affected both species of meat very similarly. No trend change in the wholesale prices, and thus the relative price of beef and pork can be noticed, which would indicate a shift in their supply curves or in consumer preferences. These findings confirm the more general point that before the 1820s there were no major changes in transportation technologies or animal husbandry that would have significantly altered urban supply conditions for butcher's meats. For Philadelphia, see Billy G. Smith, "The Material Lives of Laboring Philadelphians, 1750 to 1800," *William and Mary Quarterly* 38, no. 2 (1981), 167–71, especially, 170, table 1.

In fact, before canals and railroads connected cities to more distant hinterlands in the second quarter of the nineteenth century, livestock had to be driven to urban markets. At the same time, as Danhof and others have argued, farmers made no significant improvements to the breeding of livestock, including cattle, hogs, and sheep, prior to the 1820s. Until the mid-nineteenth century, livestock improvement was limited to a small group of farmers, many of them urban gentlemen. In short, during the Early Republic, the urban supplies of fresh beef, veal, lamb and mutton, and pork were not significantly altered by the reduction of transportation costs, nor were they affected by major productivity gains in animal husbandry or rising slaughtering weights. For the literature, see Clarence H. Danhof, *Change in Agriculture: The Northern United States, 1820–1870* (Cambridge, MA: Harvard University Press, 1969), 33–38, 52–64, 160–78; Robyn S. Metcalfe, "American Livestock Improvers and Urban Markets during the Nineteenth Century," *Journal of the Historical Society* 7, no. 4 (2007), 475–92; Eric C. Stoykovich, "The Culture of Improvement in the Early Republic: Domestic Livestock, Animal Breeding, and Philadelphia's

Urban Gentlemen, 1820–1860," *Pennsylvania Magazine of History & Biography* 134, no. 1 (2010), 31–58.

It is also true that the case for veal, and lamb and mutton, is less clear. Comparing Smith's 1772 Philadelphia figures to the 1816 and 1818 New York City estimates, the data indicate that urban consumers may have shifted their preferences from veal to mutton (see note 19 in chapter 2). Yet this is not confirmed by other sources. Archaeological data of bone remains from Boston do not provide any evidence of declining veal consumption from the late eighteenth to the early nineteenth century. American sheep stocks were also not improved for mutton production until mid-century. Moreover, bone remains from New York City indicate an overall decline in lamb and mutton consumption between the early eighteenth to the mid-nineteenth century. Besides, beef and veal prices tend to move closely together, and, as noted, wholesale beef prices did not experience any trend increase that would indicate mounting pressure on consumers to substitute mutton for veal. Most probably, for veal and mutton the Philadelphia and New York figures are not directly comparable, for Smith's data refer to a Philadelphia laborer, not the "average" consumer. It is also possible that residents in the two cities may have differed in their preferences. For the literature, see Joanne Bowen, "To Market, to Market: Animal Husbandry in New England," *Historical Archaeology* 32, no. 3 (1998), 143; Nan A. Rothschild, *New York City Neighborhoods: The 18th Century* (Clinton Corners, NY: Percheron Press, 2008), 146–49; Metcalfe, "American Livestock Improvers," 483–86.

Based on the literature, the evidence is in favor of using the 1816 ratios for veal and mutton as well. One should note, however, that even if one was to assume shifting ratios (with the Philadelphia figures as a benchmark), this would have a minor impact on total per capita meat consumption, given the much greater importance of fresh beef in the Early Republican urban diet. Nevertheless, in comparison to table 2.1, the estimates below make use of shifting consumption ratios between veal and lamb, assuming a constant rate of change between the 1772 Philadelphia and the 1816 New York City ratios. Lacking more observations, such a simple method of calculation is justifiable. Accordingly, the estimates of total per capita butcher's meat consumption (in pounds) are: 138.2 (1790), 172.4 (1795), 158.8 (1800), 164.1 (1805), 132.2 (1813), 159.3 (1816), 142.0 (1818); the same for lamb and mutton: 21.5 (1790), 28.9 (1795), 28.5 (1800), 31.2 (1805), 27.5 (1813), 34.1 (1816), 28.6 (1818); for veal: 29.1 (1790), 33.2 (1795), 27.8 (1800), 26.0 (1805), 17.5 (1813), 19.6 (1816), and 16.9 (1818). As these figures show, using shifting ratios results in a minor (at the most 6 pounds) increase in total per capita meat consumption, because veal and lamb represented only about one-third of all butcher's meats consumed.

Tables 2.1, 2.2, 2.3, and 6.1 rely on the estimation process discussed above when presenting per capita butcher's meat consumption figures for New York City between 1790 and 1818. The same is true for table 4.1 in documenting meat consumption for the city and the Catharine Market neighborhood. Similarly, figures 3.4 and 3.5 make use of these calculations to chart the monthly distribution of meat sales across the public markets (1816) and at Catharine Market (1818), and the weekly distribution of meat sales at Washington Market (1816–19). Finally, in studying weekly, daily, and hourly volumes of meat sales at Catharine Market (1818), tables 4.3 and 4.4 draw on a combination of monthly Catharine Market and daily Washington Market sales data.

Notes

INTRODUCTION

1. Free market in this book is understood in the sense of open access and free competition, ideas at the heart of antebellum debates about markets and government regulation.

2. For a selected list of books on the market revolution, see Alfred Chandler, *The Visible Hand: The Managerial Revolution in American Business* (Cambridge, MA: Belknap Press of Harvard University Press, 1977), 13–78; Charles Sellers, *The Market Revolution: Jacksonian America, 1815–1846* (New York: Oxford University Press, 1991); Winnifred B. Rothenberg, *From Market-Places to a Market Economy: The Transformation of Rural Massachusetts, 1750–1850* (Chicago, IL: University of Chicago Press, 1992); Melvyn Stokes and Stephen Conway, eds., *The Market Revolution in America: Social, Political, and Religious Expressions, 1800–1880* (Charlottesville: University Press of Virginia, 1996); John L. Larson, *The Market Revolution in America: Liberty, Ambition, and the Eclipse of the Common Good* (New York: Cambridge University Press, 2010); Michael Zakim and Gary J. Kornblith, eds., *Capitalism Takes Command: The Social Transformation of Nineteenth-Century America* (Chicago, IL: University of Chicago Press, 2012).

3. John C. Teaford, *The Municipal Revolution in America: Origins of Modern Urban Government, 1650–1825* (Chicago, IL: University of Chicago Press, 1975); John C. Teaford, *The Unheralded Triumph: City Government in America, 1870–1900* (Baltimore, MD: Johns Hopkins University Press, 1984).

4. On New York City's water supply and sanitation, see Gerard T. Koeppel, *Water for Gotham: A History* (Princeton, NJ: Princeton University Press, 2000); David Soll, *Empire of Water: An Environmental and Political History of the New York City Water Supply* (Ithaca, NY: Cornell University Press, 2013); Joanne Abel Goldman, *Building New York's Sewers: Developing Mechanisms of Urban Management* (West Lafayette, IN: Purdue University Press, 1997). For national-level studies, see Martin V. Melosi, *The Sanitary City: Urban Infrastructure in America from Colonial Times to the Present* (Baltimore, MD: Johns Hopkins University Press, 2000); Martin V. Melosi, *Precious Commodity: Providing Water for America's Cities* (Pittsburgh, PA: University of Pittsburgh Press, 2011); Carl Smith, *City Water, City Life: Water and the Infrastructure of Ideas in Urbanizing Philadelphia, Boston, and Chicago* (Chicago, IL: University of Chicago Press, 2014).

5. It is impossible to survey this vast literature. For New York City, the most important contemporary documents are Citizens' Association of New York, Council of Hygiene and Public Health, *Report of the Council of Hygiene and Public Health of the Citizens' Association of New York upon the Sanitary Condition of the City* (New York: D. Appleton, 1865); Jacob A. Riis, *How the Other Half Lives: Studies among the Tenements of New York* (New York: Dover, 1971 [1890]); Robert W. Deforest and Lawrence Veiller, eds., *The Tenement House Problem, Including the Report of the New York State Tenement House Commission of 1900* (New York: Macmillan, 1903). The seminal book on early nineteenth-century New York housing markets is Elizabeth Blackmar's *Manhattan for Rent, 1785–1850* (Ithaca, NY: Cornell Uni-

versity Press, 1989). See also Richard Plunz, *A History of Housing in New York City* (New York: Columbia University Press, 1990). Tenement housing is widely discussed in New York histories, for example: Robert Ernst, *Immigrant Life in New York City, 1825–1863* (New York: King's Crown Press, 1949); Edward K. Spann, *The New Metropolis: New York City, 1840–1857* (New York: Columbia University Press, 1981); Christine Stansell, *City of Women: Sex and Class in New York, 1789–1860* (Urbana: University of Illinois Press, 1987); Richard Briggs Stott, *Workers in the Metropolis: Class, Ethnicity, and Youth in Antebellum New York City* (Ithaca, NY: Cornell University Press, 1990); Kenneth A. Scherzer, *The Unbounded Community: Neighborhood Life and Social Structure in New York City, 1830–1875* (Durham, NC: Duke University Press, 1992); Edwin G. Burrows and Mike Wallace, *Gotham: A History of New York City to 1898* (New York: Oxford University Press, 1999).

6. For seminal books of legal history on the subject, see Oscar Handlin and Mary F. Handlin, *Commonwealth: A Study of the Role of Government in the American Economy: Massachusetts, 1774–1861* (Cambridge, MA: Belknap Press of Harvard University Press, 1969); Morton J. Horwitz, *The Transformation of American Law, 1780–1860* (Cambridge, MA: Harvard University Press, 1977); Jonathan R. Hughes, *The Governmental Habit Redux* (Princeton, NJ: Princeton University Press, 1991); William Novak, *The People's Welfare: Law and Regulation in Nineteenth-Century America* (Chapel Hill: University of North Carolina Press, 1996).

7. Novak, *The People's Welfare*.

8. The well-regulated society theory evokes other political economy frameworks, most notably E. P. Thompson's widely used notion of the "moral economy" of early-modern England or the "commonwealth" ideal of Early America developed by Oscar and Mary Handlin in *Commonwealth*. The moral economy theory in particular has been used by other historians studying Early American public markets, a subject of interpretation to be addressed in chapter 1.

9. Novak, *The People's Welfare*, 83–113, especially the section on the "urban marketplace," 95–105. For a thorough discussion of the regulatory framework of Early American public markets, see Helen Tangires, *Public Markets and Civic Culture in Nineteenth-Century America* (Baltimore, MD: Johns Hopkins University Press, 2003), 3–25, 48–68. Chapter 1 provides a more detailed treatment of the scholary debates.

10. In Tangires's words, "these facilities were more than a convenience; it was the duty of the state to ensure that the urban populace would have adequate, wholesome, and affordable supply of necessities." Tangires, *Public Markets and Civic Culture*, 3.

11. Unethical trade practices included "forestalling," "regrating," and "engrossing." Forestalling refers to the practice of buying up goods before they enter the marketplace, typically for the purpose of selling them at a higher price. Regrating describes the unlicensed trade of middlemen, such as peddlers, who would purchase goods at the market to resell at profit. Engrossing describes the illegal practice of hoarding goods and thus creating scarcity in order to drive up prices. Tangires, *Public Markets and Civic Culture*, 3–25, 5–8; 48–68; Novak, *The People's Welfare*, 95–105.

12. For a definitive reading of the Montgomery Charter, including the place of public markets within the properties and governmental powers of the corporation of New York City, see Hendrik Hartog, *Public Property and Private Power: The Corporation of the City of New York in American Law, 1730–1870* (Ithaca, NY: Cornell University Press, 1989), 13–20.

13. On the assize of bread in New York, see Teaford, *The Municipal Revolution in America*, 95–97.

14. On banking in the antebellum period, see Hugh Rockoff, "The Free Banking Era: A Reexamination," *Journal of Money, Credit and Banking* 6, no. 2 (1974), 141–67; Howard Bodenhorn, *A History of Banking in Antebellum America: Financial Markets and Economic Development in an Era of Nation-Building* (Cambridge: Cambridge University Press, 2000); Howard Bodenhorn, *State Banking in Early America: A New Economic History* (New York: Oxford University Press, 2003); Howard Bodenhorn, "Free Banking and Bank Entry in Nineteenth-Century New York," *Financial History Review* 15, no. 2 (2008), 175–201; Stephen Mihm, *A Nation of Counterfeiters: Capitalists, Con Men, and the Making of the United States* (Cambridge, MA: Harvard University Press, 2007).

15. James W. Hurst, *The Legitimacy of the Business Corporation in the Law of the United States, 1780–1970* (Charlottesville: University of Virginia Press, 1970); Susan P. Hamill, "From Special Privilege to General Utility: A Continuation of Willard Hurst's Study of Corporations," *American University Law Review* 49, no. 1 (1999), 81–177; Richard Sylla and Robert E. Wright, "Corporation Formation in the Antebellum United States in Comparative Context," *Business History* 5, no. 4 (2013), 653–69; Eric Hilt, "Corporation Law and the Shift toward Open Access in the Antebellum United States," *NBER Working Paper Series 21195* (2015).

16. George Taylor, *The Transportation Revolution* (New York: Holt, Rinehart & Winston, 1951); Carter Goodrich, *Government Promotion of American Canals and Railroads, 1800–1890* (New York: Columbia University Press, 1960); Ronald E. Shaw, *Erie Water West: A History of the Erie Canal, 1792–1854* (Lexington: University Press of Kentucky, 1966); Ronald E. Shaw, *Canals for a Nation: The Canal Era in the United States, 1790–1860* (Lexington: University Press of Kentucky, 1990); John L. Larson, *Internal Improvement: National Public Works and the Promise of Popular Government in the Early United States* (Chapel Hill: University of North Carolina Press, 1996).

17. On Manhattan's grid and the street system, see Hillary Ballon, ed., *The Greatest Grid: The Master Plan of Manhattan, 1811–2011* (New York: Columbia University Press, 2012). On Central Park, see Roy Rosenzweig and Elizabeth Blackmar, *The Park and the People: A History of Central Park* (Ithaca, NY: Cornell University Press, 1992).

18. Koeppel, *Water for Gotham*, 170–72.

19. For works focusing mainly on the cultural aspect of food history in New York City, see Annie Hauck-Lawson and Jonathan Deutsch, eds., *Gastropolis: Food and New York City* (New York: Columbia University Press, 2009); Andrew P. Haley, *Turning the Tables: Restaurants and the Rise of the American Middle Class, 1880–1920* (Chapel Hill: University of North Carolina Press, 2012); Cindy R. Lobel, *Urban Appetites: Food and Culture in Nineteenth-Century New York* (Chicago, IL: University of Chicago Press, 2014).

The framework of food access as a central issue of political economy, infrastructure, geography, and living standards in New York City in the first half of the long nineteenth century was developed in my dissertation (2009), also articulated in a *Journal of Urban History* (2013) article. Lobel's book (2014) on the food cultures of nineteenth-century New York City has built on these ideas in its introduction and especially in chapters 1–3, when discussing food markets, food supplies, and market deregulation. Her treatment of food access, however, is secondary to her original research of the city's public and private dining cultures, especially restaurants and middle-class eating habits, which is the strength of her book and its main contribution. Gergely Baics, "Feeding Gotham: A Social History of Urban Provisioning, 1780–1860" (PhD dissertation, Northwestern University, 2009); for a summary and review of the dissertation, see *Journal of Economic History* 71, no. 2 (2011), 475–80, 493–95; Gergely Baics, "Is Access to Food a Public Good? Meat Provisioning in Early New York City, 1790–1820," *Journal of Urban History* 39, no. 4 (2013), 643–68.

20. For fascinating new scholarship on the history of food systems planning, see Gregory A. Donofrio, "Feeding the City," *Gastronomica: The Journal of Food and Culture* 7, no. 4 (2007), 30–41; Gregory A. Donofrio, "Attacking Distribution: Obsolescence and Efficiency of Food Markets in the Age of Urban Renewal," *Journal of Planning History* 13, no. 2 (2014), 136–59; Domenic Vitiello and Catherine Brinkley, "The Hidden History of Food System Planning," *Journal of Planning History* 13, no. 2 (2014), 91–112; Catherine Brinkley, "Avenues into Food Planning: A Review of Scholarly Food System Research," *International Planning Studies* 18, no. 2 (2013), 243–66. Also, for two recent volumes focusing on the history of urban food infrastructures and other subjects, see Peter Atkins, Peter Lummel, and Derek Oddy, eds., *Food and the City in Europe since 1800* (Aldershot: Ashgate, 2007); Roger Horowitz and Warren Belasco, eds., *Food Chains: From Farmyard to Shopping Cart* (Philadelphia: University of Pennsylvania Press, 2009).

21. For studies directly on slaughtering, see Paula Y. Lee, ed., *Meat, Modernity, and the Rise of the Slaughterhouse* (Lebanon: University of New Hampshire Press, 2008); Paula Y. Lee, ed., *Food and History* 3, no. 2 (2005) (Special Issue on "The Slaughterhouse and the City"); Dorothee Brantz, "Slaughter in the City: The Establishment of Public Abattoirs in Paris and Berlin, 1780–1914" (PhD dissertation, University of Chicago, 2003); Dominic A. Payga, *Slaughterhouse: Chicago's Union Stock Yard and the World It Made* (Chicago, IL: University of Chicago Press, 2014); Ian Maclachlan, "A Bloody Offal Nuisance: The Persistence of Private Slaughter-houses in Nineteenth-Century London," *Urban History* 34, no. 2 (2007), 227–54. For studies not directly on slaughtering but on meat provisioning, see Roger Horowitz, *Putting Meat on the American Table: Taste, Technology, Transformation* (Baltimore, MD: Johns Hopkins University Press, 2006); Sydney Watts, *Meat Matters: Butchers, Politics, and Market Culture in Eighteenth-Century Paris* (Rochester, NY: University of Rochester Press, 2006); Robyn Metcalfe, *Meat, Commerce and the City: The London Food Market, 1800–1855* (London: Pickering & Chatto, 2012).

22. For an excellent survey of public markets in several major European cities, see Manuel Guàrdia and José L. Oyón, eds., *Making Cities through Market Halls: Europe, 19th and 20th Centuries* (Barcelona: Museu d'Història de Barcelona, 2015). On Barcelona's robust public market system, see Nadia Fava, Manuel Guàrdia, and José L. Oyón, "Public versus Private: Barcelona's Market System, 1868–1975," *Planning Perspectives* 25, no. 1 (2010), 5–27; Monsterrat Miller, *Feeding Barcelona, 1714–1975: Public Market Halls, Social Networks, and Consumer Culture* (Baton Rouge: Louisiana State University Press, 2015). On Berlin, see Andrew Lohmeier, "Bürgerliche Gesellschaft and Consumer Interests: The Berlin Public Market Hall Reform, 1867–1891," *Business History Review* 73, no. 1 (1999), 91–113. On England, see James Schmiechen and Kenneth Carls, *The British Market Hall: A Social and Architectural History* (New Haven, CT: Yale University Press, 1999); Martin Phillips, "The Evolution of Markets and Shops in Britain, 1800–1914," in *The Evolution of Retail Systems, 1800–1914*, ed. John Benson and Gareth Shaw (Leicester: Leicester University Press, 1992), 53–75; Roger Scola, *Feeding the Victorian City: The Food Supply of Manchester, 1770–1870* (Manchester: Man-

chester University Press, 1992); Roger Scola, "Food Markets and Shops in Manchester, 1770–1870," *Journal of Historical Geography* 1, no. 2 (1975), 153–68; Deborah Hodson, "The Municipal Store: Adaptation and Development in the Retail Markets of Nineteenth-Century Urban Lancashire," *Business History* 40, no. 4 (1998), 94–114; Colin Smith, "The Wholesale and Retail Market of London, 1660–1840," *Economic History Review*, new series, 55, no. 1 (2002), 31–50.

23. For a broad history on nineteenth-century public markets in America, see Tangires, *Public Markets and Civic Culture*. See also Helen Tangires, *Public Markets: Library of Congress Visual Sourcebooks* (New York: W. W. Norton, 2008); James M. Mayo, "The American Public Market," *Journal of Architectural Education (1984–)* 45, no. 1 (1991), 41–57; Candice L. Harrison, "The Contest of Exchange: Space, Power, and Politics in Philadelphia's Public Markets, 1770–1859" (PhD dissertation, Emory University, 2008). For an excellent dissertation on Early New York City public markets, see Thomas D. Beal, "Selling Gotham: The Retail Trade in New York City from the Public Market to Alexander T. Stewart's Marble Palace, 1625–1860" (PhD dissertation, State University of New York at Stony Brook, 1998). On New York, see also Lobel, *Urban Appetites*, 11–103; Suzanne Wasserman, " 'Hawkers and Gawkers,' Peddling and Markets in New York City," in Hauck-Lawson and Deutsch, *Gastropolis*, 153–73.

24. On the subject of deregulation, see Tangires, *Public Markets and Civic Culture*, 71–94; Roger Horowitz, Jeffrey M. Pilcher, and Sydney Watts, "Meat for the Multitudes: Market Culture in Paris, New York City, and Mexico City over the Long Nineteenth Century," *American Historical Review* 109, no. 4 (2004), 1055–83; Roger Horowitz, "The Politics of Meat Shopping in Antebellum New York City," in Lee, *Meat, Modernity*, 167–77; Beal, "Selling Gotham," 329–42.

25. Jared N. Day, "Butchers, Tanners, and Tallow Chandlers: The Geography of Slaughtering in Early-Nineteenth-Century New York City," in Lee, *Meat, Modernity*, 178–97.

26. See note 23.

27. One exception is Beal's unpublished dissertation, "Selling Gotham," an excellent and focused case study dealing with New York City food markets, meat shops, and groceries. Beal's study focuses mainly on the vendors and does not really engage the subject from the context of urban provisioning.

28. One element of the food system this book does not engage with is the city's emergent and increasingly important restaurant culture. On this point, the existing scholarship is already on solid footing thanks to insightful research by Lobel and others; see note 19.

29. GIS has recently gained traction with urban historians. There are only a handful of urban history books, however, that make use of GIS systematically. Olson and Thornton's demographic and social history of late nineteenth century Montreal is a model to follow for the systematic application of GIS research and analysis. Similarly, Gordon's *Mapping Decline* stands out for its rigorous and sustained deployment of GIS, both as a technology and analytical approach, to provide a novel interpretation of postwar urban decline through a case study of St. Louis. For GIS-based urban histories, see Sherry Olson and Patricia Thornton, *Peopling the North American City: Montreal, 1840–1900* (Montreal: McGill-Queen's University Press, 2011); Colin Gordon, *Mapping Decline: St. Louis and the Fate of the American City* (Philadelphia: University of Pennsylvania Press, 2009), including the website http://mappingdecline.lib.uiowa.edu/; Robert Lewis, *Chicago Made: Factory Networks in the Industrial Metropolis* (Chicago, IL: University of Chicago Press, 2008); Eric Sanderson, *Mannahatta: A Natural History of New York City*

(New York: Harry N. Abrams, 2009); Jean-Luc Pinol and Maurice Garden, *Atlas des Parisiens: De la révolution à nos jours* (Paris: Parigramme, 2009); Jordan Stanger-Ross, *Staying Italian: Urban Change and Ethnic Life in Postwar Toronto and Philadelphia* (Chicago, IL: University of Chicago Press, 2010). For the special issue "Historical GIS and the Study of Urban History," see Donald A. DeBats and Ian Gregory, guest eds., *Social Science History* 35, no. 4, 2011.

There are also a handful of websites devoted to historical GIS projects, some of which have an urban history focus. For a short selection, see the Welikia Project, http://welikia.org/; Digital Harlem, https://digitalharlemblog.wordpress.com/digital-harlem-the-site/; A Tale of Two Cities: Community Differentiation in 19th Century America, http://www.socsci.flinders.edu.au/amst/TaleofTwo Cities/; Montréal, l'avenir du passé, http://www.mun.ca/mapm/eng/about_frame.html; HyperCities, http://www.hypercities.com/; Stanford Spatial History Project, http://web.stanford.edu/group/spatialhistory/cgi-bin/site/index.php.

30. The question of social inequalities in food consumption is explored by Lobel in chapter 3 of *Urban Appetites*, with the most detailed discussions devoted to the swill milk scandals of the 1850s. Relying primarily on newspapers, surveys, and other descriptive sources, Lobel conveys more about contemporary views and debates surrounding unequal food consumption, in itself an important subject, than providing a systematic analysis of unequal access to food supplies. Addressing this issue requires a different, systematic, and quantitative source-base that grounds the analysis firmly within the economic, social, and spatial conditions of the city. Lobel, *Urban Appetites*, 73–102. On swill milk, see also Catherine Mc-Neur, *Taming Manhattan: Environmental Battles in the Antebellum City* (Cambridge, MA: Harvard University Press, 2014), 134–74.

31. For a selective publication list on the antebellum puzzle, see Roderick Floud, Robert W. Fogel, Bernard Harris, and Sok Chul Hong, *The Changing Body: Health, Nutrition, and Human Development in the Western World since 1700* (Cambridge: Cambridge University Press, 2011); Robert W. Fogel, *The Escape from Hunger and Premature Death, 1700–2100* (Cambridge: Cambridge University Press, 2004); John Komlos, "The Height and Weight of West Point Cadets: Dietary Change in Antebellum America," *Journal of Economic History* 47, no. 4 (1987), 897–927; John Komlos, "Shrinking in a Growing Economy? The Mystery of Physical Stature during the Industrial Revolution," *Journal of Economic History* 58, no. 3 (1998), 779–802; John Komlos, "A Three-Decade 'Kuhnian' History of the Antebellum Puzzle: Explaining the Shrinking of the US Population at the Onset of Modern Economic Growth," *Discussion Papers in Economics*, 2012–10, at SSRN, http://ssrn.com/abstract=2021060; Richard H. Steckel, "Stature and the Standard of Living," *Journal of Economic Literature* 33, no. 4 (1995), 1903–40; Dora L. Costa and Richard H. Steckel, "Long-Term Trends in Health, Welfare, and Economic Growth in the United States," in *Health and Welfare during Industrialization*, ed. Richard Steckel and Roderick Floud (Chicago, IL: University of Chicago Press, 1997), 47–89; Richard H. Steckel, "Biological Measures of the Standard of Living," *Journal of Economic Perspectives* 22, no. 1 (2008), 129–52; Michael R. Haines, Lee A. Craig, and Thomas Weiss, "Development, Health, Nutrition, and Mortality: The Case of the 'Antebellum Puzzle' in the United States," *NBER Historical Working Paper Series* 130 (2000); Michael R. Haines, Lee A. Craig, and Thomas Weiss, "The Short and the Dead: Nutrition, Mortality, and the 'Antebellum Puzzle' in the United States," *Journal of Economic History* 63, no. 2 (2003), 382–413; Michael R. Haines, "Growing Incomes, Shrinking People—Can Economic Development Be Hazardous to Your Health? Historical Evidence for the

United States, England, and the Netherlands in the Nineteenth Century," *Social Science History* 28, no. 2 (2004), 249–70; Louis Cain and Sok Chul Hong, "Survival in 19th Century Cities: The Larger the City, the Smaller Your Chances," *Explorations in Economic History* 46, no. 4 (2009), 450–63.

32. Thomas F. De Voe, *The Market Book: A History of the Public Markets of the City of New York* (New York: A. M. Kelley, 1970 [1862]); Thomas F. De Voe, *The Market Assistant, Containing a Brief Description of Every Article of Human Food Sold in the Public Markets of the Cities of New York, Boston, Philadelphia, and Brooklyn; Including the Various Domestic and Wild Animals, Poultry, Game, Fish, Vegetables, Fruits, &c., &c., with Many Curious Incidents and Anecdotes* (Cambridge, MA: Printed at the Riverside Press for the author, 1867). De Voe's manuscript records are held by the New-York Historical Society's Manuscript Division.

33. Through the "The New York City Historical GIS Project," funded by the National Endowment for the Humanities (NEH), the NYPL's Lionel Pincus and Princess Firyal Map Division has been creating digital resources based on its historical paper map and atlas collections. The NYPL relied on crowdsourcing to georeference maps and trace cartographic data, resources that have been made publicly available through its Map Warper website, http://maps.nypl.org/warper/. Another GIS resource used in this book for some shapefiles is the Historical Urban Ecological GIS Data Portal (HUE) of the Center for Population Economics (CPE), http://hue.uadata.org/. For a detailed discussion of the GIS data and methods used in this book, see appendix A.

34. William Perris's Atlas, completed in 1852–54 on the commission of George T. Hope, secretary of the Jefferson Insurance Company, was the first systematic fire insurance survey of any American city. Its purpose was to assist fire insurance underwriters in calculating the risk of urban properties. It provided accurate and current information, at the level of individual buildings, about the location, size, shape, use-type, and building material of each property. The Perris Atlas contains ninety-eight map sheets that have been georeferenced and made available at the NYPL's Map Warper website. Additionally, all building footprints contained in these maps have been digitized and are downloadable as a shapefile. This shapefile was used for the book's GIS analysis and to build a historical address locator. For further details on the book's GIS data and methods, see appendix A.

35. The N-YHS's collection of electronically searchable New York City directories is available through the EBSCO digital database "Gateway to North America."

CHAPTER 1: IS ACCESS TO FOOD A PUBLIC GOOD?

1. Thomas F. De Voe, *The Market Book: A History of the Public Markets of the City of New York* (New York: A. M. Kelley, 1970 [1862]), 496.

2. Ibid., 488; New York (N.Y.). Common Council, *Minutes of the Common Council of the City of New York, 1784–1831 (MCC)* (New York: M. B. Brown Printing & Binding, 1917), 8:394–98; Common Council Microfilm Database, New York City Municipal Archives (CCMD), Market Committee (1816), 59:1416.

3. Although already in March 19, 1816, the council passed an act to appropriate the lands, the initial momentum was lost due to endless bickering over compensations to landowners. De Voe, *The Market Book*, 488; MCC, 10:337–42, 10:402–5.

4. CCMD, Market Committee: New Markets, Fulton's Slip (1) (1821), 80:1713.

5. Most of the petitions articulated common concerns, such as the Fly Market butchers remonstrating against the loss of their stalls, residents worrying about no longer having convenient access to a public market, or the overall expenditures.

CCMD, Market Committee: New Markets, Fulton's Slip (1) (1821), 80:1713; Market Committee: New Markets, Fulton's Slip (2) (1821), 80:1714.

6. Up to this point, the most expensive market to build was Washington. Overall construction costs reached $22,500, that is, about 10% of the price of Fulton. *MCC*, 7:29–31, 7:163, 7:273–74, 7:657–63; 8:383–89.

7. No comparable fanfare accompanied the opening of the city's largest market, Washington, in 1813. It is also true that this was a war year, making such a spectacle less appropriate.

8. Beal documents the expansion of the market system, but he does not suggest a qualitative change in the process, nor does he study closely the building of Fulton Market. Tangires also implies continuity from the Early Republic through the mid-1830s. This is probably because they do not closely examine the financing of market construction. Thomas D. Beal, "Selling Gotham: The Retail Trade in New York City from the Public Market to Alexander T. Stewart's Marble Palace, 1625–1860" (PhD dissertation, State University of New York at Stony Brook, 1998), 309–13; Helen Tangires, *Public Markets and Civic Culture in Nineteenth-Century America* (Baltimore, MD: Johns Hopkins University Press, 2003), 3–94.

9. In Hartog's view, over the course of the first half of the long nineteenth century, the focus of the city government gradually shifted from asserting its public powers by managing its private properties, to providing public goods and services to its residents. Hendrik Hartog, *Public Property and Private Power: The Corporation of the City of New York in American Law, 1730–1870* (Ithaca, NY: Cornell University Press, 1989).

10. This wholesale market would have been bounded north and south by Seventh and Tenth Streets, and east and west by the East River and First Avenue. William Bridges, *Map of the City of New York and Island of Manhattan as Laid Out by the Commissioners Appointed by the Legislature April 3d, 1807* (New York: 1811); William Bridges, *Map of the City of New-York and Island of Manhattan: With Explanatory Remarks and References* (New York: T. & J. Swords, 1811), 27–30; Hartog, *Public Property and Private Power*, 165; Elizabeth Blackmar, *Manhattan for Rent, 1785–1850* (Ithaca, NY: Cornell University Press, 1989), 97–98; Beal, "Selling Gotham," 304–6; Tangires, *Public Markets and Civic Culture*, 75–77; Hillary Ballon, ed., *The Greatest Grid: The Master Plan of Manhattan, 1811–2011* (New York: Columbia University Press, 2012), 40–42, 106.

11. CCMD, Market Committee: New Markets, Fulton's Slip (1) (1821), 80:1713; Market Committee: New Markets, Fulton's Slip (2) (1821), 80:1714.

12. For sources and methods on how the number of butcher stalls between 1790 and 1860 was calculated, see appendix B. For the period of operation of the individual markets, De Voe's *The Market Book* was primarily used, complemented by other sources.

13. From five to six marketplaces by the end of the first decade of the nineteenth century, the council increased their number to ten during the 1810s, and between eleven to fourteen over the 1820s and 1830s. Between 1790 and 1840, the number of stalls grew more gradually, since they could be added to already existing locations. Still, one finds the same trajectory of expansion between 1814 and 1840, with the number of stalls doubling from a little less than two hundred to nearly four hundred. To what extent the market system kept up with urban growth was above all the function of how it corresponded to spatial and demographic changes in the city, in particular, to shifting local population densities.

14. This drastic interruption in the development of the public market system was widely noted by scholars. Tangires, *Public Markets and Civic Culture*, 93; Edward

K. Spann, *The New Metropolis: New York City, 1840–1857* (New York: Columbia University Press, 1981), 124–28; Roger Horowitz, *Putting Meat on the American Table: Taste, Technology, Transformation* (Baltimore, MD: Johns Hopkins University Press, 2006), 24–26; Roger Horowitz, Jeffrey M. Pilcher, and Sydney Watts, "Meat for the Multitudes: Market Culture in Paris, New York City, and Mexico City over the Long Nineteenth Century," *American Historical Review* 109, no. 4 (2004), 1064–65, 1071–73; Horowitz, "The Politics of Meat Shopping in Antebellum New York City," in *Meat, Modernity, and the Rise of the Slaughterhouse*, ed. Paula Y. Lee (Lebanon: University of New Hampshire Press, 2008), 167–77; John Duffy, *A History of Public Health in New York City* (New York: Russell Sage Foundation, 1968), 420–24.

15. One exception was Harlem Market, which between 1842 and 1857 supplied the then separate village of Harlem.

16. Looking at the number of stalls, one finds the same story, albeit the shift appears to have occurred in the early 1840s, from which point on the number of stalls decreased gradually.

17. As early as December 1839, the Common Council contemplated the repealing of the market laws. Discussions on the subject dragged on for a little over two years, and were complicated by the endless petitioning of licensed butchers, nonlicensed vendors, and neighborhood residents. The subject was also fiercely debated in the city's papers. Within the council, the Market Committee remained the last bastion to sustain the market laws. New York (N.Y.). Board of Aldermen, *Documents of the Board of Aldermen of the City of New-York* (BA Documents) (New York: 1834–68), Vol. 6, Doc. 31, 365–75; Vol. 6, Doc. 37, 405–6; Vol. 7, Doc. 55, 565–73; Vol. 7, Doc. 43, 599–606; Vol. 7, Doc. 60, 709–12; Vol. 9, Doc. 31, 257–62; Vol. 9, Doc. 45, 389–405; Vol. 9, Doc. 46, 407–24; New York Board of Assistant Aldermen, *Documents of the Board of Assistant Aldermen of the City of New-York* (BAA Documents) (New York: 1834–68), Vol. 19, Doc. 63, 265–72; Vol. 21, Doc. 50, 51–54; Vol. 21, Doc. 68, 263–73. See also Tangires, *Public Markets and Civic Culture*, 77–86, especially 83–84; Beal, "Selling Gotham," 329–42; Horowitz, Pilcher, and Watts, "Meat for the Multitudes," 1071–73; Horowitz, "The Politics of Meat Shopping," 167–77; Duffy, *A History of Public Health*, 420–26.

18. Beal, "Selling Gotham," 314–15. On the Montgomery Charter, see Hartog, *Public Property and Private Power*, 13–20.

19. New York (N.Y.), *A Law for the Better Regulating and Ordering the Publick Markets within the City of New-York* (New York: 1735); emphasis in original.

20. Beal, "Selling Gotham," 315.

21. "No Person other than a licensed Butcher, shall cut up in any of the said public Markets, or in any Street in this City, any Beef, Pork, Veal, Mutton or Lamb, or expose the same for Sale, by the Joint or in Pieces, under the Penalty of *Ten Shillings*"; emphasis in original. New York (N.Y.), *Laws and Ordinances Ordained and Established by the Mayor, Aldermen and Commonalty of the City of New-York* (New York: Hugh Gaine, 1793), 7.

22. New York (N.Y.), *Laws and Ordinances* (1793), 7. Beal provides an insightful analysis of the relationship between the market butcher and his stall. Beal, "Selling Gotham," 314–17.

23. Beal's meticulous research documents the loopholes of the public market system. Other scholars have paid less attention to the system's small accommodations. Beal, "Selling Gotham"; Duffy, *A History of Public Health*, 420; Horowitz, Pilcher,

and Watts, "Meat for the Multitudes," 1064–65; Horowitz, "The Politics of Meat Shopping," 167–77; Tangires, *Public Markets and Civic Culture*, 3–25, 48–68.

24. Country farmers, who brought to market the "meats raised and slaughtered on their own farms, but not the meat belonging to other persons," were allowed to sell those directly to customers. New York (N.Y.), *Laws and Ordinances Ordained and Established by the Mayor, Aldermen and Commonalty of the City of New-York* (New York: Pelsue and Gould, 1812), 154–64; New York (N.Y.), *A Law to Regulate the Public Markets* (New York: J. Hardcastle, 1815); New York (N.Y.), *A Law to Regulate the Public Markets* (New York: 1833), 1–18; quote on 10.

25. Shirk butchers became a problem from the 1790s, and over the next decades their numbers increased. By 1818, according to one report, shirk butchers dominated the country market sections of the Fly Market. Beal, "Selling Gotham," 317–20, notes 18–24; De Voe, *The Market Book*, 222–23; *MCC*, 10:8–9.

26. Beal diligently unearthed the documentation for such street licenses. Beal, "Selling Gotham," 323–29, notes 25–31.

27. Ibid., 329–36, notes 39, 43; *MCC*, 17:397.

28. City Clerk Filed Papers, New York City Municipal Archives (CCFP): Market Committee (1840).

29. Beal, "Selling Gotham," 333–34, notes 41–42.

30. To be fair, by the 1830s, the council was also at times lax in enforcing the market laws. Quote by Duffy, *A History of Public Health*, 422; Horowitz, *Putting Meat on the American Table*, 24–26; Horowitz, Pilcher, and Watts, "Meat for the Multitudes," 1064–65, 1071–73; Horowitz, "The Politics of Meat Shopping," 167–77; Beal, "Selling Gotham," 329–42.

31. BA Documents, Vol. 9, Doc. 46, 410.

32. Ibid., Vol. 21, Part 1, Doc. 41, 647, 744.

33. Ibid., Vol. 21, Part 2, Doc. 50, 933–40; Vol. 23, Doc. 10, 43–52. See, also, Tangires, *Public Markets and Civic Culture*, 89–93.

34. Market butchers were not a monopoly in the precise definition of the term. Even if butchers cooperated to protect their privilege to sell meat or to obtain beneficial rental and other agreements from the council, they still competed with each other at the public market. They were closer to what one may call a cartel. Yet contemporaries described all (allegedly unfair) trade restrictions as a monopoly, and thus referred to the market butcher's exclusive right to sell fresh meat as the market monopoly. To reflect the contemporary terms of the debate, the phrase is used in this meaning.

35. This explanation is especially stressed by Tangires and Horowitz. Tangires, *Public Markets and Civic Culture*, xv–xx, 3–25, 48–94; Horowitz, Pilcher, and Watts, "Meat for the Multitudes," 1055–58, 1064–67, 1071–74; Horowitz, "The Politics of Meat Shopping," 167–77.

36. Tangires, *Public Markets and Civic Culture*, 3–25, 48–68. Horowitz, Pilcher, and Watts also by and large follow this interpretation, additionally drawing on the economic anthropology literature in the tradition of Karl Polanyi. Horowitz, Pilcher, and Watts, "Meat for the Multitudes," 1055–58, 1080–82; Karl Polanyi, *The Great Transformation: The Political and Economic Origins of Our Time* (Boston, MA: Beacon Press, 1957).

37. The Croton's construction began in 1837, and it was completed in about six years. The inauguration ceremony took place on October 14, 1842. Gerard T. Koeppel, *Water for Gotham: A History* (Princeton, NJ: Princeton University Press, 2000).

38. William Novak, *The People's Welfare: Law and Regulation in Nineteenth-Century America* (Chapel Hill: University of North Carolina Press, 1996), especially 83–

113, on the "public economy" and "well-ordered market," and 95–105 on the "urban marketplace."

39. In a highly influential article, E. P. Thompson argued that eighteenth-century English food riots "operated within a popular consensus as to what were legitimate and what were illegitimate practices in marketing, milling, baking, etc. This in its turn was grounded upon a consistent traditional view of social norms and obligations, of the proper economic functions of several parties within the community, which, taken together, can be said to constitute the moral economy of the poor." The moral economy, he claimed, assumed a "paternalist model of the marketing" process based on the dual principles of "market-supervision" and "consumer-protection." It derived from a societal consensus that citizens were entitled to adequate quantities and quality of food at affordable prices. Local governments were to uphold the ethics of trade in life's necessities through a set of measures, such as price controls, the assize of bread, oversight of weights and measures, by facilitating direct exchange between producers and consumers, and imposing restrictions on middlemen. By the nineteenth century, Thompson agued, this model was replaced by a new consensus that "the natural operation of supply and demand in the free market would . . . establish the common good." "The death of the old moral economy of provision," however, was a "long-drawn-out" process, involving most of the eighteenth century. E. P. Thompson, "The Moral Economy of the English Crowd in the Eighteenth Century," *Past & Present* 50, no. 1 (1971), 76–136; quotes on 79, 83, 90, 32; John Bohstedt, "The Moral Economy and the Discipline of Historical Context," *Journal of Social History* 26, no. 2 (1992), 265–84.

Referring back to E. P. Thompson's classic formulation, Early American public markets have been interpreted in terms of a moral economy, above all, by Tangires. In a similar vein, Horowitz, Pilcher, and Watts underline the "paternalist intervention" of the state in Old Regime meat provisioning, looking at late eighteenth- and early nineteenth-century Paris, Mexico City, and New York. More recently, Lobel also describes the public markets in the moral economy framework, referring to the model as the "patrician government of the early national period," and its deregulation as the "laissez-faire machine politics of the mid- and late nineteenth century." It is not entirely clear, however, how the term patrician differs from or adds to the moral economy and paternalist interpretations. Tangires, *Public Markets and Civic Culture*, 3–25; Horowitz, Pilcher, and Watts, "Meat for the Multitudes," 1055–59; Cindy R. Lobel, *Urban Appetites: Food and Culture in Nineteenth-Century New York* (Chicago, IL: University of Chicago Press, 2014), 4, 21, 23, 57–59.

40. In Tangires's words, "the public market is a compelling demonstration of the persistence of the moral economy despite the disruptive effects of a capitalist market economy in nineteenth-century America." Tangires, *Public Markets and Civic Culture*, xvii, 3–4; quote on xvii.

41. Ibid., 3–25, 48–68; Novak, *The People's Welfare*, 1–18, 83–113, 95–105.

42. In the highly controlled spatial order of New York City public markets, butchers, members of a par excellence urban trading craft, retailed inside the market-halls from individually assigned stalls; fishmongers operated out of collectively managed stalls by the fish market; farmers, coming into town only occasionally, occupied undefined spaces by the country market or at the nearby streets; while hucksters were allowed at the marginal spaces. See chapter 4 for details.

43. For an excellent review and critique of the moral economy theory's application in the Early American context, see Naomi R. Lamoreaux, "Rethinking the Transi-

tion to Capitalism in the Early American Northeast," *Journal of American History* 90, no. 2 (2003), 437–61. It should be noted that Thompson's original formulation of the theory already contained an explicit anticapitalist tone: "It is not easy for us to conceive that there may have been a time, within a smaller and more integrated community, when it appeared to be 'unnatural' that any man should profit from the necessities of others." Thompson, "The Moral Economy of the English Crowd," 131–32.

44. It would be unfair to suggest that these authors do not acknowledge the conflicting interests between and within the different groups of vendors and consumers. Tangires does point out that the city government was put in charge to negotiate a common ground between particularistic demands, while Horowitz focuses on the guild-like privilege of the butchers, implying that the market system was in part a mechanism of rent-seeking by the licensed butchers. Still, conflict is not as central to their analysis as consensus. Tangires, *Public Markets and Civic Culture*, 4; Horowitz, Pilcher, and Watts, "Meat for the Multitudes," 1064–65; Horowitz, "The Politics of Meat Shopping," 167–77.

45. Historians have looked at this subject only tangentially, hence missing a noteworthy shift that occurred in the financing of the market infrastructure after 1812, which pushed provisioning more firmly into the realm of public goods.

46. Henry Rutgers was among the largest landowners in Manhattan in the late eighteenth and early nineteenth century, with property holdings mostly in the northeastern outskirts along the East River. On Rutgers and his real estate dealings, see Blackmar, *Manhattan for Rent*, 30, 37, 41, 101–2, 210.

47. De Voe, *The Market Book*, 341; MCC, 1:220.

48. De Voe, *The Market Book*, 341–43, 347–50, 352; MCC, 4:3; 6:154; 7:527; 8:449, 8:527; 9:15; 10:436, 10:464; 11:571.

49. It is also true that the petition was concerned with those subscribers "who have hitherto refused or neglected to pay their respective Subscriptions." MCC, 1:471.

50. Ibid., 2:54.

51. De Voe, *The Market Book*, 328.

52. Ibid., 370–71; MCC, 1:409.

53. The missing amount was not negligible: $137.95. CCMD, Markets: Stalls & Licenses (1812), 48:1200.

54. To be precise, $500 came directly from the treasury and another $557 was collected from fifty-nine voluntary subscribers. CCMD, Market Committee: Reports (1813), 51:1256; De Voe, *The Market Book*, 309.

55. The nine marketplaces that opened between 1786 and 1813 were Catharine (1786), Exchange (1789), Spring Street (1801), State Prison (1806), Corlaers Hook (1806), Duane (1807), Collect (1809), Governeur (1812), and Greenwich Markets (1813). The three that closed were Peck Slip (1793), Oswego (1810), and State Prison (1812) Markets. See also figure 1.1. The construction of the State Prison Market is unclear; it consisted of a shed rather than an actual markethouse, accommodating only two butchers, who most likely paid the costs themselves. Ibid., 375–76, 382–83, 384–85, 390–91, 396–97, 399, 404.

56. Ibid., 308.

57. The original subscriptions fell short by £50, which remained due on the bonds, and "for which a suit commenced against some of the petitioners, who prayed for aid from the Corporation." De Voe, *The Market Book*, 330; MCC, 1:463.

58. De Voe's research confirms the comptroller's assessment that all market-houses in New York City prior to Washington Market's construction in 1812–13 had

been funded by local residents. BA Documents, Vol. 21, Part 1, Doc. 41, 670, De Voe, *The Market Book*.

59. Examples are as many as there were markets. For instance, Essex Market (1818) was built in direct response to a petition by the residents of the Tenth Ward, who complained about not having convenient access to a public market. The Common Council's Special Committee validated their complaint, stating that "a large proportion of the inhabitants of this section are mechanics and laboring men, who reside from half a mile to one mile and a half from any of the markets now established; the inconvenience experienced by these citizens, whose time is of the utmost importance to them, may be easily conceived; that more accommodations of the kind can be afforded at a moderate expense; they ought to be granted." De Voe, *The Market Book*, 479.

60. James M. Mayo, "The American Public Market," *Journal of Architectural Education (1984–)* 45, no. 1 (1991), 41–57; Tangires, *Public Markets and Civic Culture*, 26–47.

61. Countless petitions document these spatial negotiations. One example is Catharine Market. In 1805 Catharine Market butchers vehemently protested against the practice of Fly Market butchers to relocate their stalls during the sickly season to Chatham Street, for they considered this as their own area of interest. The notion that two public markets should not be located too close to each other was common sense. When in 1821, certain citizens remonstrated against the replacement of Fly Market with Fulton claiming that this would become "a pretext for the removal of the Catharine-Market, the building of a new Market in the southerly part of the city," their reasoning was essentially spatial. As another group of remonstrators explained, "in removing the market to Fulton-Street, by its contiguousness to Catharine-Market, two great markets are brought very nearly together, while the whole city south of it is left destitute of any considerable market." While Catharine Market was not removed, in 1822, the council opened the new Franklin Market down south. Furthermore, the remonstrators were right, in that Fulton and Catharine Markets were too close to each other. Only three years after Fulton opened, Catharine Market butchers complained about shrinking profits and asked for the reduction of their rents, arguing that their stands "are daily decreasing in value, owing to the numerous markets, lately built in that and the adjoining neighborhoods." One petition from 1830 corroborates this complaint: Catharine Market is at a "disadvantageous location, on account of its proximity to the Fulton Market. That portion of our citizens who reside West of the New Market do not require its present location, as they . . . resort to the Fulton Market." CCMD, Market Committee (1805), 27:751; Market Committee: New Markets, Fulton's Slip (1) (1821), 80:1713; Market Committee: New Markets, Fulton's Slip (2) (1821), 80:1714; Market Committee: Stalls & Licenses (Jan.–May 1825), 98:1955; Market Committee (1827), 110:2088; Market Committee: New Markets (1830), 132:2325.

62. There is ample evidence to support this claim. For instance, in 1812, when Mr. Bergh complained about the unwillingness of local inhabitants to subscribe to the building of Governeur Market, he expected to "defray the expenses thereof more especially from the Land holders in the vicinity." His original petition, in fact, reveals that the project was designed as a real estate improvement. He and other subscribers asked for permission to erect a public market, which "would not only have a tendency to add to the Great Convenience of all. But would also inhance and increase almost ten Fold, the value of property in the Neighborhood and Vicinity thereof." Or take the case of Catharine Market. At each instance when

the council considered removing sections of the marketplace, residents, inhabitants, and property owners vehemently protested. They raised their voice in 1806, when certain groups called the fish market a nuisance. They not only refuted the charges but also questioned the legitimacy of the complainers by suggesting that one-third of them "reside at a distance from the place of which they complain." In 1824, certain "occupants of Houses and Lots of Ground" petitioned for the relocation of Catharine Market. Immediately after, seventy-five others— "Subscribers, Owners, Lessees & Occupants of Houses & Lots of ground in the vicinity of Catharine Market"—protested, saying that "we are satisfied with the present location of the Catharine Market." Then again in 1830, more than two hundred individuals proposed the same plan to relocate Catharine Market. This was swiftly blocked by the remonstrance of "owners, lessees & others interested in the property in the vicinity of Catharine Market." Whereas many found Catharine Market inadequate for its accommodations and wished for a more spacious facility, others—especially those who owned property, operated businesses, or simply lived right nearby—wanted to preserve it for the convenience of its location and also for the property values it created. CCMD, Inspector: Petitions (1806), 28:779 oversized; Markets: Stalls & Licenses (1812), 48:1200; Market Committee: New Markets (1824), 92:1888; Market Committee: New Markets (1824), 92:1887; Market Committee: New Markets (1830), 132:2325; Market Committee (1830), 132:2324; Market Committee: Petitions (1830), 132:2326.

63. Robin Einhorn refers to this model of municipal governance as the segmented system, whereby public works were funded through assessments levied on the interested properties in proportion to a project's expected benefits. Two features distinguish the building of public markets. First, subscriptions were voluntary, and only the pressure to maintain one's reputation ensured that no prominent residents would behave as free riders. Second, the model emerged about a century and a half prior to the system described by Einhorn. Robin L. Einhorn, *Property Rules: Political Economy in Chicago, 1833–1872* (Chicago, IL: University of Chicago Press, 2001), 1–27, 61–143.

64. On the use of benefits assessment for public improvements, such as street and park construction, see Blackmar, *Manhattan for Rent*, 158–69; Ballon, *The Greatest Grid*, 73–77; Catherine McNeur, *Taming Manhattan: Environmental Battles in the Antebellum City* (Cambridge, MA: Harvard University Press, 2014), 61–82.

65. See Blackmar's seminal book on the formation of the New York City real estate markets. She describes the process by which urban land became a major source of investment in New York from the second half of the eighteenth century. By the early nineteenth century, Manhattan's increasingly competitive housing market was firmly established. What made this possible was Gotham's exponential rate of growth, which made real estate the city's scarcest resource. Blackmar, *Manhattan for Rent*.

66. De Voe, *The Market Book*, 328.

67. BA Documents, Vol. 21, Part 1, Doc. 41, 657; De Voe, *The Market Book*, 129–31.

68. In 1738, the Market Committee was authorized to "enlarge, alter and support the market-houses at the expense of the Corporation." Direct municipal control, however, lasted only eighteen months and resulted in failures. Eventually, in 1741, an order was passed directing "the clerk of the Board to advertise the public markets to be let for one year, at public auction!" The Common Council auctioned the public markets to private individuals for the next nineteen years, while in 1760, an individual shopkeeper, and in 1766–67 a certain "gentleman named White," rented the markets. Flagg's account does not clarify when exactly the

council took charge of the public markets again. BA Documents, Vol. 21, Part 1, Doc. 41, 671–72.

69. Ibid., 671.

70. Ibid., 684–85; De Voe, *The Market Book*, 130–31.

71. It is unclear how fees were collected over the two or three decades when markets were leased out to private individuals. Presumably, in exchange of the lease, investors were free to keep the regular sales taxes paid by the butchers. The system of taxation through fees was temporarily altered in 1790, when the council decided to collect weekly rents from all butchers. However, in a month, this law was repealed, and the original system of collecting fees on the sales of butcher's meats was reestablished. De Voe, *The Market Book*, 183; MCC, 1:516–19.

72. The specific conditons of these sales, whether they concerned the actual stalls themselves or only the right to their uses, were subject to later debates. Either way, what is notable is that the documents specifically refer to sales and not long-term leases in the case of Fly Market stalls, a departure from the existing precedent of leasing out market cellars at public auction. BA Documents, Vol. 21, Part 1, Doc. 41, 693–95; quote on 693.

73. The conditions of these sales were specified accordingly: "no transfer of any stall so purchased to be made without leave of the Corporation. Butchers who have Stands in the upper Market & becoming purchasers in the lower Market are considered to have forfeited their Stall in the upper Market. None of the Butchers in the other Markets are to have leave to become Purchasers in the Fly Market." MCC, 2:301–2, 2:307; BA Documents, Vol. 21, Part 1, Doc. 41, 693–95; De Voe, *The Market Book*, 200–201.

74. BA Documents, Vol. 21, Part 1, Doc. 41, 694.

75. In response to Margaret Lovell's request in 1812 to inherit her deceased husband, John Lovell's, stall at Catharine Market, which she would then transfer to another relative, Robert Lovell, the Market Committee "have made due inquiry in relation to the existence of a custom set forth in the petition of the said Margaret Lovell and are fully satisfied that such custom has long existed, and which your Committee consider as laudable, and reasonable and hope it may be continued." The transfer was therefore approved. Importantly, Catharine Market stalls were neither sold nor rented in this period. Butchers, like at all other markets, paid fees after the amount of meats sold. Still, they considered stalls as their properties, if not based on legal sanction, then following custom. CCMD, Markets: Stalls & Licenses (1812), 48:1200.

76. BA Documents, Vol. 21, Part 1, Doc. 41, 691–96.

77. To be precise, the city had to pay $10,272.46 to the plaintiffs. De Voe, *The Market Book*, 201, 238–41; Tangires, *Public Markets and Civic Culture*, 73–75.

78. Market clerks kept 10% of the fees they collected. This amount never made it to the mayor or to the treasury, but was regarded as the clerks' share of the market trade. De Voe describes this method of collecting fees. According to his records, in 1790 clerks James Culbertson and Rinier Skaats performed so well in collecting the market fees that the council decided that "from that day they be allowed a commission of *ten per cent*"; emphasis in original. From 1810, deputy clerks were put in charge of collecting fees, and they were also allowed a 10% share. De Voe, *The Market Book*, 183; MCC, 6:144–46.

79. De Voe, *The Market Book*, 406; MCC, 7:29–31.

80. MCC, 7:163.

81. Ibid., 7:273–74; De Voe, *The Market Book*, 407.

82. MCC, 7:29–31, 7:163, 7:273–74, 7:657–63; 8:383–89.

83. De Voe, *The Market Book*, 407, 410.
84. Mayo, "The American Public Market," 41–46; Tangires, *Public Markets and Civic Culture*, 34–42.
85. Subscriptions would have been far inadequate to fund public works projects of this magnitude. Even for erecting Greenwich Market in 1812, which cost a total of $1,057, less than 5% of the price of Washington, donations covered only one-half of the expenses needed, while the rest came from the treasury.
86. Hartog, *Public Property and Private Power*.
87. In 1820, the total valuation of the market property was $105,639.13 or 3.1% of all public property. This relatively low ratio reflects that with the exception of Washington Market, all market-houses in the city were street markets. Indeed, Washington alone represented 75.5% ($79,713.13) of the real estate value of the entire market property, which by then consisted of ten marketplaces. New York (N.Y.). Common Council, Finance Committee, *On the Amount and Value of the Public Property of the Corporation of the City of New-York* (New York: 1820).
88. Bridges, *Map of the City of New York . . . Laid Out by the Commissioners*; Bridges, *Map of the City of New-York . . . with Explanatory Remarks*, 27–30; Hartog, *Public Property and Private Power*, 165; Blackmar, *Manhattan for Rent*, 97–98; Beal, "Selling Gotham," 304–6; Tangires, *Public Markets and Civic Culture*, 75–77; Ballon, *The Greatest Grid*, 40–42, 106.
89. For Centre (1817), the largest of the three modest markets, the council expended $5,000 to purchase the grounds and an estimated $1,000 for the facilities, whereas for Grand Street and Essex, both completed in 1818, projected costs remained as low as $700 each. *MCC*, 9:718–19; De Voe, *The Market Book*, 460, 479.
90. Their petition continues: "The inhabitants of this ward are generally persons in moderate circumstances . . . who find employment a considerable distance from home and whose daily support depends on their daily labour. . . . We hope we shall not be thought unreasonable in our request, that a market may be erected in some central part of the ward as your wisdom shall direct." De Voe, *The Market Book*, 479; CCMD, Market Committee (1818), 66:1535.
91. Estimated costs were distributed accordingly: $100,000 to purchase the ground, $50,000 for filling the lots under water, and $70,000 for construction. *MCC*, 8:394–98; 10:37–42. The actual expenses, most of which occurred in 1821–22 but stretched until 1826, were distributed in the following manner: $156,704.37 for the ground, $2,524.47 for carpenters' work and paving, $45,836.97 for construction, $104.50 for drawing and surveying, $10,272.46 for the compensation of Fly Market butchers for the loss of their stalls, and $1,324.86 for additional expenses. The total sum reached $216,767.63. *MCC*, 11:640–49; 12:637–41, 12:649–70; 13:451–58; 14:140–42, 14:242–50.
92. The exact cost of the Almshouse (built between 1811 and 1817) was $421,109.56, about twice as much as Fulton Market. Yet this sum was expended over a longer period and included additional buildings, such as the penitentiary. Similarly, in 1819, the council entertained the idea of rebuilding the Battery in an "ornamental & durable" manner to create the city's first world-class public walk. The project, which failed to materialize, was estimated to cost the same amount as Fulton Market. The treasury also expended funds for building the city's streets between May 1817 until the end of 1818, about the same amount as the cost of Fulton. The precise figure came to $226,668.35, and it included all outlays, such as mapping, opening, building, and paving, the streets, as well as the construction of monuments. *MCC*, 9:481–82; 10:201–8, 10:687–95.
93. In fiscal year 1823, city revenues and expenditures came to about three-quarters

of a million dollars. In the years 1820 and 1821, city revenues fluctuated greatly: they were $1,034,777.49 and $356,762.88, respectively. As for 1822, revenue data are difficult to compile. When comparing the figures of 1823 to those of the subsequent two years, it appears that city revenues remained stable: in 1823, they were $749,825.19; in 1824, $877,426.83; and in 1825, $778,077.82. Total expenditures in 1823 reached $724,449.92. These amounts exclude the revenues handled by the commissioners of the sinking fund, designated solely for the redemption of the city debt, which in 1823 was an additional $52,581.91. *MCC*, 11:640–49; 12:649–70; 13:451–58; 14:242–50; 15:134–43.

94. Ibid., 8:394–98; following emphasis on sinking fund in original; CCMD, Market Committee (1816), 59:1416.

95. The $140,000 received from the US government represented the last adjustment on the Defense Account of the City Corporation of New York.

96. On the details of financing and public borrowing for the Croton and Central Park, respectively, see Koeppel, *Water for Gotham*; Elizabeth Blackmar and Roy Rosenzweig, *The Park and the People: A History of Central Park* (Ithaca, NY: Cornell University Press, 1992).

97. *MCC*, 11:337–42; quotes on 338; 11:402–5.

98. Ibid., 11:402–5; De Voe, *The Market Book*, 488–90.

99. As of May 15, 1821, the exact amount of the city debt was $1,179,169.82. *MCC*, 11:539–42, 11:640–49.

100. De Voe, *The Market Book*, 490. It is also true that Fulton Market was far less expensive than America's most famous public market-hall, Boston's Faneuil Hall-Quincy Market, which was reconstructed between 1823 and 1826 for a staggering $1 million of public funds. Tangires, *Public Markets and Civic Culture*, 40–41.

101. Insofar as the exact figures can be reconstructed, the construction of the new public markets cost the following sums. Franklin Market (1822) was erected on public grounds for $2,630.34. Manhattan (1827) was also built on public grounds for $1,975. Clinton (1828) replaced the inadequate Spring Market; grounds were bought for $38,400, while construction costs were estimated at $20,450. The council then decided to advertise the contract, and by doing so possibly slightly lowered this sum. For Tompkins (1829) the city spent $20,000 for the grounds, while building costs had to be about $2,000, considering that this market had the same proportions as Manhattan. For Jefferson (1833) the council spent $32,500 for the grounds and $6,576 for construction. Weehawken (1834), which replaced Greenwich Market, was erected on public grounds for $3,475. Union (1836), replacing Grand Street Market (1836), cost $8,000 in terms of the grounds and $5,961 for construction. Finally, Monroe (1836), replacing Manhattan Market, cost $9,072 of construction money, while the corporation seems to have owned the grounds. *MCC*, 12:640, 12:637–41; 16:52–54; De Voe, *The Market Book*, 524, 527–28, 550–51, 559, 578, 580–81; New York (N.Y.), *Annual Report of the Comptroller, with the Accounts of the Corporation of the City of New York, for the Year Ending with the 31st December, 1836; Also the Account of the Commissioners of the Sinking Fund, for the Same Period* (New York: 1837), 59; New York (N.Y.), *Annual Report of the Comptroller, with the Accounts of the Corporation of the City of New York, for the Year Ending with the 31st December, 1837; Also the Account of the Commissioners of the Sinking Fund, for the Same Period* (New York: 1838), 65.

102. The three costliest expansions were those of Essex Market in 1822–23, again Essex in 1836–37, and Centre Market in 1838. The precise cost of the first expansion of Essex Market is unclear. Yet the city spent $7,000 for purchasing the grounds to enlarge both Essex and Grand Street Markets in 1822, while an ad-

ditional $8,800 was spent on the grounds for Essex in 1823. In 1836–37, the city spent a total of $90,294.71 to erect a new and more spacious market-house at Essex: $62,850 was spent on lands and compensations and $27,444.71 for construction. One year later, the council expended a similarly large sum to rebuild Centre Market: the grounds were purchased for $31,471, while construction costs reached $36,034.74. Overall, the new Centre Market cost $67,505.74. De Voe, *The Market Book*, 485, 471–72; *MCC*, 12:659, 12:649–70; 13:455, 13:451–58; New York (N.Y.), *Annual Report of the Comptroller, with the Accounts of the Corporation of the City of New York, for the Year Ending with the 31st December, 1834; Also the Account of the Commissioners of the Sinking Fund, for the Same Period* (New York: 1835), 58; New York (N.Y.), *Annual Report of the Comptroller, with the Accounts of the Corporation of the City of New York, for the Year Ending with the 31st December, 1835; Also the Account of the Commissioners of the Sinking Fund, for the Same Period* (New York: 1836), 63; New York (N.Y.), *Annual Report of the Comptroller . . . 1836*, 59, 61; New York (N.Y.), *Annual Report of the Comptroller . . . 1837*, 65; New York (N.Y.), *Annual Report of the Comptroller, with the Accounts of the Corporation of the City of New York, for the Year Ending with the 31st December, 1838; Also the Account of the Commissioners of the Sinking Fund, for the Same Period* (New York: 1839), 13, 93.

103. Another concern was that fees varied with the seasons, and the treasury needed more stable incomes. De Voe, *The Market Book*, 351.

104. The Common Council established monthly rates for the five markets based on their respective sales. Local butchers would decide how to distribute said rates among one another depending on the value of their businesses and stalls. The butchers would pay their annually fixed rents directly to the clerks. This would save money for the council by not having to share 10% of all market revenues with the market clerks. *MCC*, 1:516–19.

105. De Voe, *The Market Book*, 183; *MCC*, 1:534.

106. *MCC*, 2:301–2, 2:307; BA Documents, Vol. 21, Part 1, Doc. 41, 693–95; De Voe, *The Market Book*, 200–21.

107. In 1796, total market fees came to £1,986:3:3, after adjusting for the clerks' salaries and such expenses as sweeping. *MCC*, 2:421–23.

108. New York (N.Y.). Comptroller's Office, *Report of the Comptroller on the Establishment of a Sinking Fund for the Redemption of the City Stock* (New York: Hardcastle & Van Pelt, 1813).

109. Fourteen cellars at Washington Market, and one of each at Grand Street and Duane Markets were leased out through auctions for a five-year period to be paid in quarterly sums. De Voe, *The Market Book*, 411–12; *MCC*, 8:435–37.

110. The butchers complained that at the end of the term, just as they established their businesses, they would need to quit their stalls, not being able to bid competitively again. Stands would be purchased by speculators, while "butchers who are poor, will not be able, during their lives, to procure a stand." Tangires, *Public Markets and Civic Culture*, 74; De Voe, *The Market Book*, 411–12; CCMD, Market Committee: Stalls & Licenses (1816), 59:1417.

111. The resolution continues accordingly: "and shall go into operation, as it respects the Butcher Stalls in the present Markets on the first day of May next; and as soon thereafter as the Market Committee can complete the arrangement, as it respects the stands for the Fishermen, Country people, and sellers of Vegetables and fruit." *MCC*, 11:539–42; CCMD, Market Committee: Reports (1821), 80:1716; Market Committee: Stalls & Licenses (1821), 80:1717.

112. They managed to delay auctions at the other markets until at least Fulton Market

was completed. CCMD, Market Committee: Stalls & Licenses (July–Dec. 1821), 80:1718; De Voe, *The Market Book*, 489–93; quotes on 493. On this story, see also John C. Teaford, *The Municipal Revolution in America: Origins of Modern Urban Government, 1650–1825* (Chicago, IL: University of Chicago Press, 1975), 99.

113. Sixteen market cellars were sold for three-year leases in the value of $7,775 annually, and five others for fifteen months for $1,800 annually. The thirty-four huckster stands were auctioned for three-year leases at an annual rent of $1,320. De Voe, *The Market Book*, 494–97.

114. On market revenues, see appendix B.

115. CCMD, Market Committee: Reports (1822), 84:1766; De Voe, *The Market Book*, 497–500.

116. De Voe, *The Market Book*, 497–500.

117. Total market fees were $9,341.23 in 1816 and $9,490.70 in 1818. In comparison, total market revenues reached $28,767.32 in 1823 and $36,327.73 in 1824. The population between 1818 and 1824 increased from an estimated 107,625 to 156,583. On market revenues, see appendix B.

118. According to Pomerantz, city expenditures in 1790 reached £25,493. Given that municipal incomes, deriving from regular city revenues on the one hand, and personal and property taxes on the other, came to the same amount, while market fees were £1,097:15:1 in 1790, the market income represented about 4.3% of total revenues and expenditures. City expenditures grew more than fourfold by the end of the decade, while market fees came to £2,345:17:4 in 1800. Their share of the total consequently decreased to about 2.3%. Sidney Irving Pomerantz, *New York, an American City, 1783–1803: A Study of Urban Life* (New York: Columbia University Press, 1938), 355–71, especially 356; *MCC*, 3:186–87.

119. In 1813, overall city revenues were $464,948.34, while the income of the sinking fund was an additional $16,664.81, that is, total municipal revenues reached $481,613.15. Market fees came to an estimated $8,022.35 this year. In the fiscal year of 1818 (May 11, 1818–May 10, 1819), corporation revenues reached $682,819.51 and the sinking fund income was $43,650.56; therefore, total municipal revenues added up to $726,320.41. Market fees reached $9,490.70. *MCC*, 7:657–63; 10:382–88. On market revenues, see appendix B.

120. In 1824, overall city revenues were $877,426.83, the income of the sinking fund was $68,655.49, and total market revenues were $36,327.73. *MCC*, 14:242–50.

121. The yearly balance of revenues and expenditures between 1823 and 1845 came to $392,822.34. For sources and methods on how market revenues were estimated, see appendix B. The same municipal records contain data on market expenses as well.

122. The first deficit corresponds to the building of Clinton Market, while the second to the reconstruction of Essex and Centre.

123. Historians have not recognized this shift from neighborhood market-houses to a public market system probably because they did not look closely into the changes in public finances that sustained the city's infrastructure of provisioning. As for Tangires, she focuses mainly on auctions and premiums, and concludes that what eventually undermined the traditional moral economy of the market system was that the council violated its basic consensual principles by trying to maximize revenues through such means. She highlights how auctions and premiums were sources of tension between the butchers and the council, and that these reflected the new idea "that a market house was not a public amenity but rather an important piece of real estate." "By the 1830s the municipal corporation also had come to view markets primarily as real estate. It jealously guarded its holdings and

kept count of its market buildings and grounds—preferring to maximize revenues rather than to provide satisfactory and economical public facilities."

Tangires does have a point. But there is another side to the story as well. Looking at auctions outside of the revenue system, while giving too much credit to the butchers' complaints, she treats auctions as evidence of the government's withdrawal from finding public solutions to the challenge of feeding a growing metropolis. Certainly, by the 1810s the council found it imperative to raise market revenues, not least because from 1813 those were pledged to the sinking fund to redeem the public debt. Yet it was just as important that the city had never before been so invested in the public markets. To manage a public infrastructure of the scale and scope of the market system by the 1810s was no longer feasible through sales taxes. Tangires, *Public Markets and Civic Culture*, 73–75.

124. "Your memorialists are convinced that the tax on your markets is a great evil, calculated greatly to oppress the poor, and in the end injure the rich man. As things now are, a heavy tax, is laid upon almost everything sold in the markets, and collected by the market clerks." The petitioners suggested that "the mechanic worth $1,000 pays as much of the tax on markets as the rich man worth $100,000." CCMD, Market Committee (1830), 132:2324; emphasis in original.

125. Ibid.

126. The Law and Market Committees put forth the following argument: "Why should the Common Council collect this indirect tax from their fellow citizens? And what is it but an unequal burthen?—The poor man who buys but sparingly of poultry, deals almost every day with the Butcher. The rich man buys Butcher's meat when it suits him, and but a very small portion of it is acceptable to his palate—compared to the amount sold to the Mechanic and the working man." BAA Documents, Vol. 1, Doc. 66, 659–66; quote on 661.

127. CCFP, Markets (1836).

128. BA Documents, Vol. 5, Doc. 31, 374.

129. CCFP, Markets (1836).

130. Grocers raised their voice in part because they were worried that in the heat of the market controversy they may lose their right to retail fresh pork. CCFP, Markets (1837).

131. BA Documents, Vol. 3, Doc. 89, 599–603; Vol. 6, Doc. 25, 327–28; Vol. 6, Doc. 31, 363–77; Vol. 7, Doc. 55, 565–73; Vol. 11, Doc. 52, 517–29.

132. Ibid., Vol. 7, Doc. 43, 599–606; Vol. 9, Doc. 46, 407–24; BAA Documents, Vol. 19, Doc. 63, 265–72.

133. Even if shop butchers and grocers also had to pay store rents, the costs of which would in all likelihood be shifted to their customers, open access in theory would boost competition, putting downward pressure on retail food prices.

134. Teaford, *The Municipal Revolution in America*, 74; Kenneth Jackson, Lisa Keller, and Nancy Flood, eds., *The Encyclopedia of New York City*, 2nd ed. (New Haven, CT: Yale University Press, 2010), 521.

135. The complete sentence reads: "To a person engaged in profitable business, one hour spent in market is frequently worth more than the whole of what he purchases." Bridges, *Map of the City of New York . . . Laid Out by the Commissioners*, 27–30.

136. De Voe, *The Market Book*, 479; CCMD, Market Committee (1818), 66:1535.

137. CCFP, Markets (1837).

138. CCMD, Market Committee (1810), 40:1045.

139. Nonmarketplace butchers, operating south of these boundaries, had their businesses shut down, which they protested vehemently but in vain despite that

dozens of customers supported their cause. For instance, in 1817, John Akly, who "sold meat at the corner of Essex and Division Street . . . for three years past," petitioned for the renewal of his license, which was endorsed by twenty-one of his customers. Isaac Varian's request, who "has for some times past sold Meat at the corner of Pearl and Cross Streets in the 6th ward," was supported by twenty-two subscribers from the neighborhood. Other cases include Stephen Doan, who "sold Meat at the House No. 147 Division Street," or in 1818, Thomas Place, who "sold Meat in the neighborhood of Division and Norfolk Streets about thirty years, by which means he has been enabled to support his large family, but being deprived of that privilege," now petitioned for a stand at Grand Street Market. Many other butchers could be cited who suddenly lost their rights to retail meat at the street or from their homes, including James Gardener, Samuel Piercy, Henry M. Disbrow, or Joshua J. Place. Others used this opportunity to petition for a license to sell meat north of the market boundaries. For example, in 1817, Peter C. Chappel requested permission to set up his stall at the Bowery, which was endorsed by thirteen residents, and Thomas Morris asked for permission to sell meat at the corner of Greenwich Lane and Third Avenue, which was endorsed by fifteen residents. CCMD, Market Committee: Petitions (1817), 62:1477; Market Committee: Stalls & Licenses (1817), 62:1477; Market Committee: Stalls & Licenses (July–Dec. 1818), 66:1537; Market Committee: Stalls & Licenses (Jan.–July 1818), 66:1537; see, also, Beal, "Selling Gotham," 320–29.

140. Beal, "Selling Gotham," 335–36; CCMD, Market Committee: Reports (1827), 110:2090; Market Committee: Petitions (1828), 117:2172; Market Committee: Reports (1828), 117:2173; Market Committee: New Markets (1829), 124:2245.

141. Centre Market butchers considered outside vendors unfair competition. They not only infringed on their area, but they also did not pay rents, and hence could undersell them. In this specific case, however, street butchers at the Bowery offered the council to pay rents and "be subjected to the same regulations in all respects, as those are who complain" insofar as they could continue their businesses. CCMD, Market Committee: Petitions (1828), 117: 2172; Market Committee: Petitions (1828), 117:2172 oversized; Market Committee: New Markets (1829), 124:2245.

142. CCMD, Market Committee: New Markets (1829), 124:2245; Market Committee: Reports (1829), 124:2244.

143. CCFP, Markets (1837).

144. After the revenue system reform in 1821, it appears that these operations did not even pay taxes. This may seem an unfair advantage, but it reflects the principle that nonmarketplace butchers represented an exception to the market laws, aimed at addressing a temporary spatial problem.

145. If officials thought that in 1840 there were about thirty butchers licensed to sell meat north of Fourteenth Street, this figure was at best an estimate. CCFP, Market Committee (1840).

146. On shirk butchers, see note 25 in this chapter. Prior to the 1830s, many occasional cases of unlicensed food sales may be cited. It is noteworthy that the most often mentioned location of unlicensed meat sales was the Bowery, where an informal food market of sorts seems to have operated. This probably originated with licensed retailers, who became informal vendors once the market boundaries were pushed northward in 1817. As for the nonmarket retail of fish, the practice was probably spatially more dispersed. At least in 1825, a large number of fishermen complained to the council about "certain persons in the daily practice of hawking or peddling fish thro the streets and highways of this city." Two

years later, the fishmongers repeated the same grievances. *MCC*, 12:203; CCMD, Market Committee (1823), 88:1826; Market Committee (1823), 88:1826 oversized; Market Committee: Reports (1825) 98:1954; Market Committee (1827), 110:2088.

147. BAA Documents, Vol. 1, Doc. 66, 659–66; quote on 662.

148. BA Documents, Vol. 2, Doc. 28, 117–20; quote on 117.

149. Ibid., Vol. 2, Doc. 55, 237–39; quote on 238.

150. Ibid., Vol. 3, Doc. 89, 599–601; Vol. 3, Doc. 30, 185–86; Vol. 6, Doc. 25, 327–28; Vol. 9, Doc. 17, 161–62.

151. Ibid., Vol. 6, Doc. 37, 363–77; Vol. 6, Doc. 37, 405–6; BAA Documents, Vol. 19, Doc. 3, 265–72.

152. BA Documents, Vol. 7, Doc. 43, 599–606; Vol. 7, Doc. 60, 709–12; Vol. 9, Doc. 31, 257–62; Vol. 10, Part 1, Doc. 51, 651–58; Vol. 13, Doc. 4, 57–66; BAA Documents, Vol. 21, Doc. 50, 51–54; Vol. 21, Doc. 68, 263–73.

153. CCFP, Markets (1837). For a recent account on the bank war, see Stephen Mihm, *A Nation of Counterfeiters: Capitalists, Con Men, and the Making of the United States* (Cambridge, MA: Harvard University Press, 2007), 103–56.

154. Support for deregulation was widespread. The New York City Municipal Archives contains countless similar petitions signed by hundreds of residents from the next years, above all, from 1842. City Clerk Approved Papers (CCAP), Miscellaneous (1842).

155. They argued for the "necessity of Repealing the Law, prohibiting the Sale of Fresh Meats in private Shops at any Season." CCFP, Markets (1837).

156. In 1841, forty-eight shirk butchers from the Washington Market, while in the following year, 107 permit butchers from across the city demanded openly equal rights to the licensed butchers. CCFP, Markets (1841), Miscellaneous (1842).

157. They respectfully requested the council "to sustain the market laws as they now are—believing that the public good would be best served thereby." Similarly, in November 1842, two months before the market laws were repealed, licensed butchers unanimously protested the measure, while more than a hundred permit butchers supported it. CCFP, Market Committee (1840); BA Documents, Vol. 9, Doc. 45, 389–405.

158. CCFP, Markets (1838).

159. Duffy, *A History of Public Health*, 422; Beal, "Selling Gotham," 329–42; Horowitz, *Putting Meat on the American Table*, 24–26; Horowitz, Pilcher, and Watts, "Meat for the Multitudes," 1064–65, 1071–73; Horowitz, "The Politics of Meat Shopping," 167–77.

160. Tangires, *Public Markets and Civic Culture*, xv–xx, 3–25, 48–94; Horowitz, Pilcher, and Watts, "Meat for the Multitudes," 1055–58, 1064–67, 1071–74; Horowitz, "The Politics of Meat Shopping," 167–77.

161. Chapter 6 discusses the ethnic dimension of the market system. By and large, market butchers tended to be native-born, whereas outside vendors were often of immigrant, especially German origin.

162. BA Documents, Vol. 9, Doc. 46, 407–24; quote on 410.

163. For two examples of the Market Committee expressing this view, see BA Documents, Vol. 6, Doc. 31, 363–77; Vol. 11, Doc. 52, 517–29.

164. The comptroller's position is best summarized in BA Documents, Vol. 9, Doc. 46, 407–24.

165. Koeppel, *Water for Gotham*, especially 70–101, 104–25.

166. Jackson et al., *The Encyclopedia of New York City*, 450, 1382.

167. Even as the economic hardships of the recession of 1837–43 may have accounted

for rising welfare payments, it was much harder to explain why expenditures on street cleaning, for example, doubled between 1835 and 1838. Taxpayer, *City Finances: An Appeal to the Citizens of New-York* (New York: 1839).

168. The precise figures of city debt were as follows: $745,034.62 in 1834; $902,534.83 in 1835; $1,282,103.58 in 1836; $2,243,789.61 in 1837; $2,016,469.41 in 1838. As for the water loans, by the end of fiscal year 1838, they added up to $6,156,533.04. *City Finances*, 14; BA Documents, Vol. 6, Doc. 5, 82.

169. BA Documents, Vol. 6, Doc. 5, 37–90.

170. Ibid., 44.

171. Koeppel, *Water for Gotham*; Spann, *The New Metropolis*, 117–19; Edwin G. Burrows and Mike Wallace, *Gotham: A History of New York City to 1898* (New York: Oxford University Press, 2000), 625–28.

172. The overall costs of delivering the Croton water to Murray Hill were estimated at $4,250,709.71. An additional $1.3 million was considered necessary for building the distribution system. Yearly revenues from the Croton were projected at $310,000, sufficient to cover the annual interest of 6% assuming a $5 million budget. Insofar as the commissioners were concerned, paying off the principals was a problem left for future generations. Koeppel, *Water for Gotham*, 167–72.

173. To be precise, the outstanding debt, both permanent and temporary, came to $13,697,323.33. From this amount, the commissioners of the sinking fund held $965,805 worth of stocks, which reduced the net debt to $12,731,518.33. However, an additional $710,162.64 worth of contingent debt (fire stocks and bonds) was also issued by the corporation. BA Documents, Vol. 10, Doc. 1, 12–3.

174. Each year, when the mayor addressed the council to discuss the current state of public finances and other important matters of city governance, the public debt was treated as the most alarming subject. BA Documents, Vol. 10, Doc. 1, 12–13, 3–27; Vol. 13, Doc. 1, 4–6, 3–19; Vol. 14, Doc. 49, 705–17; Vol. 18, Doc. 1, 3–4, 1–20; Vol. 22, Doc. 1, 2–4, 1–34; Vol. 23, Doc. 10, 3–5, 1–70; Vol. 25, Part 1, Doc. 1, 4–7, 3–47; BAA Documents, Vol. 49, Doc. 1, 6–7, 3–12.

175. By then, the commissioners of the sinking fund held stocks in the amount of $3,092,345, while another $1,083,000 was funded in other ways, leaving the city debt to be redeemed at $9,710,514. BAA Documents, Vol. 49, Doc. 1, 6–7, 3–12.

176. Had the council not already authorized the reconstruction of Centre Market in May 1838, chances are that by the following year, even this last market improvement would not have been pursued. After Centre, New Yorkers had to wait until 1852 for the next noteworthy market reconstruction project, when Essex Market was again rebuilt for about $50,000. Then in 1854, Monroe Market was rebuilt, while in 1860, Tompkins Market was reconstructed for an estimated $155,371. De Voe, *The Market Book*, 471, 486–87, 555–56, 586.

177. BA Documents, Vol. 6, Doc. 55, 565–73; quote on 568.

178. Further, as Hartog argues, by the mid-nineteenth century, just as New York City became much like any other municipal corporation in America, it gradually relegated its private properties and rights. Hartog, *Public Property and Private Power*, 240–58.

179. In response to the first major debt cycle following the building of the new Almshouse and the new City Hall, the council assessed the value of all its properties in 1820. The total valuation of the market property came to $105,639.13 or 3.1% of all public property, which was assessed at $3,396,218.12. New York (N.Y.). *On the Amount and Value of the Public Property* (1820).

180. Market properties were assessed at $1,167,820 in 1838; $934,000 in 1840 (the

middle of the recession of 1837–43); and at $1,112,500 in 1843. BA Documents, Vol. 21, Part 1, Doc. 41, 665–69.

181. In 1846, the city's fourteen public markets, including Harlem, were appraised at $1,116,000, while they earned a total of $52,990.93 of revenues. The assessed value of all corporation real estate was $25,107,088.21. This consisted of $2,638,682.53 worth of "property available for the purposes of sale," and $22,468,397.68 worth of "property unavailable for the purposes of sale." Overall, the market property represented roughly 4.4% of the value of all corporation real estate, and belonged to the city's productive property, that is, unavailable with sale. BAA Documents, Vol. 29, Doc. 22, 249, 256.

182. In 1850, the city's market property, by then consisting of only twelve markets, was valued at $1,109,000. Its real estate was appraised at $19,505,410.88, not counting the properties associated with the Croton, valued at $14,327,583.95. BA Documents, Vol. 18, Part 1, Doc. 28, 577, 581.

183. According to Blackmar, by this time "political economy theory reconceptualized 'ground rent' itself to analyze not only revenues collected from tenants but even land's 'cost' to an owner-occupier who might pursue alternative investments." This was precisely the rationale Comptroller Flagg followed when he applied a standard rate of return, usually somewhere between 5 to 7%, on the market property. The important intervention on his part was to extend the real estate investment logic to evaluate the performance of municipal property, considering also opportunity costs. Blackmar, *Manhattan for Rent*, 251.

184. The lands were assessed at $925,000, while the buildings at $116,000. BA Documents, Vol. 21, Part 1, Doc. 41, 665–69, 743–44.

185. In his calculations, he assumed a 6% interest per annum, which eventually became the standard. BA Documents, Vol. 23, Doc. 10, 47; Vol. 25, Part 1, Doc. 1, 27–28; Vol. 26, Part 1, Doc. 1, 40–42.

186. BA Documents, Vol. 21, Part 1, Doc. 41, 646–47. The idea to rent out the public markets to private investors originated from similar plans implemented in New Orleans. Another approach to privatization, to charter private market corporations, was enthusiastically pursued in Philadelphia from 1859, where in three years twenty market companies were created. In the postbellum era, privatization swept through Pennsylvania. To New York City, it arrived later in 1871, when the state legislature approved a general incorporation act for private markets. The first such private market to open in 1872 was the Manhattan Market Company. For a detailed discussion of privatization in the postbellum period, see Tangires, *Public Markets and Civic Culture*, 87–89, 108–48.

187. BA Documents, Vol. 21, Part 2, Doc. 50, 933–40; quote on 933.

188. Ibid., Vol. 23, Doc. 10, 43–52; quotes on 45, 50; Vol. 22, Doc. 34, 12; Tangires, *Public Markets and Civic Culture*, 89–93.

189. Lobel links the reverse trends of municipal disinvestment in the public market system on the one hand and large-scale public works such as the Croton or Central Park on the other, drawing mainly on my dissertation. In her account, "these two large public works projects turned out to be the exception that proved the rule. Croton represented an ending, rather than a beginning—a relic of the patrician government of the early national period." As this book's introduction and this chapter have demonstrated, the opposite was the case. The Croton was not a "relic" of some "patrician government" but the first instance of a modern municipal utility, owned and managed by the city government. The construction of the Croton and Central Park demonstrate the robust expansion of city government in the midcentury, as urban historical scholarship has shown. The comparison with

the food infrastructure offers novel insights, but not because it shows that deregulation was the dominant trend. Rather, the problem at stake is why the food infrastructure had a different fate from the Croton, Central Park, or the street system, especially considering that it was one of the few public services the city had traditionally provided. The significance of this formulation lies in recognizing that it was the result of specific antebellum political economy decisions that the provisioning of food did not develop into a modern public service in the nineteenth-century American city but instead was left to free markets. Lobel, *Urban Appetites*, 98; Gergely Baics, "Feeding Gotham: A Social History of Urban Provisioning, 1780–1860" (PhD dissertation, Northwestern University, 2009).

CHAPTER 2: THE LANDSCAPE OF MUNICIPAL FOOD ACCESS

1. New-York Historical Society, Manuscript Division (NYHS-MD), "Fat Oxen" (New York: 1828) following emphasis on Monday afternoon in original.

2. The existing scholarship on urban provisioning, public markets, and food culture does not systematically engage the subject of living standards. Specifically for this chapter, the performance of public markets in the Early Republican era to fulfill their political mandate in provisioning residents has been assumed rather than carefully studied with the sources and tools available to urban social and economic historians. This is what this chapter sets out to do.

   One exception is Horowitz, whose pathbreaking work on American meat consumption over the centuries points to important questions about provisioning and food quality in nineteenth-century New York. Other scholars working entirely or partly on nineteenth-century New York City, especially Tangires and Beal, provide excellent discussions of the history of public markets, butchers, and food vendors, however, their focus is not primarily on food consumption, quality, inequality, and living standards. Such an analysis is also by and large absent from Lobel's research of New York food and restaurant cultures in the nineteenth century. As for the Early Republican era, in chapter 1, Lobel provides a useful description of the regulatory context and daily functioning of public markets, but her research does not extend to the analysis of the actual performance of the provisioning system. In general, the literature has focused primarily on what public markets were supposed to do instead of how successfully or not they achieved their mandate, a problem that requires different research strategy and source documentation. Roger Horowitz, *Putting Meat on the American Table: Taste, Technology, Transformation* (Baltimore, MD: Johns Hopkins University Press, 2006); Roger Horowitz, Jeffrey M. Pilcher, and Sydney Watts, "Meat for the Multitudes: Market Culture in Paris, New York City, and Mexico City over the Long Nineteenth Century," *American Historical Review* 109, no. 4 (2004), 1055–83; Helen Tangires, *Public Markets and Civic Culture in Nineteenth-Century America* (Baltimore, MD: Johns Hopkins University Press, 2003); Paula Y. Lee, ed., *Meat, Modernity, and the Rise of the Slaughterhouse* (Lebanon: University of New Hampshire Press, 2008); Thomas D. Beal, "Selling Gotham: The Retail Trade in New York City from the Public Market to Alexander T. Stewart's Marble Palace, 1625–1860" (PhD dissertation, State University of New York at Stony Brook, 1998); Cindy R. Lobel, *Urban Appetites: Food and Culture in Nineteenth-Century New York* (Chicago, IL: University of Chicago Press, 2014).

   Economic historians have paid far more attention to the subject of food consumption in living standards, especially in the context of the antebellum puzzle. However, their line of research does not directly address the subject of food provisioning, nor does it have a specifically urban focus. The empirical material for this book (especially in chapters 2 and 6) fills this gap between the two bodies of scholarship of food and economic history. For a select list of key publications on the antebellum puzzle, see note 31 in the introduction.

3. Meat consumption has been used by economic historians as an indicator of changing nutritional and living standards. The subject occupies a prominent place in the antebellum puzzle debate (see note 2). Scholars more directly interested in food history, such as Horowitz in the American or Otter in the British context, have also paid significant attention to how meat consumption relates to nutritional and living standards. Horowitz, *Putting Meat on the American Table*; Christopher Otter, "The British Nutrition Transition and Its Histories," *History Compass* 10, no. 11 (2012), 812–25.

4. For a discussion of public market revenue data and how these were used to estimate meat consumption figures, see appendix B.

5. It is not possible to determine how substantial this portion was. Reconstructions of John Pintard's 1811, 1814, and 1827 household budgets offer one point of reference. In 1811, Pintard spent 56.6% of his family's meat budget on butcher's meats, 28.9% on processed and preserved meats, and 14.5% on poultry, fowl, and game. The respective ratios in 1814 were 55.3, 25.3, and 19.4%, while in 1827 they were 62.4, 9, and 28.5%. Pintard's upper-middle-class family is certainly not representative. Yet the fact that his expenditures on butcher's meat were consistently between 55 and 62% underlines that red meat, while greatly important, constituted only part of an average New Yorker's meat basket. Considering that poultry, fowl, and game were relatively expensive, the meat basket of an average New Yorker probably relied more heavily on red and/or preserved meats than that of the Pintards. NYHS-MD, John Pintard, *Papers*, "Marketing Account Book, 1811–1824"; "Marketing Account Book, 1826–1830"; "Record of Household Expenses, 1826–1828," 9:1–3.

6. For a discussion of how yearly market fees (collected as excise taxes) were estimated for the period between 1786 and 1818, see appendix B.

7. Thomas F. De Voe, *The Market Book: A History of the Public Markets of the City of New York* (New York: A. M. Kelley, 1970 [1862]), 410.

8. Edwin G. Burrows and Mike Wallace, *Gotham: A History of New York City to 1898* (New York: Oxford University Press, 1999), 425–28.

9. Market fees remained stable between 1794 ($4,659.84) and 1795 ($4,669.01), when yellow fever first hit New York City after the Revolution, killing 732 people. Fees dropped sharply from $5,112.92 in 1797 to $4,384.66 in 1798, when 1,524 residents only in New York City died in the most devastating yellow fever epidemic. If one includes those who contracted illness in New York but died outside of the city, the figures reach a staggering 2,086 victims. For the 1803 epidemic, there are no corresponding market fee data available, while the much milder 1805 fever, which claimed "only" 262 lives, had no observable impact on market fees. John Duffy, *A History of Public Health in New York City* (New York: Russell Sage Foundation, 1968), 105–9, 101–23; Ira Rosenwaike, *Population History of New York City* (Syracuse, NY: Syracuse University Press, 1972), 16–19.

10. The embargo caused severe hardships to New York City's economy. Between 1807 and 1809, municipal expenditures on relief rose by 70%. Burrows and Wallace, *Gotham*, 412.

11. For a discussion of how meat consumption figures were estimated, see appendix B.

12. Two caveats are in order. First, these figures are likely to slightly underestimate per capita butcher's meat consumption for they refer to animals officially accounted for and prepared and sold by licensed butchers at the city's public markets. Given the market monopoly, this should have been the whole supply. Yet despite a well-functioning and strictly enforced public market system, there was already evidence of some informal trade. It is also unlikely that market clerks managed to count all animals sold by the butchers. Butchers paid taxes after each and every animal slaughtered, and had the incentive not to report all sales. The figures, on the other hand, may also slightly overestimate per capita consumption. By 1810, New York surpassed Philadelphia to become America's most populous city and greatest emporium of commerce. At any given day, there were thousands more in the city besides residents eating butcher's meats. It is impossible to know which factor was more important, and to what extent the two canceled each other out.

13. According to Horowitz's calculations, per capita urban meat consumption rates in 1909 ranged from an average of 136.1 pounds for lower-income families to 163.7 pounds for middle-income families, and to 201.6 pounds for higher-income families. By 1942, the Great Depression pushed total meat consumption for the respective income groups down to 107.5, 143.6, and 166.1 pounds, respectively. Yet by 1965, these rates reached record heights at 205.2 pounds for lower-income families, 219.4 pounds for middle-income families, and 230.2 pounds for higher-income families. The corresponding figures for urban beef consumption for the same groups were: 57.6, 71.3, and 88.4 pounds in 1904; 37.0, 60.0, and 65.6 pounds in 1942; and 67.5, 81.6, and 101.2 pounds in 1965. For pork: 52.9, 55.5, and 65.6 pounds in 1904; 41.5, 42.6, and 45.8 pounds in 1942; and 57.1, 58.0, and 54.1 pounds in 1965. To distinguish between these different socioeconomic groups, Horowitz used the following income gradients: in 1909, less than $1,000 for the lowest income category, between $1,000–2,000 for the middle, and more than $2,000 for the highest; in 1942, the corresponding categories were less than $1,500 (1942), between $1,500–3,000, and more than $3,000; in 1965, less than $3,000, between $3,000–6,000, and between $6,000–15,000 (for this year, Horowitz also added a separate category for those more than $15,000).

Looking at the national level for the same years, per capita beef consumption stood at 81.5 pounds in 1909, dropped to 69.4 pounds by 1942, and reached a staggering 104.7 pounds by 1965. Pork consumption declined slowly but consistently from 67 pounds in 1909, to 63.7 pounds in 1942, and to 58.7 pounds in 1965. At the same time, poultry consumption increased robustly from 14.7 (1909), to 20.7 (1942), and to 40.9 pounds (1965). Horowitz, *Putting Meat on the American Table*, 6, 11–17.

14. For a discussion of how meat consumption figures were estimated, see appendix B.

15. In 1816, the council decided to replace Fly Market with the modern Fulton Market, which opened in 1821. Butchers started to abandon Fly Market as early as 1818. Given that Fly conducted the largest volume of trade, its demise must have resulted in expanding unlicensed sales, leaving more animals unaccounted for by the market clerks. The fact that the decrease in animal counts resulted less from declining sales of beef than of "small meats" (veal, lamb and mutton, and pork), in which cases violations occurred more frequently, supports this explanation.

16. Horowitz, *Putting Meat on the American Table*, 12.

17. She finds that the yearly meat allowance of widows rose from between 120.8 and

145.2 pounds in the early eighteenth century to between 168.2 and 183.5 pounds from the middle of the century to its end, and then reached an impressive 201.8 pounds by the beginning of the nineteenth century. Sarah F. McMahon, "A Comfortable Subsistence: The Changing Composition of Diet in Rural New England, 1620–1840," *William and Mary Quarterly* 42, no. 1 (1985), 36–37, 56, table 4; Sarah F. McMahon, " 'All Things in Their Proper Season': Seasonal Rhythms of Diet in Nineteenth-Century New England," *Agricultural History* 63, no. 2 (1989), 130–51.

18. James T. Lemon, "Household Consumption in Eighteenth-Century America and Its Relationship to Production and Trade: The Situation among Farmers in Southeastern Pennsylvania," *Agricultural History* 41, no. 1 (1967), 61–63.

19. One should note that the composition of the Philadelphia meat diet closely mirrored the distribution of the four types of butcher's meats in New York City, further validating the consistency of these estimates. According to Smith's reconstructions, in 1772, an average Philadelphia laborer's supply of butcher's meats consisted of 100.2 pounds of beef, 47.0 pounds of veal, 18.2 pounds of mutton, and 9.1 pounds of pork. That is, 57% of a Philadelphia laborer's meat supply came from beef, 27% from veal, 10% from mutton, and 5% from pork. The corresponding ratios in New York City in 1816 were 58% for beef, 12% for veal, 21% for lamb and mutton, and 8% for pork, while in 1818, 60% for beef, 12% for veal, 20% for lamb and mutton, 8% for pork. The ratios for beef and pork are essentially the same for the two cities. It is also true that they considerably differ for veal and mutton, although these represented only one-third of total fresh meat consumption. For further discussion, see appendix B. Billy G. Smith, "The Material Lives of Laboring Philadelphians, 1750 to 1800," *William and Mary Quarterly* 38, no. 2 (1981), 167–71, especially, 170, table 1.

20. See note 5 on John Pintard's meat expenditures in 1811, 1814, and 1817.

21. Horowitz, *Putting Meat on the American Table*, 18–19.

22. Husson provides average yearly per capita butcher's meat consumption rates (beef, veal, and mutton) for 1781–86, 1799–1808, 1809–18. He does not specify the amounts by individual species, but he gives annual slaughter counts for the respective animals (*boeuf & vache, veau, mouton*) along with their dressed weights. From this, a simple calculation allows for establishing the ratios of the three species of meat within the whole supply, and accordingly their per capita consumption rates. The category of pork is excluded from table 2.3 because Husson does not treat pork as butcher's meat, but instead includes cured meats (*charcuterie*) under that category as well, and therefore the Parisian and New York City figures in this case are not directly comparable. Finally, data on total per capita meat consumption in France come from Brantz's dissertation. Armand Husson, *Les consommations de Paris* (Paris: Guillaumin et Cie, 1856), 142, 145, 148, 153–54, 157, 196; Dorothee Brantz, "Slaughter in the City: The Establishment of Public Abattoirs in Paris and Berlin, 1780–1914" (PhD dissertation, University of Chicago, 2003), 127–41, 138, table 2.3; Maurice Garden and Jean Luc Pinol, *Atlas des Parisiens, de la révolution à nos jours* (Paris: Parigramme, 2009), 157.

23. According to John Ramsay McCulloch's calculations, per capita meat consumption in 1837 in London, exclusive of processed meats and poultry, was 107 pounds. Similarly, Brantz finds that Berliners consumed 104.7 pounds of red meat per capita in 1845. Simon G. Hanson, *Argentine Meat and the British Market: Chapters in the History of the Argentine Meat Industry* (Stanford, CA: Stanford University Press, 1938), 22–23, notes 12, 16; Brantz, "Slaughter in the City," 295.

See, also, Peter J. Atkins, "A Tale of Two Cities: A Comparison of Food Supply in London and Paris in the 1850s," in *Food and the City in Europe since 1800*, ed. Peter Atkins, Peter Lummel, and Derek Oddy (Aldershot: Ashgate, 2007), 34–36.

24. For Barcelona, meticulous new research has reconstructed meat consumption levels from the late eighteenth through the mid-twentieth century. Manuel Guàrdia, José L. Oyón, and Nadia Fava, "Meat Consumption and Nutrition Transition in Barcelona, 1820–1935: Slaughterhouses, Public Markets and Butcher Shops" (paper presented at the Twelfth International Conference of the European Association for Urban History, Lisbon, September 2014).

25. Other scholars confirm this enormous discrepancy. In the nineteenth century, per capita meat consumption in Paris was close to 200 pounds, that is, about one-fourth higher than the amount consumed in other major cities, and about five times the level of meat consumption in rural areas. Pinol and Garden, *Atlas Des Parisiens*, 157.

26. It required all beef cattle from the Paris region to be sold at the Sceaux and Poissy provisioning markets for the exclusive consumption of the capital. If regular supplies from Normandie, Île-de-France, and Limousin proved inadequate, the government commissioned livestock purchases tapping into more distant supply regions. Horowitz, Pilcher, and Watts, "Meat for the Multitudes," 1060–61.

27. Horowitz, *Putting Meat on the American Table*, 20.

28. Indeed, meat consumption estimates for Philadelphia in 1772 and New York City in the Early Republic have yielded comparable results (see table 2.2, and note 19). Moreover, price series data (see figure 2.2 and note 30) reveal that wholesale beef and pork prices between the two cities moved closely together. This demonstrates that by the Early Republic, livestock markets were regionally integrated, indicating similar meat supply conditions for the two cities.

29. The underlying point is that New Yorkers (or American city dwellers in general) could consume such abundant supplies of meat or other provisions only insofar as the urban economy generated enough wealth to pay for these goods. Had the relative price of food to industrial goods increased, urban consumers would have found agricultural imports such as meat more expensive, and their ability to pay for them diminished, and the other way around.

30. Wholesale price indexes (base years: 1821–25) from Philadelphia and New York City reveal a strong association between the prices of barreled (= 200 pounds) beef and pork during the Early Republic, and there is no reason to believe that fresh beef and pork prices would have followed different trends. Indeed, even as beef and pork prices show much volatility, these changes affected both species of meat similarly. To be precise, the widely cited Philadelphia price indexes show a strong positive correlation between the annual wholesale prices of barreled beef and pork ("r" = 0.88) between 1784 and 1825. The two series are also very strongly correlated with the Philadelphia price index for all "meats and meat products" ("r" = 0.93 and 0.97, respectively), and thus figure 2.2 only uses this composite index. Despite their greater volatility due to external shocks and sparser price quotations, annual wholesale prices for barreled beef and pork in New York between 1796 and 1825 also show a moderately strong correlation ("r" = 0.64). In addition, there are strong correlations between beef ("r" = 0.83) and pork ("r" = 0.93) prices in the two cities, indicating that northeastern meat markets were already well integrated. Anne Bezanson et al., *Wholesale Prices in Philadelphia, 1784–1861* (Philadelphia: University of Pennsylvania Press, 1936),

1:392, 1:394; 2:9, 2:171; Arthur Harrison Cole and International Scientific Committee on Price History, *Wholesale Commodity Prices in the United States, 1700–1861; Statistical Supplement: Actual Wholesale Prices of Various Commodities* (Cambridge, MA: Harvard University Press, 1938).

31. Wholesale price indexes for barreled beef and pork in New York City, and for all "meat and meat products" and industrial commodities in Philadelphia, suggest that the relative price of meat to industrial goods remained unchanged in this period. In fact, one finds a strong positive correlation between Philadelphia meat prices and industrial prices ("r" = 0.74) between 1784 and 1825, a moderately strong correlation between New York pork prices and Philadelphia industrial prices ("r" = 0.74) between 1796 and 1825, and a weak relationship between New York beef prices and Philadelphia industrial prices ("r" = 0.22) in the same period. Overall, the relative price of beef and pork in the two cities, and most probably across the Northeast, did not undergo any trend rise or decline during the Early Republic. One should add that Komlos already brought attention to the use of relative prices in studying changing levels of food consumption. John Komlos, "The Height and Weight of West Point Cadets: Dietary Change in Antebellum America," *Journal of Economic History* 47, no. 4 (1987), 915–16.

32. Relying on the Philadelphia price data, one finds strong positive correlations between meat and grain ("r" = 0.86) and meat and fish ("r" = 0.8) prices between 1784 and 1825. Further, industrial commodity prices also strongly correlate with grain ("r" = 0.69) and fish ("r" = 0.78) prices in the same period. In other words, the relative prices of different types of provisions to industrial goods remained unchanged.

33. The full quote reads: "On the shoals of roast beef and apple pie, all socialist utopias flounder." Werner Sombart, "American Capitalism's Economic Rewards," in *Failure of a Dream? Essays in the History of American Socialism,* ed. John Laslett and Seymour Martin Lipset (Garden City, NY: Doubleday Anchor, 1974), 599.

34. Most textbooks on economic geography or urban economics include a basic description of central-place theory. The discussion here is primarily based on Berry's classic treatise of the theory and its extension to urban retail trade. Another useful introduction to urban retail geography is offered by Kivell and Shaw, while more recently an excellent brief summary is presented by Lesger in relation to his insightful case study of the locational patterns of retailing in mid-eighteenth-century Amsterdam. Brian J. L. Berry, *Geography of Market Centers and Retail Distribution* (Englewood Cliffs, NJ: Prentice Hall, 1969); Philip T. Kivell and Gareth Shaw, "The Study of Retail Location," in *Retail Geography,* ed. John A. Dawson (London: Croom Helm, 1980), 95–155; Clé Lesger, "Patterns of Retail Location and Urban Form in Amsterdam in the Mid-Eighteenth Century," *Urban History* 38, no. 1 (2011), 26–28.

35. For example, in their case study of Snohomish County, Washington, in the late 1950s, Berry and Garrison estimated the threshold population for food stores at 256, among the lowest of all businesses, whereas the same for jewelry stores (a commonly used example for shopping goods) was 827 people. Correspondingly, jewelry stores had a greater range, attracting customers from much larger distances. Brian J. L. Berry and William L. Garrison, "A Note on Central-Place Theory and the Range of a Good," *Economic Geography* 34, no. 4 (1958), 304–11. For a broader discussion of these variables, see Berry, *Geography of Market Centers,* 10–20, 42–57; Brian J. L. Berry, "Internal Structure of the City," *Law and Contemporary Problems* 30, no. 1 (1965), 116–19.

36. Berry actually distinguishes between five levels of hierarchy for shopping centers: isolated convenience stores, neighborhood, community, regional shopping centers, and the metropolitan central business district. This ranking follows the same logic of centrality that underlies the hierarchy of settlements in a region: hamlets, villages, towns, cities (small or large), and metropolises (regional or national). Berry, *Geography of Market Centers*, 17, 44–46; Brian J. L. Berry, "Ribbon Developments in Urban Business Patterns," *Annals of the Association of American Geographers* 49, no. 2 (1959), 147–49; Ross L. Davies, "Structural Models of Retail Distribution: Analogies with Settlement and Urban Land-Use Theories," *Transactions of the Institute of British Geographers*, no. 57 (1972), 64–69.

37. Several studies in historical geography demonstrate this dispersed retail pattern for food shops, including Conzen and Conzen for Milwaukee (1836–90) grocers, butchers, and other food vendors; Wild and Shaw for Kingston upon Hull (1823–81) grocers and butchers; Robichaud for San Francisco (1870) butchers; and in the case of bakers, Leesger for Amsterdam (1742), Pred for New York (1840), and Zephyr for Rio de Janeiro (1870). Michael P. Conzen and Kathleen N. Conzen, "Geographical Structure in Nineteenth-Century Urban Retailing: Milwaukee, 1836–90," *Journal of Historical Geography* 5, no. 1 (1979), 45–60; Gareth Shaw and M. T. Wild, "Locational Behaviour of Urban Retailing during the Nineteenth Century: The Example of Kingston upon Hull," *Transactions of the Institute of British Geographers* 61, no. 1 (1974), 101–18; Lesger, "Patterns of Retail Location," 32; Allan R. Pred, *The Spatial Dynamics of U.S. Urban-Industrial Growth, 1800–1914: Interpretive and Theoretical Essays* (Cambridge, MA: MIT Press, 1966), 206; Frank Zephyr, "Terrain of History," Stanford Spatial History Lab, http://www.stanford.edu/group/spatialhistory/cgi-bin/site/viz.php?id=397&project_id=0; Andrew Robichaud, "Animal City," Stanford Spatial History Lab, http://www.stanford.edu/group/spatialhistory/cgi-bin/site/viz.php?id=149&project_id=0.

38. The pattern to seek out mutually exclusive market areas is also referred to as monopolistic competition and is characteristic of retailers of convenience goods, where comparison shopping is not customary. Berry, *Geography of Market Centers*, 63.

39. For a detailed analysis on the rhythms of food shopping, see chapter 3.

40. Rosenwaike, *Population History*, 18.

41. For central-place theory, retail growth is endogenous to urban growth. On this point, see James E. Vance Jr., *The Merchant's World: The Geography of Wholesaling* (Englewood Cliffs, NJ: Prentice Hall, 1970), 140–42.

42. In other words, even as demand for retailers is a direct function of urbanization, the expansion of the public market infrastructure depends on the political process as an exogenous factor.

43. In this sense, public markets, even though supplying residents directly as retail centers, in terms of their volume of trade, resemble wholesale establishments.

44. This discussion is influenced by Vance's seminal work on the geography of wholesaling. His main insight and critique of central-place theory emerged out of his analysis of the historical development of American urban hierarchy. He argues that under the frontier conditions of America, urbanization evolved not from a gradual bottom-up development from lower to higher centrality but originated from relatively larger settlements, which served as entrepôts with wholesaling functions, anchoring the growth of their regions and organizing the territories around them. In other words, central-place development followed the settlement process initiated by gateway cities. Vance thus introduces an exogenous factor,

wholesaling agents, to explain urbanization and settlement hierarchy in frontier geographies. Without the intention of pushing the analogy too far, the public market system, for the reasons of its agglomeration economies and politically negotiated development, shares certain characteristics with Vance's model. The most relevant issue is the role that public markets played in newly urbanizing areas: the degree to which they followed or anticipated urban growth, as well as anchored and supported population settlement and business development. Vance, *The Merchant's World*.

45. For a discussion of butcher stalls data, and how annual stall counts were established, see appendix B.

46. To be precise, the ratio increased from 433 in the 1790s, to 488 in the first, and then to 498 in the second decade of the nineteenth century.

47. For a discussion of the sources and methods used to produce the maps, see appendix A.

48. In fact, Fly, Bear, and Catharine Markets were located in close proximity to one of the four ferry lines that connected Manhattan to Brooklyn or New Jersey.

49. In addition, at the southeastern tip of Manhattan, the recently opened Franklin Market (1822) also served residents.

50. For example, in 1818 the volume of trade of the individual marketplaces and the population density of their wards show a strong positive correlation ("r" = 0.71).

51. For sources and literature, see note 10 in chapter 1.

52. The Market Committee articulated the case for public health most clearly in its report of Dec. 2, 1839, in response to widespread debates about the legitimacy of the public market system: "The various and important duties which are now performed by the Superintendents and the Deputy Clerks of the Markets, in guarding the public health, by examining as to the wholesomeness of provisions; whether stale, or blown, plaited, raised or stuffed, measly or affected by disease; and whether proper cleanliness is observed; and as to other important Police regulations, as to weights, measures, &c., if the business of vending meats, &c., is not confined to the Public Markets, become entire vain and nugatory . . . The health of our city is a matter of the highest consideration; and the cleanliness, upon which it mainly depends, and which now characterizes our public Markets, cannot possibly be preserved, if the business of dealing in all kinds of meats be diffused throughout the city." Historians have similarly argued that public markets were an essential infrastructure for Early American cities to maintain control over the quality of food supplies. For a discussion on deregulation and public health, see chapter 6. New York (N.Y.). Board of Aldermen, *Documents of the Board of Aldermen of the City of New York* (BA Documents) (New York: 1834–68), Vol. 6, Doc. 31, 363–77; quote on 375; Duffy, *A History of Public Health*, 50–52, 83–86, 222–27, 420–39; Tangires, *Public Markets and Civic Culture*, 15–17, 3–25, 71–94, 132–48.

53. For more on public health regulations, see New York (N.Y.), *Laws and Ordinances* (1793), 6–10; New York (N.Y.), *Laws and Ordinances* (1812), 154–64; New York (N.Y.), *A Law to Regulate the Public Markets* (1815); New York (N.Y.), *A Law to Regulate Fulton Market, and for other Purposes; Passed Dec. 13, 1821* (New York: Printed by G. L. Birch, 1821). On oysters specifically, see Thomas F. De Voe, *The Market Assistant, Containing a Brief Description of Every Article of Human Food Sold in the Public Markets of the Cities of New York, Boston, Philadelphia, and Brooklyn; Including the Various Domestic and Wild Animals, Poultry, Game, Fish, Vegetables, Fruits, &c., &c., with Many Curious Incidents and Anecdotes* (Cambridge, MA: Printed at

the Riverside Press for the author, 1867), 306–8; quote on 306. The 1839 ordinance prohibited the sale of oysters from May 1 through September 1, corresponding to the established wisdom to eat oysters only in months with an "R."

54. Arthur O'Sullivan, *Urban Economics* (Homewood, IL: Irwin, 1990), 28–29; Asher
Wolinsky, "Retail Trade Concentration Due to Consumers' Imperfect Information," *Bell Journal of Economics* 14, no. 1 (1983), 275–82.

55. On the term "market monopoly," see the discussion in chapter 1.

56. Beal, "Selling Gotham," 317–20.

57. New York (N.Y.), *Laws and Ordinances* (1812), 157.

58. Despite profound changes in the structure of work in the first half of the nine-
teenth century, butchers remained one of the last traditional trading crafts in
American cities. On the erosion of traditional crafts and the formation of New
York's working class in the antebellum era, Wilentz's seminal book provides the
best treatise. For the butchers' case specifically, see Sean Wilentz, *Chants Demo-
cratic: New York City and the Rise of the American Working Class, 1788–1850* (New
York: Oxford University Press, 1984), 55, 137–39, 262, 270, 315–16; Tangires,
Public Markets and Civic Culture, 61–63, 64–68, 71–94; Burrows and Wallace,
Gotham, 402, 632, 740, 1086.

59. Butchers maintained informal control of the everyday social and spatial order of
the marketplace. They also effectively represented their corporate interests in
city politics, and exhibited their corporate identity at public events such as city
parades. The fact that butchers succeeded in protecting their retail privilege until
1843 is testimony to their high-level trade organization.

60. De Voe was undoubtedly an exceptionally erudite butcher. His published works
are testimonies of an old tradition of urban craftsmanship, and the public purpose and collective identity of generations of butchers. *The Market Book* contains
detailed biographies of New York's more reputable butchers as if their public role
competed with that of the city's officeholders. *The Market Assistant*, in essence a
guide for households, describes every aspect of the butcher's craft, including the
preparation and handling of meat, the various kinds of cuts, and their qualities.
De Voe, *The Market Book*; De Voe, *The Market Assistant*.

61. For further discussion about the butchers and their stalls, see chapter 1.

62. As some petitions testify, and was noted in chapter 1, some butchers found ways
around the system. A butcher could manipulate the market for stalls by recom-
mending a successor to the Common Council, or by exchanging his stall for another with the consent of another butcher and the council, or by informally
subleasing it. Still, such practices could only have small impact on a real estate
market that was largely controlled by the municipality, and that created artificial
barriers for butchers to relocate their businesses.

63. Data on butcher stalls at the more prominent markets confirm that the butcher's
trade was spatially stable. While the data come from the 1820s and 1830s, they
can be regarded equally relevant for the early nineteenth century. Accordingly,
42% of the butchers between 1818 and 1828, and 44% of them between 1828
and 1838 continued to work at their original marketplaces. Furthermore, over
the five-year period between 1832 and 1836, 58% of the stalls were held continu-
ously by the original butchers, 23% had one, 11% two, and 7% had three occupancy changes. One should note that out of these occupancy changes, 9% of
transfers occurred between immediate relatives, 7% refers to a butcher's move
from one stall to another within the same marketplace, while many others must
have occurred between distant relatives, friends, or master butchers and appren-

TABLE A. Butchers Retailing Meat at Same Stall over Ten Years,
1818/28 and 1828/38

Market	1818/28	1828/38
Catharine	32%	32%
Centre	57%	45%
Franklin	NA	50%
Fulton	NA	50%
Washington	36%	40%
Clinton (1829/38)	NA	46%
Average	42%	44%

Sources: See note 63 appendix B.

TABLE B. Number of Occupancy Changes at Butcher Stalls, 1832–36

Market	"0"	"1"	"2"	"3"
Catharine	55%	26%	15%	4%
Centre	54%	42%	4%	0
Essex	56%	33%	0	11%
Franklin	75%	0	25%	0
Fulton	58%	30%	8%	3%
Grand	50%	0	20%	30%
Washington	58%	31%	7%	4%
Average	58%	23%	11%	7%

Sources: See note 63 appendix B.

tices. The data are summarized in the two tables above. For a discussion of butcher stalls data, see appendix B.

64. For example, De Voe's 1849 petition to the council to obtain a stall at Jefferson Market was signed by 107 regular customers. NYHS-MD, De Voe, *Manuscripts*, "New York City markets collection, ca. 1817–ca. 1878," 1.

65. In the colonial period, the Common Council confined slaughtering to the area around the Collect Pond, outside of the city's densely populated wards. The right of slaughtering was periodically sold to one individual, and licensed butchers were required to kill and process their animals at this Public Slaughter-House under the supervision of city officials, the keeper of the slaughterhouse, and the so-called slaughter farmer. De Voe, *The Market Book*, 366–68; Roger Horowitz, "The Politics of Meat Shopping in Antebellum New York City," in Lee, *Meat, Modernity*, 171; Jared Day, "Butchers, Tanners, and Tallow Chandlers: The Geog-

raphy of Slaughtering in Early Nineteenth Century New York City," in Lee, *Meat, Modernity*, 180–85.

66. Offal, bones, hides, and blood were either discarded or sold to soap makers, bone boilers, fat renderers, or tallow chandlers. For more on slaughter and the nuisance trades in late eighteenth- and early nineteenth-century New York, see Day, "Butchers, Tanners, and Tallow Chandlers," 180–90, Horowitz, "The Politics of Meat Shopping," 169–71.

67. For sources and methods used to produce these maps, see appendix A.

68. Nineteenth-century European cities increasingly opted for government control by erecting modern centralized public slaughterhouses (abattoirs). Most famously, in 1810, Napoleon I ended the practice of slaughtering in Paris, requiring that five municipal abattoirs be erected outside of the city, which opened for business in 1818. Horowitz, Pilcher, and Watts, "Meat for the Multitudes," 1074–75; Paula Y. Lee, "Siting the Slaughterhouse: From Shed to Factory," in Lee, *Meat, Modernity*, 50–51, 52–62.

69. One clue indicates that the butcher drawing the map, in fact, may have been Ernest Keyser. Specifically, among the butchers listed on the sketch and the final map, only in his case did the author write "Ernest Keyser born" and "Ernest Keyser born Old House," which building he also marked up carefully. Further, Ernest Keyser's home addresses as listed in the city directories match up reasonably well with the butcher's houses between 1815 and 1823 as marked on the map. Unfortunately, the correspondence is not perfect, thus the identity cannot be confirmed with certainty. David Longworth, *Longworth's American Almanac, New York Register, and City Directory, for the Thirty-Seventh Year of American Independence* (New York: David Longworth, 1812), 172; Thomas Longworth, *Longworth's American Almanac, New-York Register, and City Directory, for the Sixty-Sixth Year of American Independence* (New York: Thomas Longworth, 1841), 408; John Doggett Jr., *The New-York City Directory, for 1849–1850* (New York: John Doggett Jr., 1849), 239; New York (N.Y.). Common Council, *Minutes of the Common Council of the City of New York, 1784–1831 (MCC)* (New York: M. B. Brown Printing & Binding, 1917), 6:611; 7:77, 7:134.

70. The note "1797" on the map indicates that the butcher most probably worked from the Taylor-Roberts map of 1797. Another note, "1820 to 1840," suggests that he used a second map for the missing streets, which also helps explain why the map contains features from two different periods.

71. For sources and methods used to produce this map, see appendix A.

72. For a discussion on the market revenue system and its changes in 1822, see chapter 1.

73. In 1818–19, there were only three men listed among the city's 193 licensed hucksters. An 1827 list identifies 22 men out of 185 hucksters. Huckster women usually emphasized their desperate financial situation when petitioning for a license. Widows, especially if their husbands had been market vendors, often pursued this strategy. Out of Fulton Market's approximately 69 huckster women in 1827, 31 were widows. Common Council Microfilm Database, New York City Municipal Archives (CCMD), Market Committee (1818), 66:1535; Market Committee (1819), 72:1595; Market Committee (1827): Market Committee Reports, 110.2090.

74. Needless to say, the public market system did not counterbalance all sources of inequality in provisioning.

75. For sources and methods used to produce these maps, see appendix A.

CHAPTER 3: CONSTRAINTS OF TIME

1. John Pintard, *Letters from John Pintard to His Daughter, Eliza Noel Pintard Davidson, 1816–1833* (New York: Printed for the New-York Historical Society, 1940), 1:35. Also quoted by Thomas D. Beal, "Selling Gotham: The Retail Trade in New York City from the Public Market to Alexander T. Stewart's Marble Palace, 1625–1860" (PhD dissertation, State University of New York at Stony Brook, 1998), 381.

2. Ibid.

3. Beal, "Selling Gotham," 392–94.

4. To the extent possible, purchases made at groceries and bakers or for foodstuff not typically sold at public markets were excluded from these counts. New-York Historical Society, Manuscript Division (NYHS-MD), John Pintard, *Papers*, "Marketing Account Book, 1811–1824"; "Marketing Account Book, 1826–1830"; "Record of Household Expenses, 1826–1828," 9:1–3.

5. David Longworth, *Longworth's American Almanac, New-York Register, and City Directory, for the Thirty-Sixth Year of American Independence* (New York: David Longworth, 1811), 230; David Longworth, *Longworth's American Almanac, New-York Register, and City Directory, for the Thirty-Ninth Year of American Independence* (New York: David Longworth, 1814), 219; Thomas Longworth, *Longworth's American Almanac, New-York Register, and City Directory, for the Fifty-First Year of American Independence* (New York: Thomas Longworth, 1826), 381; Thomas Longworth, *Longworth's American Almanac, New-York Register, and City Directory, for the Fifty-Second Year of American Independence* (New York: Thomas Longworth, 1827), 390; Thomas Longworth, *Longworth's American Almanac, New-York Register, and City Directory, for the Fifty-Third Year of American Independence* (New York: Thomas Longworth, 1828), 470; Beal, "Selling Gotham," 380, 393. In between these two more permanent residences, for two years (1824–25), the Pintards also lived on 540 Broadway, about 1,500 feet away from Centre Market. Thomas Longworth, *Longworth's American Almanac, New-York Register, and City Directory, for the Forty-Ninth Year of American Independence* (New York: Thomas Longworth, 1824), 346; Thomas Longworth, *Longworth's American Almanac, New-York Register, and City Directory, for the Fiftieth Year of American Independence* (New York: Thomas Longworth, 1825), 340.

6. Beal, "Selling Gotham," 394–430.

7. The journey to work in the nineteenth-century city became a central subject for the "new urban history" in the 1970s. Scholars have paid comparatively little attention to the provisioning journey. On the journey to work, see Kenneth T. Jackson, "Urban Deconcentration in the Nineteenth Century: A Statistical Inquiry," in *The New Urban History: Quantitative Explorations by American Historians*, ed. Leo F. Schnore (Princeton, NJ: Princeton University Press, 1975), 110–42, especially 133–40; Theodore Hershberg, Dale Light Jr., Harold E. Cox, and Richard R. Greenfield, "The 'Journey to Work': An Empirical Investigation of Work, Residence and Transportation, Philadelphia, 1850 and 1880," in *Philadelphia: Work, Space, Family and Group Experience in the Nineteenth Century*, ed. Theodore Hershberg (New York: Oxford University Press, 1981), 97–109.

8. Marc Bloch in the *Historian's Craft* makes the case for the multiplicity of historical time, arguing that "each type of phenomenon has its own particular dimension of measurement." Fernand Braudel expands on this idea, arguing that the world can be described by three different rhythms. Life's episodic aspects, the so-called *histoire événementielle*, are to be captured by the short timespan; the cyclical

movements of social and economic life, the so-called structures and conjunctures, are to be understood in terms of the *moyenne durée*; while the most slowly changing aspects of human life are to be measured by the *longue durée*. Braudel organized the three volumes of *The Mediterranean* to correspond to these three rhythms. While "the *longue durée*, the conjuncture, the event all fit into each other neatly and without difficulty, for they are all measured on the same scale," Braudel's preference for the *moyenne durée* and the *longue durée* is evident. This chapter's time-analysis focuses on the second category of structural time. Marc L. B. Bloch, *The Historian's Craft* (New York: Knopf, 1953), 184; Fernand Braudel, "History and the Social Sciences: The Longue Durée," in *On History* (Chicago, IL: University of Chicago Press, 1980), 48; Fernand Braudel, *The Mediterranean and the Mediterranean World in the Age of Philip II* (New York: Harper & Row, 1972).

9. For its methodology, the chapter pursues what Henri Lefebvre termed as rhythmanalysis: to deconstruct time patterns of urban everyday life in order to shed light onto their underlying social structures and processes. Henri Lefebvre, *Writings on Cities* (Oxford: Blackwell, 1996), 219–27.

10. John Pintard's letters to his daughter, written between 1816 and 1833, and his marketing books, produced between 1811 and 1829, have also been examined by Beal in his dissertation. This chapter borrows from Beal's exhaustive reading of Pintard's letters, while it pursues a more systematic analysis to the marketing books. Beal, "Selling Gotham," 379–94.

11. Evert Bancker Jr. lived on 3 Fair Street, two blocks away from Oswego Market, which was the city's second largest in terms of its number of butcher stalls and volume of trade in the late 1780s and early 1790s. David Franks, *The New-York Directory* (New York: Loudons, 1787), 7. For more information on Bancker, see Beal, "Selling Gotham," 236–37.

12. Pintard was a politically involved citizen: he was assistant alderman for the East Ward (1789–92), was a member of the Council Committee entrusted to reform the public markets, and served as a city inspector in 1806. His commitment to the public market system was not only driven by personal interest but also by public duty. Beal, "Seeling Gotham," 379–80.

13. See, on this point, Elizabeth Blackmar, *Manhattan for Rent, 1785–1850* (Ithaca, NY: Cornell University Press, 1989), 97. In Blackmar's view, the commissioners in charge of the 1811 grid plan were sensitive to the time savings offered by a free-market system of provisioning relative to the public markets, in part because they had in mind other men, in particular, busy merchants undertaking the daily task of marketing.

14. Beal makes extensive use of both Bancker's and Pintard's accounts to study the daily routines of household provisioning. There are, however, three considerations that warrant a different examination of the sources. First, Beal focuses exclusively on monthly variations in the frequency of marketing trips, yet weekly cycles were also important. Second, he did not enter into spreadsheets each and every food item purchased in the selected years, but aggregated market transactions into specific categories of foodstuff. The problem is that some of his categories, such as "meats and poultry," hide important seasonal fluctuations in food provisioning and consumption. Third, and most important, Beal undercounted Pintard's marketing trips. Pintard began each line of his accounts with a date, then listed item by item his individual purchases quoting the prices, and at the end of each line, summed up the prices. Beal counted the number of marketing trips based on the dates listed on the left margins of the account books. However, most of the lines contain small dates immediately above the specific food items,

dividing each line into additional dates of marketing. In other words, one line usually comprised several different days of marketing, and in all cases, the dates are given in small letters above the purchases. Another additional source of possible undercounting stems from that on certain days Bancker and Pintard may have visited the market more than once. Beal, "Selling Gotham," 238, 382, 385, 236–41, 379–94.

15. NYHS-MD, Evert Bancker Jr., "Household Account Book of Evert Bancker, Jr., 1772–1776"; "List of Proprietors, Account and Survey Book, 1784–88."

16. NYHS-MD, Pintard, *Papers*, "Marketing Account Book, 1811–1824"; "Marketing Account Book, 1826–1830"; "Record of Household Expenses, 1826–1828," 9:1–3.

17. In both Bancker's and Pintard's accounts, many of the years available are incomplete or difficult to read. For Pintard, his 1828 market purchases were also entered into a spreadsheet, but this year seems the least reliable. As for Bancker, the 1787 account was chosen since these records are complete and are the closest to this book's time range.

18. For a discussion of public market revenue data, specifically original market returns, see appendix B.

19. On Clinton Market revenues, see appendix B.

20. The notable dip in Pintard's marketing trips in the summer of 1827, to be more precise, between July 14 and August 15, is because the family left New York City for Bath during this period. There Pintard continued to record his food purchases, however, not with the same precision and detail as he normally did.

21. In Bancker's case it is sometimes difficult to identify the dates of his individual shopping trips, and to distinguish between purchases made at the public market versus the grocery store. In particular, his supplies of cured pork and beef, some of which came from grocers, are difficult to decipher from his purchases of fresh butcher's meats.

22. In fact, the correlations between Pintard's and Bancker's weekly marketing trips and the revenues collected at Clinton Market (1847) are reasonably strong: Bancker 1787 ("r" = 0.48), Pintard 1811 ("r" = 0.57), Pintard 1814 ("r" = 0.66), Pintard 1827 ("r" = 0.47), Pintard 1828 ("r" = 0.56).

23. Technological change transformed the ice industry. Commercial ice became increasingly available after 1827, with the invention of the ice cutter and improvements in icehouses. Large ice companies began to harvest and distribute ice to consumers across the country. By the 1850s, the largest company to supply New York City was the Knickerbocker Ice Company, but it also had other competitors. The increased availability of ice contributed to the more widespread use of refrigeration in restaurants and hotels, by food purveyors and also by private homes. By the 1860s, refrigerator boxes were generally used by food vendors, as well as better-off households. For more on refrigeration, see Cindy R. Lobel, *Urban Appetites: Food and Culture in Nineteenth-Century New York* (Chicago, IL: University of Chicago Press, 2014), 46–48.

24. The graphs are limited to Pintard's 1811 and 1814 accounts, which have proven the most reliable for the rhythm-analysis. However, one finds the same seasonality in the amounts expended for each marketing trip to a similar or lesser extent in Bancker's 1787 and Pintard's 1827 accounts.

25. In all of Bancker's and Pintard's accounts, even as late as 1827, marketing purchases are given in pounds, shillings, and pence. On the contrary, purchases of groceries and bread are usually entered in dollars and cents by Pintard. In con-

verting all expenses into dollars, the conventional rate by the Common Council of 0.96 pence to a cent was used.

26. To compute the marketing budget, purchases for groceries, cereals, and bread, essentially food items not typically bought at public markets, were excluded. However, processed and cured meats, even though these were often also sold by grocers, were included. Accordingly, in 1811 the Pintards expended 29% of their marketing budget on butcher's meats, 15% on cured meats, 8% on poultry and fowl, 6% on fish, 6% on shellfish, 9% on vegetables, 2% on fruits, 23% on milk and dairy products, and 2% on eggs. Their 1814 budget was nearly identical: 29% spent on butcher's meats, 13% on cured meats, 10% on poultry and fowl, 4% on fish, 5% on shellfish, 7% on vegetables, 4% on fruits, 26% on milk and dairy, and 1% on eggs. With the exception of processed meats, their expenses in 1827 were also very similar: 27% on butcher's meats, 4% on cured meats, 12% on poultry and fowl, 4% on fish, 5% on shellfish, 9% on vegetables, 6% on fruits, 31% on milk and dairy, and 3% on eggs. As for cured meats, a considerable share of these were probably listed under groceries and thus are left out of the analysis. It is even more interesting to find significant consistency between Pintard's and Bancker's accounts. For Bancker, it is not possible to distinguish between purchases of fresh and cured meats. Still, the marketing budget looks very similar: in 1787, the Banckers expended 47% of their marketing on fresh and cured meats, 6% on poultry and fowl, 4% on fish, 3% on shellfish, 15% on vegetables, 3% on fruits, 21% on milk and dairy, and 1% on eggs. Overall, the evidence suggests a significant degree of commonality in the composition of New Yorkers' diets.

27. Prior to the 1820s there were no major changes in transportation technologies or animal husbandry that would have significantly altered urban supply conditions for the four sources of fresh protein. Certainly, from the mid-1820s the Erie Canal drastically reduced transportation costs for a wide range of agricultural products, especially grains. However, New York continued to rely for its meat supplies on livestock driven alive into the city, where they were slaughtered and prepared by the butchers for consumption as fresh meat. For further detail, see chapter 2 and appendix B.

28. On the seasonality of food supplies, including meat, and their connection to agricultural production cycles, see Sarah F. McMahon, " 'All Things in Their Proper Season': Seasonal Rhythms of Diet in Nineteenth-Century New England," *Agricultural History* 63, no. 2 (1989), 130–51; J. Ritchie Garrison, "Farm Dynamics and Regional Exchange: The Connecticut Valley Beef Trade, 1670–1850," *Agricultural History* 61, no. 3 (1987), 1–17; Lorena S. Walsh, "Feeding the Eighteenth-Century Town Folk, or, Whence the Beef?" *Agricultural History* 73, no. 3 (1999), 267–80; David B. Landon, "Seasonal Slaughter Cycles and Urban Food Supply in the Colonial Chesapeake," in *Case Studies in Environmental Archaeology*, ed. Elizabeth Reitz, C. Margaret Scarry, and Sylvia J. Scudder (New York: Springer-Verlag, 2008), 375–90.

29. The relatively stable consumption of fresh red meat through the twelve months of the year was the direct outcome of urban agglomeration effects. Urban populations generated constant demand for fresh meat, which could be satisfied only by tapping into all available supplies from the hinterlands. The complementary seasonal cycles produced a smoothing effect, reducing the variation in the total monthly supply of butcher's meat. In fact, the standard deviation in the monthly supply of butcher's meat was only 2.8 pounds in 1816.

30. In fact, very strong correlations are found in the monthly sales of butcher's meats between the 1816 market returns and the 1818 Catharine Market returns: beef

("r" = 0.89), veal ("r" = 0.98), lamb and mutton ("r" = 0.94), pork ("r" = 0.96). It is also true that these correlations are somewhat exaggerated, because for 1816 estimates had to be made for the missing months of November and December, and in the case of Catharine Market, the 1818 monthly returns were used to generate the results. The effect of this, however, should be small; it only concerns two months in 1816 and is limited to Catharine Market, which represented about one-fifth of all meat sales in the city in that year. For the estimation process, see appendix B.

31. Not surprisingly, given the lack of strong seasonality in the supply of beef, correlations between monthly sales as recorded by the 1816 market returns and monthly expenditures as registered by the household accounts are weak: Bancker 1787 ("r" = 0.36), Pintard 1811 ("r" = 0.38), Pintard 1814 ("r" = 0.27), Pintard 1827 ("r" = 0.16).

32. As expected, much stronger correlations are found for veal, whose supply followed well-defined seasonal cycles: Bancker 1787 ("r" = 0.82), Pintard 1811 ("r" = 0.59), Pintard 1814 ("r" = 0.54), Pintard 1827 ("r" = 0.88).

33. Similarly, strong correlations are found for lamb and mutton: Bancker 1787 ("r" = 0.95), Pintard 1811 ("r" = 0.81), Pintard 1814 ("r" = 0.63), Pintard 1827 ("r" = 0.40). One exception is Pintard's 1827 account book, in which case lamb and mutton consumption began one to two months earlier than in the other years.

34. Finally, with the exception of Bancker's accounts, the correlations are convincing for pork as well: Bancker 1787 ("r" = -0.02), Pintard 1811 ("r" = 0.57), Pintard 1814 ("r" = 0.54), Pintard 1827 ("r" = 0.91).

35. In 1811, Pintard settled his accounts for bread every other month; in 1814, he seems to have made one large disbursement for the entire year; in 1827 and 1828, he usually paid at the end of each month. Bancker's accounts seem incomplete as for his bread purchases.

36. Whereas in 1811 and 1814 Pintard paid for milk in large disbursements, in 1827 and 1828 he settled his accounts at the end of each month. Bancker's accounts for milk contain both small and large payments. As for butter, individual payments for small amounts and larger disbursements covering several months are both found in Pintard's records. Bancker's accounts include only case-by-case purchases. Overall, the records do not suggest any evident seasonality for either milk or butter. Quote from Thomas F. De Voe, *The Market Assistant, Containing a Brief Description of Every Article of Human Food Sold in the Public Markets of the Cities of New York, Boston, Philadelphia, and Brooklyn; Including the Various Domestic and Wild Animals, Poultry, Game, Fish, Vegetables, Fruits, &c., &c., with Many Curious Incidents and Anecdotes* (Cambridge, MA: Printed at the Riverside Press for the author, 1867), 400.

37. Ibid., 405.

38. Across Pintard's accounts, one finds increased egg consumption in the spring, while a secondary cycle in the fall is also noticeable. In fact, the fall cycle appears more pronounced in 1811 than the spring one. As for Bancker, the records do not indicate any evident seasonality for eggs.

39. De Voe, *The Market Assistant*, 27.

40. William Cronon, *Nature's Metropolis: Chicago and the Great West* (New York: W. W. Norton, 1992), 207–60.

41. Looking at the figures of the Crescent City Slaughterhouse Company, one finds no seasonality at all in the supplies of veal, lamb and mutton, and pork, while in the case of beef, only a slight summer dent can be detected, indicating the ab-

sence of the fresh red meat cycle by the 1870s. For data, see Lindgren Johnson, "To 'Admit All Cattle without Distinction': Reconstructing Slaughter in the *Slaughterhouse Cases* and the New Orleans Crescent City Slaughterhouse," in *Meat, Modernity, and the Rise of the Slaughterhouse*, ed. Paula Y. Lee (Lebanon: University of New Hampshire Press, 2008), 208.

42. See also Roger Horowitz, *Putting Meat on the American Table: Taste, Technology, Transformation* (Baltimore, MD: Johns Hopkins University Press, 2006), 18–19.

43. More precisely, 19% of Bancker's marketing trips in 1787 occurred on Saturdays. The same for Pintard was 19% in 1811, 25% in 1814, and 21% in 1827.

44. From Pintard's weekly marketing expenditures, Saturdays represented 32% in 1811, 35% in 1814, and 28% in 1827.

45. The precise Saturday figures were 30% of meat sales at Washington Market in 1816–19, and 34% of market revenues at Clinton Market in 1847.

46. For market schedules, see New-York (N.Y.), *Laws and Ordinances, Ordained and Established by the Mayor, Aldermen and Commonalty of the City of New-York, in Common Council Convened, for the Good Rule and Government of the Inhabitants and Residents of the Said City, Passed during the Mayoralty of De Witt Clinton; to which Are Added, the Health Laws of the State of New-York* (New York: Pelsue and Gould, 1812), 154, 156; New York (N.Y.), *A Law to Regulate the Public Markets* (New York: Office of the Examiner, 1814), 3, 5–6; New York (N.Y.), *A Law to Regulate Fulton Market, and for Other Purposes* (New York: G. L. Birch, 1821), 4.

47. There are minor variations to the daily market schedule between the laws. The 1812 and 1814 market laws define the end of sales time for the butchers as 1:00 or 2:00 p.m. (depending on the season), whereas the Fulton Market law sets the closing time of the market in general at 2:00 or 3:00 p.m. (depending on the season). The 1812 and 1814 market laws mark October 1 as the cut-off date between summer and winter schedule, while the Fulton Market law defines the same to be November 1. The daily market schedule described in this paragraph represents a combination of these different laws. New York (N.Y.), *Laws and Ordinances* (1812), 154, 156; New York (N.Y.), *A Law to Regulate the Public Markets* (1814), 3, 5–6; New York (N.Y.), *A Law to Regulate Fulton Market*, 4.

48. De Voe, *The Market Assistant*, 21; emphasis by De Voe.

49. On the point of food shopping being conducted by men, see Blackmar, *Manhattan for Rent*, 97; Jeanne Boydston, *Home and Work: Housework, Wages, and the Ideology of Labor in the Early Republic* (New York: Oxford University Press, 1990), 102–3, 132–34.

50. For a seminal study of antebellum housework and its political economy, see Boydston, *Home and Work*, especially 75–141, for food shopping specifically, 102–3, 132–34. See also Christine Stansell, *City of Women: Sex and Class in New York, 1789–1860* (Urbana: University of Illinois Press, 1987), 41–62, 155–68.

51. De Voe, *The Market Assistant*, 21; emphasis by De Voe.

52. Thomas F. De Voe, *The Market Book: A History of the Public Markets of the City of New York* (New York: A. M. Kelley, 1970 [1862]), 346.

53. New York (N.Y.), *Laws and Ordinances* (1812), 156; New York (N.Y.), *A Law to Regulate the Public Markets* (1814), 6.

54. De Voe, *The Market Assistant*, 25.

55. "Proof of the Comfortable Situation of the Working-Classes in our City," *American*, April 6, 1825. Quoted in De Voe, *The Market Book*, 354.

56. Ibid.

57. George G. Foster, *New York by Gas-Light and Other Urban Sketches* (Berkeley: University of California Press, 1990), 192.

58. De Voe, *The Market Book*, 346.
59. In De Voe's account, refrigerator boxes came into more widespread use by retailers and housekeepers after 1835. *The Market Book*, 346–47.
60. Ibid., 346; emphasis by De Voe.
61. Home delivery also meant that the modern retail butcher had more to worry about than selling meat. It became customary for several butchers to work at one stall, and to employ a few apprentices whose responsibility was to deliver goods to the customer's address. According to De Voe, the new custom of home delivery required "*extra* help, *extra* space, *extra* carts and wagons, *extra* patience; and with all, and the worst of all, *extra expense.*" Moreover, the process inevitably opened up space for the middlemen, undermining the direct relation between vendors and customers. *The Market Book*, 346–47; emphasis by De Voe.
62. De Voe, *The Market Assistant*, 21.
63. Ibid., 22.
64. From the second quarter of the nineteenth century, the Pintards, and thousands of other families, increasingly complemented and substituted their journeys to the public market with quick visits to the retail grocer, whose stock-in-trade increasingly included fresh provisions. On this subject, see Beal, "Selling Gotham," 390–94.
65. Ibid., 350–51, 407.
66. This conclusion may appear counterintuitive at first. In many ways, modern urbanization can be seen as a historical process by which societies gained ever greater control over a variety of natural constraints, including time. Cities have long been at the forefront of taming seasonal and daily time patterns, taking advantage of a variety of technologies and services from heating to street lighting or transportation. At the same time, in the context of food provisioning, the urban variable seems to have amplified agricultural time, at least until later into the nineteenth century. The evidence suggests that the protein and fresh meat cycles defined the temporal relations of urban provisioning in America from the colonial era through the antebellum period. Improvements in transportation technologies and refrigeration by the mid-nineteenth century gradually smoothed out the supply cycles of meat consumption. From the late nineteenth century, by tapping into global supply chains, consumers gained access to all varieties of fresh foodstuff independent of the seasons. Indeed, the gradual weakening of the butcher's meat cycle from the mid-nineteenth century onward may have presented the first step in the two-centuries-long history of eliminating much of seasonality in fresh food consumption.

Chapter 4: Catharine Market and Its Neighborhood

1. Thomas F. De Voe, *The Market Book: A History of the Public Markets of the City of New York* (New York: A. M. Kelley, 1970 [1862]), 344–45, 355–56.
2. In the early nineteenth century, the traditional slave festivals of the Northeast were Pinkster in New York and New Jersey, and Negro Election Day in New England. Pinkster is a variation of the Dutch word *Pinksteren*, which means Pentecost. Originally, Pinkster was a religious holiday for the Dutch, while for their African slaves it was a time free from work. Filled with music, dance, festivities, and even ritual mimicking and mocking of white culture, Pinkster was arguably the most important African American holiday in Early America. Shane White, " 'It Was a Proud Day': African Americans, Festivals, and Parades in the North, 1741–1834," *Journal of American History* 81, no. 1 (1994), 15.

3. De Voe, *The Market Book*, 344.
4. It is reasonable that slaves or free blacks with a talent for dancing made the most of this opportunity to earn some pocket money. But apart from fame, why did they dance for the prize of a bunch of eels? As eels were considered a delicacy, it is conceivable that they served as a currency, and so after the dancing contests, the winners could exchange them for money. But eel-skin also carried value in itself. According to De Voe, the Jersey slaves "were known by their suppleness and plaited forelocks tied up with tea-lead," whereas the Long Islanders "usually tied theirs up in a cue, with dried eel-skin; but sometimes they combed it about their heads and shoulders, in the form of a wig, then all the fashion." For its soft texture, unique definition, and rich variations in color, eel-skin was also widely used as a substitute for leather. And for African Americans, hairstyle and clothing were essential forms of self-expression. Besides, it was a precious item of folk medicine: tied around various parts of the body, eel-skin was believed to cure headache, rheumatism, and cramps; relieve wrist and back pains; and, most important, make one's hair grow faster. De Voe, *The Market Book*, 344–45; Shane White, "A Question of Style: Blacks in and around New York City in the Late 18th Century," *Journal of American Folklore* 102, no. 403 (1989), 23–44.
5. De Voe, *The Market Book*, 344–45.
6. My reading of the image in the next pages borrows considerably and builds on Lhamon's rich interpretation of the same drawing, especially as it pertains to the artist's position, the staging of the dancers and their performance, and the spectator crowd. W. T. Lhamon Jr., "Dancing for Eels at Catharine Market," in *American Literary Studies: A Methodological Reader*, ed. Michael A. Elliott and Claudia Stokes (New York: New York University Press, 2003), 159–62.
7. Shane White, "The Death of James Johnson," *American Quarterly* 51, no. 4 (1999), 753–95, image on 767.
8. From the 1790s, the city's black population increased rapidly: at the turn of the century, 5,865 African Americans lived in New York (9.7% of the population), by 1820 their number reached 10,886 (8.8%), and in 1840, the black community peaked at 16,358 (5.2%). As these numbers also show, from the 1810s black population growth lagged behind overall population growth. The disintegration of slavery in New York was painfully slow. In 1790, two-thirds of the city's black residents were in bondage. By the turn of the century, slaves represented 44%; by 1810, 16%; and by 1820, less than 5% of New York City blacks. By 1827, ten years after the second New York State Gradual Emancipation Law (1817) completed the legal process of emancipation, slavery had become a matter of the past. But emancipation was not this gradual. In the 1790s, the absolute number of slaves still increased to decline only from the next decade. Hence, when in 1799 the state passed its first Gradual Emancipation Act, slavery was still on the rise. This underlines that the dynamic growth of New York's free black population derived chiefly from immigration and not from manumission. Freed slaves from the countryside, Southern fugitives, and slave owners with their slaves from Saint Domingue fleeing during the 1793 slave revolt were the sources of growth of New York City's black population. Graham Russell Hodges, *Root & Branch: African Americans in New York & East Jersey, 1613–1863* (Chapel Hill: University of North Carolina Press, 1999), 163, 193, 230, 279–80; Shane White, " 'We Dwell in Safety and Pursue Our Honest Callings': Free Blacks in New York City, 1783–1810," *Journal of American History* 75, no. 2 (1988), 448–51; Shane White, *Somewhat More Independent: The End of Slavery in New York City, 1770–1810* (Athens: University of Georgia Press, 1991), 24–55; Leslie M. Harris, *In the Shadow of*

Slavery: African Americans in New York City, 1626–1863 (Chicago, IL: University of Chicago Press, 2003).

9. *Nomen est omen*; the bobolink is a species of bird that exhibits sexual dimorphism in pluming. In the nonbreeding season, the male bobolink resembles the female and is relatively drab, while during the nuptial the male puts on the blackface and turns black overall. Furthermore, the name recalls the word *bobolition*, a common mockery of abolition at the time. When cultural historian Lhamon refers to Jack, Ned, and Bob as "proto blackface performers," he captures the social mechanisms at play in their performances; on Catharine Market's incidental stage, these black performers showed their skills within the confines of exploitation and patronage. Lhamon, "Dancing for Eels at Catharine Market," 155.

10. De Voe, *The Market Book*, 344–45; emphasis by De Voe. In an interesting parallel to the farmer De Voo's alleged gesture to fit out Jack in a new suit, the conventional agreement required the master artisan to provide a full suit of clothes to his apprentice at the end of the term. Elizabeth Blackmar, *Manhattan for Rent, 1785–1850* (Ithaca, NY: Cornell University Press, 1989), 57–58.

11. De Voe ends his account on a bitter note. "Knowing something of the history of their former generations, although slaves, when all were instructed, well-fed, and dressed, with the merry laugh, song, and dance, and withal trusted with their masters' business and the proceeds of their sale—and then turn and look on these poor, squalid, dirty, half-dressed, ill-fed and bred, and some no doubt with a strong inclination to be thievish—by their looks—I felt that when Government made them free, Government should have removed some of the obstacles which interfered with the intellectual progress and the domestic comfort of the newly liberated African race." De Voe, *The Market Book*, 370.

12. Ibid., 369–70.

13. A wide range of scholarship has inspired the analysis of Catharine Market as public space. Here only a few works are cited. Low's anthropological study of the plaza at San José, Costa Rica, presents a model to follow from a historical perspective. Anderson's ethnographies of street society serve as guidance to study social behavior in public space. Lofland's book offers theoretical framework. Whyte's studies of the uses of public space in New York City underscore the importance of the built environment. Three classical works have also oriented the approach taken here: Simmel's brilliant essays on urban life, and the idea of the stranger as the par excellence urban type, Goffman's sociological studies of social behavior in public space, and Sennett's influential book on public and private sociability. Setha M. Low, *On the Plaza: The Politics of Public Space and Culture* (Austin: University of Texas Press, 2000); Elijah Anderson, *Streetwise: Race, Class, and Change in an Urban Community* (Chicago, IL: University of Chicago Press, 1990); Lyn H. Lofland, *The Public Realm: Exploring the City's Quintessential Social Territory* (Hawthorne, IL: Aldine de Gruyter, 1998); William H. Whyte, *City: Rediscovering the Center* (New York: Doubleday, 1988); Georg Simmel, *On Individuality and Social Forms, Selected Writings* (Chicago, IL: University of Chicago Press, 1971), 43–69, 143–49, 324–39; Erving Goffman, *Behavior in Public Places: Notes on the Social Organization of Gatherings* (New York: Free Press of Glencoe, 1963); Richard Sennett, *The Fall of Public Man* (New York: Knopf, 1977).

14. De Voe, *The Market Book*, 341; New York (N.Y.). Common Council, *Minutes of the Common Council of the City of New York, 1784–1831 (MCC)* (New York: M. B. Brown Printing & Binding, 1917), 1:220.

15. Brown's was the second busiest ferry on the East River connecting Manhattan to

Brooklyn. *MCC*, 3:456; 4:3; 5:645; 7:785–86; 8:459; 9:687; 10:333–34; 11:61, 11:105–6; 14:756–57; 18:188.

16. De Voe, *The Market Book*, 341.
17. Ibid., 342–43.
18. Ibid., 347–48.
19. Ibid., 349–50; *MCC*, 8:449–50.
20. De Voe, *The Market Book*, 354–56, 359–61; *MCC*, 14:638, 14:704; 19:401–2; New-York Historical Society, Manuscript Division (NYHS-MD), Thomas F. De Voe, *Manuscript Records*, "Ground Plans of the Public Markets in New York City, 1694–1866"; "List of Butchers in the City with some Biographical Notes, 1656–1844"; "New York City Markets Collection, ca. 1817–ca. 1878," 1–2.
21. *MCC*, 6:154; Common Council Microfilm Database, New York City Municipal Archives (CCMD), Market Committee (1810), 40:1045.
22. The others were Division, Chatham, and Pearl Streets. De Voe, *The Market Book*, 350; *MCC*, 7:527; 9:15.
23. De Voe, *The Market Book*, 352; *MCC*, 10:436, 10:464; 11:571.
24. In 1809, Fly Market had seventy-one, Bear Market forty, and Catharine Market twenty-four butcher stalls, while the rest of the seven markets had thirty-four additional stalls in total. For sources and methods on how butcher stalls were counted, see appendix B.
25. In 1816, the estimated revenues generated were $3,309.88 for Fly, $2,384.14 for Washington, and $2,282.18 for Catharine Market. The rest of the markets earned an additional $1,365.03 for the city in that year. In 1818, Fly Market generated $3,200.96, Washington $2,286.53, and Catharine $2,470.06 of tax revenue, while the rest of the markets contributed $1,533.18 to the city coffers. For sources and methods on how market revenues were estimated, see appendix B.
26. Catharine Market with its forty-seven butcher stalls produced $3,110 of annual rents; Washington, which had fifty-four butcher stalls, generated $3,010 of rents; and Fly's forty-eight stalls earned $2,434 of rents. Average rents, therefore, were $66.17 for Catharine, $55.74 for Washington, and $50.71 for Fly Market. Catharine Market was by far the most expensive for butchers to retail from. It is also true that Fly's meager performance partly had to do with the fact that it was soon to be replaced by Fulton Market, making many butchers abandon their stalls. CCMD, Market Committee: Stalls & Licenses (Jan.–June 1821), 80:1717.
27. *MCC*, 14:704; De Voe, *The Market Book*, 354.
28. De Voe, *The Market Book*, 348.
29. Ibid., 354.
30. De Voe, *The Market Book*, 347–48; CCMD, Market Committee: Market (1802), 22:623; Market: Petitions (1803), 23:658, oversized.
31. CCMD, City Inspector: Petitions (1806), 28:779, oversized.
32. For example, in a similar debate in 1822, residents again stood up against an attempt to remove the fish market, thus protecting their market's profitable fish trade. CCMD, Market Committee: New Markets (1822), 84:1767.
33. CCMD, Market Committee (1817), 62:1476.
34. CCMD: Market Committee (1818), 66:1535.
35. CCMD: Market Committee: New Markets (1824), 92:1888.
36. CCMD: Market Committee: New Markets (1824) 92:1887.
37. Ibid.
38. In addition, the Common Council proceedings refer to several other petitions from 1826–28 on the same subject of hucksters and farmers selling their goods on the streets. As one group of petitioners argued in 1828: "The Country People

should not be confined with their produce to the Lower end of the market," but should be permitted "to stand at such places as may suit their convenience." *MCC*, 15:466, 15:489; 16:338; 17:280; De Voe, *The Market Book*, 355; CCMD, Market Committee: Petitions (1826), 104:2020; Market Committee: New Markets (1827), 110:2089; Market Committee: Petitions (1828), 117:2172.

39. CCMD, Market Committee: Petitions (1828), 117:2172.

40. De Voe, *The Market Book*, 360; CCMD, Market Committee: New Markets (1830), 132:2325.

41. CCMD, Market Committee (1830), 132:2324; Market Committee: Petitions (1830), 132:2326.

42. Fast-forward a decade: the same round of petitions occurred in 1839–41, with the familiar complaints and requests but little change to the overall layout of Catharine Market. This time, the petition to relocate the market was signed by 119 residents. As one group described: "the Farmer is excluded altogether from shelter as the covered part of the Market is appropriated and occupied wholly by the Butchers, Hucksters, & forestallers, and the Producer is compelled to expose his vegetables in the Public street thus injured and rendered unwholesome from the effects of the weather, that he is taxed full market fees for the privilege of obstructing the Public thoroughfare." Of course, several ideas emerged: one crowd proposed the addition of a shed along the market-houses, while another one suggested that the fish market be appropriated for the farmers. To free up space for the farmers at the fish market section, they suggested, the fishmongers should be moved into a new building between the lower market and their current location. Little surprise, the fishmongers swiftly remonstrated. So the spatial battles continued throughout the 1840s. For this round of petitions, see City Clerk Filed Papers, New York City Municipal Archives (CCFP), Markets (1839); Market Committee (1840); Markets (1841). For subsequent rounds, see CCFP, Markets (1842); Markets (1844); Markets (1845).

43. See also Helen Tangires, *Public Markets and Civic Culture in Nineteenth-Century America* (Baltimore, MD: Johns Hopkins University Press, 2003), 61–63.

44. Two sets of licensed huckster lists were found in the archives. The first one is from 1818–19 for Fly (76 hucksters), Washington (59), Catharine (48), Centre (8), and Duane Markets (2), listing a total of 193 hucksters. Additionally, a few more hucksters had to be licensed for the small Spring, Greenwich, Grand Street, Essex, Governeur, and Corlaers Hook Markets. In the entire list, only 3 hucksters were men. The second set is from 1827. It includes lists for Fulton (approximately 89 hucksters), Catharine (45), Washington (33), Grand Street (7), Franklin (7), Essex (3), and Governeur Markets (1), but not for Duane, Spring, Greenwich, Centre, and Manhattan. Out of the 185 hucksters included, only 22 were men. On women hucksters petitioning for a license, see chapter 2 and note 73 there. CCMD, Market Committee (1818), 66:1535; Market Committee (1819), 72:1595; Market Committee: Reports (1827), 110:2090.

45. One should note that farmers often hired agents to sell their produce on their behalf. De Voe occasionally includes biographical sketches for individual farmers, a sign of respect that he normally reserves for fellow butchers. In the case of Catharine Market, he details one of the farmers' petitions, also briefly commenting on the life of farmer Jacob Van Alst. De Voe, *The Market Book*, 344–45, 355–56.

46. The spatial analysis that follows borrows from the theoretical framework of critical urban geographers. According to their approach, under capitalism, land is estranged from its social environment and transformed into an abstract and mea-

surable concept, bought and sold like any other commodity. Hence, the laws of market exchange function as the organizing principle for the production of space. Likewise, one key mechanism behind the sociospatial organization of public markets was the division of market space into rentable stalls. In a sense, market stalls operated much like urban real estate. This was the council's rationale, for example, when to maximize revenues it pushed for a system to auction stalls for premiums from 1822, or when it regularly assessed the relative rental value of stalls within and across the marketplaces. In turn, by paying annual rents to the council, the butchers secured control over specific pieces of market space. Acquiring a strategic location was the butcher's single largest capital investment. Henri Lefebvre, *The Production of Space* (Oxford: Blackwell, 1991); Henri Lefebvre, *Writings on Cities* (Oxford: Blackwell, 1996); David Harvey, *The Urban Experience* (Baltimore, MD: Johns Hopkins University Press, 1989); David Harvey, *Spaces of Capital: Towards a Critical Geography* (New York: Routledge, 2001); David Harvey, *Paris, Capital of Modernity* (New York: Routledge, 2003).

47. The image is from Thomas F. De Voe, *The Market Assistant, Containing a Brief Description of Every Article of Human Food Sold in the Public Markets of the Cities of New York, Boston, Philadelphia, and Brooklyn; Including the Various Domestic and Wild Animals, Poultry, Game, Fish, Vegetables, Fruits, &c., &c., with Many Curious Incidents and Anecdotes* (Cambridge, MA: Printed at the Riverside Press for the author, 1867), frontispiece.

48. Whether assembled in pairs or standing independently, this linear configuration remained standard at most public markets.

49. It appears that the Common Council tried to change this custom for all the markets in 1839 as it had done earlier at Fulton Market, where wholesale fishermen had individually assigned stalls. In an 1839 petition, some of the Catharine Market fishermen asked the council to uphold the tradition of distributing stalls between each other by drawing. It is also true that in the next year another group petitioned for the exact opposite, that they could continue to hold on to their stalls instead of redrawing them. Eventually, the council seems to have pursued its original plan to establish greater order, and, as an 1840 list suggests, all fishermen by then retailed from individually assigned stalls. CCFP, Markets (1839); Markets (1840).

50. For a discussion of the market revenue system and its changes, see chapter 1.

51. According to a report by the Joint Committee on Markets, the total number of butcher stalls in 1845 was 365, out of which 116, or nearly one-third of them, was sold at auction as premium stands between 1822 and 1835. After the repeal of the market laws in 1843, Clinton Market butchers, the most affected by the premium system, tried in vain to get refunded for their premiums even as the value of their stalls diminished due to growing competition from meat shops. In a stream of petitioning and responses between 1843 and 1846, the council eventually established that the sale of stalls was limited to their leases, and thus the city was not bound legally to compensate the butchers. New York (N.Y.), *Annual Report of the Comptroller, of the City of New York, of the Receipts and Expenditures of the Corporation, for the Year 1853* (New York: 1854), 663–64, 726–31; New York (N.Y.). Board of Aldermen, *Documents of the Board of Aldermen of the City of New-York* (BA Documents) (New York: 1834–68), Vol. 10, Part 1, Doc. 51, 651–58; Vol. 11, Doc. 52, 517–29; Vol. 13, Doc. 4, 57–66; De Voe, *The Market Book*, 528–29, 532–48.

52. For a discussion of the sources and methods used to produce these maps, see appendix A.

53. This list refers to all street markets between 1818 and 1833. Extending the chronology to 1836 would add to the list Monroe, Union, and Weehawken Markets.

54. As the map shows, in 1832, the upper market generated $1,864 (46.5%) and the lower market $1,140 (28.5%) of butcher rents. The country and fish market together produced $1,003.62 of market fees (25%), hence the value of $501.81 for the two sections separately. For rent per square feet, the amount of yearly revenues earned at the specific market sections was divided by their area (forty-nine cents for the butchers' markets; twenty-five cents for the country and fish market sections), a reasonable but imperfect approach. The valuable space of the market was not the entire market space itself but rather the stalls. Further, while the exact proportions of the two market-houses are known, the country and fish market sections are approximations. Neither of these facts should alter the conclusion that the meat markets dominated Catharine Market's space, which earned about twice as much rental value as the country and fish markets combined. For market revenues, see appendix B.

55. To be noted, Catharine Market rents declined between 1828 and 1838. However, the Market Committee decreased rents on almost every stall at the same time and proportionately, thus these adjustments did not change the relative value of market space in the period.

56. To chart the relative value of space at the public markets, the same set of sources were used as for drawing the Catharine and Fulton Market maps. See appendix A.

57. For sources and methods used to produce these maps, see appendix A.

58. The number of butcher stalls finalized at forty-seven after one was removed to make space for the public scale. Complete butcher lists for Catharine Market for 1818, 1820, 1824, 1828, 1832–36, 1838, 1840, and 1854 were entered into a spreadsheet. The analysis here was limited to the period between 1818 and 1836, which is a sufficiently long time; besides, in 1837, Catharine Market was again enlarged to include eight additional stalls, resulting in their spatial reorganization and renumbering, which renders the continuation of the analysis difficult. Since the data are not continuous, the estimate of an average length of business for five years and one month is an approximation. For example, when the same butcher was found in 1824 and 1828, he was assumed to have stayed in business for five years. Of course, it is possible that he did not work as a butcher for a period, in which case the stability of his business is overestimated. It is also possible that he had started his trade before 1824, in which case it is underestimated. Chances are that over 133 cases, these factors balance each other out. In three cases, the same butcher was found at two distinct moments in time apart from each other. One possibility is that the same butcher moved to another marketplace or stopped working for a while. Another is that the observations may have referred to two different butchers, father and son. For sources on butcher stalls, see appendix B.

59. For simplicity, everyone with the same last name was assumed to be related. This method is likely to somewhat overestimate the extent of kinship relations.

60. The Martins, Tiers, and Valentines had four, while the Varians had seven different members of their families retailing meat at Catharine Market at some point between 1818 and 1836. Additionally, for each year observed, there were two or three Varians holding stalls simultaneously at the marketplace.

61. Emphasis in original. NYHS-MD, De Voe, *Manuscripts*, "New York City Markets Collection, ca. 1817–ca. 1878," 2.

62. Tangires, *Public Markets and Civic Culture*, 16.

63. For Max Weber, "classes, status groups and parties are phenomena of the distribution of power within a community," where power is the "chance of a man or a number of men to realize their own will in a social action even against the resistance of others who are participating in the action." Classes are defined by the distribution of economic power, which dominates in market situations, especially under capitalism. Status groups are determined by the distribution of social honor, and reflect, among others, shared occupational prestige and lifestyles. Even if status groups may stem from economic relations, shared class position in and of itself does not constitute a status group, according to Weber. The hierarchy of market vendors, even if economic relations certainly mattered, most closely reflected the distribution of social honor at the marketplace. Therefore, status order appears the most suitable way to describe the internal power relations among Catharine Market vendors. Max Weber, "Distribution of Power: Class, Status, Party," in *Economy and Society: An Outline of Interpretive Sociology*, ed. Max Weber, Guenther Roth, and Claus Wittich (Berkeley: University of California Press, 1978), 926, 927, 926–35.

64. *MCC*, 3:456; 11:61; 18:138.

65. "Neighborhood" is a frequently used term, especially in American urban history, perhaps because of the enduring legacy of the Chicago school of urban sociology, which defined urban communities by connecting the social to the spatial via this concept. The idea of a neighborhood may refer to widely different sociospatial realities within the same urban context. One useful framework comes from urban sociologist Albert Hunter, who distinguishes between three meanings of the term: the ecological (who lives in a specific area), the symbolic (representing the awareness of residents of the social divisions of their city), and the social (referring to the institutions and networks that tie people together). In an excellent book, historian Kenneth Scherzer applies Hunter's conceptual framework to explore New York City's neighborhoods in the mid-nineteenth century. Similarly, the discussion here considers all three aspects of the term. Establishing the spatial boundaries of the area supplied by Catharine Market captures the ecological neighborhood. The marketplace was also an institution that tied residents together through the vital routine of household provisioning, while also serving as the neighborhood's symbolic center of sociability. When local residents petitioned the council regarding some concern about Catharine Market, they acted upon their membership in the public market's ecological and symbolic community. Similarly, when they procured provisions or attended the public dancing contests of African Americans, they partook in the social life of the marketplace. Robert E. Park, Roderick D. McKenzie, and Ernest Burgess, eds., *The City: Suggestions for the Study of Human Nature in the Urban Environment* (Chicago, IL: University of Chicago Press, 1925); Albert Hunter, *Symbolic Communities: The Persistence and Change of Chicago's Local Communities* (Chicago, IL: University of Chicago Press, 1974), 3–16, 173–97; Kenneth Scherzer, *The Unbounded Community: Neighborhood Life and Social Structure in New York City, 1830–1875* (Durham, NC: Duke University Press, 1992), 13–15, notes 61–65; Robert J. Sampson, *Great American City: Chicago and the Enduring Neighborhood Effect* (Chicago, IL: University of Chicago Press, 2012).

66. For further discussion of the sources and methods used to produce the map, see appendix A.

67. Interestingly, a large cluster of the 1839 petitioners resided in the Chatham Street area.

68. To estimate this figure, the following method was used. To calculate the city's

population in 1818, census data from 1816 and 1820 were used, assuming a constant rate of growth between the two observations. To compute the population of the Catharine Market wards in 1818 (for which there are no matching data from 1816), the same ratios of growth were applied, counting back from the 1820 ward-level censuses. Finally, based on the estimated catchment area, the entire population of ward 4, one-half of wards 6 and 7, and 20% of ward 10 were included as Catharine Market's customer base. For census data, see Ira Rosenwaike, *Population History of New York City* (Syracuse, NY: Syracuse University Press, 1972), 16–19.

69. For sources on butcher stalls and how they were counted, see appendix B.

70. For hucksters, see note 44. According to a list of fishermen's stalls from 1840, Fulton Market had 44, Washington 29, Catharine 25, Centre 23, Clinton 20, Essex 14, Union 12, Monroe 10, Jefferson 8, Tompkins 6, Governeur 6, Franklin 4, and Greenwich 2 licensed fishmongers. CCFP, Markets (1840).

71. De Voe, *The Market Book*, 355.

72. For market revenue data, including how excise taxes and meat consumption figures were estimated, see appendix B.

73. The close proximity of the Catharine Market figures to those of the city's averages further confirms the validity of the method used to project the market's catchment area and customer base.

74. It is also true that the 1818 figures may slightly underestimate overall meat consumption in New York, as discussed in chapter 2, including note 15.

75. For estimating the number of customers at Catharine Market, the following method was used. First, Catharine Market's customer base was calculated at 24,756 people. Obviously, not all residents did marketing, hence, one shopper for every four inhabitants was assumed. Second, the frequencies of John Pintard's 1811, 1814, and 1827 shopping trips to Fly and Centre Markets (as studied in chapter 3) were considered as representative. In order to correct for possible data problems, the averages of the three accounts were used. Based on these figures, the total number of monthly, weekly, and daily (weekday versus Saturday) visits could be estimated, again, extrapolating from a population of 24,756 and a one-to-four ratio of shoppers. For hourly rates, the marketplace was assumed to stay open for seven hours on weekdays (from sunrise till 1:00 or 2:00 p.m., when the butcher stalls closed). All estimates are reported seasonally, accounting for the significant fluctuations of customer traffic, and at the level of the entire market and an "average" butcher. Hourly rates for Saturdays are not included; since the market stayed open from sunrise until night, and customer traffic varied greatly through the day, the average hourly rate would not provide a useful measure. For Pintard's accounts, see note 4 in chapter 3.

76. De Voe, *The Market Book*, 346.

77. Calculations for tables 4.3–4.4 are based on the following method. The market clerk's 1818 accounts contain complete monthly figures for the sale of cattle, calves, sheep, and hogs at Catharine Market. Additionally, the reports include, incompletely, daily sales for the four categories of livestock at Washington Market in 1816–19. First, monthly sales at Catharine Market were converted into weekly rates. Second, the Washington Market daily rates were used to distribute weekly figures into weekday and Saturday sales at Catharine Market. Last, estimates are expressed at the level of the marketplace and per butcher, by the number of livestock and the corresponding pounds of meat, by the seasons, and by weekdays and Saturdays. Additionally, hourly sales per butcher for a weekday

are also included. For the clerks' original returns and how meat consumption was estimated, see appendix B.

78. De Voe, *The Market Book*, 354.
79. This figure matches remarkably well the earlier estimate of 417 visitors per hour in the spring season. It is also true that the journalist likely slightly undercounted the number of customers, as he probably missed out on some of those who did not enter the market-houses but simply came to purchase fish or other provisions.
80. For the fascinating world of black dancing cellars in early nineteenth-century New York, see White, "The Death of James Johnson," 753–59, 758; Shane White, *Stories of Freedom in Black New York* (Cambridge, MA: Harvard University Press, 2002), 28–29; Ned Buntline, *The Mysteries and Miseries of New York: A Story of Real Life* (New York: Berford, 1848), 89–90; Charles Dickens, *American Notes for General Circulation* (London: Penguin Books, 2000), 102; George G. Foster, *New York by Gas-Light and Other Urban Sketches* (Berkeley: University of California Press, 1990), 140–19, 183; Harris, *In the Shadow of Slavery*, 92. For minstrelsy more generally, see Vera B. Lawrence, "Micah Hawkins, the Pied Piper of Catharine Slip," *New-York Historical Society Quarterly* 62, no. 2 (1978), 138–65; Allan W. C. Green, " 'Jim Crow,' 'Zip Coon': The Northern Origins of Negro Minstrelsy," *Massachusetts Review* 11, no. 2 (1970), 385–97; Hans Nathan, *Dan Emmett and the Rise of Early Negro Minstrelsy* (Norman: University of Oklahoma Press, 1962); Eric Lott, *Love and Theft: Blackface Minstrelsy and the American Working Class* (New York: Oxford University Press, 1993); W. T. Lhamon Jr., *Raising Cain: Blackface Performance from Jim Crow to Hip Hop* (Cambridge, MA: Harvard University Press, 1998); W. T. Lhamon Jr., *Jump Jim Crow: Lost Plays, Lyrics, and Street Prose of the First Atlantic Popular Culture* (Cambridge, MA: Harvard University Press, 2003); Lhamon, "Dancing for Eels at Catharine Market," 152–81.

CHAPTER 5: WITHDRAW THE BUNGLING HAND OF GOVERNMENT

1. New York (N.Y.), *Annual Report of the Comptroller, of the City of New York, of the Receipts and Expenditures of the Corporation, for the Year 1853* (New York: McSpedon and Baker, 1854), 649.
2. Ibid., 646–47.
3. Ibid., 648–49; emphasis in original.
4. Ibid., 649.
5. Ibid.
6. Charles R. Rode, *The New-York City Directory, for 1854–1855* (New York: Charles R. Rode, 1854).
7. New York (N.Y.), *Annual Report of the Comptroller . . . 1853*, 652–53.
8. Ibid., 647.
9. Rode, *The New-York City Directory, for 1854–1855*.
10. For the case of Clinton Market butchers, all of whom obtained their stalls through the premium system, and thereby were especially hurt by deregulation, see note 51 in chapter 4.
11. For a discussion of butcher stalls data and how annual stall counts were established, see appendix B.
12. Assuming that the average ratio of 491 residents per butcher stall between 1800 and 1820 was a constant, this number was used as the base to calculate the number of stalls missing from the system between 1820 and 1843. Accordingly, by the 1830s the public market system lacked about 37% of the retail capacity

needed. While this figure cannot be equated with the level of unlicensed trade, because butchers could increase their daily turnover by a certain margin, it is reasonable to suggest that the share of the economy outside of the formal system reached about 20 to 25% of the meat trade.

13. For a discussion of the sources and methods used to produce these maps, see appendix A.

14. Washington and Fulton Markets were the only exception to the west-to-east pattern, which reflects their reorientation to wholesale trade by this period.

15. Earnings from butcher rents were much more evenly distributed between marketplaces, corresponding more closely to the number of butcher stalls. This also suggests that the same hierarchy of wholesale and retail trade was not yet as firmly established in the meat industry, or at least, it did not center to the same degree on Washington and Fulton Markets but probably operated more directly out of larger slaughtering facilities. For a discussion of the geography of slaughtering, see chapter 6.

16. In an assessment of the Committee on Markets of the Board of Aldermen, "Washington market is the great depot, receiving the produce from all sections of the country, by land and water, and diffusing and distributing it to the consumer through the other markets and market places in the city, nearly all of which derive their supplies from this source, besides furnishing as it does the shipping in port, with most of its fresh provisions." New York (N.Y.). Board of Aldermen, *Documents of the Board of Aldermen of the City of New York* (BA Documents) (New York: 1834–68), Vol. 18, Part 1, Doc. 10, 690.

17. Further, Washington Market's share of the revenues increased dynamically, year by year. New York (N.Y.), *Annual Report of the Comptroller of the City of New York, of the Receipts and Expenditures of the Corporation, for the Year 1855* (New York: McSpedon and Baker, 1856), 53.

18. For an informative discussion of restaurants in antebellum New York, including their different varieties, customers, and locations, see Cindy R. Lobel, *Urban Appetites: Food and Culture in Nineteenth-Century New York* (Chicago, IL: University of Chicago Press, 2014), 103–38, including 110–11 for maps showing their exact locations in 1835 and 1865.

19. The Committee on Markets in its 1851 report, for example, refers to the massive increase of trade on the western riverfront as one of the main reasons why to rebuild Washington Market. "It is a conceded fact that the augmentation of the commerce of this city has driven many of our ships and much of our shipping trade from the east to the west side of New York. This growth of our commercial marine, and its change of location, naturally draws the merchant after it; in consequence of which, the business of the west side of the city, in the First, Third and Fifth Wards, is very largely increased and constantly increasing." BA Documents, Vol. 18, Part 1, Doc. 10, 688.

20. Rode, *The New-York City Directory, for 1854–1855*, appendix 51; Kenneth Jackson, Lisa Keller, and Nancy Flood, eds., *The Encyclopedia of New York City*, 2nd ed. (New Haven, CT: Yale University Press, 2010), 1075–81.

21. Jackson et al., *The Encyclopedia of New York City*, 1075–81.

22. According to the Market Committee of the Board of Assistant Aldermen, "the immense quantity of the different kinds of produce, the vast number of people congregated to buy and sell, not only occupy all the market grounds, but extend to blocks around, where the streets are so filled as to be impassable for any vehicle in the busy time of marketing." New York (N.Y.). Board of Assistant Alder-

men, *Documents of the Board of Assistant Aldermen of the City of New York* (BAA Documents) (New York: 1834–68), Vol. 37, Doc. 4, 54–55.

23. In 1854, no less than 81% of bakers, 61% of retail grocers, and 46% of shop butchers resided on the premises of their stores, according to the directory. These numbers probably underestimate the degree to which home and workspace was the same in the food retail sector, for they are based only on those entries where both home and business addresses are listed. Doggett, *Doggett's New-York City Directory, for 1845 & 1846*; Rode, *The New-York City Directory, for 1854–1855*.

24. Thomas D. Beal, "Selling Gotham: The Retail Trade in New York City from the Public Market to Alexander T. Stewart's Marble Palace, 1625–1860" (PhD dissertation, State University of New York at Stony Brook, 1998), 330–35.

25. New York (N.Y.), *Annual Report of the Comptroller . . . 1853*, 649.

26. Thomas F. De Voe, *The Market Book: A History of the Public Markets of the City of New York* (New York: A. M. Kelley, 1970 [1862]), 369–70, 584.

27. Debates about the rebuilding of Washington Market in 1850–51 left a considerable paper trail. BA Documents, Vol. 18, Part 1, Doc. 10, 685–724; Vol. 18, Part 2, Doc. 61, 1097–1131; Vol. 18, Part 2, Doc. 62, 1133–34; Vol. 20, Part 2, Doc. 66, 1263–66; BAA Documents, Vol. 36, Doc. 12, 169–76; Vol. 37, Doc. 4, 53–62; Vol. 38, Doc. 12, 178–80; Vol. 44, Doc. 15, 327–54. See also Helen Tangires, *Public Markets and Civic Culture in Nineteenth-Century America* (Baltimore, MD: Johns Hopkins University Press, 2003), 136–37.

28. New York (N.Y.). City Inspector, *Annual Report of the City Inspector of the City of New York, for the Year Ending December 31, 1860* (ARCI) (New York: 1804–60), 23.

29. Ibid., 22.

30. Other scholars have also discussed the decline of the public market system, in particular, the absence of market facilities in urbanizing northern districts. The most attuned to the geographic consequences of inadequate system expansion and the rise of unregulated food markets is Beal's dissertation. Beal, "Selling Gotham," 333, 335, 345–54; Tangires, *Public Markets and Civic Culture*, 93; Roger Horowitz, Jeffrey M. Pilcher, and Sydney Watts, "Meat for the Multitudes: Market Culture in Paris, New York City, and Mexico City over the Long Nineteenth Century," *American Historical Review* 109, no. 4 (2004), 1071–73; Roger Horowitz, *Putting Meat on the American Table: Taste, Technology, Transformation* (Baltimore, MD: Johns Hopkins University Press, 2006), 167–77; Lobel, *Urban Appetites*, 64–68.

31. Hitherto the only attempt to study the geography of food retail in New York City is Beal, "Selling Gotham," especially chapters 5–7.

32. On central-place theory and its application to retail geography, see discussion in chapter 2, including notes 34–38 for references.

33. For data on food vendors and clothing shops, a consistent series of city directories (specifically Doggett, Doggett & Rode, and Rode) was consulted. Their time frame spans between 1842/43 and 1854/55, corresponding to the years 1842 to 1854 in figure 5.3. A variety of controls were used to arrive at accurate estimates for the number of residents per retail unit. For instance, in the case of butchers both market and shop butchers were included. For shop butchers, duplicates, that is, two butchers working in the same shop were counted as one because the analysis is concerned not with the number of vendors but the number of shops. Also, late butchers or butchers without a business address were discounted. This method to correct directory counts was completed for 1845 and 1854, and then

the ratios by which these two directories overcounted meat retail outlets were applied to all the other years.

The same process to account for both market- and shop-based retail, and to eliminate all overcounting was followed for fish, oyster, and fruit vendors. For bakers, grocers, and milk vendors, there was no need to worry about market-based retail, but the same method was applied to eliminate double counts. Figure 5.3 reports thresholds for butchers, bakers, grocers, and all food vendors (this last category also includes dealers of fish, oysters, fruits, and milk). To establish threshold figures for clothing, the data include shops selling clothing, boots and/ or shoes, and hats. The same corrections to the counts were applied, also eliminating irrelevant speciality clothing shops. Overall, the approach taken offers sound, perhaps slightly conservative, estimates of different types of retail activity in the city, based on their listings in the directories.

For sources, see John Doggett Jr., *The New-York City Directory, for 1842 & 1843, Containing Fifty-five Thousand Names: Together with Other Valuable Information* (New York: John Doggett, 1842) and subsequent editions with slight variations of title covering years 1842/43 to 1850/51; John Doggett Jr. and Charles R. Rode, *The New York City Directory, for 1851–1852* (New York: John Doggett, 1851); Charles R. Rode, *The New York City Directory, for 1852–1853* (New York: Charles R. Rode, 1852), and subsequent editions for 1853/54 and 1854/55.

34. For an excellent discussion (relying on a close study of account books) on how groceries increasingly became "indoor markets," directly competing with public markets from the second quarter of the nineteenth century, see Beal, "Selling Gotham," 394–413.

35. The slightly higher ratio by the mid-nineteenth century is easily explained, on the one hand, by possible undercounting in the directories, and on the other, that in the new unregulated environment nothing stood in the way of groceries to directly compete with butchers, capturing a considerable share of the fresh meat trade.

36. For a discussion of the sources and methods used to produce these maps, see appendix A. For a detailed GIS analysis of land use and population density in mid-nineteenth-century Manhattan, see the forthcoming article, on which the following discussion of land-use patterns is also based: Gergely Baics and Leah Meisterlin, "Zoning before Zoning: Land Use and Density in Mid-Nineteenth-Century New York City," *Annals of the American Association of Geographers* (2016).

37. For a discussion of New York City's early to mid-nineteenth-century commercial geography, especially the segregation of land uses and the consolidation of the commercial center, see Mona Domosh, *Invented Cities: The Creation of Landscape in Nineteenth-Century New York and Boston* (New Haven, CT: Yale University Press, 1998), 15–25. For an excellent discussion of the commercial development resulting from Manhattan's midcentury boom, focusing primarily on the postbellum period, see David M. Scobey, *Empire City: The Making and Meaning of the New York City Landscape* (Philadelphia, PA: Temple University Press, 2002), 89–120. For a more general treatment of central business district development and functional segregation in the nineteenth-century American city, through a case study of Boston, see David Ward, "The Industrial Revolution and the Emergence of Boston's Central Business District," *Economic Geography* 42, no. 2 (1966), 152–71; David Ward, *Cities and Immigrants: A Geography of Change in Nineteenth-Century America* (New York: Oxford University Press, 1971), 85–103.

38. In his seminal book on the working class of early nineteenth-century New York City, Wilentz describes the dominance of small-shop production, often located in

dwelling structures, as a "peculiarly metropolitan form of industrialization." For the discussion of industrial land use, this presents an important caveat: specifically, the map ignores a variety of industrial activities, for these were not registered by the Perris Atlas. As a consequence, the map probably underestimates the intensity of industrial uses in densely built working-class areas. Sean Wilentz, *Chants Democratic: New York City and the Rise of the American Working Class, 1788–1850* (New York: Oxford University Press, 1984), 32.

39. For an evocative description of the mixed-use city of the mid-nineteenth century, see Sam Bass Warner, *The Urban Wilderness: A History of the American City* (Berkeley: University of California Press, 1972), 81–84.

40. For a brief discussion of land-use development and industrial locations in Manhattan around the 1860s, see Scobey, *Empire City*, 129–31. For detailed analyses of the industrial geography of other North American cities in the mid-nineteenth century, see, for example, Edward K. Muller and Paul A. Groves, "The Emergence of Industrial Districts in Mid-Nineteenth Century Baltimore," *Geographical Review* 69, no. 2 (1979), 159–78; Robert Lewis, "The Development of an Early Suburban Industrial District: The Montreal Ward of Saint-Ann, 1851–71," *Urban History Review* 19, no. 3 (1991), 166–80; Robert Lewis, "A City Transformed: Manufacturing Districts and Suburban Growth in Montreal, 1850–1929," *Journal of Historical Geography* 27, no. 1 (2001), 20–35.

41. These percentages were obtained from the building use–type designations of the digitized Perris Fire Insurance Atlas. Besides residential, commercial, and industrial uses, New York also had a fair number of public (government, educational, or religious) buildings. For data, see appendix A.

42. For a discussion of the sources and methods used to produce the map, see appendix A.

43. There is yet limited scholarship on the retail geography of mid-nineteenth-century Manhattan. For a discussion of the consolidation and development of Manhattan's commercial center and its cultural geography over the mid- to late-nineteenth century, see Domosh, *Invented Cities*, 35–64. For the earlier period, drawing on the 1845 directory, Beal presents a detailed analysis of the development and agglomeration of retail activity in specific areas, especially Chatham Square, Catharine Street, the Bowery, and Broadway; Beal, "Selling Gotham," 440–506. In general, the historical geography of nineteenth-century urban retail remains an understudied subject; for two excellent studies, see Gareth Shaw and M. T. Wild, "Locational Behaviour of Urban Retailing during the Nineteenth Century: The Example of Kingston upon Hull," *Transactions of the Institute of British Geographers* 61, no. 1 (1974), 101–18; Michael P. Conzen and Kathleen N. Conzen, "Geographical Structure in Nineteenth-Century Urban Retailing: Milwaukee, 1836–90," *Journal of Historical Geography* 5, no. 1 (1979), 45–60.

44. This argument is especially stressed by Reps, Spann, Marcuse, and Scobey. For a select historiography on Manhattan's 1811 grid, see John W. Reps, *The Making of Urban America: A History of City Planning in the United States* (Princeton, NJ: Princeton University Press, 1965), 296–99; Edward Spann, "The Greatest Grid: The New York Plan of 1811," in *Two Centuries of American Planning*, ed. Daniel Schaffer (Baltimore, MD: Johns Hopkins University Press, 1988), 11–39; Peter Marcuse, "The Grid as City Plan: New York City and Laissez-Faire Planning in the Nineteenth Century," *Planning Perspectives* 2, no. 3 (1987), 287–310; Elizabeth Blackmar, *Manhattan for Rent, 1785–1850* (Ithaca, NY: Cornell University Press, 1989), 94–100; Reuben Rose-Redwood, "Rationalizing the Landscape: Superimposing the Grid upon the Island of Manhattan" (MS thesis, Pennsylvania State

University, 2002); Reuben Rose-Redwood, "Mythologies of the Grid in the Empire City, 1811–2011," *Geographical Review* 10, no. 3 (2011), 396–413; Scobey, *Empire City*, 120–31; Hillary Ballon, ed., *The Greatest Grid: The Master Plan of Manhattan, 1811–2011* (New York: Columbia University Press, 2012); Marguerite Holloway, *The Measure of Manhattan: The Tumultuous Career and Surprising Legacy of John Randel, Jr., Cartographer, Surveyor, Inventor* (New York: W. W. Norton, 2013); Gerard Koeppel, *City on a Grid: How New York Became New York* (Boston, MA: Da Capo Press, 2015).

45. The Commissioners' Plan did not include any specific land-use requirements, a point also made by Spann, "The Greatest Grid," 22–23. The grid incentivized commercial development on the avenues as opposed to the streets based on three spatial variables. First, the rectangular shape of the blocks created more frequent intersections on avenues than streets. Second, the relatively greater width of avenues increased their volume of traffic, an argument also made by Blackmar, *Manhattan for Rent*, 96–97. Third, buildings on avenues were usually at least three stories, making them more conducive to accommodate ground-floor retail. For a discussion of how these three parameters of the grid incentivized land-use development, see Baics and Meisterlin, "Zoning before Zoning."

46. For sources and methods used to produce these maps, see appendix A.

47. Hitherto two partial efforts have been made to map the locations of food shops in antebellum New York. For bakers in 1840, see Allan R. Pred, *The Spatial Dynamics of U.S. Urban-Industrial Growth, 1800–1914: Interpretive and Theoretical Essays* (Cambridge, MA: MIT Press, 1966), 206. For butchers and grocers in 1845 in the Lower East Side, and by tabulating their numbers by street, see Beal, "Selling Gotham," 346, 353, 423–23, 427.

48. See also Domosh, *Invented Cities*, 19, 22; Scobey, *Empire City*, 114–20.

49. For details on how elite residential neighborhoods were developed—in areas like Gramercy Park, Washington, Union and Madison Squares, or Fifth and Madison Avenues—by using restrictive covenants, financing the construction of park space, lobbying the council to promote real estate interests by diverting public funds, or altering the grid's original layout, see Blackmar, *Manhattan for Rent*, 183–212; Ballon, *The Greatest Grid*, 115, 103–25; Scobey, *Empire City*, 126–29; Catherine McNeur, *Taming Manhattan: Environmental Battles in the Antebellum City* (Cambridge, MA: Harvard University Press, 2014), 45–94.

50. For sources and methods used to produce these maps, see appendix A.

51. For the geography of slaughter, see chapter 6.

52. See note 37 in chapter 2 for similar studies establishing a uniformly dispersed pattern for bakers.

53. In fact, the Kernell density analysis documents a significant clustering of private butcher shops in this rapidly consolidating working-class immigrant zone.

54. The concentration of groceries in wards 4 and 6 is also significant by the Kernell density measure.

55. For sources and methods used to produce the subsequent maps, see appendix A.

56. Beal, "Selling Gotham," 407.

57. For a discussion of public market revenue data, see appendix B.

58. De Voe, *The Market Book*, 346–47.

59. For an earlier attempt to map butchers and bakers in the area in 1845, see Beal, "Selling Gotham," 353, 427.

60. For market revenue data, see appendix B.

61. On the basis of a list of market law violations in November to December 1841, the Lower East Side, especially near the Bowery, was the most affected area. City

Clerk Filed Papers, New York City Municipal Archives (CCFP), Markets (1843), rolled document, "Violations of Market Laws, Nov.–Dec. 1841." For a map of these violations and discussion, see Gergely Baics, "The Geography of Urban Food Retail: Locational Principles of Public Market Provisioning in New York City, 1790–1860," *Urban History* (2015), 15–16, available on CJO 2015, http://dx.doi.org/10.1017/S0963926815000176.

62. For market revenue data, see appendix B.

63. De Voe, *The Market Book*, 369–70.

64. For a discussion of Catharine Market customers, see chapter 4.

65. For battles over space at Catharine Market, see chapter 4.

66. In a typical battle of petitions in 1839–41 (for details and sources, see note 42 in chapter 4) over the use of space, some voiced their concern that such fighting might hurt Catharine Market's entire economy. Property owners and residents in particular worried that "the Public dependent on Catharine Market for a supply of Provisions are put to great inconvenience by being compelled to resort to other markets to procure country produce and vegetables." They well understood that the Achilles' heel of the public market was its business agglomeration. If customers had to walk to another marketplace or to private shops to procure certain provisions, Catharine Market's monopolistic position would be broken.

67. They vehemently remonstrated against the vending of meat "by saddles, quarters and the whole of the carcass . . . by speculators purchasing Hogs, sheep and calves, and offering them for sale there and other places contrary to the regular rules and laws of the corporation." Common Council Microfilm Database, New York City Municipal Archives (CCMD), Market Committee (1823), 88:1826; New York (N.Y.). Common Council, *Minutes of the Common Council of the City of New York, 1784–1831* (*MCC*) (New York: M. B. Brown Printing & Binding, 1917), 12:203.

68. Whereas the market laws prohibited the sale of fresh meat "in quarters, joints and pieces," the law did not explicitly forbid the same for whole animal carcasses. To resolve this issue, the council rephrased the market laws accordingly: "No person or persons whomsoever shall sell or expose for sale any fresh meat of any description in any street or place in this city other than in the public markets or the streets adjoining or contiguous thereto used for such purposes, under the penalty of Ten dollars for each offence." CCMD, Market Committee (1823), 88:1826.

69. The earlier cited 1841 document (see note 61), listing fifty-nine cases of market law violations with locations identifies several incidents of unlicensed meat sales falling within Catharine Market's catchment area. Further, when in 1843 and 1844 meat shop licenses were newly issued, their addresses often coincided with the sites of former market law violations, indicating the persistence of these operations over the years. CCFP, Markets (1843); Markets (1844).

70. CCFP, Markets (1842).

71. De Voe, *The Market Book*, 370.

72. In 1825, for example, only eighty independent retail stores selling attire (clothing, boots and/or shoes, hats) were found in the Longworth city directory. For a sector-by-sector comparison of Gotham's retail industry in 1800 and 1845, demonstrating the remarkable expansion of stores selling dry goods, different types of clothing, and other specialized goods between the two periods, see Beal, "Selling Gotham," 451. Thomas Longworth, *Longworth's Directory for the Fiftieth Year of American Independence, 1825–26* (New York: Thomas Longworth, 1825).

73. De Voe, *The Market Book*, 369–70.

74. Domosh, *Invented Cities*, 35–64; Christine Stansell, *City of Women: Sex and Class*

in New York, 1789–1860 (Urbana: University of Illinois Press, 1987), 89–100; Edwin G. Burrows and Mike Wallace, *Gotham: A History of New York City to 1898* (New York: Oxford University Press, 2000), 690–711.

75. Late Retailer, *A Peep into Catharine Street, or the Mysteries of Shopping* (New York: John Slater, 1846), 3. See also Beal on this document, "Selling Gotham," 463–65.
76. Late Retailer, *A Peep into Catharine Street*, 3.
77. Ibid.
78. Ibid.
79. Ibid., 8.
80. A schematic map of Catharine Street businesses in 1845, along with a discussion of the street's retail agglomeration, had also been developed by Beal. He also conducted similar analyses of Broadway and the Bowery. Beal, "Selling Gotham," 456–98, especially 463–66.
81. For sources and methods used to produce this map, see appendix A.
82. *MCC*, 9:15. Rode, *The New-York City Directory, for 1854–1855*, appendix, 30–31.
83. Late Retailer, *A Peep into Catharine Street*, 6.
84. Ibid.; emphasis in original.
85. "The risk of business was slight because of its known reputable principles," he added. Ibid.
86. Ibid., 5.
87. Ibid., 7.
88. Ibid., 8.
89. Ibid., 5.
90. Ibid., 6–7.
91. Ibid., 15–16, 19–20, 21–23; emphasis in original.

CHAPTER 6: THE PRICE OF DEREGULATION

1. Citizens' Association of New York, Council of Hygiene and Public Health, *Report of the Council of Hygiene and Public Health of the Citizens' Association of New York upon the Sanitary Condition of the City* (New York: D. Appleton, 1865).
2. Public health reformers, historians have rightly argued, were misguided in their assumption that fixing environmental problems would amount to uplifting Gotham's working-class residents. Fixating on housing also distracted from the more basic issue of workers' inadequate pay. These should, however, not prevent one from recognizing the sanitary movement's intellectual achievements. Elizabeth Blackmar, "Accountability for Public Health: Regulating the Housing Market in Nineteenth-Century New York City," in *Hives of Sickness: Public Health and Epidemics in New York City*, ed. David Rosner (New Brunswick, NJ: Rutgers University Press, 1995), 42–64; John Duffy, *A History of Public Health in New York City, 1625–1866* (New York: Russell Sage Foundation, 1968).

   For an excellent discussion on nuisance regulation and animal agriculture in four major American cities from the eighteenth century, examining land use, food supplies, and public health, see Domenic Vitiello and Catherine Brinkley, "From Farm to Nuisance: Animal Agriculture and the Rise of Planning Regulation," *Journal of Planning History* 13, no. 2 (2014), 113–35. On animals and environmental reform in antebellum New York, see Catherine McNeur, *Taming Manhattan: Environmental Battles in the Antebellum City* (Cambridge, MA: Harvard University Press, 2014), 6–44, 134–74.

3. Government withdrawal from food provisioning is also noted by Blackmar, "Accountability for Public Health," 59.
4. Citizens' Association, *Report of the Council of Hygiene and Public Health*, xxii.
5. Ibid., xxiv, xxvii.
6. The twenty-nine districts consisted of thirty-one zones, with two districts being divided into separate halves. Ibid., xxii.
7. They first had to draw up plans of their districts, then begin their surveys at one corner, making their way from one block to the next until the end, then move on to the next "belt of squares," and so on until reaching the last corner. Ibid., xxv.
8. The city block "constitutes in itself a small sanitary district, and should be considered a distinct entity," the instructions explained. Ibid., xxv.
9. Ibid.
10. Ibid., xxiv–xxv.
11. This should come as no surprise, for the report's premise was to map urban disease environments. The environmentalist view, however, was not absolute either, as the document effortlessly switched over to contagionist etiologies of disease. Smallpox, for example, was recognized as spreading directly between individuals. Yet even in this case, the inspectors were directed to document its concentration in specific buildings, like much fretted "fever-nests." Ibid., liv–lv.
12. These were listed in twenty-two points. Ibid., xxvii.
13. Inspectors were to record all relevant issues, ranging from elevation to the nature of the ground and soil, vacant lots, streets, courts and alleys, the type of pavements used, or the extent and quality of the water and sewerage networks.
14. In particular, their physical attributes, street frontage or rear location, exterior and interior spaces, access to sanitary infrastructures, ease of ventilation, and crowdedness were to be considered.
15. Brothels, crowded facilities in general, stables, and bone and offal processing plants were also singled out.
16. They were instructed to describe archetypal sanitary risks, such as "fever-nests," typically tenements of extreme crowding, without proper sanitation, lacking ventilation and often situated on rear lots. These "insalubrious quarters" were given close attention, warranting detailed reports for each district, with their own set of questions to nail down "the statistics, distribution, and grouping of pestilential diseases." Other notorious "nuisances" were also exposed, especially unsanitary slaughter pens, wanting of drainage and sewer connections, emanating stench to their vicinities, spreading pests carried by livestock kept in tight quarters or driven across the streets. Ibid., xxviii–xxx.
17. In the age of statistical thinking, when surveys, tables, and charts came to explain reality, the inspectors were required to follow standardized methods of data collection. Besides the route of their surveys, their daily system of record taking was also specified. In addition, a "summary of the week's labors" had to be written up to be discussed at weekly councils on Saturday evenings for "the comparison of results, and for advice from a committee of the Council of Hygiene." Ibid., xxvi, xxxi. On the rise of statistics as a study of society and population, see Theodore M. Porter, *The Rise of Statistical Thinking, 1820–1900* (Princeton, NJ: Princeton University Press, 1988).
18. Ibid., xxxvii–cxliii.
19. For example, Ezra R. Pulling's survey of the Fourth District is a model of nineteenth-century sanitary science: it exhausts all themes, is systematic and detailed, balances penetrating case studies with statistics, and achieves the ulti-

mate feat of drawing up the ward's "sanitary and social" map, with labels to each sanitary hazard building by building. Ibid., 43–65.

20. Some sketchier reports include those of either section of the Fifth District, leaving one to wonder how closely the two inspectors studied their areas. Indeed, the original notebooks of the inspectors confirm that while they followed the premise of block-by-block visitation, they did little more than the minimum required. Again, there were other reports that shone not so much for their evidence but for their erudite musings on sanitary debates. For example, Twentieth District inspector E. H. Janes filled up pages of wisdom on garbage boxes and the proper design of sewers, while James L. Little of the Twenty-First District boasted his expertise on ventilation, specifically, the necessary amount of cubic air per person and its relevance for tenement design. At times, the field notes are more interesting than the summaries. Guido Furman of the Seventeenth District based his average final report on a meticulous survey, containing beautiful hand-drawn, color-coded charts of each block, followed by detailed records on all themes. Overall, the sanitary report was the product of the time, when public health research was becoming a comprehensive enterprise of urban social geography. Still, individual skills and biases got in the way, and the council was unable to force its team of inspectors to submit to the straitjacket of its survey design. Ibid., 66–69, 70–72, 195–205, 226–54, 255–67; New-York Historical Society, Manuscript Division (NYHS-MD), *Citizens' Association of New York, Council of Hygiene and Public Health, Record of Sanitary Inquiry, 1864–1865,* "Fifth District Sections I–II," "Seventeenth District."

21. The analysis was also colored by the report's anti-intemperance instincts, which made it equate groceries with liquor stores, not an unfair connection, but also dismissive of their vital function to distribute food supplies to residents.

22. Citizens' Association, *Report of the Council of Hygiene and Public Health,* xciv–xcv.

23. Ibid., xciv–xcv.

24. Ibid., xcv.

25. Ibid.

26. Ibid., 59.

27. Ibid., 250–51.

28. Ibid., 201–2.

29. Ibid., 311.

30. Expanding on the original dissertation research, chapter 6 in this book brings new evidence to bear on the little understood relationship between food access, living standards, and social inequality in antebellum New York City. Lobel's book, especially its chapter 3, engages with the subject, also placing the question of food quality in the context of laissez-faire markets. However, by relying mainly on narrative sources, its treatment of food inequality remains anecdotal. It reveals more about reformers' and journalists' concerns about low-quality food and its risks, rather than providing a comprehensive account of how structural inequalities in food access worked, and what role they played in contributing to unequal living and health standards. Lobel's most interesting discussions focus on the role of groceries as liquor shops in poor areas, a frequent concern among health and social reformers, and the notorious swill milk scandals of the 1850s, which gained a great deal of publicity at the time. The argument of this chapter rests on different historical material and types of analysis: it exhausts a systematic and quantitative source base with the tools of GIS to map and explain how food access emerged as a structural condition of inequality in the nineteenth-

century American city. Cindy R. Lobel, *Urban Appetites: Food and Culture in Nineteenth-Century New York* (Chicago, IL: University of Chicago Press, 2014), 73–102. On swill milk, see also McNeur, *Taming Manhattan*, 134–74.

31. Declining physical stature for cohorts born from about 1830 to 1860 was first noted among white Union Army recruits, and has later been found for several other samples, including West Point cadets, free blacks in Maryland and Virginia, Georgia convicts, and Ohio National Guardsmen. Further research confirmed that the phenomenon was not confined to the United States, but body heights declined in the United Kingdom, Sweden, the Habsburg Monarchy, and Bavaria in the mid- to late-eighteenth century, while the American cycle in the mid-nineteenth century also had its European counterparts, affecting among other countries Britain and the Netherlands. Dora L. Costa and Richard H. Steckel, "Long-Term Trends in Health, Welfare, and Economic Growth in the United States," in *Health and Welfare during Industrialization*, ed. Richard Steckel and Roderick Floud (Chicago, IL: University of Chicago Press, 1997), 47–89; John Komlos, "Shrinking in a Growing Economy? The Mystery of Physical Stature during the Industrial Revolution," *Journal of Economic History* 58, no. 3 (1998), 779–802; John Komlos, "A Three-Decade 'Kuhnian' History of the Antebellum Puzzle: Explaining the Shrinking of the US Population at the Onset of Modern Economic Growth," *Discussion Papers in Economics*, 2012–10, at SSRN, http://ssrn.com/abstract = 2021060; Michael R. Haines, "Growing Incomes, Shrinking People—Can Economic Development Be Hazardous to Your Health? Historical Evidence for the United States, England, and the Netherlands in the Nineteenth Century," *Social Science History* 28, no. 2 (2004), 249–70; Roderick Floud, Robert W. Fogel, Bernard Harris, and Sok Chul Hong, *The Changing Body: Health, Nutrition, and Human Development in the Western World since 1700* (Cambridge: Cambridge University Press, 2011), 296–363.

32. Since adult body height is positively related to meat consumption levels at infancy, childhood, and adolescence, it can serve as a proxy for studying living standards. Research corroborates that assuming an ideal body mass, taller people tend to have more robust immune systems. John Komlos, " 'The Height and Weight of West Point Cadets': Dietary Change in Antebellum America," *Journal of Economic History* 47, no. 4 (1987), 897–927, especially 908–19. Robert W. Fogel, *The Escape from Hunger and Premature Death, 1700–2100* (Cambridge: Cambridge University Press, 2004); Floud et al., *The Changing Body*.

33. Komlos's reasoning was that since the agricultural labor force grew relatively slowly, and productivity gains in agriculture remained limited, the availability of food supplies lagged behind demand from rapid population growth and urbanization. Per capita food output declined, while rising relative food prices pushed consumers to substitute carbohydrates for meat. Komlos, "The Height and Weight of West Point Cadets," 908–19; quote on 919.

To this, he added secondary explanations. He argued that the recession of 1837–43 negatively impacted household food budgets. He also stressed that rising income inequality must have disproportionately decreased meat consumption for low-income populations. Moreover, he emphasized that city dwellers, a rapidly rising share of the population, paid a premium for having to import food from growing distances. Until the invention of refrigerated railcars and ships, transportation technology was not adequate to ensure the shipment of fresh meat and milk over long distances at sufficiently low prices to offset this trend. Komlos, "Shrinking in a Growing Economy," 783–93.

34. For data, Komlos relied on production figures from the federal censuses. One

issue was that this left the period before 1839 unaccounted for. There are also methodological concerns, including the reliability of early census figures, the problem of using production data for studying consumption, or converting animal counts into pounds, calories, and proteins. The latter issue triggered a lively debate between Komlos and Gallman. Robert E. Gallman, "Dietary Change in Antebellum America," *Journal of Economic History* 56, no. 1 (1996), 193–201; John Komlos, "Anomalies in Economic History: Toward a Resolution of the 'Antebellum Puzzle,' " *Journal of Economic History* 56, no. 1 (1996), 202–14.

To reach further back in time, Haines exploited the New York State censuses, which contain production figures from 1825. When calculating per capita selected livestock, milk, and milk products, he excluded New York City, as it imported most of its food supplies, and much of it from out of state. It is also unclear what percentage of the livestock was consumed locally or exported to cities. Haines's figures hence do not refer to actual consumption rates but instead indicate relative consumption. Michael R. Haines, "Health, Height, Nutrition, and Mortality: Evidence on the 'Antebellum Puzzle' from Union Army Recruits in the Middle of the Nineteenth Century," *NBER Historical Working Paper Series* 107 (1998), 27, table 3.

More recently, Floud et al. published new consumption figures based on the federal censuses, also making estimates for the preceding decades. Their data also offer international comparisons. Floud et al., *The Changing Body*, 310, table 6.4.

35. Further, and not unrelated, access to transportation networks resulted in higher mortality. More directly relevant, the data did not bear out a relationship between falling per capita nutrition and higher mortality. However, a small positive relationship was found between regional agricultural specialization and mortality. The explanation is that commercial farming resulted in more specialized, that is, less diversified regional agricultural production, which in turn contributed to the deteriorating composition of local diets. Better access to regional transportation networks increased county-level crude death rates by about four per thousand, while a 10 percentage point increase in the share of a county's urban population increased mortality by about 1.3 to 1.4 deaths per thousand. Michael R. Haines, Lee A. Craig, Thomas Weiss, "Development, Health, Nutrition, and Mortality: The Case of the 'Antebellum Puzzle' in the United States," *NBER Historical Working Paper Series* 130 (2000), 11–14; Michael R. Haines, Lee A. Craig, and Thomas Weiss, "The Short and the Dead: Nutrition, Mortality, and the 'Antebellum Puzzle' in the United States," *Journal of Economic History* 63, no. 2 (2003), 396–98.

36. For studying physical stature, they turned to data on white Union Army recruits. They found that both the quantity and the variety of the food supply mattered. Growing up in a county with a net surplus of protein increased adult body height, whereas greater agricultural specialization had a small negative impact. Haines, Craig, and Weiss, "Development, Health, Nutrition, and Mortality," 11–14; Haines, Craig, and Weiss, "The Short and the Dead," 404–7.

37. "It seems that the growing prosperity of the United States in the antebellum period was partly purchased at a price of some deterioration of the biological standard of living." Haines, Craig, and Weiss, "The Short and the Dead," 409.

38. To cite a few relevant studies from this vast literature: Simon Szreter, "Economic Growth, Disruption, Deprivation, Disease, and Death: On the Importance of the Politics of Public Health for Development," *Population and Development Review* 23, no. 4 (1997), 693–728; Simon Szreter and Graham Mooney, "Urbanization,

Mortality, and the Standard of Living Debate: New Estimates of the Expectation of Life at Birth in Nineteenth-Century British Cities," *Economic History Review* 51, no. 1 (1998), 84–112; Michael R. Haines, "The Urban Mortality Transition in the United States, 1800–1940," *NBER Historical Working Paper Series* 134 (2001); Louis Cain and Sok Chul Hong, "Survival in 19th Century Cities: The Larger the City, the Smaller Your Chances," *Explorations in Economic History* 46, no. 4 (2009), 450–63; Floud et al., *The Changing Body*, 320–29; Sherry Olson and Patricia Thornton, *Peopling the North American City: Montreal, 1840–1900* (Montreal: McGill-Queen's University Press, 2011).

39. For a discussion of market revenue data and how they were used to estimate meat consumption figures between 1790 and 1818, see appendix B. To estimate meat consumption in 1836–38, the Market Committee's 1839 report gives annual counts for beef cattle for these years. For 1842, the comptroller provides estimates for the number of cattle and the total number of "small livestock" slaughtered in the city. In distributing small livestock into the relevant categories of veal, lamb and mutton, and pork, the 1818 ratios for the same animals were used. For sources, see New York (N.Y.). Board of Aldermen, *Documents of the Board of Aldermen of the City of New York* (BA Documents) (New York: 1834–68), Vol. 6, Doc. 31, 374–75; Vol. 9, Doc. 46, 412. For estimates on national-level meat production and consumption, see Komlos, "The Height and Weight," 913, table 9; Floud et al., *The Changing Body*, 310, table 6.4.

40. See Horowitz's figures (chapter 2, note 13) on falling meat consumption during the Great Depression. Roger Horowitz, *Putting Meat on the American Table: Taste, Technology, Transformation* (Baltimore, MD: Johns Hopkins University Press, 2006), 11–17.

41. "The decline in heights of the second half of the 1830s may very well have been caused, or at least exacerbated, by the recession of 1837." Komlos, "Shrinking in a Growing Economy," 788.

42. Data on premiums are not available for 1822–29. For sources and methods of obtaining annual public market revenue data, see appendix B.

43. Looking for comparison farther afield, the city of Boston and its agglomerations, more persistent records from the centralized Brighton livestock market show a similarly declining trend in annual beef cattle sales from 1836. For the data, see David C. Smith and Anne E. Bridges, "The Brighton Market: Feeding Nineteenth-Century Boston," *Agricultural History* 56, no. 1 (1982), 20–21.

44. Specifically, Komlos's calculations of per capita beef and mutton production in 1839 are very close to the 1838 and 1842 New York figures, and the same can be said about the estimates of beef and veal by Floud et al., *The Changing Body*. As for mutton, the New York figures and those of Komlos are considerably different from the ones offered by Floud et al. Unfortunately, it is not possible to directly compare fresh pork consumption in New York City and total pork production nationally.

45. One should add that this decline was further exacerbated by the Civil War, lasting for another decade. Komlos's estimates for beef, pork, and mutton production, and overall meat consumption after the Civil War, are as follows: for beef: 56 (1869) and 64 (1879) pounds; for pork: 61 (1869) and 88 (1879) pounds; for mutton: 12 (1869) and 11 (1879) pounds; for overall meat consumption: 130 (1869) and 161 pounds (1879). Komlos, "The Height and Weight," 913, table 9.

46. This is consistent with other records, such as Haines's data on declining livestock production in New York State, starting before the recession and continuing until after the Civil War, or stagnant annual livestock sales at Boston's Brighton Market

lasting well past the recovery. Based on the state census, Haines shows that per capita production of hogs, cattle, and sheep in New York State (minus New York City) began to decline already between 1825 and 1835. His figures between 1821 and 1840 are as follows: 0.973 cattle and 1.719 sheep (1821); 1.013 hogs, 1.045 cattle, and 2.414 sheep (1825); 0.815 hogs, 0.989 cattle, and 2.235 sheep (1835); 0.898 hogs, 0.903 cattle, and 2.419 sheep (1840). Haines, "Health, Height, Nutrition, and Mortality," 27, table 3; Smith and Bridges, "The Brighton Market," 20–21.

47. Wholesale price indexes of beef, pork, and meat in general, two other key food groups, grains and fish, and industrial commodities are charted in figures 6.2–6.3. Like in figure 2.2, industrial goods are included to indicate changes in relative prices between food imports and industrial exports. The more limited New York records are again complemented by the more widely used Philadelphia price indexes.

Meat prices in the two cities moved closely together during the forty years covered. Prices again refer to barreled (= 200 pounds) beef and pork. For New York, the figure uses beef and pork prices, while for Philadelphia they also include "meats and meat products," a more comprehensive category, which strongly correlates with beef and pork prices in Philadelphia ("r" = 0.86, "r" = 0.97, respectively) and New York ("r" = 0.80, "r" = 0.89) between 1826 and 1859. Additionally, New York and Philadelphia beef ("r" = 0.81) and pork ("r" = 0.95) prices are strongly correlated (1826–59), and so are beef prices between Boston and New York ("r" = 0.94) or Philadelphia ("r" = 0.89) from 1826 until 1842, when Boston quotes are available (these are not used in the figure given their limited timespan).

The evidence is clear that the region's meat markets were closely integrated, with wholesale prices following the same trends of supply and demand. Generally better price data for Philadelphia can be taken as indicative of supply conditions in New York as well. Further, the available grains, fish, and industrial commodities prices for Philadelphia, allow for broadening the picture to other foodstuff while also assessing the changing terms of trade between wholesale prices for industrial exports and agricultural imports. Here the more comprehensive industrial commodities index is used, which strongly correlates with the price of textile fabrics ("r" = 0.74). Anne Bezanson, Robert Davis Gray, and Miriam Hussey, *Wholesale Prices in Philadelphia, 1784–1861* (Philadelphia: University of Pennsylvania Press, 1936), 1:392, 1:394; 2:9, 2:171; Arthur Harrison Cole and International Scientific Committee on Price History, *Wholesale Commodity Prices in the United States, 1700–1861: Statistical Supplement; Actual Wholesale Prices of Various Commodities* (Cambridge, MA: Harvard University Press, 1938).

48. BA Documents, Vol. 6, Doc. 31, 374.

49. The full quotation reads, "The general trend of food production prior to the Civil War was not favorable. Rapid population growth by urbanization and immigration had fettered food supplies per capita for major foodstuffs, though their gross levels were increasing." Floud et al., *The Changing Body*, 316, 332. It should be noted that this was essentially the original argument posited by Komlos, which was later reaffirmed by Floud et al. based on more extensive data. Komlos, "The Height and Weight," 920.

50. Even assuming a 20–25% drop in meat consumption (relying on the New York City estimates), the actual health effects of reduced protein intake may have not been unambiguously negative.

51. The secondary literature addressing rising inequality and poverty in antebellum

New York City is vast. A short selection of key works includes: Edward Pessen, "The Egalitarian Myth and the American Social Reality: Wealth, Mobility, and Equality in The 'Era of the Common Man,'" *American Historical Review* 76, no. 4 (1971), 989–1034, especially 1019–31; Sean Wilentz, *Chants Democratic: New York City and the Rise of the American Working Class, 1788–1850* (New York: Oxford University Press, 1984); Christine Stansell, *City of Women: Sex and Class in New York, 1789–1860* (Urbana: University of Illinois Press, 1987); Elizabeth Blackmar, *Manhattan for Rent, 1785–1850* (Ithaca, NY: Cornell University Press, 1989); Richard Briggs Stott, *Workers in the Metropolis: Class, Ethnicity, and Youth in Antebellum New York City* (Ithaca, NY: Cornell University Press, 1990); Kenneth A. Scherzer, *The Unbounded Community: Neighborhood Life and Social Structure in New York City, 1830–1875* (Durham, NC: Duke University Press, 1992). Also, parts of these books deal with the subject: Edward K. Spann, *The New Metropolis: New York City, 1840–1857* (New York: Columbia University Press, 1981); Edwin G. Burrows and Mike Wallace, *Gotham: A History of New York City to 1898* (New York: Oxford University Press, 1999); David M. Scobey, *Empire City: The Making and Meaning of the New York City Landscape* (Philadelphia, PA: Temple University Press, 2002).

52. The earliest representative consumer expenditures for families by income are available for Massachusetts wage earners (397 families) in 1874–75 based on data from the Massachusetts Bureau of Statistics of Labor, and for workers in nine basic industries across the United States (2,562 families) in 1901 using data from the US Bureau of Labor. Both tables were compiled by Lee A. Craig, "Consumption Expenditures of Families, by Income Class: 1874–1875 [Massachusetts Wage Earners]," table Cd456-464, in *Historical Statistics of the United States, Earliest Times to the Present: Millennial Edition*, ed. Susan B. Carter, Scott Sigmund Gartner, Michael R. Haines, Alan L. Olmstead, Richard Sutch, and Gavin Wright (New York: Cambridge University Press, 2006), available from http://hsus.cambridge.org/HSUSWeb/toc/tableToc.do?id = Cd456-464; Lee A. Craig, "Consumption Expenditures of Families, by Income Class: 1901," table Cd474-482, in *Historical Statistics of the United States*, ed. Carter et al., available from http://hsus.cambridge.org/HSUSWeb/toc/tableToc.do?id = Cd474-482.

53. On rising rents, especially after the end of the recession of 1837–43, see Robert A. Margo, "The Rental Price of Housing in New York City, 1830–1860," *Journal of Economic History* 56, no. 3 (1996), 605–25; Carlos Villareal, "Where the Other Half Lives: Evidence on the Origin and Persistence of Poor Neighborhoods from New York City, 1830–2012," Working Paper, 2014.

54. For a discussion of the sources and methods used to produce these maps, see appendix A. For further detail on the block-level GIS analysis of population density and tenement crowding in mid-nineteenth-century New York informing the discussion here, see the forthcoming article, Gergely Baics and Leah Meisterlin, "Zoning before Zoning: Land Use and Density in Mid-Nineteenth-Century New York City," *Annals of the American Association of Geographers* (2016).

55. On elite residential enclaves, see Scobey, *Empire City*, 114–20; Burrows and Wallace, *Gotham*, 712–34; McNeur, *Taming Manhattan*, 45–94.

56. On the Manhattan real estate and housing market, see Blackmar, *Manhattan for Rent*.

57. Not surprisingly, the Metropolitan Board of Health also experimented with a block-level density map to explain unequal cholera mortality in 1866. The map uses seven shades to differentiate density levels: New York (State), Metropolitan Board of Health, *Second Annual Report of the Metropolitan Board of Health of the*

State of New York (Albany, NY: Charles Van Benthuysen & Sons, 1868), map between 452–53.

58. For a discussion of the sources and methods used to produce these maps, see appendix A.
59. "In the early decades of the nineteenth century, then, Manhattan's housing market developed above all else as a market in health." Blackmar, "Accountability for Public Health," 48.
60. The sanitary report, following other public health and social reform treatises from the time, provides ample evidence of groceries operating as liquor shops, especially in tenement districts: Citizens' Association, *Report of the Council of Hygiene and Public Health*, 26–27, 40, 54, 58, 67, 71, 77, 137, 186, 191, 276, 311. The same point has been made by historians, including Howard B. Rock, *Artisans of the New Republic: The Tradesmen of New York City in the Age of Jefferson* (New York: New York University Press, 1979), 297; and, more recently, Lobel, *Urban Appetites*, 76–81. Indeed, for many grocers, retailing alcohol was a key business, while selling foodstuff may have been more like window-dressing. It is also true, as Beal correctly points out, that focusing too much on the aspect of liquor sales by grocers in tenement districts distracts from their more fundamental role of provisioning residents with daily food supplies. Thomas D. Beal, "Selling Gotham: The Retail Trade in New York City from the Public Market to Alexander T. Stewart's Marble Palace, 1625–1860" (PhD dissertation, State University of New York at Stony Brook, 1998), 396, 435n24. In addition, it also plays into the temperance sentiments of middle-class reformers.
61. This was a point already asserted by Komlos in his original formulation of the nutritional thesis. Komlos, "Height and Weight," 919–22.
62. The hindquarters were considered the choice quarters, which were separated into smaller cuts to form sirloin or rump roasts. Roasts from the first nine ribs of the forequarters were also much valued. The other premium cut from the loin was the steak, which was served mostly in eating houses or broiled over open fires. As a smaller cut, it was accessible even to working-class residents on rare occasions. Most New Yorkers, however, could not afford expensive roasts or steaks but depended on tougher and bonier cuts eaten largely in stews or soups. These included the flank and the rounds from the hindquarters, and the brisket and plate from the forequarters, eaten mostly in stews, as they needed to be cooked longer in water. Bony meats, such as the neck, shoulder, and thigh, were mainly served in soups, while beef livers and kidneys were eaten both in stews and soups. The cheapest cuts were the beef shins, which, according to De Voe, were good for nothing but stock for soup, while beef brisket and plate were used chiefly for cured beef.

A similar, albeit less elaborate hierarchy existed for the other butcher's meats as well. For veal, the hindquarters, divided usually in the loin and the leg, were the choice pieces, commanding the highest prices, while the forequarters, containing the shoulder, neck, and breast were less popular, and were often used for stewing. Similarly, for mutton and lamb, the leg and loin were the choice pieces, and for pork, the loin was considered the best meat. Horowitz, *Putting Meat on the American Table*, 22–24; Thomas F. De Voe, *The Market Assistant, Containing a Brief Description of Every Article of Human Food Sold in the Public Markets of the Cities of New York, Boston, Philadelphia, and Brooklyn; Including the Various Domestic and Wild Animals, Poultry, Game, Fish, Vegetables, Fruits, &c., &c., with Many Curious Incidents and Anecdotes* (Cambridge, MA: Printed at the Riverside Press for the author, 1867), 29–59, 65–73, 76–84.

63. BA Documents, Vol. 6, Doc. 55, 571–72.

64. Ibid., 567–68.

65. In fact, the ordinance that abolished the market laws, drafted in October 1842, and signed into law January 20, 1843, extended the same sanitary regulations to shop butchers that applied to market butchers. It even entrusted the same authorities to enforce those, including the superintendent of markets, the alderman, assistant alderman, street inspector, and health warden of each ward. BA Documents, Vol. 9, Doc. 31, 258–59.

66. "The sale is not limited to hucksters, and peddlers, it is sold in our markets by the quantity, and is extensively retailed in basements throughout the city. On Saturday nights our avenues and minor streets are traversed with wagons and hand carts laden with it." New York (N.Y.). City Inspector, *Annual Report of the City Inspector of New York for the Year Ending December 31, 1855 (ARCI)* (New York: 1804–60), 190–91.

67. Citizens' Association, *Report of the Council of Hygiene and Public Health*, 54.

68. Ibid.; emphasis by Pulling. Slunk veal refers to soft or watery meat in this context. Moreover, Pulling comments on adulteration, not only of milk or alcohol but of all types of foodstuff regularly retailed in local shops. Whether an urban legend or reality, he warns about the ragpicker's "fragments of bread and other farinacious food, decaying potatoes, cabbages, &c., interspersed with lifeless cats, rats, and puppies, thus introduced to a post mortem fellowship," which find their "occasional metamorphosis . . . into the familiar sausage," or enter into the "composition of bread puddings" (59–61).

69. Ibid. "They constitute the food of thousands of prematurely-aged men and women, who seek relief from the poisonous effects of such viands in the more poisonous stimulants which are vended side by side with them" (59–60).

70. Ibid. Further, "it is impossible that the milk of a mother or a nurse residing in one of these wretched hovels or dungeons, can be of good and sufficient quality and quantity for the nurseling; it must produce a faulty alimentation or assimilation, and become the predisposing, if not the exciting cause of cholera infantum, which is fully developed by meteorological influences during the summer months" (201–2).

71. Ibid., 245.

72. Ibid. In explaining substandard nutritional levels, he deemed "the laborer's remuneration inadequate to the bare necessities of life" (250).

73. Ibid. He was especially concerned about "swill milk," obtained from cows stabled in the city, which "increases the number and severity of cases of cholera infantum," and about "pork raised in the city and its environs," which "is consumed in the shanties and tenant-houses." "The drab and mottled appearance and peculiar oily and disagreeable flavor of this meat, renders it probable that it is not a wholesome article of diet" (311–12).

74. Ibid.; emphasis by Field. "One side of the house through, from front to back, is all that is required to set-up an establishment of this kind; the front room being thrown open for a store, and the back room reserved for the '*grocer's*' family" (214–15).

75. Death rates in New York also exceeded those of comparable cities like Philadelphia or Boston, albeit the trends were parallel. Crude death rates in American cities over the long nineteenth century were compiled by Haines. I thank Michael Haines and Joseph P. Ferrie for giving me access to the data, used for Boston and Philadelphia. For New York, crude death rates were calculated based on the annual number of deaths compiled by Ira Rosenwaike. Haines, "The Urban Mortal-

ity Transition"; Ira Rosenwaike, *Population History of New York City* (Syracuse, NY: Syracuse University Press, 1972), 176.

76. Data on the number of deaths from specific causes, including dysentery and diarrhea, are available from the city inspector's reports: *ARCI* (1860), 253–64.

77. Besides, misdiagnosis of diseases was not uncommon. Kenneth F. Kiple, *The Cambridge World History of Human Disease* (Cambridge: Cambridge University Press, 1993), 676–80.

78. Gerard T. Koeppel, *Water for Gotham: A History* (Princeton, NJ: Princeton University Press, 2000), 285–87.

79. Ibid., 287.

80. For a discussion of the sources and methods used to produce these maps, see appendix A.

81. It is hardly surprising that tenement crowding coincided with areas of high population density; after all, the two measures are related. Overbuilt blocks, with residential structures occupying back lots, exploiting every nook of space, were by definition high-density localities. In fact, they represented the very bottom of the rental housing market, where only the poorest lived, for overcrowding, darkness, and lack of ventilation were considered the witch's brew of health threats. Even in high-density districts, only certain blocks were burdened by an excessive number of rear-lot tenements.

82. For sources and methods used to produce this map, see appendix A.

83. Ibid.

84. The urban history of cholera is well documented. Important books on the subject for New York and other cities include: Charles E. Rosenberg, *The Cholera Years: The United States in 1832, 1849 and 1866* (Chicago, IL: University of Chicago Press, 1962); Duffy, *A History of Public Health*; Alan M. Kraut, *Silent Travelers: Germs, Genes, and the "Immigrant Menace"* (New York: Basic Books, 1994), 11–30; Louis Chevalier, *Laboring Classes and Dangerous Classes in Paris during the First Half of the Nineteenth Century* (London: Routledge & Kegan Paul, 1973); Francois Delaporte, *Disease and Civilization: The Cholera in Paris, 1832* (Cambridge, MA: MIT Press, 1986); Richard J. Evans, *Death in Hamburg: Society and Politics in the Cholera Years, 1830–1910* (Oxford: Clarendon Press, 1987); Frank M. Snowden, *Naples in the Time of Cholera, 1884–1911* (Cambridge: Cambridge University Press, 1995).

85. Linking cholera to local environmental conditions (crowding, tenement housing, inadequate sanitation) permeates the pages of contemporary public health reports. The annual reports of the Metropolitan Board of Health offer examples of the continued influence of this view, well after John Snow's well-known demonstration in 1854 that cholera was waterborne. New York (State), Metropolitan Board of Health, *Annual Report of the Metropolitan Board of Health* (Albany, NY: Van Benthuysen & Sons, 1867); New York (State), *Second Annual Report of the Metropolitan Board of Health*, especially 271–81.

86. On the complex relationship between nutrition and health standards, see Floud et al., *The Changing Body*.

87. For example, in opposing deregulation, the city's butchers cited an 1842 medical report by Drs. M. Post, Hosack, and Chilton, which offered "irresistible and conclusive proof of the absolute necessity of protecting our citizens against the fatal results consequent upon the sale and consumption, as an article of food, of the flesh of diseased animals—a fraud so easily detected under the present system of the Public Markets." The original report detailed a recent incidence of smoked-beef poisoning. Based on thorough medical examination, the experts established

that the source of the disease, affecting a family of seven, all of whom showed alarming symptoms of food poisoning, was a neighborhood grocer selling smoked beef. Three years later, city inspector Cornelius B. Archer returned to this report to make the case for a rigorous system of livestock and meat inspection. BA Documents, Vol. 9, Doc. 34, 279–304; Vol. 9, Doc. 45, 395; *ARCI* (1845), 175–76.

88. Gardiner Harris, "Poor Sanitation in India May Afflict Well-Fed Children with Malnutrition," *New York Times*, July 14, 2014; "Sanitation in India: The Final Frontier," *Economist*, July 19, 2014.

89. The First Tenement House Act of 1867, directly influenced by the Citizens' Association, *Report of the Council of Hygiene and Public Health*, while timid and ineffective in improving tenement living conditions, at the least set a precedent for reform. Still, it took another half century until the first effective housing legislation was passed with the Tenement House Act of 1901. As for water, in 1842 New York City completed its gargantuan public works of the Croton aqueduct. For a discussion about its importance and financing, see introduction and chapter 1. For a detailed history, see Koeppel, *Water for Gotham*.

90. On the broader political economy context, and the negotiations and shifting balance of public and private goods, see introduction and chapter 1.

91. On the problem of increasingly frequent moving, as often as annually among wage-earning tenant populations, as well as the practice to move on the same day of May 1, when leases were up, see Blackmar, *Manhattan for Rent*, 104, 213–16.

92. Some skilled butchers transferred to the shop system, for they could not obtain legitimate stalls. But thousands of others, without appropriate skills or training, now ventured into the retail of perishable and delicate foodstuff, often selling them from groceries.

93. For sources and methods used to produce these maps, see appendix A.

94. Robert Ernst, *Immigrant Life in New York City, 1825–1863* (New York: King's Crown Press, 1949); Stott, *Workers in the Metropolis*, 191–211; Scherzer, *The Unbounded Community*.

95. The Germans far outrivaled the Irish in the food trades. Representing 15.7% of the population, they represented a remarkable 36.7% of the city's food dealers, whereas the Irish, 28.2% of the population, gave only about 21.9% of the food dealers. Ernst, *Immigrant Life*, 87, 193, 214–17.

96. This was a point also asserted by Horowitz: Roger Horowitz, Jeffrey M. Pilcher, and Sydney Watts, "Meat for the Multitudes: Market Culture in Paris, New York City, and Mexico City over the Long Nineteenth Century," *American Historical Review* 109, no. 4 (2004), 1073.

97. Ernst, *Immigrant Life*, 87, 214–17.

98. Citizens' Association, *Report of the Council of Hygiene and Public Health*, xciv–xcv.

99. On colonial era slaughtering and its deregulation, see Thomas F. De Voe, *The Market Book: A History of the Public Markets of the City of New York* (New York: A. M. Kelley, 1970 [1862]), 366–68; Roger Horowitz, "The Politics of Meat Shopping in Antebellum New York City," in *Meat, Modernity, and the Rise of the Slaughterhouse* ed., Paula Y. Lee (Lebanon: University of New Hampshire Press, 2008), 171; Jared Day, "Butchers, Tanners, and Tallow Chandlers: The Geography of Slaughtering in Early-Nineteenth-Century New York City," in Lee, *Meat, Modernity*, 180–85. See also chapter 2, including figure 2.5 on the geography of slaughter in Early Republican New York.

100. Citizens' Association, *Report of the Council of Hygiene and Public Health*, xxvii.

101. Ibid., xciv.

102. Ibid., 86.
103. Ibid., 87.
104. Ibid., 86–88.
105. Unlike the other inspectors, he took a measured approach. He did not declare all slaughterhouses unsanitary but singled out the most offensive ones. Citizens' Association, *Report of the Council of Hygiene and Public Health*, 155.
106. Ibid., 154–63.
107. Ibid., 168.
108. Ibid. He pronounced most slaughterhouses in his district "excessively filthy, and utterly reckless of any regard to sanitary regulations or the laws of decency" (175–76).
109. Ibid., 261–62, 264–66 (for the Twenty-First District), 277–78 (for the Twenty-Second District), 294 (for the Twenty-Fourth District). Even the wealthy ward 15 (Twelfth District) had one killing shed "in rather a dilapidated condition" (138), albeit not in a prominent location.
110. For sources and methods used to produce these maps, see appendix A.
111. In fact, judging not by the number of facilities but by their overall areas, a potentially better indicator of scale and capacity, the largest agglomerations of slaughterhouses were along the Hudson River, and certainly not in these centrally located districts.
112. Nor were population density, tenement crowding, and mortality the best predictors of the geography of slaughter. Rather, the clustering of slaughterhouses was the result of their historical concentration in that central area, dating back to the early nineteenth century, and supply-side agglomeration effects elsewhere. This helps explain why Inspector Derby did not find his smoking gun of a direct correlation between killing sheds and high disease rates. It is also true that the center city cluster did correspond to a high mortality area, with its fair share of cholera and diarrhea-related mortality in 1866.
113. Citizens' Association, *Report of the Council of Hygiene and Public Health*, xciv–xcv; emphasis in original. Even Inspector Newman, who held more lenient views on private slaughtering, added that all practical reforms "would not exclude other improvements, nor the introduction of abattoirs." Ibid., 156.
114. Griscom's best-known work acknowledges his intellectual debt to Chadwick in its title: John H. Griscom, *The Sanitary Condition of the Laboring Population of New York, With Suggestions for Its Improvement; A Discourse (with Additions) Delivered on the 30th December, 1844, at the Repository of the American Institute* (New York: Harper & Brothers, 1845).
115. *ARCI* (1842), 181–85; quote on 184.
116. Archer also included the abatement of nuisances in his discussion as a secondary consideration. He reiterated his views in his next annual report, adding another interesting point about the detrimental effects of nuisances on local property values. *ARCI* (1845), 172–83; (1846), 397–402, on property values 397.
117. Emphasis in original. *ARCI* (1845), 172–83; quote on 173, 175–76.
118. Ibid., 182.
119. Ibid.; emphasis in original document. For further discussions on slaughtering in Paris, see Dorothee Brantz, "Slaughter in the City: The Establishment of Public Abattoirs in Paris and Berlin, 1780–1914" (PhD dissertation, University of Chicago, 2003); Sydney Watts, "The Grand Boucherie, the 'Right' to Meat, and the Growth of Paris," in Lee, *Meat, Modernity*, 13–26; Kyri Claflin, "La Villette: City of Blood (1867–1914)," in Lee, *Meat, Modernity*, 27–45. The same edited volume by Lee contains other excellent essays on slaughtering in German, British, and

American cities. Additionally, see Ian Maclachlan, "A Bloody Offal Nuisance: The Persistence of Private Slaughter-Houses in Nineteenth-Century London," *Urban History* 34, no. 2 (2007), 227–54.

120. *ARCI* (1845), 181.
121. City Clerk Filed Papers, New York City Municipal Archives (CCFP), Special Committee on Slaughter-houses (1850), 271; BA Documents, Vol. 16, Doc. 21, 256.
122. Ibid., 248–51.
123. Ibid. To which "the law affords redress" (243–47).
124. He gained experience by having previously sought the courts to close down a slaughterhouse in his neighborhood.
125. His proposal was accompanied by a discussion of the scheme's public health benefits, detailed cost and revenue estimates, construction plans, and responses anticipating a range of counterarguments with intelligence and wit.
126. CCFP, Special Committee on Slaughter-houses (1850), 271, "Joseph L. Frame's Proposal for Public Slaughter-houses," quote on 14 in handwritten essay. See also related documents in same folder.
127. Ibid., quote on 21–22 in handwritten essay.
128. BA Documents, Vol. 11, Doc. 63, 683–84; *ARCI* (1849), 508–12; BA Documents, Vol. 18, Part 1, Doc. 23, 463; Vol. 19, Part 1, Doc. 17, 473–74; *ARCI* (1852), 282–83; (1855), 203–4; (1856), 200–201; (1859), 11–12; (1860), 51–52, 55–57.
129. To illustrate the scale of the problem, if an 1851 police report found that Gotham's then 206 slaughterhouses generated an estimated 375,000 carcasses, the 173 such facilities by 1864 must have produced at least twice that amount. The slight decrease in the number of slaughtering establishments between the two dates only reflected the consolidation of the industry into the type of private abattoirs, also escaping government inspection, about which Frame cautioned against, and the maps of figure 6.5 documented.
130. About the case, see McNeur, *Taming Manhattan*, 140–48; Duffy, *A History of Public Health*, 380–81. For broader discussions about related nuisances, see Duffy, *A History of Public Health*, 380–84; Burrows and Wallace, *Gotham*, 786–87; Spann, *The New Metropolis*, 129–30; Horowitz, "The Politics of Meat Shopping," 167–77; Day, "Butchers, Tanners, and Tallow Chandlers," 178–97.
131. Thomas F. De Voe, *Abattoirs: A Paper Read before the Polytechnic Branch of the American Institute* (Albany, NY: Charles van Benthuysen & Sons, 1866), 22–23.
132. A less effective but still feasible strategy would have been to inspect food at a central wholesale market, similar to the Halles Centrales in Paris. By the 1840s, as the spatial analysis in chapter 5 showed, Washington Market fulfilled such a role. However, as discussed, efforts to rebuild the dilapidated Washington Market in 1851 did not materialize, and, finally, in 1854 Mayor Wood vetoed the ordinance to reconstruct Washington Market. For sources, see chapter 5, including note 27.
133. By 1860, city inspector D. T. Valentine declared Washington and Fulton Markets beyond repair, and the market system in general a "disgrace." One year later, the superintendent of markets suggested the sale of the property and the building of a new market at the nearby site of West-Washington Market, "now covered by all kinds of sheds, intersected by filthy paths." While his proposal no longer envisioned a splendid wholesale market, under the era's liberal provisioning regime, even this modest plan failed to move forward. *ARCI* (1860), 22–24; (1861), 283–98; quote on 283.
134. They protested loud and organized at their corporate meetings. De Voe got in-

volved, disputing reformers' claims about the health risks of slaughterhouses, on historic and scientific grounds in an erudite paper read at the Polytechnic Branch of the American Institute and other occasions. Others took the case to court, if not derailing at least delaying reforms. De Voe, *Abattoirs*; NYHS-MD, Thomas F. De Voe, *Manuscript Records*, "Scrapbook of Notes and Clippings about Butchers."

135. They claimed that slaughterhouses were not a nuisance per se, unless kept unsanitary, while abattoirs were not by necessity sanitary, and those already in use proven to be a disaster. Further, they denied any link between slaughterhouses and higher disease rates, and to prove this point, they referred to themselves, strong and healthy fellows, not victims of their facilities' foul air. They also stressed that distancing their slaughterhouses from their homes presented an unfair burden on their livelihood. Ibid.

136. New York (State), *Second Annual Report of the Metropolitan Board of Health*, 31–32; New York (State), Metropolitan Board of Health, *Third Annual Report of the Metropolitan Board of Health of the State of New York* (Albany, NY: Charles Van Benthuysen & Sons, 1868), 37–39.

137. NYHS-MD, De Voe, *Manuscripts*, "Scrapbook of Notes and Clippings about Butchers."

138. New York (State), *Annual Report of the Metropolitan Board of Health*, 44.

139. Ibid., 44–46; New York (State), *Third Annual Report of the Metropolitan Board of Health*, 37–39.

140. De Voe, *Abattoirs*, 22–23. De Voe was hardly an impartial observer, having witnessed the board close down his two slaughterhouses, both located on West Nineteenth Street, in 1867. NYHS-MD, De Voe, *Manuscripts*, "Scrapbook of Notes and Clippings about Butchers."

141. Ibid.

142. For an excellent survey of market systems in major European cities, see Manuel Guàrdia and José L. Oyón, eds., *Making Cities through Market Halls: Europe, 19th and 20th Centuries* (Barcelona: Museu d'Història de Barcelona, 2015). For a survey of urban slaughtering, abattoirs, and municipal reforms in Europe and the United States, see Lee, *Meat, Modernity*.

CONCLUSION

1. For a survey of market systems in European cities, see Manuel Guàrdia and José L. Oyón, eds., *Making Cities through Market Halls: Europe, 19th and 20th Centuries* (Barcelona: Museu d'Història de Barcelona, 2015).

2. On Barcelona's market system, see Nadia Fava, Manuel Guàrdia, and José L. Oyón, "Public versus Private: Barcelona's Market System, 1868–1975," *Planning Perspectives* 25, no. 1 (2010), 5–27; Nadia Fava, Manuel Guàrdia, and José L. Oyón, "The Barcelona Market System," in Guàrdia and Oyón, *Making Cities*, 261–96; Nadia Fava, Manuel Guàrdia, and José L. Oyón, "Barcelona Food Retailing and Public Markets, 1876–1936," *Urban History* (2015), available on CJO 2015, http://dx.doi.org/10.1017/S096392681500022X; Monsterrat Miller, *Feeding Barcelona, 1714–1975: Public Market Halls, Social Networks, and Consumer Culture* (Baton Rouge: Louisiana State University Press, 2015).

3. Definition by United States Department of Agriculture.

4. New York City, Department of City Planning, "Going to Market: New York City's Neighborhood Grocery Store and Supermarket Shortage" (2009), http://www.nyc.gov/html/dcp/html/supermarket/presentation.shtml.

Index

Page numbers in *italics* indicate illustrations and tables.